# WALLABY
## *Greats*

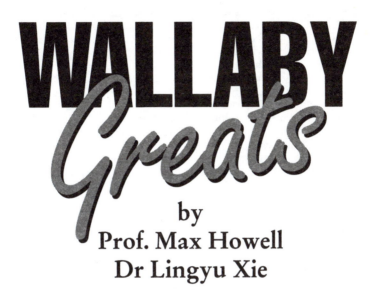

# WALLABY Greats

by
Prof. Max Howell
Dr Lingyu Xie

rugby publishing limited
Auckland, New Zealand

# Acknowledgements

THE authors are particularly grateful to Bill Honeybone, Bob Howitt, Warren Adler and the other staff at Rugby Press.

The authors would also like to express their appreciation to the following individuals who were willing to be interviewed for *Wallaby Greats*: the daughter of Bill Cerutti, Virginia Convoy, and her husband; Cyril Towers' wife, Rita, and her son Tom; Trevor Allan; Sir Nicholas Shehadie; Cyril Burke and his wife Marge; Colin Windon, his daughter Julie and her husband; John Thornett; Jules Guerassimoff; Ken Catchpole; Geoff Shaw; Tony Shaw; John Hipwell; Greg Cornelsen; Mark Loane; Chris Handy; Simon Poidevin and his wife; Roger Gould; Andy McIntyre; Andrew Slack.

In addition, interviews were conducted for the book *Bledisloe Magic* with individuals who provided information which was utilised in this book: All Blacks and New Zealand rugby personalities such as Alf Waterman, Noel Bowden, Tane Norton, Doug Bruce, Charlie Saxton, David Kirk, Eric Watson, Ray Harper, Peter Johnstone, Hugh McLean, Terry McLean, Leicester Rutledge, Duncan Robertson, Graham Mexted, Ces Blazey, Ian MacRae, Brian Lochore, Johnny Simpson, Frank Oliver, Gary Knight, Rod McKenzie, Jack Finlay, Bruce Robertson and Fred Allen.

Others in Australia interviewed were Ken Kearney, Bob McMaster, Dr Alex Ross, Keith Windon, Graham Cooke, John Solomon, Daryl Haberecht, Dr 'Chilla' Wilson, Dick Tooth and Des Connor.

The scrapbooks of Graham Cooke, Cyril Towers, Jules Guerassimoff, Colin Windon, Trevor Allan, Keith Windon, Cyril Burke, Greg Cornelsen and Bill Cerutti were invaluable in piecing the biographies together.

There were many sources that were utilised and the authors would like to acknowledge these outstanding works: Bob Dwyer (1992) *The Winning Way*. Auckland: Rugby Press; Alex Veysey (1974) *Colin Meads All Black*. London: Collins; Gordon Bray (1995) *The Spirit of Rugby*. Sydney: Harper Collins; Mark Ella and Terry Smith (1987) *Path To Victory*. Sydney: ABC; Peter FitzSimons (1993) *The Authorised Biography of Nick Farr-Jones*. Sydney: Random House; Greg Growden (1995) *With the Wallabies*. Sydney: ABC; Terry Cooper (1985) *Victorious Wallabies*. Waterloo Press; Jim Webster (1990) *For Love Not Money*. Sydney: ABC; Steven O'Meagher (1984) *Fronting Up - The Sean Fitzpatrick Story*. Glenfield: Moa Beckett; Paul Lewis (1991) *Brothers in Arms - The Alan and Gary Whetton Story*. Auckland: Moa; Jack Pollard (1994) *Australian Rugby - The Game and The Players*. Chippendale: Ironbark; Mark Ella (1995) *Running Rugby*. Sydney: ABC; Greg Growden (1991) *The Wallabies' World Cup*. East Melbourne: The Text; Roger Rollin (1973) *Hero/Anti-Hero*. N.Y: McGraw-Hill; Max Howell, Lingyu Xie and Peter Horton (1995) *Bledisloe Magic*. Auckland: Rugby Press; Ian Diehm (1994) *Giants in Green and Gold*. Brisbane: Boolarong; Lindsay Knight (1986) *The Geriatrics*. Auckland: Moa; Bret Harris (1959) *Maurauding Maroons*. Cammeray: Horwitz; Spiro Zavos (1995) *The Gold and the Black*. St Leonards: Allen and Unwin; Bert Bickley (1982) *Maroon*. Herston: Queensland Rugby Union; Keith Willey (1968) *The First Hundred Years: The Story of Brisbane Grammar School*. Brisbane: Macmillan; Alex Veysey (1985) *Ebony and Ivory: The Stu Wilson, Bernie Fraser Story*. Auckland: Moa; R.H. Chester and N.A.C McMillen (1994) *Men in Black*. Auckland: Moa; Don Clarke and Pat Booth (1966) *The Boot: Don Clarke's Story*. Wellington: AH and AW Reed; Chris Laidlaw (1973) *Mud In Your Eye*. Wellington: AH and AW Reed; Malcolm Spark (1989) *The 1947-48 Wallaby Tour*. Yorkshire: M.S. Spark; Phil Wilkins (1986) *The Highlanders*. Gordon: Gordon Rugby Club; Maxwell Price (1969) *Wallabies Without Armour*. London: Bailey Bros. and Swinfen; John Thornett (1967) *This World of Rugby*. Sydney: Murray; Winston McCarthy (1968) *Haka! The All Blacks Story*. London: Pelham; H.H. Moran (1946) *In My Fashion*. Sydney: Dymock's; Herbert H.Moran (1939) *Viewless Winds*. London: Peter Davies; Herbert H. Moran (1945) *Beyond The Hill Lies China*. London: Peter Davies; David Campese and Peter Bills (1991) *On A Wing and A Prayer*. London: Queen Anne Press; Norman McKenzie (1961) *On With The Game*. Wellington: AH and AW Reed.

©1996 Max Howell and Lingyu Xie.
First published in 1996 by Rugby Publishing Ltd,
67-73 View Road, Glenfield, Auckland 10, New Zealand.

Layout/design by Sportz Graphics Ltd, Takapuna, Auckland.
Typeset by Sportz Graphics Ltd.
Printed by Australian Print Group, Maryborough, Victoria, Australia.

Rugby Publishing Ltd is a member of the Medialine Group of Companies.
P.O. Box 100-243, North Shore Mail Centre, Auckland10, New Zealand.

ISBN 0-908630-60-3

# Contents

## Dedication

To Dr Reet Howell, who died unexpectedly of cancer on June 10, 1993:
international scholar, author, athlete, role model in her profession,
a person of high principles who was universally beloved.

# Foreword

Each person who puts on a Wallaby jersey is changed forever. He is a Wallaby for the rest of time, it can never be taken away. No amount of money can ever substitute for the never-to-be-forgotten feeling when one runs on the field as a Wallaby for that initial encounter.

As a youngster, I stood in centre field, ready to play for Australia, waiting for the kick-off and watching the awesome antics of the All Blacks doing their inspired haka, and chills ran up and down my spine. Fear was mixed with nervousness. I wondered: What am I doing here? Will I make a bloody fool of myself? I must show courage, I must play till I drop for my country. I looked down at the Australian crest on my green sweater, and knew that I must never yield, no matter the odds.

Hundreds of other Wallabies have reacted in a similar way since test rugby in Australia first began in 1899. It would be nice to say visions of former great Wallabies danced before my eyes before my initiation into rugby manhood, but it would be a falsehood. My thoughts related to myself, not letting my country down, and for that matter my family and my friends. You are never an isolate when you play, your responsibility extends beyond all those present. It is a fearsome responsibility, and has occasionally crushed those unable to handle the pressure of such an occasion.

Rugby is a team game, every person a vital cog in a machine. If one part breaks down, the whole edifice may crumble. The dilemma facing teams like the Springboks and the All Blacks over the years was that they had no weaknesses, whereas in past years, certainly not now, we must be truthful and admit to some Australian players being of insufficient international standard. However it was not their fault they were picked, for most times they were the best players available.

Because rugby is a team game, when the baptism of fire is over there is a mateship, a camaraderie, that lasts until death. Your team is like a family, and you become a member of a larger family, that of other Wallabies who likewise endured and gave their all for their country.

Though a team game, the simple fact is there are those who are the shining lights, the stars, the match-winners. In my lifetime there have been players who are electric when they receive the ball, the crowd sensing that anything might happen when they have the ball in hand. These are the Campeses, the Ellas, the Allans, the Towers of this world. Every Wallaby by a matter of selection is a great, but we all acknowledge there are super-greats, whose performances exceed that of the other greats.

This volume is an attempt to put the record straight. Bob Howitt wrote two volumes called *New Zealand Rugby Greats* and H. Tillman *Great Men of New Zealand Rugby*, Chris Greyvenstein penned *20 Great Springboks* and Paul Dobson *30 Super Springboks*. Apart from that most worthy production, Jack Pollard's *Australian Rugby: The Game and The Players*, there is not a similar work on the Wallabies.

Rugby is often held to be a middle and upper class sport, but until recent years there has been a void in rugby literature. The captain of the 1908 Wallabies, 'Paddy' Moran, wrote three books: *Viewless Winds, In My Fashion* and *Beyond The Hill Lies China*, and though well written they are mainly autobiographical, one chapter in *Viewless Winds* leaving the reader in a state of despair over not what was written, but what was not.

Apart from newspaper articles by ex-players like Tom Richards, Cyril Towers and so on chronicling their exploits, it was not fashionable or profitable to write books on rugby in Australia, though there was a flourishing literature in the British Isles, and more particularly in South Africa and New Zealand.

John Thornett, one of Australia's greatest leaders of men, wrote *The World of Rugby* in 1967, and the *Rothmans Australian Rugby Yearbooks*, edited by Jim Shepherd and initiated in 1981, offered a tentative history of the game.

There was then a hiatus in Australian rugby literature, influenced to some extent but not solely on the antiquated rules permeating rugby officialdom which declared an individual a professional if he profited from the game, and this included writing.

It is only in recent years that such veils of hypocrisy have been dropped, and we are at last treated with a plethora of works for the rugby devotee. Some of them have been Jeff Sayle, Chris Handy and John Lambie, *Well I'll Be Ruggered*; Spiro Zavos, *The Gold and the Black*; Max Howell, Lingyu Xie and Peter Horton, *Bledisloe Magic*; Bob Dwyer, *The Winning Way*, Jim Webster, *For Love Not Money: The Simon Poidevin Story*; Mark Ella, *Running Rugby*; Greg Growden, *The Wallabies' World Cup*; Thomas Hickie, *They Ran With The Ball*; Ian Diehm, *Giants In Green and Gold*; Phil Wilkins, *The Highlanders: The First Fifty Years* of *The Gordon Rugby Football Club*; Andrew Slack, *Noddy: The Authorised Biography of Michael Lynagh*; David Campese with Peter Bills, *On A Wing And A Prayer*; Peter FitzSimons, *Nick Farr-Jones*; Terry Cooper, *Victorious Wallabies: UK Tour 1984*; Greg Growden, *With The Wallabies*; Bret Harris, *The Marauding Maroons: The Rise of Queensland Rugby*; Malcolm McGregor, *Paul McLean*; Mark Ella and Terry Smith, *Path to Victory: Wallaby Power in the 1980s*; Bert Bickley (ed.) *Maroon: Highlights of One Hundred Years of Rugby in Queensland*; Peter FitzSimons, *Rugby Stories*; Gordon Bray, *The Spirit of Rugby*; and so on. It is a new world for rugby literature in Australia, and it is well overdue.

This book is a modest attempt to bridge another gap, to present biographies of some of the legends of the game. It first of all should be noted that present players are not included. Their careers are still in progress. As for the selection, as they say, it is 'dealer's choice'. The players selected are not meant necessarily to be the greatest in the game, but certainly they are all super-greats. There has been an attempt to obtain a smattering from different time periods, but scarcity of information even after considerable research has ruled out some candidates.

Like all countries, Australia must have its heroes and heroines. These should be from the past as well as from the present. This volume will hopefully do a little to alleviate this problem as far as rugby is concerned. Some of those super-heroes of yesteryear will hopefully shine once more.

# Trevor Allan

Australia has been blessed with gifted centres, going back to Stan Wickham, 'Boxer' Russell, 'Dally' Messenger and 'Larry' Wogan in the early 1900s, Sid King and Cyril Towers in the twenties, Dave Cowper, 'Dooney' Hayes, Tom Pauling and Gordon Sturtridge in the thirties, John Solomon, Rod Phelps and Herbie Barker in the fifties, Dick Marks, Beres Ellwood, John Brass and Phil Smith in the sixties, Dick L'Estrange and Geoff Shaw in the seventies, Andrew Slack, Michael O'Connor and Michael Hawker in the seventies and eighties, and Tim Horan and Jason Little in the nineties.

In the forties it was all Trevor Allan. Australia was searching for heroes after the Second World War, and Trevor, or 'Tubby' as he is more familiarly known, fitted the bill perfectly. He was good-looking, well-mannered, a virtual tee-totaller but not a 'wowser', was poised beyond his years and met people well.

Above all, he was an exceptional athlete who covered the ground magnificently, being particularly devastating in cover defence. He looked an athlete from head to toe.

'Tubby' resembled a gazelle or an antelope on the field, though one with a scrum helmet on, and it made him stand out. The spectators, and the selectors, could see that scrum helmet bobbing up all over the field.

The Wallaby backline of 1946, 1947 and 1948 were actually a fearsome-looking lot, Trevor in his helmet, and inside centre Max Howell and winger Terry MacBride wearing aluminium noseguards that almost covered their faces. They obviously meant business when they ran on the field, resembling commandos sent in to completely disrupt the enemy. As well, the veteran from Queensland, the mighty Graham Cooke, used broad tape over his enormous ears, and because of this you could see 'Cookie' at his best and also during his most malevolent moments.

There were some who disliked such distinctiveness, hooker Ken Kearney being among them. 'Killer' Kearney was to be a rugby union and then a rugby league great. In those days the Australian sox were bright green and gold bands, resembling hornets on the rampage. Hookers are all individualistic types who really are not particularly interested in the grand design of games, even winning and losing. They are all in seeming need of psychological counsel, their limited minds only concerned with the scrum count that day.

If a major earthquake occurred during a Wales-Australia game, with thousands injured and dead, 'Killer's' only memory would be that he was leading in the scrum count 28 to 25. 'Killer' was absolutely fanatical about the Wallaby sox. He figured it brought two to three penalties a game. He wanted some subdued colour, so that when he cheated - or struck faster than his opponent as he would say - the referee would not immediately know who had won the ball. Distinctiveness, then, might have been good for some, but not others.

The thing about Trevor is that he never gave up. He did not know how to. He was also unselfish, truly one of the greats of the game.

Trevor was born in Bathurst and came to Willoughby at an early age. One brother was a fine all-round athlete, who captained North Sydney Tech., and played first grade football as well as opening for Gordon in cricket, and his example motivated Trevor. His brothers called Trevor 'Fatty' as he was a little chubby, and this later became 'Tubby'. He started playing rugby league at Willoughby Primary, and in sixth class was fortunate enough to come under the influence of Wal Thom, a former Sydney Grammar Teacher, who instructed him in the fundamentals, the key to success at every level of the game. Thom started the school on rugby union. 'Tubby' was soon scoring a prodigious number of points. He was a veritable schoolboy prodigy. His five stone seven pounds team, in eight matches, scored 312 points to their opponents' three.

Trevor's father 'Slab' was not too interested in sport to this point, but soon became Trevor's alter ego, masterminding in many ways his son's progression. He was quite a controversial character.

His real name was Herbert, but he was no Herbert, he was called 'Slab', like a slab of teak or iron. He was a strong personality who did not mince his words, hence he was not everyone's cup of tea.

He falsified his age to enlist in the first World War, and though he was 17 years of age he signed that he was 18. His brother was supposed to look after him, but he was captured by the Germans. 'Slab' won the British Military Medal at Pozieres and the French medal L'Militaire at Bullecourt, a decoration that could be categorised with the Victoria Cross. He was badly injured in tank action during the Battle of the Hamel, and received back wounds that were so serious he was left for dead. For the rest of his life he had shrapnel in his body, and it was possible to put a fist in the hollow of his back. He was hit in the leg as well.

He had a long convalescence in London before coming back to Australia, and was then still only twenty years of age. He was eventually to have three sons.

Phil Wilkins wrote of him in *The Highlanders*, a history of the first fifty years of Gordon Football: "Slab had an acutely retentive mind and a cutting tongue. He was articulate and well-read in the classics. He could speak refined English and he used the most profane, raw Australian. "I don't give a thrush's prick - and that's a little bit of meat - if you can't take what I'm telling you. But you were awful today, bloody awful!" he would say.

"But, with a do-as-I-say, not do-as-I-do policy, Slab drew the line at his players speaking offensively in mixed company. Though he often addressed players as if they were navvies, he insisted: 'I'm a foul-mouthed bastard, but I won't have anyone singing dirty songs after the game, not with women and children outside the room.'"

Trevor went to North Sydney Technical High School, and represented Combined High Schools in 1944 and 1945 against Sydney University, Duntroon Military College and Combined GPS. In 1945 North Sydney Tech. were undefeated. The coach was now 'Slab', assisted by mathematics master Tom Haron.

'Tubby' was a pretty fair schoolboy athlete. Coached by his father, he won the CHS 440 yards title in 1944, but was outgunned by John Treloar in the 110 and 220 yards. Treloar was one of the finest sprinters ever produced in Australia. Trevor also played one game with the CHS cricket team, being a medium-pace bowler.

After high school in 1946 Tubby was faced with a dilemma, as the North Sydney Rugby League Club were after his services. In many ways the league game suited him more than rugby union, as there was more space in which to work with four players, the breakaways, off the field. His father, however, was adamant. As reported in *The Highlanders*, 'Slab' said: "You're not going there. You're going to Gordon. If you don't get big-headed and stupid, I can see you playing for Australia in the near future. You can forget about that if you go to league. There's no coming back. Go to Gordon and see how good you are."

Tubby's precocious talent was soon recognised and he went straight to first grade. In his third match he received a severe blow to the head, and from then on started wearing his trade-mark headgear. There had been another famous footballing back wearing a scrum helmet in the past, Rugby League immortal Dave Brown who, however, donned it because of premature baldness. Trevor wore it for protection.

He had a dream run in 1946, as he went immediately into first grade, scoring 101 points that season, was selected for NSW and toured Queensland after six games, and was playing for Australia in August in New Zealand, after only twelve first-class games. It was quite a year for a young boy who had never been outside of Sydney, except for his early period at Bathurst.

He was not the 'baby' of the 1946 team. That dubious honour went to inside centre Max Howell, one of three 19-year-olds on the squad, the other youngsters being Trevor and Terry MacBride. 'Tubby' turned 20 years of age on tour. The captain of the Wallabies was ex-commando Bill McLean, of that remarkable rugby family.

When interviewed, Trevor said: "I can still recall as if it was yesterday getting the Australian jersey at Whangarei, the scene of our first game. It was a tremendous feeling. I kept putting it on and taking it off." He went on: "New Zealand represented something I had not experienced before. It was a real rugby nation. As you walked down the street all the heads would turn, you'd hear them say: 'The Wallabies'. They would stop you for autographs, and you would hear rugby songs being sung. This is rugby, I thought. I had never experienced anything like it."

There is a remarkable transition from high school to club to state and then international rugby, and some never can handle the ever-increasing demands as each level of play is faced. Many a young prodigy has been brought quickly down to earth. The speed of the game, the quality of the tackling, the skills of the opponents are, understandably, just that much higher. Only a few of the 1946 Wallabies had ever played international rugby, Keith Windon and Graham Cooke being the most notable. Many had never ever seen an international team in action. That 1946 team was an untried Wallaby team, and an air of anxiety hung over the team as it had its opening foray against North Auckland at Whangarei.

The Australian team on that historic day for Trevor was: Brian Piper, Charlie Eastes, Trevor Allan, Jimmy Stone, Mick Cremin, Paul Johnson, Cyril Burke, Wally Dawson, Kev Hodda, Bob McMaster, Keith Windon, Graham Cooke, Ernie Freeman, Alan Livermore and Arthur Buchan. There were a few outstanding players that day representing North Auckland: centres J.B. Smith and Peter Smith, and five-eighth Ike Proctor. The fullback Hook was an All Black trialist in 1937, and the front-rower Squire had been on the New Zealand Services team in the British Isles and France.

J.B. Smith was the real threat, and he was up against Trevor. Renowned broadcaster Winston McCarthy wrote of him: "Johnny remains among the unforgettable players, a player who had everything, plus an ice-cold brain while on the field. So great a player was he that he could make a mediocre wing look the tops...He was just as liable to go right into a tackle before releasing the ball to his winger as pass it to him while ten years from an opponent. Big in the thighs he could break a tackle by an imperceptible lengthening of stride. He had a terrific fend, a two-footed sidestep and an educated boot."

In fairness, the great 'J.B.' got the better of 'Tubby' in this initial encounter, but the New Zealand press put his maiden appearance into perspective. 'Cantab' wrote: "Of the Australian players, the youthful T. Allan, at centre-threequarter, created a good impression. He was marking a very experienced player in J.B. Smith, who beat him on occasions, but this was no disgrace. Allan scored a splendid try in the second spell, when he ran strongly from his own twenty-five. With J. Stone, wing, in support, he sold a dummy and ran over near the posts. At this stage Smith, who had received a knock on the arm, had dropped to fullback. Allan is speedy and covers well on defence."

Australia was devastated in its opening, receiving a fair thrashing, going down 32 to 19. Trevor had his wrist in plaster after the game and a cut over his eye, inside centre Paul Johnson and winger Jimmy Stone suffered muscle injuries, vice-captain Keith Windon was ruled out of the tour with an inflammation of the lower right leg, hooker Kev Hodda was unable to bend his knee and captain Bill McLean was limping badly. Replacements were requested from Australia. It was a torrid introduction to international rugby.

Trevor's injury kept him out of the next six games, but he was picked against the All Blacks for the first post-war test, at Carisbrook. His nemesis, the great J.B. Smith, was at centre.

It was a decisive win for the All Blacks, to the tune of 31 to 8. Trevor had to leave the field in the second half with a sprained ankle but he had again created a fine impression. *Cantab* wrote: "Allan played well at centre-threequarter and his try, when Cremin made a fine opening from a defensive position, was spectacular. Allan's defence was more sound than in his first match of the tour and, by his speed and anticipation, showed he is a player of class." Though perhaps still overshadowed by the great 'J.B.', 'Tubby' showed he had a never-say-die attitude and was on a steep learning curve.

The second test was acclaimed as a 'moral victory' for Australia, though they were defeated by 14-10, fullback Bob Scott kicking 11 of New Zealand's 14 points. Johnny Smith was unable to play, his place taken by Morrie Goddard. As E.W. Kann put it, the "better team lost".

In 1947 the All Blacks toured Australia, and were beaten by NSW at the Sydney Cricket Ground. Trevor had an ankle injury, and watched from the stands. Alan Walker took his place in the first test team, but 'Tubby' recovered to play in the second match at the Sydney Cricket Ground, which was the final hit-out before the 1947-48 tour was due to be announced. He was honoured to be named vice-captain in this match, a precursor of things to come. Though Australia lost in this last game, 27 to 14, Tom Goodman wrote: "Trevor Allan was the brains of the Australian backline. He again showed himself a fine defensive player and was always dangerous in attack."

He was at home when the touring team to the British Isles, France, Canada and the United States was announced, and when he heard his own name he was overjoyed. His father said: "Are you happy, Trevor?"

'Tubby' remembers his reply: "Bloody oath I am!"

"And how do you feel about the vice-captaincy?" his father asked.

"The what?" queried Trevor.

"The vice-captaincy! You're the vice-captain."

So there he was, at 20 years of age, the vice-captain of Australia in 1947, for its 9-month tour. He had come a long way since graduating from North Sydney Tech. at the end of 1945.

There had not been too much money in the family, his father also liking the occasional bet and a drink with his cobbers, so Trevor had been working part-time in 1946 at an ice factory to help out financially, delivering 25 pound blocks of ice via a truck. It was great fitness training, running up blocks of flats with the ice, but a bit tough on Saturdays as he went to the games after the ice run.

In 1947 his boss retired and Trevor took over the lease of the truck, working 5.5 days a week to salt away some money on the likelihood of going overseas with the Wallabies. Trevor, who has remained a fitness advocate throughout the years, recalls that period with some nostalgia. "You know," he said, "I was running all the time. I now regard those days as the best of my business life. It was cash money, too."

'Tubby' turned 21 on the third match of the Wallabies tour. They lost their fifth match, an unbelievably rugged encounter with Cardiff at Cardiff Arms Park, by 11 to 3, Australia for a period only having eleven men on the field. The most serious injuries were to Wal Dawson, hooker, with a torn muscle and injured ribs, and Nick Shehadie and Eric Tweedale with dislocated shoulders. There were many other less serious injuries, including a back injury to Trevor.

At one stage a pitiful five players packed down for a set scrum, front rower Bob McMaster taking over as hooker. He looked up to see malicious grins from the Welsh front row. He said to them: "Okay, you pit ponies, we'll see what you can do!" He crashed into them, Roy Cawsey put the ball in, and Australia won it.

The next game, against Combined Services, is one that Trevor will never forget in his life time. Phil Tressider wrote about it many years later: "Like a broken sapling, the crack of the Australian captain's leg reverberated around the cavernous stands at Twickenham. Australian reserve players and supporters, scattered among the pockets of onlookers, winced.

"Out in the field on this greyest of dank London days, Wallaby and Combined Services players disentangled themselves from a maul, then huddled anxiously over a lone, prostrate figure.

"The Wallaby tour of 1947-48 was barely six weeks old but for Bill McLean, teak-like Queensland forward and tour leader, it was all over.

"Trevor Allan helped colleagues and opponents place the stricken skipper on a stretcher and move him to the touchline.

"Then Allan walked back to join the silent team-mates. Suddenly, the full significance hit him. He was captain of the Wallabies. He needed to say something, to start directing.

"He remembers turning to the boys and urging them, 'Let's get on with the job.'

"Trevor Allan was just 21 years and five days, a boy captain among the oldest, most hard-headed Australian Rugby team ever assembled. Many had seen service in World War II, one had been a prisoner at Changi."

He may not have been the youngest to ever captain Australia, that honour going to one 'Jimmy' Flynn, who was age 20 years and seven months when he captained Australia against New Zealand in 1914. But he was certainly the youngest-ever touring captain. In the next game, against Northumberland and Durham at Newcastle, a woman was heard to say as he led the Wallabies out on the field: "Why, he's only a baby."

'Tubby' was not worried about captaincy, as he had always been the captain of teams he played for. But this was different, there were some real tough and rugged veterans among the Wallabies. He worried if the older players would accept him.

There is something in the character of Aussies that they respond to a crisis, and the Wallabies reacted like the true champions they were. Little was said, but by common consent it was as Trevor said: "Let's get on with the job".

As for the service types, they were used to taking orders whoever was in charge. 'Tubby' was the captain, they were prepared to charge with him into the valley of death. There never was, for a second, a question mark about the new Wallaby captain.

The Wallaby tour was arguably the most successful Wallaby tour in the history of the British Isles. They did not win the Grand Slam, losing to Wales on two penalty goals, but their overall record surpassed that of the Grand Slam

Wallabies. And they never had their line crossed in a home international, a record that can never be bettered. Trevor led the team all the way, playing more matches than anyone else (32), and being the second leading point scorer with 86, behind Brian Piper (94). The Wallabies played 41 games, winning 35 and losing 6, and scored 712 points to 276.

There have been many highlights for 'Tubby', on top of being captain. There were the victories in the internationals against Scotland, Ireland and England, and the superlative match at Oxford, which was a brilliant exposition of the rugby code. Even the unlucky loss to Wales figures among his great memories, for the heroic defensive battle, a game in which neither fullback tackled because of the fierceness and closeness of the other tacklers. He remembers how well the Australian centres stale-mated their legendary counterparts, Dr Jack Mathews and Bleddyn Williams.

He will also always remember a particular moment against England when he single-handedly kept Australia's line intact. The English winger Swarbrick had breached the defence, and was putting the ball down over the goal-line, when 'Tubby' hit him with a copybook dive-tackle and knocked the ball loose.

The 1947-48 tour carved forever his name in the history of the game.

When he came back he married his long-time girlfriend Judith Knuckey, and they have been inseparable ever since.

In 1949 there were three games against a visiting Maori team, and Trevor captained Australia in each of them. Then it was off to New Zealand for the Bledisloe Cup. The team had an ideal management team with a couple of experienced hard-rocks, Ron Walden and Bill Cerutti, and a core of experienced players in Nev Emery, Roy Cawsey, 'Barney' Piper, 'Breeze' Windon, Eddie Broad, Don Furness, Nick Shehadie and 'C.T.' Burke. There were also a few exciting newcomers in Rex Mossop, Ralph Garner and Dave Brockhoff.

New Zealand had thirty players touring South Africa at the time, but all the Maori players were at home, and there were some formidable ones among them, Alan Blake, Ben Couch, Vince Bevan, Johnny Smith and Ron

Bryers. The Wallabies won 11 of their 12 games, and the two tests. They were the first Wallaby team to come home from New Zealand with the coveted Cup, and it was the first time Australia had defeated New Zealand twice in one season. Trevor was chaired off the field after the last test. Les Ryan wrote: "Wallaby captain Trevor Allan played a match-winning game in marking Smith. Allan's cover defence was amazing, the more so because he injured his shoulder in the first half."

The pinnacle of Trevor's career came with the possession of the Bledisloe Cup, and then being selected, along with Ralph Garner and Rex Mossop, as one of the five players of the year by the *Rugby Almanack of New Zealand*.

The British Lions came to Australia in 1950, and though selected in the tests 'Tubby' was unable to play because of his hamstring injury. His career in rugby union ended, therefore, in New Zealand in the second test. He had played 14 tests, and captained Australia 10 times.

His epitaph could not have been written better than that in *The Rugby Almanack of New Zealand*: "Captain of the 1949 Australia touring side, Allan on his second trip to this country confirmed the good opinions entertained concerning him three years earlier. An extremely speedy and elusive centre, 'Tubby' Allan puts every ounce of energy into his football, one minute in a terrific and startling burst through the opposition, the next saving brilliantly on defence. He achieves the almost impossible, by being brilliant both on attack and defence. Never stinting himself Allan does the work of two men, his cover defence and his backing-up being outstanding. A deadly tackler, Allan is always in the thick of the fray, and is ever ready to open up an attack with one of his devastating straight dashes up field; often he has caught the defence on the wrong foot by a sudden change of direction, and flashed through to either score a try or make one possible."

Over the years 'Tubby' had received many

offers to go to rugby league, and with his own economic situation he could no longer refuse. He went to the cotton-mill town of Leigh in Lancashire. It was a record signing-on fee, 6250 pounds sterling, tax free, with additional match payments for a win, a loss and a draw, accommodation and employment in Leigh, and first-class return fares for himself and his wife on the *Orcades*.

His decision created an unbelievable controversy in 1950. The NSWRU, within a week, expelled him from the game. Many years later this was rescinded, but at the time it left a bitter taste in many people's mouths, considering the outstanding service that Trevor had given to the game.

His league career in England was successful as he scored 52 tries in 97 games for Leigh, and played for Other Nationalities. He had a four-year contract, but left England after 3.5 years because of a severe ankle injury, which required six months of rest. His father died in 1951 at 52 years of age, while Trevor was in England.

When he returned to Australia he coached Gordon in 1955, and then played rugby league for North Sydney before recurring injuries got the better of him and he retired in 1958. The North Sydney experience was in retrospect the biggest disappointment of his life, as he felt frustrated he could no longer do justice to himself and his team.

In 1959 he found himself again, as a part-time ABC announcer in rugby league, from 1959-70, and when Cyril Towers retired he became 'the voice of Rugby' from 1970 to 1986.

Trevor is and always has been a credit to his family, and to sport generally. He remains today remarkably young-looking, giving every impression that he could still take off in cover defence and haul down the best of them. A boy prodigy, he became a man overnight with the responsibility of captaincy, and handled himself always with class and poise. No one ever doubted his sincerity and commitment on the field of play.

# Cyril Burke

There have been some fantastic scrum halves in Australian rugby, from Chris McKivatt and Fred Wood in the 1908 Wallabies, to Wally Meagher and Sid Malcolm in the Waratah time period, to Ken Catchpole, John Hipwell and Nick Farr-Jones in more modern times. Today the Australian tight-five matches any in the world, and scrum halves work on at least fifty percent possession.

It was not so in the early years, when rugby in Australia was fighting hard to maintain respectability in the international arena, and players were severely outgunned by the superior arsenal available among South African and New Zealand teams, in particular. The scrum halves were lucky if they received thirty percent possession in those times, and were often receiving the ball behind a retreating scrum or from a lineout an elephant could get through.

Cyril Burke was **the** Wallaby scrum half of the forties and fifties, and he copped canings that were horrible to witness, being regularly kicked from goal-post to goal-post. If he had been a boxer the referee would have stopped the slaughter. Not that Cyril would have ever allowed such intervention. Arguably he may not have had the longest pass of any Australian scrumhalf before or since. Maybe that honour would go to Nick Farr-Jones. Ken Catchpole might have been quicker, and John Hipwell might have been a better cover-defender. It is a never-ending debate.

What is not open to conjecture is that Cyril Burke had a heart like a lion, never took a backward step in his life, and took unmerciful punishment without blinking an eyelid. Ask any player who played with him: "Who would you want with you in the trenches when the going was rough?" The answer always comes post-haste: "Cyril!"

Some called him 'Squirrel', others 'Burkey' and 'C.T', while Phil Hardcastle managed a dragged out 'Cirr-hale'. He was always pretending to be 10 stone but carefully avoided the scales and was 5'7" when he had a profusion of hair.

He was not only gutsy beyond belief, he had the moves of a magician. Those who were lucky enough to have seen him in action have the same vision of him, Cyril breaking from the scrum base with mutates all round him, and him leaving them floundering in his wake as he gave them his trade-mark sidestep that left them all grabbing helplessly at thin air. No one side-stepped quite like Cyril Burke. No one ever had his audacity. During a run he would throw one, then another and then another sidestep. It was rugby magic, and all from this whipper-snapper who probably should have been a jockey. Many a great player has been reduced to a blabbering idiot by the boy from Newcastle.

Cyril is a living legend, and when he inevitably does depart this life it will occasion the biggest funeral ever held in Newcastle, because Cyril has helped so many throughout his life, and done so much for those around him. When he coached his beloved Waratahs, and won five out of six premierships, his wife Marge rightly said: "They'd do anything for Cyril." It is so true. There are many around who would do anything for Cyril.

John Hipwell will shudder when he hears again what happened in the sixth premiership game, one that the Waratahs lost. With the game wrapped up, Hippie - a living legend just like Cyril, and just as sincere - uncharacteristically booted the ball with his left instead of his right foot, and the consequence was disastrous. The kick did not reach halfway, and a late penalty bounced off the cross-bar for the opposition to win the game. Cyril never forgot such a misdemeanour, even when his best friend was involved.

With the passage of time the normal memory dims, tours merge into one another, glorious days on the rugby field are erased forever from the mind. Not so with Cyril, to the chagrin of those around him, for not only does he remember the passage of events, he can recall the errors that we all hope have been long forgotten.

It is amazing to listen to him. "Yes, you remember, Max, we were on the twenty-five, and I put the ball in the scrum, and Ken Kearney won it because Tweedale brought his leg over to help. Cookie trapped it in the scrum for a while, but he couldn't trap anyone offside, so he gave it to Buch, who heeled it to me. Chucker was on my left and I was tempted to go left, but I noticed Neville was flatter than normal so I let it out to him…etc, etc." Absolutely amazing, considering the game he is describing occurred about fifty years ago. He has a virtual photographic memory when it comes to games, to the absolute horror of those who do not desire such accurate recall.

The author recalls Cyril on the 1947-48 tour, aboard the *Orion*. Cyril is sitting on a deck-chair, writing letters back to his girl, Marge, who he married on his return. It was rumoured that Cyril used up all the writing pads and the pens on the *Orion*. He was one of the great letter writers of all time. But he knew what he wanted, and he got it. As he said, when interviewed, "I won the Lottery once in my life - I won it when I married Marge. Can't do better than that - Max, I won the Lottery." And so he did!

Cyril actually has three loves in his life, his wife Marge, who perplexes him only when she regularly thrashes him in lawn bowls, *his* club, the Waratahs Rugby Club, and his grandchildren.

In 1940 the Newcastle Rugby Union organised a schoolboy competition, which was played on Saturday mornings. The competition was restricted to boys 6st 7lb and under, with the average weight of the players not to exceed 5st 7lb. There were five teams entered, and one was from Waratah Primary School. The Waratah team could not cope with the older boys in the Saturday competition. Enter Cyril Burke from Newcastle Boys' High and Waratah schoolboy Keith Taylor to assist the team, but they were well rolled.

When the primary school boys were debarred from Saturday competition, Taylor and Burke recruited players from Central High School (now the Broadmeadow School) and Newcastle Boy's High (now Waratah High School).

The team did not have a win to this point, and played the undefeated leaders, Dangar Park. The Waratahs won. Ex-NSW hooker Ern Howarth offered to coach, and Cyril's father Norman came forward to manage the kids. That was the beginning of the 'Waratahs'. Many of the players in those first years gravitated eventually to the first team and to representative rugby. The first club pocket was designed by Cyril's father, and his mother was one of the organisers for the first players' dinner. It was called a "party" in deference to the age of the team.

The first international from the Waratah Club was Cyril Burke, who attained that honour for the first time in 1946. The second international from the club was in 1949, Jack Marshall. Ron Harvey was the third, in 1957, and the fourth, in 1968, the phenomenal John Hipwell, who attributes his success to Cyril. Then came Peter Horton, Michael Fitzgerald, Declan Curran and Dominic Vaughan.

One club highlight was in 1954, when five from the Waratahs, Ray Frost, 'Bluey' Riley, Ken Chambers, Ron Harvey and Cyril Burke, were in the Country team that defeated Sydney for the first time in 29 years.

Cyril would not know how to cheat if he tried, being as honest as the day is long. He was, however, known to use the rules to his advantage, as well as a little guile.

The Waratahs were playing a closely-contested and important game, and Cyril whispered to his team-mate Ray Frost: "At the next 25 drop-out go down injured for a few minutes." Dutifully, Ray followed orders. While everyone was surrounding the supposedly injured player, 'C.T.' took the ball and went to the sideline, still on the 25 yard line, and talked to the linesman. Frost recovered miraculously, and then the referee yelled: "Where is the ball?"

Cyril, on the sideline, yelled: "It's here, sir!", tapped it over the line and streaked down the sideline, scoring a glorious try. The referee, doubtless miffed, ruled no try, saying Cyril did not ground the ball properly. This decision incensed the Waratahs, who then took the control of the game and won it handily.

In another Grand Final game, he asked his second rower Jim Garven to stand off the scrum, and Cyril fed him. He had the try for certain, and dropped the ball. There was another scrum, and Cyril told Garven to stand off the scrum again. Unbelievably, it was another knock-on. Cyril did not give up easily, and when they won the ball again all the opposition rushed towards the second rower, Cyril faked the pass, and with his patented sidestep was over the line. A little guile from a little player was never out of place in any rugby game.

Dr Gordon Kerridge has been a good friend and supporter of Cyril's throughout his career, and was in the Royal Newcastle Hospital when Cyril was brought in with a dislocated hip, one of the worst injuries that can occur in rugby. He had the unhappy task of telling Cyril, who would assuredly still be playing otherwise, that he could never play again.

Cyril said, simply: "You're the expert, Doctor. If that's what you say, that is what I'll do." There was no fuss, no tears. He just accepted it and went on with his business. That was Cyril.

A few days after the injury Cyril was down at his beloved Waratahs Club, working, walking stick in hand, helping to build the squash court. There was no stopping Cyril, and the fact is he did sneak in an occasional game, "when we were short".

He maintained his contribution at the club when his playing days were over, being highly successful as a coach and imparting to many a youngster his deep love of the game.

Cyril was the second great half to come from Newcastle, Sid Malcolm being the first. Myth has it that Cyril was coached by Sid, but it was not so, though he went to Sam Malcolm's home when he was young and Sid would occasionally be there. Nothing enthralled Cyril more than "talking football" with his father and the Malcolms.

Football was in Cyril's blood, and when he enlisted in the Air Force at 18 years of age he sought every opportunity to get a game. When there was calisthenics to toughen them up Cyril gave it his all, as he felt it would "help my football". He did all he could to "get two weekends in a six-day leave", for, with travelling time, it meant two games.

There was a bit of luck in Cyril's career, and part of it was to be in Sydney in 1944 at the embarkation depot when Newcastle was playing a representative game. Cyril arrived at the match-with his boots, of course-and they put him in the game at half-time. He was selected, after an impressive performance, in the state team to play Army. There were some Wallaby greats on the field, such as Ron Rankin and Max Carpenter.

As he was not yet 19, and the rules at that time required one to be 19 years of age to be sent overseas, he found himself in Townsville, and played rugby league for the Air Force in the local competition. The army teams were always particularly rugged encounters, as they were fit and had a few internationals in their ranks. One local bet 25 pounds that one Army team would beat the Air Force, a fair sum of money in those days, and Cyril, who never bets, scored three tries and was the principal architect in an unexpected Air Force victory. As Cyril said: "That fellow wasn't too happy with me."

He did actually get overseas, his first landing in Borneo being on Labuan Island. He was with a Fighter Control Unit. They then went to Sarawak in another landing and set up at Lutong, which was virtually a suburb of Miri at the very north of Sarawak. The Air Force always came in after the Army and it was generally not too dangerous, though once there was some shooting and Cyril's remarkable sidestep even fooled the Japanese.

While working at Lutong in Sarawak three young boys came up to talk to him. They were 11, 13 and 15 years of age and they spoke fine English. As it turned out their families had been moved from Singapore by the Japanese to operate an oil refinery.

"Where are you living?" asked Cyril.

They pointed to a broken-down shack, which housed thirty to forty people.

"Where are your fathers?" said Cyril.

They hung their heads. "We don't know, the Japanese took them away."

A few days later fourteen males were found slaughtered, the fathers of the boys being among them.

Cyril is and always has been a caring person, and he wrote home to his mother and food parcels dutifully arrived. On top of that a Liberty ship had hit a mine and appeared with damaged food supplies, and Cyril presented them to the family.

In later years Cyril brought members of this family out to Newcastle, and they lived with Cyril and Marge, the boys being educated in Australia. "They became part of our family," said Cyril, who himself was not very well off. He and Marge changed the lives of that family. Cyril is just that kind of person.

Another item of luck occurred for him. The Commanding Officer back in Labuan after Japan surrendered told Cyril he was going to make him a corporal, and Cyril said facetiously: "Who, me?" Somewhat chagrined, the CO gave the promotion to someone else. This meant Cyril got back to Australia in January 1946, which allowed him into the Australian trials for the first post-war tour, to New Zealand in 1946. The corporal got back to Australia in 1947, after the Wallabies had left for the British Isles, France, Canada and the United States, with Cyril cavorting on board. Such is fate!

Cyril made the tour to New Zealand in 1946, going away as the second scrum half to the more experienced Bernie ('Chappie') Schulte from Queensland, who had been a Japanese POW. Every tour Cyril seemed to go away as second choice and had to fight his way back to number one.

When Cyril was in New Zealand in 1946 the team at one time was having a bad run, and after a Saturday loss the manager, Dr Ward, announced that all functions were cancelled and the team had to report to a certain meeting room.

It was a thoroughly chastened, indeed silent, team that sat there, knowing that they were going to be lashed by a 'disgrace to Australia' speech. Dr Ward walked in, followed by the assistant manager, Harry Crow.

Dr Ward walked around the room, the heads bowed ready for the onslaught. Dr Ward drew himself up and declared: "I've taught you mob everything I know [which was not much, a few conjectured]. I've tried everything. There's one thing I haven't tried. No-one - and I mean no-one - leaves this room until they're dead drunk." An 18 gallon keg of beer was rolled into the room, then the manager locked the door.

The team sat first of all in stunned disbelief, then let out raucous yells, 'you bloody beaut' being the common consent. It did not take long for the lads to be tossing down the amber fluid with rare abandon, Wallabies throughout history being particularly adept at demolishing free grog. It was not long before the room resembled a mad-house. Sitting to one side with disgusted looks were the avowed teetotallers of the team, Cyril Burke, Graham Cooke, Max Howell and Trevor Allan, all willing to follow any orders except these. They went to Dr Ward, himself in the middle of downing one, who simply said: "And I mean no-one!"

After another ten minutes of increasing mayhem the wowsers approached assistant manager Harry Crow, who had a more kindly disposition towards the youngsters, and he quietly let them out the door. They had a splendid night at the local picture show.

The enigma is that the team embarked on a winning streak after this eccentric approach. So much for the science of coaching!

This was the same Dr Ward who was the first Patron of the Waratahs Club at Newcastle, where Cyril was an inspiration throughout the years. 'Bertie', as Dr Ward was known familiarly, was a Victorian who became interested in rugby while in that State. One time, while he was at a presentation ceremony at the club, which he was chairing, he managed on two separate occasions to have poured over him (and his very elegant suit), trays of Cyril's sarsparilla with ice and beers. In the first instance, the waiter took one beer off the tray and it unbalanced the tray, and 'Doc' copped it down the back. Having wiped 'Doc' down the waiter returned with the same drinks and when behind 'Doc' put his foot on a piece of Cyril's ice and 'Doc' copped it once more. As Cyril said: "Charlie Chaplin could not have done it better." 'Doc' did not manage to have a drink all night, and was taken home by his good friend Dr Gordon Kerridge. As they got to his home the pair were laughing hysterically, and with the smell of the assorted beverages his poor wife assumed he was in an alcoholic haze. It took some time before she could be convinced that all the alcohol was on the outside and not on the inside.

To show what a good sport the genial Dr Ward was, during the meeting he got hold of the drink waiter who had done the deed, and with his arms around him sang: "For He's a Jolly Good Fellow".

One of Cyril's biggest thrills in his endeavour to prove he was big enough for international rugby was the Wallaby victory over a star-studded Wellington team. During the game, at a crucial moment, Cyril was covering desperately, and the ball was kicked over his head. Cyril dropped the kicker in his tracks. There was a penalty, but no score. It saved the game for the Wallabies. 'Bluey' Nicholls came into the dressing room afterwards and said: "You won the game for Australia today!"

Cyril clawed his way into the second test team by brilliant displays, at the same time demonstrating unbelievable guts behind retreating packs. During the second test, again at a crucial time, Cyril went for the line, and put the ball down. It would have meant victory for Australia. Instead, the referee called Cyril for barging, Cyril, who had difficulty running into the teeth of a New Zealand breeze. "Just imagine," intoned Cyril, "me being called for barging. Just think of me barging 'Killer' Arnold, Johnny Simpson and the like - they'd have killed me. You know, there are good refs and bad refs, and occasionally some who will cheat. I leave you to make up your mind about the ref that day." Australia lost the game, though it was generally acclaimed as a 'moral victory'.

On his next tour to New Zealand a man came up to him and gave him a paua shell kiwi brooch for his wife with a cardboard inscription. He said: "I saw you play, and you scored that try. This is to remember it." That reminder is one of Cyril's most treasured possessions.

Cyril made the fabulous nine month long 1947-48 tour of the British Isles, France, Canada and the United States, perhaps the greatest rugby tour in history. He went away as number two scrum-half to Randwick's Roy Cawsey, but after a series of stunning and intelligent displays was the choice in each of the tests.

While in London, there was a sister of a Newcastle friend, Ted Raisbeck, singing in 'Rigoletto' at Covent Garden, and Cyril rang up Covent Garden and received tickets. There were not too many takers for the 'Culture Club', so the tickets went to Col Windon, Neville Emery, Roy Cawsey and himself. When it was time to leave for the hotel Cawsey and Emery had not appeared, so Col and Cyril departed anyway. They bumped into the others on the way out. Cyril said: "Get changed and we'll see you outside the ticket office at 'Rigoletto'."

When they got to Covent Garden, they waited and waited but the other two did not show, and finally they went in, whingeing about them. What had happened was that Cawsey and Emery had changed quickly, jumped into a taxi and yelled: "Rigoletto! Rigoletto!" The driver drove them to 'Rigoletto', all right, but to the Cambridge Theatre, where it was also playing. Cyril had forgotten to mention Covent Garden.

As can only happen with touring teams, Cawsey and Emery went to the box office, and asked for tickets for the Wallabies, which of course were not there. They were about to leave when the manager came out crying: "Wallabies! Wallabies", and took them into a private box, the best seats in the house. So there were Cawsey and Emery, at the Cambridge Theatre, whingeing about Windon and Burke, while Windon and Burke were at Covent Garden, whingeing about Cawsey and Emery. Later Cyril dined with Rossina Raisbeck and her husband.

When he was in Paris on that same tour, Cyril bought a fairly expensive technical drawing set for a friend, which was no mean feat considering his limited control of the French language. He took it back to the hotel, and Wal Dawson, a graduate engineer, examined it with great interest and inadvertently broke the compass. Cyril did not know what to do, but set off with Neville Emery to find the shop again, which they eventually did. The salesgirl and Cyril were getting nowhere as he was gesticulating and trying to explain about the broken compass, and he could not see a similar set in the shop. However, there was a much more expensive one in the window.

Finally, the manager came out, and somehow got the idea. "Wallaby, Wallaby," he said excitedly. Cyril nodded. The manager took the broken compass, reached into the front window, grabbed the more expensive set, handed it to Cyril, and patted him on the back. Cyril's knowledge of the French language was soon apparent. "Merci, merci", said Cyril with a delighted grin on his face.

One of the sad moments of Cyril's life occurred a day after he arrived back from the Wallaby tour. His father had broken his leg, and died of post-operative shock. He had been a great supporter of Cyril's during his career.

One of the highlights of his rugby was winning the Bledisloe Cup in 1949, and in New Zealand. It is true that thirty of New Zealand's finest were in South Africa at the same time, but it must be remembered that the Maoris were not allowed to tour because of apartheid, and there were some mighty Maori players at the time. There was the legendary centre J.B. Smith and his brother Peter, Ron Bryers, Vince Bevan and Ben Couch.

Led by 'Tubby' Allan and Col Windon, there was a perfect blending of youth and experience. There were 'Tubby', Col, Neville Emery, Roy Cawsey, Nick Shehadie and Cyril from the famous '47-'48 mob, and youngsters like Rex Mossop ready to make their mark. Brian Piper was badly injured in a hotel escapade, and managers Ron Walden and Bill Cerutti, two old campaigners themselves, refused to send for replacements. Roy Cawsey, a long-passing scrumhalf, was put into fullback, and became a Wallaby hero through his exploits. History was made when New Zealand lost two tests, the other in South Africa, on the same day.

In one game, at Greymouth, the referee himself said before the game: "You're playing against the local sixteen again." During the game Cyril made one of his patented side-stepping sorties from the scrum base, and put the ball down cleanly over the line. The referee, who was the local publican and bookmaker at Westport and a hail-fellow-well-met, cancelled the try and had Cyril put the ball in the scrum again. The Wallabies understandably lost the game, the only loss of the tour.

That referee came to Australia years afterwards, and met a Sydney group from the tour: "Let bygones be bygones," he said to them. Cyril was not impressed when he was told about it.

One of the reporters had this memory of 'Burkey' in 1949: "Calling on Snow McQueen, who had been appointed masseur to the visitors, at his hotel at Whangarei just before the Australians' opening match, I found him giving ministrations to one who I thought was a local Grammar Schoolboy, and not a very robust one at that. I was on the point of saying, 'Hello, son, what's wrong with your heel?' when Snowy saved me by remarking, 'Paddy, meet Cyril Burke, the Australian halfback for this afternoon'."

There were games in Australia against the touring Maoris in 1949. "They nearly murdered me," said Cyril. Then there was the 1950 Lions tour.

The next highlight was going to South Africa in 1953, so he completed the Big Three in those years, New Zealand, the British Isles and South Africa. Those games against the Springboks were among the toughest he ever played.

When Cyril was in South Africa in 1953 he was after some silver spoons to take home as presents to the Waratah Ladies' Committee, but could not find them anywhere. He was directed to the South African mint, but was told they did not produce such. When a man there found out he was a Wallaby, he said: "Just leave it to me."

Some days later a person came up to him in the hotel, and left, saying: "This is for you." Cyril opened the package up, and it was a magnificent set of silver spoons, with a Springbok head on each. The Ladies' Committee got other presents, and Cyril kept them for his wife Marge. Cyril always cites this as an example of how Wallabies on tour are treated.

Before a game at Potchefstroom in South Africa he was very nervous as he wanted to impress to make the test team, and 'Spanner' Brown and he decided to go to bed early. He was dreaming of the South African pack and what he had to do on the morrow, and simply tossed and turned, a deep sleep evading him.

Before he knew it there was a tap, tap on the door.

Cyril pulled the pillow over his head, and ignored it.

Again there was this tap, tap, tap.

He ignored it.

The tap, tap, tap became more insistent. Then he heard a voice: "Want a cup of tea, mastah?"

Cyril yelled, at the top of his voice: "Drop dead!" It was an expression he normally never uses.

He heard the sound of running feet, and manager Johnny Wallace came in laughing. He said: "That was the first white negro I've ever seen in South Africa!"

Many of the team had heard the ruckus, and they were soon all in Cyril's room, laughing. That was the end of his sleep.

Cyril played the next three tests, and stated what many of the players of the day believed: "We would have won more tests with a kicker. We never took specialist kickers in those days."

In 1952 Cyril was picked to go to New Zealand again. He actually played for the Waratahs on Saturday afternoon and raced to the station to get the train to Sydney to fly to New Zealand on the Sunday morning.

In 1954 Cyril captained the NSW Country team to New Zealand, and Harry Crow was the manager. Harry did virtually no coaching on the tour, his main contribution being in public relations. As Cyril put it: "Muggins here did the coaching." The team rallied behind him.

Early on in the 1955 tour to New Zealand the assistant manager, Bill Cerutti - who was on his sixth New Zealand tour - asked the 'Dirt Trackers' to assemble for a 7am climb of Mount Te Aroha.

When Burke failed to appear, Cerutti went to his room to wake him. The door was locked and there was no response from inside.

Not to be outdone, the wily Cerutti climbed a balcony, entered the window and aroused the somnolent Burke.

As the party was almost to move off, Burke again was missing. This time Cyril had sought refuge in Cerutti's own bed in an effort to escape the mountain climb. 'Wild Bill', expecting this, quickly found the elusive Burke and soon had him back with the party.

Cyril played inside centre for the first test against the All Blacks in 1955 and scrum half for the other two.

Before South Africa arrived in 1956, Cyril went to a meeting, one of five Waratah representatives at the Newcastle Rugby Union Annual Meeting, when the NSW Country itinerary for the year was produced. It had been drawn up by Harry Crow. It showed NSW Country playing Sydney in a curtain-raiser to the NSW-Springbok game. Cyril got up and expressed his view that the game should be earlier, and at another place, to provide Country players with a chance of making the State team. That was all very well, except that a young 16-year-old reporter, Jimmy Armstrong, wrote "Cyril Burke Slates Country Rugby Union."

Harry Crow, who was paymaster of the railways and chairman of the Country Rugby Union, happened to be in Newcastle the day the paper came out, and was incensed. Moreover, Crow was talking to one of the Newcastle players and said that he, Crow, did all the coaching in New Zealand. The player put matters right in a very blunt and forthright manner, and this apparently soured Crow on Cyril. He was heard to say that Cyril would not go to England on the 1957-58 tour. Crow was an Australian selector.

Cyril appealed to Arnold Tancred, ex-Waratah and erstwhile manager of the 1947-48 team. Arnold checked it out and told him: "What you said is right. Harry has been saying what you said. But don't worry. It'll be all right."

Cyril made the Possibles v Probables final match before selecting the 1957-58 tour, and had the game of his life. When the team was announced, Cyril was not included.

It was a bitter blow to Cyril, who would have been repeating the tour of tours ten years apart. It would have been, according to him, "icing on the cake". Arnold Tancred rang him later and stated: "They assured me the team would be picked on merit. It was not!"

Some years later he ran into another of the selectors for that tour, ex-Wallaby Max Carpenter. Carpenter said: "You should have been on that England tour, Cyril. Harry Crow kept you out."

It was a disastrous tour, the Bob Davidson-led side desperately needing people with Cyril's experience and fortitude to bind them together.

Cyril captained NSW in 1958, but his career finished with the dislocated hip injury he got on Anzac Day, 1959. He was scoring a try, when the tackler grabbed his collar, and Cyril twisted his body to get the ball down, causing the dislocation.

This did not altogether stop Cyril, as he coached his beloved Waratahs for many moons to come.

His was a magnificent career. He never captained Australia, surprisingly, though he was vice-captain many times. He did captain NSW, NSW Country and the Waratahs. He played 137 games for the Waratahs, and 93 games for Australia, including 26 tests. His 26 appearances broke the Australian record held by Brisbane hooker Eddie Bonis. His good friend Nick Shehadie was to exceed his record. He regards his greatest achievement, however, being always available to front up for a game from 1944 to 1959.

Cyril received the British Empire Medal in 1954, was a Life Member of the Waratahs, won the best and fairest player in Newcastle seven times, and was elected to the Hunter Region Hall of Fame in 1993. He was very honoured to be the only Australian in a World XV selected by Wallace Reyburn in the sixties. The team was:

**Fullback**
Don Clarke (NZ)
**Threequarters**
Tony O'Reilly (Ireland) Bleddyn Williams (Wales)
Jack Matthews (Wales) Ron Jarden (NZ)
**Halves**
Jackie Kyle (Ireland)
Cyril Burke (Australia)
**Front Row**
H.P.J. Becker (S.A)    Bryan Meredith (Wales)
Wilson Whinerary (NZ)
**Second Row**
Colin Meads (NZ)      Tiny White (NZ)
**Flankers**
Waka Nathan (NZ)   Michel Crauste (France)
**No. 8**
Hennie Muller (SA)

Cyril Burke travelled the world, at times being treated like a king. Despite the considerable adulation that came his way, he never changed one iota. He is the same Cyril Burke as he ever was, modest and unassuming, yet confident about his own ability and knowledge on the rugby field. There have been many who have had the smile wiped off their faces as this skinny runt came running at them and then left them for dead with his amazing sidestep. The worst part of it was that Cyril would remember what he did, and was liable to remind you of it every now and then.

# Ken Catchpole

*It is certainly not difficult to decide that Ken Catchpole has been the outstanding scrum-half of the last decade. Others have made contributions to techniques in passing, kicking, and running, but as the supreme exponent of all the skills Catchpole stands beyond rivalry. Not only was he quicker of thought, action and reaction, but a judicious kicker and more subtle runner than either Going or Edwards. It is amusing today still to hear the know-alls of scrum-half play preaching the long pass and the high kick over the forwards. Both have been virtually phased out. Catchpole was years ahead of his time. His pass was never long - he considered that a waste of time. It was, however, phenomenally fast and his technique of delivery perfect. No elegant dive pass, no laboured swivel to avoid passing off the weak arm - just a flash of light to his flyhalf.*
*    - Chris Laidlaw, Mud In Your Eye*

Laidlaw, himself a scrumhalf of no mean capabilities, stated emphatically: "Only a fool would name any scrumhalf before Ken Catchpole, and certainly no Australian ever would."

Born in the Paddington Hospital for Women, he was brought up in Randwick, his father being employed in the woollen mills at Alexandria. He had one brother four years older than himself, and enjoyed being brought up in an extended family, with his grandmother, cousin and aunt. This situation remained the same almost until he left home.

Both parents were from Victoria, mother being a pretty fair schoolgirl sprinter in her early years, whose uncles and forebears played Australian Rules for Collingwood and Western Australia. His father's brothers were into cricket.

Ken suffered from infantile eczema and asthma from birth and sport, particularly swimming, contributed to controlling the asthma until it ceased to be a problem in his early teens. The positive aspect was a significant increase in lung capacity.

His early education was at Randwick Public School, and then his parents sent him to Coogee Preparatory School, where the principal Bill Nimmo was an extraordinary character. A chain smoker, he taught classes at all levels, and emphasised an ethic of high academic achievement and participation in sport. He believed in 'mens sano in corpore sano' - 'a sound mind in a sound body'. He might have been considered by some as eccentric, but to Catchy's eyes he was "an old-fashioned headmaster, strong on self-discipline".

While at school he played five or six sports of which tennis was, and still is, his favourite, and on a Sunday his father would take him down to Maroubra, where he did boxing with ex-Australian champion Mick Lacey. Mick would pepper poor Ken's face with lefts and rights. As he said: "It was probably good for rugby, as I learned to avoid being hit." However he was not overly good at it, for Rob Heming later informed him he had astigmatism, which fortunately did not interfere with his rugby. Afterwards he would go swimming to Maroubra Baths.

Coogee Preparatory School went on to year 7, and after that he got a scholarship to Scots College. He was there from second year to the end of high school.

He soon got involved in rugby, playing scrum half in the under-14s, and then, with Barrie French as coach, inside centre, because there was another scrum half in Jack Corner. He felt, later, that the experience at inside centre was invaluable, as it taught him the value of getting the ball early.

'Catchy' was all of nine stone and some 5ft 5in then, and one of the masters, Norm Pinwell, came up to him and put his hand on his shoulder. He said: "Catchpole, I'm sorry to have to tell you this, but I'm going to have to put you in the first team." He was genuinely sorry for the youngster.

He was three years in the firsts, making the GPS thirds in his first year, and GPS firsts in the two remaining years. One year was repeated at school so that he could get a Commonwealth Scholarship.

Though he grew up in Randwick, he was not an avid follower of the famous 'Flying Greens', as he had been too busy playing sport to be a spectator. He entered Sydney University and did Science, and probably would have played for the University, but instead trundled down to Randwick as they had an Under-21 team in 1958.

While at Randwick he immediately came under the influence of the two gurus of the Randwick Club, Wally Meagher and Cyril Towers, and took very little convincing that 'the running game was where it was at'. The running style was really Ken's instinctively. Randwick provided the framework.

In 1959, after one year in the under-21s, they recognised his latent talent and he found himself straight in first grade, alongside greats such as Ken Thornett and Peter Johnson. With very few first grade games under his belt, he soon found himself in the NSW team playing the British Lions. He was all of 19 years of age. There were some handy players in the Lions team, such as Tony O'Reilly, Dick Marques, Ron Dawson,

Bev Risman, Dickie Jeeps and Peter Jackson. The NSW game was the Lions only loss on tour, the Blues beating then 18-14, and though Ken Catchpole was outstanding in his debut alongside Arthur Summons, the national selectors stuck with the more experienced Des Connor from Queensland. He was a reserve for both tests.

In 1960 the All Blacks played against NSW on their way to South Africa, and 'Catchy' fronted up against them. The Blues were given a hiding by a very hungry All Black team.

Fiji came to Australia for three tests in 1961, and Ken was the Australian scrumhalf on each occasion. The Australian team for his first test was: Rod Phelps, Michael Cleary, 'Jimmy' Lisle, 'Harry' Roberts, Ted Magrath, 'Sparrow' Dowse and Ken Catchpole; Ted Heinrich, John O'Gorman, Terry Reid, Dick Thornett, 'Butch' Macdougall, Tony Miller, Peter Johnson and Jon White. Australia won the first test 24 to 6 at Brisbane, the next at the SCG 20-14 and in a novel departure the third, at Olympic Park, Melbourne, was drawn 3-3.

The same year he was selected to go on a short, six-match tour to South Africa, of all things as captain, and coach. Though flattered, he now realises how it was somewhat illogical, or at the very least awkward. He was only 21 years of age, the youngest captain ever appointed to lead an Australian team overseas. He had not even been captain of NSW, Scots College, Australia or his club. He was an undoubted genius, but it was really expecting too much. Some of the veterans on hand who were not chosen for the captaincy were John Thornett, Peter Johnson and Tony Miller. The manager of the team was Bjarne Halvorsen, and Arthur Henry accompanied the side as a representative of the ARFU. It was a tall order for the youngster, and certainly no surprise as Australia lost both tests, 3-28 and 11-23, and won only 3 and drew 1 of their other games.

The overall experience, however, socially and rugby-wise, was a profound one. From the point of view of rugby, the pack in particular learned more of the science of scrummaging, and this education provided a platform for Australia's scrum play for the next ten years. Socially, it was a grand tour, the players being particularly impressed with the cultural shock at Windhoek, present-day Namibia. In the game there, the spectators were 90 percent white and 10 percent black, and when Michael Cleary scored, the blacks jumped the fence and embraced him. Visiting teams were always hailed by the black minority in South Africa.

A visit by France rounded off 1961. It was a terrible day for the test against them, the rain pouring down, and 'Catchy' was ill and should not have played. The Wallabies went down at the SCG 8-15, due in no small measure to the efforts of 'Monsieur Le Drop', Pierre Albaledejo, who kicked two dropped goals to secure the victory.

There was a considered opinion among the national selectors at the time that 'Catchy's' pass was not long enough, so in the off-season he worked strenuously at this supposed deficiency to prepare for the 1962 season. It was to be an unusual year, New Zealand firstly coming to Australia for two tests, and then Australia touring New Zealand and playing three tests there. Des Connor, former Wallaby, was now the All Black scrumhalf.

The Australian team was unsettled at the time, particularly with respect to the captaincy. Hooker Peter Johnson was captain in the first test, fullback Jim Lenehan in the second and John Thornett the remainder, which finally provided welcome stability.

The switching and changing by the selectors was not restricted to the captaincy. In the first test, John Thornett was inexplicably dropped, and 'Catchy' was picked even though he had played only one competition game that season because of a torn hamstring. The Connor-Catchpole match-up was eagerly awaited. Norm Storey was the new Wallaby five-eighth, and Queensland's Lloyd McDermott was selected on the wing, thus becoming the first Aboriginal to play rugby union for Australia. The All Blacks won the first test 20 to 6, dominating the set pieces to such an extent that Catchpole and the Aussie backs had little opportunity to show their flair.

The dropping of Norm Storey after the first test is a decision that has always puzzled Catchpole, who of all people should be able to judge a five-eighth. He said: "It was a mystery. He absolutely annihilated his opponent and was dropped." Beres Ellwood, though a centre, was brought in to replace him. The second test was closer, but the All Blacks emerged as 14 to 5

victors.

Then a 25-man Wallaby team, under John Thornett, went to New Zealand for a 13-match tour. A big surprise and a severe disappointment for 'Catchy' was being dropped for the first New Zealand test. He was replaced by Ken ('Nipper') McMullen from Wagga Wagga, who had flaming red hair and, though only five foot seven inches, weighed in at a solid 11st 7lbs. There was no doubting the ability of the young country lad.

The New Zealand tests were close encounters, the first at Athletic Park, Wellington, being a draw, 9-all, the second at Carisbrook, Dunedin, a narrow 3-0 All Black victory, and the third, at Eden Park, Auckland, a hard-fought 16-8 win for New Zealand. 'Catchy' fought his way back into the team for the second test which, like the first test, Australia was unlucky to lose. At a crucial time in the match 'Catchy' picked up a ball following a tackle, and gave it to a player who scored between the posts. The referee ruled incorrectly that Catchpole had picked the ball out of a ruck, though later apologised over the error. It would probably have won the game for the Aussies. Former Kiwi captain Charlie Saxton said: "You were unlucky to lose." Catchpole was the mainspring of the Wallabies' repeated thrusts at the All Blacks' goalline.

Ken Catchpole was ruled out of the final test because of a badly bruised hip, and 'Nipper' McMullen replaced him. The Wallabies of 1962 were praised by the local media. One editorial in the *New Zealand Herald* said it all: "Rugby has never become the national game in Australia that it is in New Zealand or South Africa, yet this young team has thoroughly tested three All Black sides and forced us into the process to rediscover the virtues of intelligence and intuition as a relief from the drilled automatism of recent years. Let us hope the lesson lasts."

The captaincy of John Thornett continued during the 1963 tour of South Africa called, by Ian Diehm, the author of *Giants in Green and Gold*, "the tour of tours". 'Catchy' said: "John (Thornett) was a terrific bloke, and much admired. He gave us at last a stable captaincy." The tour was the most successful of all Australian tours to South Africa, and during it Catchpole was hailed as the world's greatest scrumhalf. It was the pinnacle of his distinguished career.

'Catchy' was unable to play in the first test because of a fractured metacarpal bone in his hand, but was on deck for the next three. The first test was lost by the Wallabies 3-14, but at Newlands the Wallabies triumphed 9 to 5. It was the first time Australia had beaten South Africa in ten years.

South Africans were stunned when Australia won a hard-fought third test by 11 to 9. Ian Diehm wrote about this historic test: "Thus Australia became the first touring team to win two consecutive test matches in South Africa since 1896, which assured these Wallabies of immortality. Yet they would not have won but for the great goal-kicking of Terry Casey. Ken Catchpole was at the height of his very considerable powers and the forwards were outstanding. Paul Irwin suggested in the *Sunday Times* - 'When Catchpole goes home they should make him a Life Member of the Sydney Life Savers - for that's what he was at Ellis Park!'"

All South Africans held their collective breaths in the count-down to the final test. It was an unparalleled situation for them, 2-1 down, and to the lowly-ranked Aussies. Danie Craven, a master tactician, was quoted in the paper as saying that Australia was cheating in the set pieces, and this certainly seemed to have an effect on the referee, Captain Myburgh. In the first half the Wallabies could not get any momentum through the tooting of his whistle. Catchpole said: "It was staggering. We would have won the game otherwise."

With the score 9 to 6 and South Africa leading late in the second half, Beres Ellwood miskicked and South Africa counter-attacked and scored right in front of the stand reserved for blacks. The blacks jumped the fence, and an extraordinary riot ensued, with police forcing the spectators back. Shots were fired. Australia never recovered from this point on, and finally went down 6 to 22. Still, the performance of the Wallabies on that 1963 tour was one of the greatest-ever by an Australian team, and the star was undoubtedly Ken Catchpole. He and five-eighth Phil Hawthorne were acclaimed the best combination in the world in their positions.

One person can never dominate an international rugby game, however. The success of the team was its all-round strength, with a lineout jumper of the quality of Rob Heming, breakaways who put fear into the opposition as Greg Davis and Jules Guerassimoff did, a fine hooker in Peter Johnson, an outstanding prop forward in Jon White, a superb leader in John Thornett, and great backs in Phil Hawthorne and Beres Ellwood.

Thornett next led the team to New Zealand in 1964. The All Blacks had been tour-toughened as well, winning 34 of 36 games in the British Isles. The Meads brothers, John Graham, Ken Gray, Chris Laidlaw, Kel Tremain and 'Spooky' Smith were very experienced campaigners. The mighty fullback Don Clarke was unavailable through injury in the first test, but was back into the side for the final two tests.

The All Blacks won the first test 14 to 9, Wallaby lock Dallas O'Neill going over the line in the final minutes, but the try was disallowed. It might have been a draw otherwise. In the second test former Wallaby Des Connor replaced Chris Laidlaw as the All Black scrumhalf and was a crucial factor in an 18-3 New Zealand victory. The Bledisloe Cup thus remained in New Zealand's hands.

As so often happens with the Aussies, they bounced back to win the third test easily, by 20 points to 5. It was the heaviest defeat inflicted upon an All Black team in a full-scale international. 'Catchy' cleverly engineered the first try when he flashed to the blindside and, when checked, sent Stewart Boyce on his way. It was the only score up to half time.

South Africa came to Australia in 1965, their principal objective playing for the mythical 'world championship' against New Zealand. The Australian squad against the Dawie de Villiers-led team was not markedly different from that which drew 2-2 in the series in 1963. It was not a happy tour for the Springboks, as they won only three of six games in Australia, losing the two tests 18-11 and 12-8, and being beaten by NSW to the tune of 12 to 3. John Thornett was chaired from the field after the final test. Beres Ellwood, Phil Hawthorne, Jim Lenehan, Greg Davis and Ken Catchpole were the pick of this Wallaby team that took Australian rugby to unprecedented heights.

The 1966-67 tour to the British Isles, France and Canada was next, and though there were disappointments, it was, according to

Catchpole, "a marvellous tour, four-and-a-half months in length. You can't do that now".

There were some positive highlights of the tour. They were the first Australian team to beat Wales, they defeated England and the Barbarians. They lost, however, to Ireland, Scotland and France, and in fact won only 19 of 36 matches and drew three.

The negative aspects of the tour were the impetigo that sidelined the captain, John Thornett, which led to him being dropped from key tests; and the sending home of hooker Ross Cullen after the infamous Oxford ear-biting incident, which had an unsettling effect on the team.

Jack Pollard, in *Australian Rugby: The Game And The Players* had this to say about Catchpole on the 1966-67 tour: "Ken Catchpole was the team's finest player, and deserved fully the praise given him at the dinner following the test against England when the president of the Rugby Football Union, Duggie Harrison, toasted the Wallabies in these words: 'I have become very fond of our Australian friends and have had hours of enjoyment out of the magnificent type of football they play. I have also had the pleasure of watching the greatest halfback of all time!"

As for his personal memories of the tour, 'Catchy' will never forget playing Wales, and the Barbarians, at Cardiff Arms Park. The singing of the 50,000 plus crowd held no fears for him, instead "it uplifted me, it stimulated me". Though the Welsh did not sing for the Australians in the international, they did when it came to the Barbarians game, the sound of 'Waltzing Matilda' remaining an indelible memory.

The team was the first to fly overseas for the long tour, and they stopped at Hong Kong and Italy, both firsts for the much-travelled 'Catchy'.

"You know", said Ken, "I always loved the movie *Love is a Many Splendoured Thing*, with William Holden and Jennifer Jones. Tony Moore and I sought out the hill where they had their tryst, dying to see the tree on top of the hill. When we got there, no tree was to be seen. A big disappointment."

John Thornett retired after the 1966-67 tour, and Ken came back as Australian captain for the one-off test in New Zealand in 1967 to commemorate the 75th Jubilee of the founding of the New Zealand Rugby Union. It was a rare thrill for him to be there and at the Jubilee Dinner, attended by some 300 surviving All Blacks. There was also a parade of past All Blacks before the game, led off by three of the remaining members of the original All Blacks, the 1905 team: Billy Wallace, 89 years of age then, George Nicholson (89) and Bunny Abbott (85). The Wallabies lost the Jubilee match by 9 to 24.

Brian Lochore led the All Blacks to Australia in 1968, no one realising the drama that was to soon unfold. Ken Catchpole was again the Australian captain, and considered to be the best in the world at the time.

With approximately thirty minutes of the second half gone in the first test at the SCG, Catchpole was taken off the field in agony. It was to be his last international game, the injuries being so horrendous. The All Blacks had been continually twisting the scrums and rucks, and 'Catchy' kept hanging on to the players to prevent it, and at times pulled them down in the process, frustrating the All Blacks.

One fateful time he went down, the ball trapped under him. He reflected on the situation: "As I went down I was driven into a splits position under enormous pressure. I could feel the muscles stretch like rubber bands reaching the end of their elasticity and snapping. It really hurt. There was no chance of my staying on. Then when the whole area went numb I knew it was something serious." It was All Black Colin ('Pine Tree') Meads pulling at his leg that increased the severity of the damage, and the act horrified the crowd at the Cricket Ground.

Colin Meads explained his side of the story in Alex Veysey's *Colin Meads All Black*: "You might see it in any club match or test. It has been done to me. But 'Catchy's' other leg was trapped and that I didn't know. It was a game in which our forwards were going pretty well. The Australians were getting some lineout ball but we were able to chop 'Catchy' off from passing it. This happened three or four times and he was turning back on us, ducking down and hanging on to the ball so that we were getting nothing. It ran through my mind, because it was a thing that had happened regularly to me. 'Look, if he's coming through there, he's got to be put on the ground so we can have a go at the ball!' Then, there he was again, wrapped up among his own players, tucking the ball beneath him. I grabbed his leg because he was stopping us from getting rucked ball, and I tried to flip him over. I did not give his leg a yank which was any stronger than I have given at other times. But his other leg was jammed, he did a sort of splits and was in a lot of pain. I felt terribly sorry about it. The referee did not penalise me but in the eyes of the Australians I was just a dirty big bastard. I knew 'Catchy' as a man and he was a fine halfback, yet I could feel no guilt about it because it was the sort of thing that happens in any club match. All Australia thought I was a bloody criminal and I know Australia has still got this against me."

The incident caused a sensation in Australia, no punches being pulled by the public and sportswriters in their assessment of the deed. The fact is, it looked terrible. Ex-Wallaby Keith Cross sent Meads a note attached to a newspaper cutting, which read: "Colin, are you proud of this effort?" Meads was vilified.

There are certainly no grudges about what happened on 'Catchy's' part, and the pair have met several times since. 'Catchy' simply says: "I think he was stupid."

It shortened 'Catchy's' career, but on the other hand it was a challenge for him to get his leg back into working order. It took him a year, and he started playing fifth grade for Randwick, but coach Jack Hovey eventually picked him in the firsts without consultation. In 1970 Randwick were beaten on their way to the finals, and so 'Catchy' decided to give the game another year.

South Africa came out in 1971, and he was picked to play for Sydney against them. In a game beforehand, against Eastern Suburbs at Coogee, he received a kick in the hand and had to rule himself out of the Springbok game. That effectively ended his distinguished career.

In all, he played 27 tests for Australia, 13 as captain, and over 180 games for Randwick. As John Thornett put it, he "has always been a model in speedy clearances no matter how awkwardly the ball came to him. He knows that a long, rhythmical passing swing may look attractive but is not as vital as moving the ball quickly, with a minimum of wasted time and movement".

No one had the speed of release of 'Catchy'. He was a veritable genius on the field, electrifying players and spectators alike by his particular blend of wizardry and magic.

With John Thornett, he became an inaugural member of The Sport Australia Hall of Fame in 1988.

# Bill Cerutti

**B**ill Cerutti was Australia's most popular rugby personality in the thirties, forties and fifties. Whenever rugby teams travelled, they would always be asked: "And how's Bill Cerutti?" And before they knew it, they would be listening to and telling stories about the most garrulous character ever to don the green and gold. He was the Stan Pilecki of yester-year.

There is something about front row forwards. They're all slightly crazy, and Bill was no exception. Why else would you want to bind arms with two fellow mutates and feel others pushing into your bum and your side, and look across at eight ugly faces determined to squash you like a bug? He used to say he packed down in over 10,000 such scrums. Front rowers all seem to have a screw loose, and after the game they are the ones socialising, drinking, cavorting, singing, laughing and generally making idiots of themselves.

Bill Cerutti was the son of an Italian immigrant, who began a wood-turning business on arrival in Australia. Bill was born on May 7, 1909, and died at 56 years of age on July 3, 1965.

Phil Tressider wrote, following his death: 'Wild' Bill Cerutti-you can select your sport and choose your era, there never was a sporting character to match him. The sports world mourns his death. He was a man of unbounded good humour and enthusiasm, and his influence bubbled over far and beyond the confines of rugby union football, which was always his first love.

Footballer, captain, coach, manager, selector, administrator - you name it and he was all of these. He played with his socks dangling around his ankles, the tail of his sweater falling out over his shorts, and he scorned such refinements as shin pads, headgear and mouthguards. He scuttled about the field on short, thick legs like a late-for-an-appointment crab, and he was as hard as nails, as any doughty All Black or Springbok forward would willingly vouch. He was not a big man as test forwards go, unless you measure your forwards by the size of their hearts, in which case he was a giant. He was a man's man, who found in the amateur rugby game the qualities of a great physical trial of strength together with teamship and good fellowship that he treasured so much.

In all, he represented Australia in 24 tests, played in 46 interstate games and an incredible 247 first-grade matches.

The author remembers playing against him while Bill was in his late thirties, in 1945. It was Randwick versus St George, and Bill was still battling on with lowly-placed St George. There was a ruck near the Randwick goal-line, and this voice boomed out from the ruck: "Let go of the ball, Randwick! Let go of the bloody ball!"

The ruck broke up, and there was Bill, alone, cradling the ball, yelling: "Let go of the ball, Randwick! Let go of the bloody ball!" Everyone burst out laughing as Bill looked up sheepishly.

He went to school in a rough part of Sydney, Newtown Public School, and while there showed he was pretty adept at soccer, never witnessing a rugby game. When he went overseas in 1933 he was asked what school he went to, and replied, "New 'ton College!"

His friend Dinny Love overheard Bill's answer and said to him later, "You didn't go to Newtown College, Bill."

"No," replied Bill, "but when you fellas were saying Grammar, Scots College, Riverview College, Shore, Joeys, I thought I'd better make it Newtown College. Sounds pretty good, don't you reckon?"

He played soccer when he left school and it was fate that led him to rugby union. The year was 1925, he was 15 years of age and his soccer team had a bye. He was on his way to a practice run at a local park and a friend persuaded him to spend the afternoon watching rugby union.

Bill went along and was immediately fascinated by the rucks, scrums and lineouts, and decided he wouldn't mind having a go, so he contacted a former school mate, Alan Beattie, who was playing for YMCA, then in the top Sydney competition.

The coach of the YMCA third team, Bill Fry, offered Bill a game in the second row.

"But I don't know the rules," said young Bill.

"Never mind about the rules, son. Wherever the ball is, you be there," replied Fry.

It was this sage advice that Bill was to pass on to hundreds of other young players during his career.

In 1926, Bill was at the YMCA pre-season trials, relishing the physicality of the new game, and played in the thirds, the seconds and the firsts on the same day.

Because he was still 17 they made him play two second grade games, but after that he was in the first team. Ironically he replaced his old friend Alan Beattie.

The word soon spread about this tough, squat character with a fair turn of speed, and he was picked in a metropolitan team to tour NSW country districts.

When playing a match at Walcha he grabbed the loose ball at a ruck and went over the line from 15 yards out. The try was disallowed as he had touched down over his own line.

Bill often said he was considered too young

to go with the Waratahs to the British Isles in 1927 and was thought to be too old in 1939 to go to England. The family, incidentally, remain convinced to this day that Bill did not make the 1939 Wallaby tour - which did not play a game because war broke out - because of the prevailing anti-Italian sentiment sweeping Australia.

Anyhow, in 1928 Bill was picked to play against the famous Waratah team on its return from the British Isles. He was playing for the Rest of NSW.

In his customary fashion he was all over the field knocking famous players down like nine-pins. A spectator asked another: "Who's that wild bastard racing around out there?"

A newspaper reporter heard the query, and nicknamed him 'Wild Bill' Cerutti. It stuck. The rugby world thereafter knew him as 'Wild Bill' Cerutti.

Bill Cerutti and Aub Hodgson, an electrifying forward, were the closest of friends until Bill died, yet their friendship had an unlikely beginning. Aub in 1930 was picked to play for Manly first as a frontrower, though he later became famous as a backrower. His opponent was the Glebe-Balmain frontrower Cerutti, who was considered the toughest in the land.

Bill loved dealing with youngsters thirsting to topple him off his crown, and immediately set about teaching Aub a few tricks of the trade, and an occasional right cross to keep the youngster alert. Every time Bill threw one Aub would surge out of the scrum, going after Bill with surprising ferocity. Though bloody of face, the young Aub gave as good as he got, and impressed the selectors. They figured correctly that anyone who could stand up to the awesome Bill would not back down against anyone in the world. Aub made the state team, and Bill and Aub became lifelong friends. Nothing like a punch or two for enduring mateship.

Aub remembered another encounter with him that season in a club match. Aub and Bill were having a little contact in the lineout.

In came the ball and down crashed Cerutti on Hodgson's feet.

Next lineout, Hodgson let fly with a right cross.

At half-time Cerutti sought out the youngster and said: "You know, son, a youngster like you shouldn't start this sort of thing. Let's call a truce."

Hodgson agreed readily.

At the first lineout after the break, Hodgson prepared to jump, and Cerutti felled him with an horrendous right.

"I thought you said we had a truce?," Aub called out from the ground.

'Wild Bill' just smiled at Aub. "That's lesson number one, sonny. Never trust your opponent."

Once, when they were in New Zealand to play tests, 'Bubs' Knight, an All Black prop who had indulged in a few wars with the Aussies, sent a peace offering. He was a butcher so he sent ten pounds of the best New Zealand steak to Aub and Bill.

They ate nine pounds of the steak, but cut off one pound and left it on the roof of the hotel. By game time it was a putrefying mess.

When the first scrum was about to go down in the test Bill pulled the evil-smelling steak from the pocket of his shorts and shoved it in Knight's face, with the words: "Here's your bloody steak, Knight!"

The All Black was furious, and spent all the game futilely endeavouring to catch up to Aub and Bill. Australia won the test. Nothing like a psychological ploy or two to throw off your opposition.

Bill was a tough customer, but he had a heart of gold and was universally beloved. A game in 1930 demonstrated exactly what kind of a player he was.

The British team was visiting Australia, and they had a rugged Irishman named Jimmy Farrell lining up against 'Wild Bill'. Early on Farrell let fly with a vicious uppercut, and Bill's head shot out of the scrum with the force of the blow.

As soon as the scrum went down again Bill returned the compliment, and Farrell fell out of the scrum with blood flowing from his nose. Bill was left alone the rest of the game.

At the post-match dinner Bill immediately went up to his antagonist, as was his wont, and had a beer with him, saying after a time that he was rather surprised to be on the receiving end of the Farrell right.

Farrell grinned and said: "Sure, Bill, I was just testing you out. If you hadn't come back to me I'd have been after you all day." They

both laughed, and tossed down a little more of the amber fluid. Front rowers, as stated earlier, are all slightly berserk.

Bill was in the first Bledisloe Cup game in 1931. It was on New Zealand soil, and was the last time that New Zealand would play the 2-3-2 formation, so two All Blacks, 'Beau' Cottrell and Ted Jessep - the latter going on to play for Australia and coach Eastern Suburbs - lined up against the Wallaby front row of Bill, Eddie Bonis and Malcolm Blair.

There were some immortals in that 1931 Wallaby touring team: fullback Dr Alex Ross, centres Cyril Towers and Dave Cowper, captain and halfback Sid Malcolm, and five-eighth Jack Steggall. Despite a star-studded team, the All Blacks won by 20 to 13.

Bill next year played in the three tests when the All Blacks, captained by scrumhalf Frank Kilby, toured Australia. In the first match at the Sydney Cricket Ground the Wallabies stunned the All Blacks to the tune of 22 to 17. Bill scored two tries, surprising everyone by his burst of speed.

The All Blacks surged back to win the remaining two tests, but Bill Cerutti covered himself with glory. He proved he could match it with the toughest in the world.

In the third test 'Weary' Dunlop replaced Max White. Dunlop was later to spend three years in Japanese prison camps, and his medical expertise saved hundred of lives. He was later to become Sir Ernest Dunlop, CMG, OBE, KS.

With the Wallabies leading 5 to 3, in the third and deciding test in 1932, 'Wild Bill' was concussed after a bruising encounter. At first he refused to leave the field, but when he copped another punch he was forced to leave for treatment, and Australia for a time played a man short. Bill pushed the ambulance men aside and ran back on the field, to a tremendous ovation, as he was a very popular figure. An announcer, who kept making inane comments throughout the match, said: "He doesn't know where he is half the time". His friends stated later that this meant Bill was back to normal. The All Blacks won the decider 21 to 13.

Bill was an automatic selection for the South African tour in 1933. The authors were fortunate to meet Bill's daughter Virginia Conroy, who has kept Bill's clippings and memorabilia, and even his diary for 1933.

The diary provides a few clues about Bill. His statistics were there for all to see: size collars 17.5; shirts 8; shoes 10; weight 13st 7; height 5 ft 10.5. It is the diary of a young sportsman enjoying life to the full, with reminders about people's birthdays, visiting All Black 'Jock' Richardson in the hospital, having the boys out home, lottery numbers, Drummoyne Club Committee meetings, surf carnivals he was in at Manly, Wollongong, Queenscliff, Freshwater, Newcastle, Coogee and Bondi, rugby games and practices, and send-offs to the Wallabies given by the Rugby Union, and Newtown, Drummoyne and Manly Clubs.

Even his favourite songs were included, which pointed out a romantic side to the burly footballer: Goodnight Sweetheart, Tenderly, Sweet Jamie Lee, Dream a Little Dream, Bye Bye Blues, You're the One I Care For, Cabana Love Song, Sweet and Lovely, Just a Little Closer, Little White Lies, Beneath Thy Window, You're Driving Me Crazy and Walking My Baby Back Home. With this line-up of songs, it was no accident that Bill proposed to his future wife from South Africa.

Bill was never reticent when it came to entertaining others, and needed little encouragement before taking over the baton from the band leader, or the microphone, piano or saxophone. Extrovert, he certainly was.

He was also an inveterate gambler, there being daily references to card games and race meetings, his wins and losses dutifully tallied. He was also a heavy smoker, a pipe being constantly in his mouth.

The team left for South Africa on the *Ulysses* on April 30, 1933, and Bill and the rest of the Wallabies plunged into the social life available on the boat. His roommate, 'Bimbo' White, thought he heard a scream one night as he was sleeping, grabbed his life-belt and started running. Bill had to hold on to him.

There were many keen surfers among the Wallabies, and they decided to form a Life Saving Squad Drill Team, which duly practised, and gave successful public demonstrations throughout their tour. The nature of the fun-loving and gregarious Cerutti sneaks through in the brief references.

**May 14** Played Slippery Sam at night, won 10/-. Slept out on deck and it was lovely.

**May 15** Race meeting at night. Lost 3/6.

**May 16** Had a few drinks today and was told off about making a row - told a few off properly and woke the ship up a bit - Had a great night.

**May 17** Boxing contests tonight - they weren't much good - no blood spilt.

**May 19** I was in bed by 10.30 but talked until 12.30.

**May 20** Dinner and dance tonight. I went as the "Tiger Man", Dinny as "Married Love". Had a singsong in the saloon and the Bishop came in and called us "Savage Barbarians". Had a great night and the passengers were very amused.

**May 24** I won the final of the Peg Quoits today. Tonight we had the best show since being on board - it was a fancy dress ball. I went as a Parson leading a team of Barbarians. It was a great turnout and a lot of people said it was "the best they had ever seen". John Ritter as a tramp smoked a pipe and made himself sick.

**May 26** We packed up this afternoon and are getting our voices and right elbows ready for tonight - the manager has a Cocktail party arranged for tonight - a great success - a dance after but I didn't go. We sang in the bar until 12, had supper in the kitchen and then woke everybody up.

On May 27 the Wallabies arrived in Durban for the beginning of their great rugby adventure, one which was to make Bill Cerutti one of the legends of the game. It started off badly for him, as two days after arrival he hurt his back and then got knee trouble, his early days being spent with the physiotherapist. Bad luck dogged the team as captain Dr Alex Ross was operated on for appendicitis. But Bill never worried unduly, he felt that fate was simply playing its hand.

Bill quite liked going to the movies, or picture shows as they called them in his day. He particularly enjoyed the South African ones. In one of his letters home he wrote: "Darkest Africa! Don't you believe it! There are bars in the picture shows. If you don't like the picture you don't have to leave the theatre."

Once at Ellis Park there was a charity match going on, and three of the Wallabies volunteered to play in the second half. This unexpected development was hailed by the organisers. However, they could not find boots for the volunteers, Bill, Aub Hodgson and Dinny Love. That did not bother them, they simply played bare-footed.

There were five tests in South Africa in 1933, and Cerutti played in them all. He became one of the game's true greats by his exploits. South Africa won the first test 17 to 3 in a fierce encounter.

Sir Nicholas Shehadie recounts a story that the South Africans and Wallabies were brought together after the match because of the over-aggressive and vicious tactics being used by both teams. The officials spoke long and hard about the poor example that had been set for the youth of South Africa, and proclaimed that from that moment on good sportsmanship and ethical conduct would prevail.

Both teams, thoroughly chastened, sheepishly left the room and two players accidentally bumped into one another. As they did, words were exchanged, and Bill said: "To hell with the test, let's settle this bloody thing now!" And both teams went at one another, punches coming from all directions. It took a while to break it up, as there were some very tough boys on both teams. So much for speeches on sportsmanship and ethics.

After the test in South Africa when mayhem had been the order of the day, the Wallabies gave it everything in the second test, and led 16-6 in the second half.

One monstrous Springbok, who had been a source of worry for the Wallabies, ran into a stunning Cerutti tackle executed, shall we say, with more than a modicum of unnecessary vigour.

As the South African hit the ground, Bill realised the best thing he could do to avoid the referee's wrath was to "collapse" with his opponent.

He was lying on the ground when he heard the referee's voice: "All right, Cerutti, you can get up now. You've done South African football a good turn today."

The Wallabies upset the pundits and emerged victorious to the tune of 21 to 6.

In the third test in Johannesburg a scrum went down near the South African line, and 'Boy' Louw, the massive front-rower marking Cerutti, bored into him and Bill's face was almost on the ground.

The Wallaby half back, Gordon Bennett, was about to put the ball in, and Bill and the hooker knew that they had no chance to win it with Bill in such a position. Cerutti screamed his head off.

The referee blew his whistle and broke up the scrum. The ref said: "What's wrong, Cerutti?"

Bill simply turned to his second rower, 'Bimbo' White, and moaned: "Aw come on, Bimbo, put your shoulder under me backside and give me a bit of weight."

The scrum reformed, and it went down just the way Bill liked it. Australia won the feed, and Dave Cowper dived over the line to score.

The South Africans, however, won the third match 12 to 3, and the fourth 11 to 0, but Australia salvaged some pride, perhaps bolstered by the return of captain Dr Alex Ross, and ended their tour with a 15 to 4 win.

One famous story about Bill occurred during a later match at Bloemfontein in the Orange Free State, where things weren't going too well for the Aussies in the scrum.

Bill suggested to Eddie Bonis, the hooker, that just before the ball entered the scrum they should stir up the thick red dust with their feet.

It was unorthodox, but it worked, and the Aussies started getting possession.

Another famous Cerutti story was after one of his many epic struggles against the well-known Cape Town slugger, Ossie van Eyssen. After he clashed with him in the match against Western Province, he walked into the enemy's dressing room and said to his rival: "I've come to bury Caesar. It's like this, Os, I'm not going to apologise for hitting you, cobber, as you certainly asked for it, but I think on a couple of occasions I did put too much sting into my returns, so I'd just like to let you know I'm apologising only for the ones when I hit too hard.

"Dinkum, I'm sorry, pal."

The formidable Os turned the joke on Bill when he went to his coat pocket and brought out a ticket, remarking: "Here you are, Bill. I'm sure this will interest you." The ticket was a pass for a boxing contest.

On the tour of New Zealand in 1936, in the very first game of the tour against Auckland, Cerutti got a fractured jaw and was unable to play thereafter, which was a severe blow to Australia's hopes. Cerutti never divulged who did the hatchet job on him, he figured it was just part of his trade.

Bill wasn't the only practical joker on

Wallaby touring teams. Sometimes the boys got their own back on him. When he was managing the Wallabies in New Zealand in 1949 through the absence of E. Gordon Shaw, who was hospitalised, the team leaked a report to the press that Bill's wife was touring with him. Bill immediately got hold of the press and told them fearfully: "If that report gets back to my wife I'll really get it!"

In 1937, after touring New Zealand the previous season, the Springboks visited, and Bill resumed his long-running feud with 'Boy' Louw.

Their first encounter was at the Sydney Cricket Ground, when NSW emerged victors on one of the foulest days Sydney could recall. The players were ankle-deep in mud at times, and yet NSW emerged with a brilliant 17 to 6 victory.

The South African props were the twins, Fanie and 'Boy' Louw. After a few hectic scuffles, 'Boy' Louw traded positions with Fanie to get some relief. Bill always figured he'd finally won out over the famous 'Boy' Louw.

In 1947 he was the liaison man with the visiting All Black team, the first since the war. Winston McCarthy, the legendary New Zealand announcer, had this to say of Bill in *Listen...! It's a Goal!:* "He was a wonderful person, a ball of energy, had a tremendous sense of humour and was always 'one of the boys'. It didn't matter what kind of society he was in, Bill was soon on a Christian name basis with everyone.

"At Canberra (on the 1947 trip) we were taken under the wing of the then NZ High Commissioner, Jim Barclay, a real man's man, and I knew that Cerutti and he would get on like a house on fire. Just after he had been presented to Mr Barclay, I drew him aside and warned him not to get too down to earth with our representative, as he was a funny sort of bloke. 'You see, Bill', I told him with my tongue in my cheek, 'he is a Labour man and very conscious of his high position and is full of protocol. I would hate to see you get a knock back from him if you call him 'Jim'. About half a dozen of us, including Cerutti, were invited to the Official Residence for dinner. Imagine my surprise when, after a few whiskies, we went in for dinner to hear Cerutti say to the High Commissioner, 'Where do you want us to sit,

Jim?' I shook my head at him, but was not astonished to hear the reply, "Oh, there is nothing formal about this Bill. Just sit where you like'. Good old Bill, he was one up on me. Jim Barclay told me later that Cerutti had gone to him and said that 'McCarthy had bet me a quid that I am not game to call you Jim, nor will you call me Bill'. See what I mean? I was starting from behind scratch."

Bill had a bit of an affliction, being possessed of a nervous twitch, his eyes blinking away most of the time as fast as a Gatling gun. During his successful managerial stint with the Wallabies in New Zealand in 1959, the team arrived in one town and the room allocations were read out. "Room 242, Shehadie and Furness."

Bill interrupted the proceedings. "Shehadie and Furness? No way you two bastards are rooming together. Shehadie, you're with me."

Nick moved off dutifully with the coach, who had by this act shown to all that he was in charge of discipline. The trouble was, there was only a double bed in Bill's room, and poor Nick had to clamber in at night with Cerutti. One of the team took a photo of the two of them in bed together arm in arm. Though faded, it is a classic. Shehadie says: "You know, when I woke up that first morning I was blinking, just like Bill. I swear it!"

On the 1949 tour the team were having breakfast and Bill saw that Trevor Allan was having some difficulty. It turned out his dental plate had broken in two pieces. He explained it to Bill, who immediately said: "Tell no-one, and put it in your mouth at practice. I'll do the rest!"

Anyhow, as soon as the practice started, with the New Zealand liaison officer standing by, Bill ordered the backs away, and told Trevor to take the high ball when it came to him.

He turned to the pack and said: "Look, I'm going to kick this bloody ball as high as I can. I want you to take Trevor down and give him a real work-out. He needs a little rough stuff."

They really nailed Trevor, who came up holding his broken dental plate. Bill turned to the NZ liaison officer. "Bloody shame! Won't be able to play as he is. Get him fixed up as soon as you can, will you? The boys can get a bit too rough at practice sometimes."

When the Wallabies won the Bledisloe Cup in 1949 the Australian High Commissioner Sir Roland Cutler was rejoicing with the team. Bill swapped his pork pie hat for the High Commissioner's homburg.

Bill, as stated, was considered too young for the Waratah tour in 1927, and in 1939 was thought too old to go to the British Isles. He did not agree, of course, and did not turn his back on the game. Rather, he kept playing club football until 1948. He was 39 years old and still formidable.

1n 1952 he was managing a team of Petersham Junior players during a tour of Western Australia. When a number of the team came down with influenza, Cerutti put his togs on to fill the gap. It was the Petersham Juniors versus Western Australia at the University of WA ground.

The referee, one Eddie Edwards, had just arrived in Australia from England, and after a while gave up on Bill's continuing tirade. Every decision was questioned, and constant advice to the ref was forthcoming.

Following a lineout infraction where Bill was holding one opponent and none-too-gently massaging another, the referee gave Bill his marching orders. Bill was then 43 years of age, an Australian selector, and it was to be his last game of rugby.

Bill never held grudges, and was a great post-match party animal. He sat next to Edwards at the table, tossed down a few with him, and was soon arm-in-arm. Feeling none the worse for wear, Edwards said: "If I had known you were such a good bloke, I wouldn't have sent you off."

There never has been another character in the game like 'Wild Bill' Cerutti. He was a man's man all the way. He was suited like no other to the world of the rugby tourist. He was as tough as nails, was never bested in his career, and never

took a step backwards. There was no malice in the man, and he was universally beloved because of it. As a technician in his position he was second to none. He was strong, fearless and surprisingly fast in the loose. Maybe he threw the occasional punch first, but for Bill it was a manhood thing, and there was no greater test of that than in an international rugby scrum. Bill loved the physicality of it all, he gloried in it. Like the boxer getting high on the smell of liniment, Bill got his jollies as he bound with such as Eddie Bonis and 'Bimbo' White and eyed off his malevolent opponents before the power surge as the packs collided.

Let's hope there is a game in heaven. If so, Bill's packed down in about 30,000 scrums by this time. They'd still be shaking their heads up there at this dynamo, who could both take as much as could be given and dish it out in more than equal measure.

And when the games are over up there, Bill would be leaving the field with his arms around his opponent, laughing and enjoying the brotherhood and mateship of it all. Then the caps of beer would be off, and Bill would be singing:

The bubbles on the beer
Keep haunting me
Every time I have a drink
I'm as happy as can be, etc.

Soon he would be at the piano, or the drums, and maybe a game of cards through the night. With his mates. For he had no enemies. They all would know that underneath it all 'Wild Bill' was just a big pussycat, loving life and loving rugby. They simply don't make them like Bill any more. When he died, some of the toughest men in the world wept openly. He was that kind of man. A legend.

# Graham Cooke

You see, he was bred in a bangalow wood,
And bangalow pith was the principal food
His mother served out in her shanty.
Henry Kendall's *"Jim the Splitter"*

Graham Cooke was born in Nanago, and whether there were bangalow or iron-bark trees there is open to conjecture, but what is not is that he was, arguably, the toughest second rower ever to play for the Wallabies. The saying is he was tough as teak, but bangalow and iron-wood can be adequately substituted.

He could never in any stretch of the imagination be called handsome, but his 6' 2.5" unbelievably lean frame was certainly distinctive. His hands were immense, like grappling irons, and the knuckles were enormous. They stood out like a series of stony ridges. His ears were like dinner plates. There were no visible scars on his face, perhaps signifying that he was rarely hit. It was no wonder, as there was dynamite in each hand, and a simplistic ethos in his brain that related to survival of the fittest.

There was not an ounce of fat on his body, his stomach muscles rippling even in his advanced thirties. There was however a strangeness to his body, the broad shoulders and narrow waist tapering to unusually thin legs for a giant, and when he ran, it was with a distinctive, mincing gait.

Off the field, 'Cookie' was a pussy-cat. He did not drink or smoke. "A wowser", he called himself. His decision to abstain was not out of any great self-rightousness. His father died at an early age and smoked heavily, and his mother did not like the noxious weed. It was as simple as that, and 'Cookie' was a simple man.

On the field, 'Cookie' was a smouldering keg, which would explode only if circumstances demanded it. He believed in an eye for an eye and a tooth for a tooth, though in actuality he himself never lost either. His opponents were not so fortunate.

One time, in an Australia versus The Rest game in Sydney to select the 1947-48 Wallaby team to tour the British Isles, France, Canada and the United States, cagey second rower Dr Phil Hardcastle kept holding Graham in the lineout. Graham gave the stuttering Phil the obligatory warning. After all, it is a gentleman's game. Hardcastle ignored the warning and held again. Cookie whirled around with those monstrous mitts and let fly. Unfortunately or fortunately, Hardcastle, a University man, ducked ahead of the Les Darcy-like blow, and front rower Eric Tweedale was carted off the Sydney Cricket Ground that day, oblivious to what had happened. Even Cookie made mistakes in the heat of the moment.

Anyhow, young Graham was born in Nanago in Queensland, near Kingaroy, in what is called 'Joh's Country' out of respect for the New Zealand - born premier Joh Bjelke-

Bill Cerutti and 1946-47-48 Australian captain Bill McLean tossing a few down at Bill's Brisbane pub.

Nick Shehadie, Dr Danie Craven, Cyril Burke and another Wallaby comparing silver mugs.

**Graham Cooke Showing he can handle more than a scrum.**

Greg Cornelsen (headband) and Stan Pilecki break from a scrum against the New Zealand Maoris.

Scrumhalf Ken Catchpole looking for support.

Queensland flankers Tony Shaw and Bruce Kennon tie up All Black halfback David Loveridge at Brisbane in 1980.

Nick Farr-Jones on the burst. With Nick in your team it was like having a third breakaway.

Cyril Burke passing to Nev Emery during the 1949 New Zealand tour.

Andrew Slack with the ball, Michael O'Connor and Brendan Moon in support – Queensland against Manawatu in Palmerston North.

Mark Ella tackling, Simon Poidevin, Andy McIntyre and Michael Lynagh preparing to assist.

**Two Queensland stalwarts celebrating a win – Roger Gould and Paul McLean.**

**Chris Handy outside his Jubilee Hotel.**

Petersen who dominated Queensland politics for all-too-many years. While a babe in arms, the family left there to temporarily settle in Thornville on a small country farm. Cookie was there until about 9 years of age, his father dry farming, that is existing on a property with about 20 milking cows, everyone depending for survival on the 20 demanding beasts. The cream was taken daily three miles to the station, and thence to the Oakey butter factory.

'Cookie's' father was born in the Downs, at Mossvale, and one of his forefathers was stoned to death in northern Ireland. His old man was about 6' 3" and 16 stone. Cookie's mother was about 5' 10", tall for that time period, and was born in Lincoln, England. She was a good horsewoman and would travel throughout the district giving private music lessons, which would often require her to stay overnight.

'Cookie's' parents had five children, three boys and two girls. They were all tall and rangy, but opportunities for sport were limited in those days. Only his older brother displayed any particular facility, playing top-grade tennis in Toowoomba with the likes of the great rugby league scrum half, Duncan Thompson.

'Cookie' himself played little sport early on, going for long bushwalks to Table Mountain and Hell Hole, and fishing for yabbies. His father, who next moved to Toowoomba, was engaged in the woodcutting business. The kids would all co-operate in the cutting and the stacking of the firewood, and Cookie and the rest of the family would handle the deliveries.

When 'Cookie' was fourteen his father died, and despite the protestations of his teacher, he left school to go to work. He started out delivering papers, but from then on, as he put it: "You name it, I did it!" He worked as a blacksmith striker, erected windmills and built tanks, until finally he got apprenticed as a carpenter, a trade qualification he eventually completed.

Graham was big for his age, and tough, and he was prevailed upon when 17 years of age to try his hand at rugby in south Toowoomba, though he had no prior experience at the game. Toowoomba at the time was one of the hot-beds of rugby league, but the players at South End all switched to rugby union. But for that switch he might have been a rugby league convert. However, Graham asked his mother if he could play rugby, and she said he could not. Reluctantly, she agreed he could play when he was 18.

One story told to the author by an ex-rugby league great and Kangaroo captain Herb Steinohrt before he died, was that one day a youngster approached him and said: "Mr Steinohrt, one day I am going to play for Australia just like you." Steiney patted him on the head and said: "I'm sure you will, son." That boy was Graham Cooke.

Anyhow, Graham threw his hat in with the Toowoomba South End boys when he was 18 years of age, a complete neophyte in the game. Graham reflected that the South End boys were a "lot of louts, the roughest and drunkenest bunch, there were many larrikans in the area. They called them the South End push. They actually turned out, however, to be a fine bunch."

Graham stood out in stark contrast to his compatriots, as he was and has always been a strict teetotaller. Graham's idea of a big night was a double sass and a squash and lemon.

In his first year, 1938, Graham made the Toowoomba representative team, and played against Warwick and Dalby. He was on his way, but his first big break came when he went to Brisbane and came up against two big city second rowers. They tried to show Graham a thing or two about rough tactics, and they quickly learned what many others did over the years, that when provoked 'Cookie' had a right hand that could have graced the boxing rings of the world. He said, in a matter-of-fact manner: "I didn't back down. I knocked one fella's tooth out."

'Cookie' had served notice that he would not be intimidated. He was now 6' 2.5" and 14 stone, with no superfluous fat on his body. He was selected in the Queensland team that year, though he was still living in Toowoomba. The manager was a dentist by the name of Darville Hunt, who took a liking to the young country giant. It has been stated facetiously that Hunt liked him because 'Cookie' was sending so much business his way.

Hunt gave 'Cookie' an old dress suit later on, which 'Cookie' not only wore on his overseas tours, but still possesses. In recent years he won a pair of slacks from Rothmans in a contest for the oldest pair of trousers, and he submitted those from the dress suit. 'Cookie' never was one to throw things away - except opponents.

Following the interstate games, 'Cookie', at 20 years of age, was selected to play for Australia in Sydney against the All Blacks. It was the second year of the Bledisloe Cup, and the first time it was held in Australia. There were some legendary players in that Wallaby team: frontrower 'Wild Bill' Cerutti, hooker and fine all-round athlete Eddie Bonis, Victorian breakaway Owen ('Lanky') Bridle, halfback Sid Malcolm, winger Dave Cowper, fullback Jack Steggall, centre Sid King and captain Tommy Lawton.

The All Blacks also had stars aplenty: hooker Ted Jessep, who was to play for Australia and New Zealand and successfully coach Eastern Suburbs; breakaway Hugh McLean, brother of famous NZ journalist T.P. McLean; breakaway Jack ('Lugger') Manchester, whose ears rivalled 'Cookie's'; captain and scrum half Frank Kilby; five-eighth 'Rusty' Page; second five-eighth 'Bunk' Pollock, and winger Arthur Bullock-Douglas.

Australia won the first test 22 to 17, the All Blacks the second 21 to 3, and the decider went with the All Blacks by 21-13. 'Weary' Dunlop from Victoria came into the final test. During the war Dunlop spent three years in Japanese prison camps, and his medical training saved hundreds of lives. He became a legend, and was to be Sir Ernest Dunlop, CMG, OBE, KS. Two future knights of the realm were in this test, New Zealand's 'Pat' Caughey and the Aussie 'Weary' Dunlop. 'Cookie' was an indispensable part of the Wallaby team, playing in all three tests.

Graham was an automatic choice to go to South Africa in 1933. It was only the fourth time a team from any country had visited South Africa, and the first tour by an Australian team to that area of the world. These were the good old days when teams travelled by ocean liner, in this case the *Ulysses*, and Cookie revelled in the experience, doubly secure in that his donated evening suit would do him justice at the evening dinner-dances. There was no coach those days, the manager Dr W.F. ('Wally') Mathews and the captain Alex Ross being responsible for training and tactics. Some of the past heroes were Malcolm, Cerutti, Bridle, the

'idol of Manly', Bob Loudon, Bonis, Steggall and Cowper; the legends-to-be were 'Cookie' himself, winger Doug McLean of the famous McLean rugby dynasty, winger 'Jockey' Kelaher and the ubiquitous Aub Hodgson.

Injuries did not aid the Wallaby cause, Aub Hodgson fracturing a wrist and Sid Malcolm breaking a collar-bone early on. Disaster really struck when the captain, Dr Alex Ross, was operated on prior to the first test for appendictis.

Graham was selected for the first rugby test ever played by an Australian team in South Africa, but the Wallabies, captained by Dave Cowper, went down by 17 to 3. The rugby immortal Danie Craven played scrum-half for the Springboks. *The Star* of July 10 reported that Cooke "was excellent in the lineout".

The second test at Durban resulted in an emphatic and surprising Wallaby win by 21 to 6, Graham again playing in the second row and dominating the lineout. The Springboks struck back at Ellis Park, winning 12 to 3. Graham, with a sprained ankle, missed the fourth and fifth tests which the Springboks won by 11 to 0 and 15 to 4.

All in all, the 20-year-old had a fine tour, playing in three of the tests and holding up physically against the most powerful pack in the world.

When he returned to Australia, Graham was in need of a job, and he was offered one in the mines of South Africa. He remained there from 1934-37 and during that period played for the East Rand Pty. Mines Club, and the New State Areas Mines Club, which had the honour of being the Transvaal Provincial team for the four years he was playing in that country. When one realises that the South African forwards were considered the finest and the toughest in the world, and 'Cookie' more than held his own with them, it is obvious at this period of his life he was playing magnificently.

When he returned to Brisbane in 1938 he played for Mayne Junction Club, and the following year changed to the YMCA team, for whom he played in 1939-40-41. He represented Brisbane and Queensland in this period, but the irony is that he was not selected in the Wallaby team of 1939 that went to the British Isles. He was considered "too old". The team did not play a game, war being declared soon after their arrival in England.

In 1946, at 34 years of age, Graham made one of rugby union's most famous comebacks when he was selected on the first post-war Wallaby tour, a six week jaunt to New Zealand. It was there that Cookie got the nick-name of 'Kiwi', which he has been called ever since by his rugby associates. He had last played against the All Blacks in 1932, 14 years previously.

He was Australia's best tight forward on that tour, demonstrating for all to see unbelievable fitness for his age, superb cunning and ruggedness in the lineout and remarkable strength in the set scrums. He was a forward who would have graced any Springbok or All Black scrum, a modest country man with very few complexes. He was a man's man in every respect.

It has to be said that he was not everyone's cup of tea. Even his own team shunned him when he illegally flattened the great Maori scrum-half Dr Manahi Paewai in the Wellington match. Graham had a rather simplistic approach to the game, and he reasoned that Paewai was running rings around the Wallabies. After a 'Toowoomba hello' from Graham, all the 'Doc' saw was stars. The traditionalists among the Wallabies were not amused.

Graham was not picked for the first test, won easily by New Zealand 31 to 8, but common sense prevailed in the final test, which Australia lost 10 to 14, the Wallabies claiming a moral victory. Graham stiffened the pack.

The 'baby' of the team was Max Howell, and he was forever grateful for Graham's presence. Every time Max was flattened by an over-zealous or late tackler, 'Cookie' was over in a flash, and with steel in his eyes would say: "Leave the kid alone or you'll answer to me!" No one ever challenged 'Cookie' when his dander was up.

The year 1947 was a crucial year in Australian rugby, as the Wallabies were to embark on a 9-month tour of the British Isles, France, Canada and the United States. This was the grand-daddy of all tours, and it came up only every ten years.

The All Blacks were sent over to Australia to give all the aspirants a going over to test their mettle. Cookie was on the outer again in 1947, despite his heroics the previous year. It was a combination of age and his deserved reputation to use his infamous equaliser, a fantastic right hand, in emergency situations. He did not make the first test in his home town, but was given a run as an eighth man, certainly not his preferred position, in the final test.

When the team was announced, 'Cookie' made it, at 35 years of age. E.W. Kann, probably Australia's premier rugby writer of the time, lamented the selection, saying that 'Cookie' was much too old for such an arduous tour.

Nothing was further from the truth, as the freakish Graham became the first Australian to play against all the then major rugby-playing countries of the world. He had played against New Zealand and South Africa, and on this, his final tour, he was selected against England, Ireland, Scotland, Wales and France. And on top of that he had the greatest longevity of any rugby player in history, representing his country's interests. Only John Hipwell rivals him from 1932 to 1948. He also played 23 matches on tour. So much for being too old.

Graham had a central role in the infamous 'Battle of Llanelli' at Stradey Park in 1947, after which Ivor David never refereed another international match. Time and again David brought the two packs together to warn them. The game however got completely out-of-hand, the level of thuggery being ridiculous, so much so that Australian manager Arnold Tancred tried to get on the field to cancel the game. This would have been unparalleled in international rugby history. The Wallabies forced him back, one player saying sharply: "They started it, we'll finish it."

'Cookie', who was not the captain, turned to the team and said: "This is it, lads!" He calmly went into the next ruck and threw his lethal short right. One player went down as if he was pole-axed. Another came at him and down number two went. A third went the way of the other two.

The strident whistle of the referee signalled an end to the mayhem, and his arm pointed to the stand. It was a send-off, not the first in international rugby history, but a rarity nevertheless. 'Cookie', head bowed, walked towards the pavilion.

As he retreated he bumped into another player, Col Windon, who was headed in the same direction. 'Cookie' said: "Col, what are you doing?"

Windon said: "I've been bloody-well sent off, that's what!"

"You?" queried 'Cookie', "I thought it was me!"

"No, 'Cookie', it was me," said Windon, and kept walking. The referee had seen an incident involving Windon, and missed 'Cookie's' one-man war.

'Cookie' returned to the fray. With due respects to Windon, who was a runner in the war, in these circumstances we preferred to have the assault troops.

Australia won the game, 6-4, in a dramatic finish.

Noted Welsh writer J B G Thomas gave his version in *the Western Mail and South Wales News*, in masterly understatement: "Forward it was a terrific battle, but I would rather forget some of the acts by players of both sides during the heated melees. The referee, Mr Ivor David, had a difficult task, but did it well. Rugby was never intended to be a game of play the man but one of play the ball, and this game contained too much feeling."

Graham Cooke at 36 came back to Australia as the outstanding tight forward on the Wallaby team. Perfectly conditioned, tough as nails, he was a man who did not relish defeat, and played every game to the limit. He was not an enforcer, and usually asserted himself only when the opposition had deviated from the rules. His jumping skills were amazing, aided by the sharpest elbows in the business and hands that were frightening in their giantism. When he came back from the Wallaby tour he had done it all.

On the return of the Wallabies from their grand tour Graham linked up with Southern Districts, but was unavailable for selection for the state. It was his intention to retire from football, but when the Police Club was admitted to first grade Brisbane rugby he was persuaded to reconsider his decision and was appointed as captain and coach.

During his years in the game 'Cookie' had never had a serious accident, but such are the vagaries of sport that in his very first match with his new team he broke his arm, and had to have a plate inserted. It forever limited his range of movement and, in the long haul, through nerve damage and consequent wasting, the enormous strength in that arm diminished. His career was over.

One honour that was bestowed on him in 1949 was becoming the honorary manager of the Australian team during their visit to Ballymore.

He came to live with Max Howell for six months in his later years, and at one stage got alarmingly ill. Max was in fear of Graham losing his life, so he called Dr Clem Windsor, a 1947-48 team-mate and highly respected surgeon, to check him over. Graham's face was as white as a sheet, and he really looked as if he were on his last legs. His eyes were closed.

Max walked into the room and said, quietly, "Graham, I've brought Clem Windsor in to see you."

Graham's eyes opened, and he beckoned Clem to his side, and whispered weakly in his ear.

Clem got up with a big smile, shaking his head. "What did he say, Clem?" Max asked.

Dr Windsor said: "'Cookie' said he didn't kick me in the head that day." We both laughed. 'Cookie' must have mistaken the medical examination for absolution on his death bed.

'Cookie' passed away while this book was going to press. He had lived at Coolum on the Gold Coast. A rugby rarity, he was a physical freak, and Australia may never see his like again.

# Greg Cornelsen

Greg Cornelsen is modesty personified, a veritable giant in body build with an underlying shyness that marks him irrevocably as a country boy. One of his early coaches, doughty ex-scrum half 'Barney' Walsh, had difficulty remembering his name, but had played against his father, so he named him 'Rudy'. 'Corney' was another obvious nickname that was used, but it was the appellation 'Every Mother's Son', or the abbreviated 'EMS', that stuck throughout his career. Wallaby front rower Chris ('Buddha') Handy gave it to him. His quiet and unassuming manner, his kindness, good manners, and his country-boy courtesies made the designation completely appropriate.

He was born in Randwick of athletic parents, his mother being outstanding in a number of sports, a 'natural' at tennis and golf, and father Rudy a rangy forward for Randwick who was not only good enough to win state selection in NSW in the post-war forties but was a fair to middling cricket player as well. In appearance Rudy was like a young giraffe, but he got around the field like a gazelle. The author, at 18 years of age, alongside Rudy made his first grade appearance with Randwick and remembers clearly being protected by him and a behemoth called Bernie Jones whenever he was being attended to in an over-officious manner in club games. One's confidence rose when one heard them cry: "Leave the kid alone or you'll answer to me."

Rudy always had a yearning for country life and so he left the die-casting factory his father had started to his manager and headed out of 'the big smoke' to a property 40 miles east of Armidale at Jeolga. Greg, who was born 29 August 1952, was now five years of age. It did not take long for the youngster to settle into the exacting but exotic world of the 'bushie', the wallabies and kangaroos, the cockatoos, crows and galahs being his constant companions. The biggest influence on his life was his father Rudy. Greg said: "He was supportive though he didn't overly push me in any way. He just encouraged me. He felt correctly that the secret in any sport was the basics, tackling, catching, kicking and passing."

He went to the local one-teacher twenty-student mixed school at Jeolga, and played his first rugby, rugby league, when he was nine years of age. Because of the limited number of boys available, his school supplied the forwards and a school ten miles out of Armidale the backs, and they played against St. Mary's school in Armidale. Greg said: "We were all very excited, and when we ran out on the field the other team gave us three cheers. No one had told us about anything like that. We felt like real dills."

He was at the back of the scrum in his first match, and his father had taught him how to tackle low. Greg laughed as he reminisced: "I remember it as clear as a bell and so can Dad, who reckons it was the best tackle I ever made, before or since. The winger got away and I was on the right line or whatever, and I tackled him low, and as I got up everyone cheered. The best tackle I ever made."

At age ten his parents sent him to boarding school at 'TAS', The Armidale School. The facilities and teachers there were excellent, and his athletic prowess soon became apparent, as he captained the under 11s, 12s, 13s, and 14s, in turn. He didn't play in the under 15s as the coach of the school second team gave him a run in 1967, and he then had three seasons in the firsts, in 1968, 1969 and 1970. He recalls vividly the support and encouragement of the school coach who brought him along. In 1969 he made the second combined GPS team, and the Australian Schoolboys Under 17 team to South Africa. He was on his way. In 1970 he made the GPS firsts and captained the school. He was outstanding in other sports as well. He high-jumped 5'10" using the scissors because he was jumping into saw-dust, and was second in the GPS hurdles, breaking the previous record in the process. He also played first team cricket and swam for the school. A strapping country boy, he was 14.2 stone and 6'2".

After high school Greg went to the University of New England, studied economics, and played for Royal Page College for four years in the New England competition. His team won the premiership each year. He made it into the New England combined team in his first year and they triumphed in the Country Week competition. This was a period of resurgence in country rugby, and much of the credit lies at the doorstop of Daryl Haberecht and Newcastle lawyer Ross Turnbull. They were later to make up the highly successful management team for the Wallaby team of 1978 during their tour of New Zealand. Greg made the Country second team following the Country Week tournament, to be coached by future national coach Haberecht. He was switched to breakaway at this point.

The 18-year-old got a run against Queensland for Country firsts in that year, 1971, and he went up against the ageing former Wallaby super-star, breakaway Jules Guerassimoff. "He nearly took my ear off when his tag slid along my head," Greg recalled.

In 1972, 'Rudy' was picked out of the Country seconds to play for an international team against France in Noumea. Four

Australians and five New Zealanders were sent. "We were thrashed, but it was a great experience," Greg reminisced.

In 1973 he was fulltime into the Country firsts as well as the NSW team, and played against Tonga. The Country team beat Sydney and Queensland that year, and most of them made the NSW team.

In 1974 'Rudy' injured his ankle playing against Queensland, and missed all the preliminary games against the visiting All Blacks. However, he was selected as a reserve in the muddy first test in which Mark Loane broke his hand. 'Loaney's' injury was that stroke of luck that allowed him to ease his way into the Australian team in the following test.

It was to be Greg's first of 25 tests. He regards himself, with the benefit of hindsight, as being rather fortunate, as he feels his play still possessed at the time an element of immaturity. He believes he was too young at 21 years of age to enter the big time.

On Wednesday prior to that first test the team got together for their initial meeting, and an extremely anxious and nervous youngster listened to the proceedings with awe. John Hipwell was the captain and Stuart ('Grunter') MacDougall was the vice-captain. The genial Bob Templeton was the coach. 'Tempo' talked about the previous game and how Australia should play the dreaded All Blacks, and 'Hippie' also said a few words. It needs to be added that Greg was never a violent player, use of the knuckle never being part of his repertoire. MacDougall, as captain of the forwards, soon made his position clear: "Fellas, I think the only way we're going to beat this mob is to take them on in the forwards and start a 'blue' in the first lineout." 'Jeezez!' thought Greg. He felt like saying that maybe there was another way. All he could think of was that he was marking one of the all-time great All Blacks, the tough Ian Kirkpatrick, and somehow he didn't feel as if it was a reasonable match-up between himself and this icon.

Before the game, with Greg understandably as nervous as a kitten, he was approached by MacDougall, who Greg feels was "a great vice-captain, he'd throw punches at anybody, no matter their size, he'd never back down". MacDougall said to Greg: "The difference in test match rugby is essentially that it's played at a higher intensity, but if you make a mistake it can really cost you as they can score from it."

Greg was still somewhat confused and anxious about the mid-week pronouncement re the impending stoush. At the very first line-out, however, absolutely nothing happened. Ray Price, a rugged performer whose body was put on the line every match he ever played, confronted MacDougall. "What about the bloody fight?" he asked. All Greg could think of was 'Shut up, Pricey, you stupid bastard!'

At the following lineout MacDougall threw a punch and everyone was into it. Greg looked over anxiously to Ian Kirkpatrick, who was also not interested in the engagement. They "were the only two not having a go!" Kirkie after a time quite calmly called out: "Yeah, come on, that's enough. Let's break it up."

Greg eagerly added his own comments. "Yeah, fellas, let's break it up!" The game proceeded with scarcely an incident, much to Greg's evident relief. It was a drawn game at Ballymore, 16 to 16, Paul McLean missing a kick at the end that would have won it for the Wallabies.

The third test was a well deserved and clear victory for the All Blacks in Sydney, 16 to 6.

In 1975 Greg was in the NSW side and England was on tour. He did not play well for NSW against them, but had a blinder as Country took their scalps in a mid-week game. Test selection, however, did not come his way, though rugby immortality awaited him when Country played City. The country coach was again Daryl Haberecht, who, though he stressed the fundamentals, was also a master of innovation, introducing the 15-man scrum and the 'up the jumper move' to the sport.

The 'up the jumper move' was designed as a surprise following a free kick, and the Country team practised it assiduously. 'Hippie' would take the tap, and then join thirteen of the players in a horse-shoe formation with all the players with their rears to the opposition. Only the full back did not participate. The ball was then passed along the formation until it came to Cornelsen, who was to stuff the ball up his jumper. He and the rest of the team would then put their hands up their jumpers, break formation and run towards the opposition.

Before the match, Greg really did not believe the move would ever be called, and had some trepidation if it ever was. All he dreamed of was the ball being trapped up his jumper and being kicked to death at the bottom of some ruck.

He was quite relieved as 'Hippie' never called the move. The game was almost over, with City narrowly ahead of Country at the Eastwood ground. A penalty was awarded Country on their own 10 metre line, right next to where Daryl Haberecht had placed himself. "Tap five!" Haberecht yelled urgently, "Tap five!" Greg's anxiety level suddenly rose as the fateful move was called.

'Hippie' followed the coach's orders, the team went into the horseshoe formation, rears to their opponents, 'Hippie' tapped the ball, then ran into the formation, the ball passed through various players until Greg got it and forced it into his jersey. All hands went up their jumpers, then they all dispersed and ran at their opponents. Pandemonium and bewilderment reigned on the other side. They simply had no idea where the ball was. Greg ran 30 yards from the left hand touchline and pulled the ball out earlier than planned, in fear that he might indeed finish up at the bottom of a ruck. The opposition then saw the ball, and the cover defence herded him towards the touch-line. Greg saw Geoff Shaw and threw the ball back inside to him. 'Bunter' got to five yards from the tryline and gave the ball to Brian Mansfield, who crashed over and scored. Country had now drawn level with City, and Jimmy Hindmarsh kicked a glorious conversion from the sidelines, for Country to win the match 22-20.

The City team was dumbfounded at this unexpected, indeed unparalleled, course of events, and at the after-match function Ron Graham observed dryly that 'Ass always beats class'. The skullduggery occupied the attention of a news-hungry press over the ensuing weeks.

The Japanese came the next year, 1976, and Country played them at Moree, thrashing them unmercifully 97-20, Greg scoring five tries. "My form was reasonable", Greg quipped with his usual understatement. He made the second test team in Brisbane, which Australia won comparatively easily by 50 to 25.

One of the ambitions of Greg's life was getting picked to go to the U.K. in 1975. Twelve of the Country team made the tour: Geoff Shaw, Jim Hindmarsh, John Hipwell, Greg Cornelsen, John Lambie, Brian Mansfield, Peter

Horton, Michael Fitzgerald, Bill McKid, Laurie Weatherstone, Gareth Grey (replacement) and Glen Eisenhauer. It was no longer the nine month tour of earlier years, but it was nevertheless a good three months long, and he gloried in his journey back into antiquity. He particularly loved wandering around Oxford and having to bend to get into the door of an ancient pub. For a young boy from the bush, it was a rare trundle back into history. Any building in his neck of the woods was viewed with horror if it was still standing after a hundred years, and in England he was viewing architecture and artifacts hundreds, indeed thousands, of years old.

Hippie was the captain of that young team and the flamboyant ex-Wallaby breakaway Dave Brockhoff the coach. It was not a successful tour, the Wallabies winning 19, losing 6 and drawing 1, the team being a trifle light in the forwards. Cornie was selected for the first three tests against Scotland, Wales and England. He was dropped against Ireland, and laughingly observed, "That was the only one we bloody-well won!"

He was enraptured by the Sportsman's Luncheon at the Savoy Hotel in London, crowded with dignitaries a-plenty, such as Sir Douglas Bader. He says in reflection that the tour was a fantastic experience, travelling with great mates and characters like 'Shawie', 'Lambie' and MacDougall. As he said: "It was magic staying with your best mates and at the best hotels". There were no other hangers-on as the team went by bus. There were no doctors, physiotherapists, and sport psychologists in those days, just the team, the manager and the assistant manager, who by this time was in actuality the coach. Each member of the team was asked to take a thousand dollars spending money, and each was given two pounds a day 'wine money' by the Home Union. His father bank-rolled his own adventure. Now he realises how absurd it all was, the players putting out such money, with a 60,000 crowd at Twickenham. But one never thought about it in those days, it was just the way it was. "It was a nonsense," he now states.

Greg has many great memories of that tour, One was when they were playing Swansea. The referee was an Englishman, and the Welsh crowd was giving the arbiter 'heaps'. Swansea in those days was captained by the great Mervyn Davies. It was a terrible day, the pitch wet and the wind whistling down the ground. Australia was narrowly ahead with just a few minutes to go, and they were awarded a penalty. This further infuriated the hostile mob. Paul McLean did not overly hurry as he placed the ball on a mound, went back for the kick, rolled up his socks, and advanced towards the ball. The wind blew the ball over, so McLean repeated the procedure, the crowd's ire rising by the moment. The ball fell over again, and again. The crowd was beside itself. As Greg said they "went off their face". The English referee turned to Paul and calmly said: "Take as long as you like. I really hate these bastards."

The highlight of a basically unsuccessful tour was meeting the Queen, Prince Charles and Princess Anne at Buckingham Palace. The bus drove them into the palace gates, and they walked up the steps, mesmerised by the rarity of the occasion, in awe of the history and the pageantry of it all. They were introduced, and the team then dispersed into various groups. He was first of all in the group with Princess Anne, and felt embarrased as the Sydney boys asked inane questions like how many horses did she have and what did they eat.

He then walked over to the Queen's group, and he felt she was absolutely magnificent, asking the players in turn what they did. Ken Wright was the youngest and she was particularly interested in him, and that he was a University student. As the team left she said: "Where is that young man I was talking to?" A pale Ken Wright signified that he was the one. She said, simply, "Best of luck in your exams."

Greg said: "She was a magic lady, just like a normal Mum, talking about kicking the balls around with her children when they were young."

Stuart MacDougall was the real character of the tour, and during the reception there was raucous laughter from his side of the room, where he was with Prince Charles. He had hold of Prince Charles' tie and was playfully endeavouring to get it off. "Come on", he said to the Prince, "I'll swap you ties". Charles explained he couldn't because he'd only been given it by someone else a few days previously. The knot on Charles' tie by this time was about one-third the original size from the tugging.

MacDougall, ever a magnanimous fellow, said, "That's all right!" He reached into his pocket and pulled out his business card. "Look, here's my card. Next time you're in Sydney give me a call and I'll show you a great time at King's Cross."

In 1976 there was a separate tour to France and the Wallabies played an Italian XV on the way back. France was very strong at the time and they beat the Wallabies, 18-15 and 34-6. They had a huge pack and dominated Australia, particularly in the second test. Steven Finnane was called 'Monsier le Gunfire' on the French tour, being possessed of a lethal right that only travelled about six inches with rare effectiveness. In the first game Finnane was easily bested in the initial scrum. He turned to Greg and said, "Just hang around, there might be a bit of a blue on after this." He then went 'whack' and down his opposite prop went. The balance of power immediately shifted, Finnane's performance in the scrums being supreme as his counterpart no longer wanted a part of the action.

In 1977 Greg moved to Queensland. He could have gone to Sydney, but many country players had and were never heard from again. So he became a vital cog in the Queensland revival, with Bob Templeton at the helm. He dedicated the three years he was there to rugby, playing club rugby for Teachers' Norths, who espoused the running game, a credo that stirred his imagination and matched his own attitudes. He worked during the period for Macquarie Counsellors, which specialised in superannuation, and they allowed him time off for his rugby commitments.

Wales came through in 1978, and at Ballymore Australia gained revenge for the thrashing they had received in Wales in 1975, when they lost 28-3. The game was called 'the battle of Brisbane', and Australia won 18 to 8. The second test the Wallabies won 19-17, Graham Price having his jaw shattered by Finnane in this match. The wins not only restored Australian prestige but were a psychological boost to the Wallabies who then toured the land of the long white cloud.

Greg became a rugby immortal in New Zealand in 1978, reaching a pinnacle of fitness and ability attained by so very few. He was selected as one of the five players of the year by the *Rugby Almanack of New Zealand* and the *Rugby Annual*. Bob Howitt wrote of him: "Even before he etched his name in the record books with four tries in the third test Cornelsen had stamped himself as one of the most talented and constructive No. 8s to tour New Zealand. Fast and strong he got through a terrific amount of ball with minimum effort and maximum efficiency."

New Zealand won the first test narrowly 13 to 12, Ken Wright narrowly missing a penalty kick which would have provided Australia, led by Tony Shaw, with the first opportunity to go one-up in a series against the All Blacks since 1949. It was only later that it was realised that referee Dave Millar had awarded an all-important penalty at the wrong spot. It should have been 10 metres infield. 'Axle' Knight was the culprit, barging the Aussie giant Garrick Fay in the lineout.

Haberecht said: "I wanted like hell for the kick to go over, but I also felt deeply for Ken because suddenly the outcome of the whole test rested with him." The New Zealand captain Frank Oliver couldn't bear to watch and instead faced the goalposts. He looked at Andy Haden's face, which as it lit up told him that the kick had missed. Australia had in this test served notice of their long-range intentions, and the 'awful Aussie's' tag of 1972 was a thing of the distant past.

The All Blacks re-asserted themselves in the second test at Christchurch, winning 22 to 6, to devastate Australia's hopes. The 'up the jumper trick' was even used by the Wallabies, to be snuffed out with disdain by the All Blacks, who never ever practised frivolities in their never-ending march towards world rugby supremacy.

Daryl Haberecht's heart attack prior to the third test seemed to galvanise the Wallabies into action. They closed ranks, resolving to do or die for Haberecht and their country. They won an astonishing match at Eden Park, Auckland, by 30 to 16, Greg Cornelsen scoring four tries in the encounter. He had played 12 tests to this point and had never scored. The feat was a combination of luck, opportunism and genius. Greg himself said three of the tries were pure luck. Maybe so, but the brilliant player seems to have the knack of getting into the right place at the right time.

'Rudy' said: "The first one came when the ball bounced off the goalposts straight into my arms - that wouldn't happen again in a hundred tests.

"I got the second one because I was late to a ruck and the ball suddenly popped out in front of me."

"And I got the next one because Gary Seear knocked a pass across the goalline, again right in my path."

"I couldn't believe my luck."

The fourth came after fine lead up work by a tour late replacement, John Hipwell, after a brilliant blindside sortie. Cornie tailed 'Hippie' and finished the move off with a well-deserved try.

Greg shaved off his beard after the match. He said: "It was the best tour I ever had for the Wallabies. It was my best year. It showed to us all we could beat the bloody All Blacks."

In 1979 the Irish came out to Australia and Queensland beat them 29 to 26. Ollie Campbell dominated both the tests, which Ireland won 33-13 and 32-18, their defence being magnificent.

Then came the All Blacks in a one-off test, which Australia won 12 to 6. Loane and Handy had blinders, putting their lives on the line, they were so totally and absolutely committed. The match was a turning point in Bledisloe Cup history, as New Zealanders were completely unused to the Wallabies running around the field brandishing the Cup after a glorious victory. "We hardly even realised it was the Bledisloe Cup," said Cornelsen.

That same year the Wallabies toured Argentina, Greg being particularly beguiled at Mendoza, at the foot of the awe-inspiring Andes. The Wallabies have always found Argentina to be a tough opponent, and Hugo Porta seemed to be ever their nemesis. After losing the first test they were in danger of losing the second, for with time running out Argentina had the feed with the scrum in front of the posts. Porta was already smiling as he lined up for the inevitable drop-kick. Wallaby hooker Bill Ross won a remarkable tight head, and Paul McLean punted the Aussies out of trouble.

In 1980 Greg went back to his father's property. He had virtually retired, but was still playing club rugby. Mark Loane, however, had

gone to South Africa, so Bob Templeton prevailed upon him to come back if he could, as Australia needed a few old heads. Greg resumed sprint training up the main road near the country property. He played for Country, but they were beaten by Sydney. Not one of the Country team was picked in the NSW side. He said: "Thank Christ I didn't go to Sydney in the first place. That's why I didn't go." At least he and Hippie should have been picked, Hippie playing particularly well.

Greg then played for NSW seconds against Wellington, then for Country against the All Blacks, and slowly his big-match fitness came back. 'Tempo' came up to him and said: "Will you be fit for the first test Saturday week?" He replied that he would, so he was picked. "I've got to thank Tempo," Greg reflected, "he always had faith in me. Blokes like him had a big influence on my life. He came to me. I played in that first test at Ballymore. Gould had a fantastic series. He was kicking the ball 50m to repel the All Blacks. We won that test 13 to 9. Steve Williams' jaw was broken by 'Cowboy' Shaw in the second test at Ballymore, which we lost 12 to 9, but Hika Reid scored a sensational try from the other end of the field to turn the game around.

"We won the third test comfortably 26-10 to clinch the series. Two Bledisloe Cups in a row. We had lost a lot - players going to league, and retirements, but players came through, Mitchell Cox, Michael Hawker and so on. There is always someone else who takes up the slack."

Greg wanted to go Britain in 1980. Though his stepmother was having heart problems, his father insisted he should go for it would be his last opportunity. The Wallabies beat Ireland and lost the other three tests. Fundamentally they could not match their opponents in the lineouts. The Wallabies scored more tries but did not kick well. It was a disappointing end to a brilliant career.

Thereafter Greg played some club rugby, but nothing serious. He moved on, his father sold the property and he went back to Sydney, and later to the Gold Coast, where he now lives.

When asked what his main qualities were, Greg said: "I was fast over the paddock. Loaney said I had the best cardiovascular system he'd ever seen. I loved fitness and training. That's why in Britain in 1980 I decided to give it up. I know age catches up, I was approaching 30 and I got sick and tired of training. I used to love it. I ran every day. I particularly loved hill sprints. Another of my strengths was my ability in lineouts. I was a high jumper and was effective at the back of the lineout."

Greg Cornelsen enjoyed playing flanker, as he loved backing up and was always on hand for a pass. Queensland had to change their tactics when he left, as when he ran he would not lope or lumber along like many players, but would 'pin his ears back'.

Australia has had outstanding breakaways throughout the years: Owen Bridle, Keith Windon, Colin Windon, Dave Brockhoff, Jeff Miller, Chris Roche, Simon Poidevin, David Wilson, and Willie Ofahengaue. Some might have been faster to the break, though that is arguable, but few matched his combined speed, power and lineout skills. What is for certain is that he was part of the most outstanding triumvirate in Australian history: Mark Loane, Tony Shaw and himself. There was rare strength and dedication among this trio, each playing his heart out for his country.

Greg reflected on what the sport had done for him: "I was a shy country boy. I am still quite shy, but rugby provided me with confidence. I believe rugby improves everyone's life. There is a position for every body build. A lot of the senior people in my day were great role models and helped me. Rugby is fantastic. What better thing is there than to travel with your best mates and play sport?"

Those who toiled him on the playing field will say that one of his greatest talents was his after-match rendition of 'I Did It My Way', and he was also quite famous for his rendition of 'Charity'…'When I am a child, etc.' Someone should write some time about the odd antics that go on in football changing rooms and after-match functions. Sociologists call them male bonding rituals, but for Greg it was all so very natural.

His team-mate Dr Peter Horton had this to say of him: "He was the product of everything that is good about NSW Country rugby. Greg was surely one of the greatest natural athletes to ever play for Australia and stands to this day as the greatest all-round backrower to come from Country. When Greg first came into the representative scene he was a somewhat wiry, extremely fit and explosive support-playing flanker. As he matured, hardened from his work on the family property at Jeogla, he turned into the complete backrower. He retained his speed and expansive game but could also exert a tremendous presence in the mauls - powered by his massive hands and upper body strength, and at the lineout he was superb.

"The trio of Mark Loane, Tony Shaw and Greg Cornelsen is, I feel, a backrow that is without peer in Australian rugby. This combination of talents provided a chemistry that was perfectly suited to the game as it was played in the 70s and 80s, and even in the current days of juggernaut rolling mauls I am certain they would be just as awesome, particularly with the more intense weight-training programs now used.

"A great rugby man, and the epitome of the archetypal Australian."

# Mark Ella

Occasionally a genius trips across the world's stage, and they astound the world in a whole range of human endeavours, from politics to sport. We think of Winston Churchill, Charlie Chaplin, Dame Nellie Melba, Enrico Caruso, Albert Einstein and so on, all defying norms of the time and recording unique achievements in a world of mediocrity.

There have been some in sport, like Johnny Weismuller, Jesse Owens, Carl Lewis and Babe Didricksen, who have performed feats of such legendary proportions that their names are still conjured up when people reflect on the truly greats. Australia has also had its share of heroes and heroines who have stood the test of time: Dally Messenger, Les Darcy, Don Bradman, Rod Laver, Herb Elliott, Stan McCabe and so on.

Mark Ella was an undoubted hero. Roger Rollin wrote, in *Hero/Anti-Hero*: "The hero is less important to us as an individual human being than he is as an embodiment and focal point of our emotions. We perceive in him things that we deeply feel. The feelings we project onto the hero are positive ones, and while some of them may be instinctive (like aggressiveness), they may also have their 'philosophical' aspects, having to do with our values (such as love of country). Whatever we value in the way of human qualities - courage, strength, high-mindedness, dynamism - is embodied in our heroes or in our images of them. Whether they actually possess such

qualities may be less important to us, at least on the emotional level, than our *belief* that they possess them.

"This is not to suggest that the hero is merely an image of our own creation, without any real substance. He may be, but most 'public' heroes have achieved that status through some visible action. We are what we do, not what we think. The hero, then, must be someone who has *done something*, something special, which others feel has positive value and meaning."

Heroes can be unifying figures in society. They provide links between us and our society, between our personal values and those of the public realm, between our dreams and our realities. Mark Ella seemed to do all of that. There was almost an 'Ella cult', who worshipped at his shrine, in so far as rugby was concerned. His selection, but more particularly his omission from teams, raised public passion to an unprecedented level.

He was an undoubted genius. The way he did things had no parallel. There was a nonchalance about it all, a fluidity, an air of relaxation that transcended pressure and occasion. Famous writer Neville Cardus used to write ecstatically about the great cricketer Victor Trumper, waxing lyrically about how when he batted there was a certain majesty about it all, and others appeared as drones before such brilliance. There was the same feeling surrounding Ella when he played. There was an unconscious rhythm and beauty to it all. We may never see his like again, and more's the pity. Stephen Spender once wrote a poem, *I Think Continually of Those Who Were Truly Great.* Its concluding lines were:

"Born of the sun, they travelled a short while toward the sun,

And left the vivid air signed with their honour."

Mark Ella was a genius as an individual, but when he played with his brothers Glen and Gary they *all* smacked of genius. Whereas the others did not attain the same high standard at the international level, who is to say what might have happened if the combination had been retained at test level? When they played together for Randwick it was a thing of beauty, a joy forever. Those privileged to have seen them recall with great nostalgia their rare understanding of the others' games, and the miraculous patterns they wove.

They were unlikely candidates for rugby union, as there were five girls and seven boys in this remarkable Aboriginal family. They were the sons of Gordon and May Ella, itinerant workers who moved around the east coast until settling at La Perouse. They were the great grandsons of Alfred Ella, an Englishman who worked in a woolshed in Sydney, then married a part-aboriginal woman and went to live with her among the aborigines in Yarra Bay.

Mark was born about half an hour before his twin brother Glen, and Gary was born twelve months later. They went to school at Matraville, and it was not long before their sporting talents were recognised. Their coach there was Geoff Mould, who was to coach the 1977 Schoolboys team. As Mark said in *Running Rugby*: "Many of the backline moves that the Australian team used at the test level in the early 1980s, moves such as the bafflers, the waggas, the cut-outs, the loops, were moves that we had used in the Matraville under-fifteens. We just took them with us as we moved up the ladder - to Australian Schoolboys, then to Randwick, and finally, to the Australian side."

Five of the Matraville team made the Schoolboys tour, but not Lloyd Walker, who Mark considers the best ball-player in all the years that he watched the game.

There were certainly some outstanding players on that 1977-78 Schoolboys tour to Japan, France, Britain and Holland. There were

Gary, Glen and Mark, Michael O'Connor, Wally Lewis, Michael Hawker, Tony Melrose, Chris Roche, Shane Nightingale and Tony D'Arcy. The team scored 553 points and had 97 scored against them, and won all of their 11 games.

Geoff Mould, their school and Schoolboys coach, was influenced by the great Randwick and Wallaby centre Cyril Towers, who came to see the Ellas often and recognised their potential. Randwick coach Bob Dwyer heard about them from Towers, and went to see them play the powerful St Joseph's team. As he put it in *The Winning Way*: "The first thing that struck me was the difference in appearance of the two teams. The St Joseph's boys were fine physical specimens - clean-cut, well-muscled and generally well turned-out. The Matraville team was, by comparison, a sorry sight - a mob of skinny, little ragamuffins. There were, I also noticed, eight or nine Aboriginal boys among them. With the exception of one red-haired winger, all the backs were Aboriginal. I heard later that Matraville did not have a backline but a 'blackline with a red tip'.

"Then I began observing their play. It was worth travelling far to see. The Matraville boys were not merely having the better of the contest. They were running rings around their opponents. For once, a St Joseph's first XV looked entirely bewildered. No matter what they did, they could not stop tries being scored. The scruffy Matraville High boys outclassed their opponents quite brilliantly and, moreover they did it with ease. I was impressed. Nine of their team would play first grade, and four would play for their country."

Bob Dwyer understandably wanted to harness all this talent for Randwick, and went to La Perouse with Gary Pearse. He knew he was at the right home when he saw about ten pairs of football boots on the verandah. There was no question that they would not be playing for Randwick, the issue was whether they would play for the colts team or in grade.

Dwyer put it this way in *The Winning Way*: "We talked to two of the brothers in the living room. The third brother - I think it was Glen - stayed in a bedroom reading a book. I remember one of the brothers saying something like, 'I couldn't give a damn whether I played colts or grade', whereupon May Ella called out from some other part of the house, 'Don't use that language in this home, thank you!' At once, I knew we were dealing with my kind of people. I told the two boys in the living room that they would be wasting their time playing colts. They would be so much better than the others, I said, that their talent wouldn't be extended, and they would risk developing wrong technique. The two brothers agreed, and one of them called out to the third brother (we will assume it was Glen) in the bedroom. 'Hey, Glen. We're playing grade'. A voice in the bedroom answered back, 'Okay'. And so it was settled."

They started off in second grade at Randwick, but first Gary and then the twins were in the firsts. In their initial match together, against Northern Suburbs, Randwick won 63 to 0. Randwick was always known as a running team, but with the Ellas running became an art form the like of which was without parallel in the club's history. Five successive premierships were won when they were at their peak.

Mark's first trip overseas with a full Australian team was to Argentina in 1979 and he gained invaluable experience, but was an understudy to the brilliant Tony Melrose. The All Blacks, under 'Trapper' Loveridge, then came to Australia in 1980 for three tests and Mark was the five-eighth for all of them. The Wallaby team for his inaugural test was: Roger Gould, Brendan Moon, Michael O'Connor, Michael Hawker, Mick Martin, Mark Ella and Phil Cox; Stan Pilecki, Bill Ross, Chris Handy, Simon Poidevin, Steve Williams, Duncan Hall, Tony Shaw (capt.) and Greg Cornelsen.

Australia won the first test 13-9 at the SCG, lost the second at Ballymore 9-12, and won the decider at the SCG 26-10. It was not only a highly successful debut, Australia had won the coveted Bledisloe Cup.

All Black Murray Mexted, who was in those tests, wrote about Mark in *Pieces of Eight*: "There is a lasting memory for me, too, of one of the finest of all individuals I have played against. Mark Ella retired when I judged him to be at the peak of his skill for he seemed to me to improve every time I played against him. In the early matches he was just good. In the end he was magnificent. He added shrewdness to his extraordinary ball skills, balance and rhythm."

Then he was off to the British Isles with his

two brothers on Tony Shaw's team of 1981-82. Paul McLean, who was viewed in Queensland with the same reverence as Mark in New South Wales, was the test five-eighth, and was an automatic selection because of his superior goal-kicking prowess. The team results were disappointing, with a sole win against Ireland in the internationals. Mark did however force his way into the test against England, with Paul McLean moving to fullback, and against Scotland, with Paul at inside centre.

In 1982 Scotland came to Australia for two test matches. With new coach Bob Dwyer at the helm, he gambled on his own coaching beliefs and picked Glen Ella to play fullback instead of Queensland's Roger Gould, and Mark ahead of Queensland's super-hero Paul McLean. The match was, of all places, at Ballymore. Australia went down 7 to 12, and the 'Ballymore mob', used to 'booing a blue', in an unprecedented outburst booed the Ellas, Glen in particular.

Bob Dwyer spoke of the matter in *The Winning Way*: "I do agree Australia may have fared better in that test if we had chosen Gould as fullback instead of Glen Ella. This was not because Gould necessarily deserved to be chosen ahead of Ella. Rather, it was because of the intense hostility directed at Ella by the Brisbane crowd, which, I believe, had a very negative effect on him during the match. Mark Ella told me later being conscious of this he felt under pressure throughout the match to do things which involved Glen. The reception Glen Ella received from the crowd and also from the Brisbane media was disgraceful. Glen was booed when he ran on to the field, and he was jeered repeatedly early in the game. Michael O'Connor has since described this as the most unpleasant moment he has known in sport. I should have foreseen it, but I didn't, and that was my mistake."

There is little doubt that Dwyer's moving too fast and too soon was a fundamental reason why he was soon to lose the coaching position to Alan Jones.

Mark and Glen were dropped from the second test, won in glorious fashion by Australia to the tune of 33-9. Gould, McLean and O'Connor scored all the points, and Paul McLean announced his retirement.

In 1982 Mark Ella captained the Wallabies

on their New Zealand tour. He had not even been in the previous test side. Tony Shaw and Mark Loane, the two principal challengers, declared their unavailability. Nine Queenslanders and one New South Welshman withdrew from the touring party. Bob Dwyer therefore took what he called "A team of unknowns" into enemy territory. Ella was fundamental to Dwyer's plans, as he represented above all the Randwick style of play that he wanted Australia to play under his stewardship. Some of the newcomers in the Australian team were David Campese, Andy McIntyre and Steve Tuynman. The three Ellas were in the touring party.

The first test was won by the All Blacks 23 to 16, and then the "Unknown Wallabies" struck back in the second, with Mark at five-eighth and Gary at centre, as they had been in the first test. Australia won 19 to 16. Mark Ella was ecstatic. He said: "Maybe now the critics will give us a break. We've been condemned ever since the team was chosen."

The first Australian try demonstrated the Ella touch. The All Blacks tried to move the ball in their own 22 and Mark Taylor was trapped with the ball. The brilliant Mark Ella secured the ball and ran with it, the long-striding Roger Gould coming in as an extra man. The ball then went to the mercurial David Campese, who left Graham Mourie standing with a flashing sidestep and passed to Gary Ella, who scored in the corner.

Despite a fantastic double cut-out play devised by Dwyer which resulted in a Gould try to start the game, Australia went down in the third test by 18 to 33. It was a successful tour, more so because of the dramatic circumstances relating to Wallabies dropping out of consideration.

In 1983 Argentina came to town, and the Wallabies were found to be lacking in the front-row. The Pumas prop, 'Topo' Rodriguez was, in particular, causing all kinds of problems. Australia lost the first test at Brisbane 3-18, but rebounded to win the second 29-13. This was the match featuring a controversial penalty try awarded by Welsh referee Clive Norling, who had seen an indiscretion 40 metres away from the goal-line.

A tour of France followed in 1983, a tour characterised by excessively rough play. After

drawing the first test, Australia lost the second. Some of the 'new boys' on that tour were Tommy Lawton, Michael Lynagh and Jeff Miller. Mark, according to Bob Dwyer, did not have the best of tours. As he wrote: "Mark Ella was outstanding in defence throughout the tour, but I have never seen him so far off his game in attack."

There was a single test against New Zealand that year at the SCG, the Aussie media hyping up the game as the "test of the century" and the "world championship of rugby". Australia lost 8-18. Campese had the kicking duties that day, and was unsuccessful. As he wrote in *On A Wing And A Prayer*: "I felt like kicking myself, but I probably would have missed."

It was the end of the road for the time being for coach Bob Dwyer, and one of Alan Jones' first decisions was to replace Mark Ella as captain with Queensland's Andrew Slack. The All Blacks, led by Andy Dalton, came to Australia in 1984. Australia surprisingly won the first test at the SCG 16 to 9, then lost the second 15-19 at Ballymore. The Bledisloe Cup hinged on the third match at the SCG, which Australia lost 24-25. One minute from fulltime Mark Ella tried a dropped goal, which would have won the series, but it sliced off his foot. The disappointment was that Australia rarely got the ball to its world-beating wings, Brendan Moon and David Campese. It was not the fault of Jones, whose strategy was to move the ball out to them.

Mark was bitterly disappointed, and he expressed what he felt in *Path to Victory*: "Jonesy and I spoke after the test. I said it was utterly useless for me to play for Australia if we went that way again. There was no place for the support game at which I think I'm best.

"We decided then that I'd call the shots in the British Isles irrespective of who was the captain. Whenever I was on the field, as the first toucher of the ball, I'd dictate how it was used. We were disgusted with the options we'd chosen against the All Blacks, I had no authority, and it just wasn't working with Slacky calling the moves from out in the centres."

Thirty players were selected for the fateful 1984 tour of the British Isles. History was made when the Wallabies recorded the first Grand Slam in its rugby history, and Mark Ella created his niche in the record books by scoring a try in each of the internationals.

The first test match was against England at Twickenham, and the Wallabies were firmly in control, winning 19 to 3. Michael Lynagh was brought into the game as inside centre to Mark for his first test, and the experiment was successful, though Michael Hawker had every right to consider himself unfortunate as he had been playing well. It was Nick Farr-Jones's first test as well. With the score 3-all after an exchange of penalty kicks, Mark looped around Michael Lynagh in a move called 'Leaguie' and sliced through the English centres. He went in for the try under the goal-posts, and Australia were in front, 9-3, in the 44th minute, a lead they were never to relinquish. The only sour note was a severe injury to Brendan Moon, one of the greatest wingers ever in the game.

The next test was against Ireland at Lansdowne Road in Dublin. It was 3-0 at halftime, 'Noddy' Lynagh having kicked a penalty, but soon after the restart Mark kicked a dropped goal to make it 6-0, and that seemed to have closed the door on the Irish. The Greens are always known for their fighting spirit, and invariably cause Australian teams all sorts of trouble, and they struck back, from three Michael Kiernan penalties, to lead 9-6. With about fifteen minutes to go, Mark kicked a dropped goal from 30 metres out to level the scores.

With five minutes left in the match Steve Cutler won the ball and gave it to Farr-Jones, who rifled it to Mark Ella, and on to Lynagh. It looked as if the loop was on again, and instead 'Noddy' went on his own, and linked with winger Matt Burke, who was Moon's replacement. 'Burkey' gave it to Campese, and when he realised he could not make it he drew two defenders and shot the ball to Ella, who scored. It was 13 to 9, and as the game was drawing to a close 'Noddy' kicked a penalty, to make the final score 16 to 9. Round 2 was over in the Grand Slam.

Then came Wales, the match crowd at Cardiff Arms Park, and the singing of 'Land of My Fathers' which sends chills up the spine of every rugby player.

The highlight of the game was the pushover try by the Wallabies. It was nicknamed 'Samson' by the Aussies, and when Steve

Tuynman fell on the ball and a try was awarded, the Welsh were 'shot'. It was the ultimate humiliation, a sight never before witnessed at the famous ground. It was their day of infamy. Wales was soundly thrashed, going down 9-28. With the score in Australia's favour 22-9, the game was over, as time was running out. The Welsh team never stopped trying, and right near the finish were 'giving the ball air'. Mark suddenly intercepted a pass from Eddie Butler and ran quite nonchalantly to the goal-line, virtually unopposed, and Gould converted. It was round 3 in the Grand Slam.

The Wallabies were housed at the North British Hotel in Edinburgh for the final show-down, and Mark felt there was an omen when he was given the key to room 358, as he had scored three tries and he was a five-eighth. Despite having the wind behind them, the Wallabies held on to a slender 12-9 lead at the half. The Scots were going down fighting, as they always did at fabled Murrayfield. Two penalties from Lynagh then made the score 18 to 12.

From a ruck, the Wallabies won the ball and Farr-Jones sent it to Roger Gould on the blind-side. As the opposition closed, Roger had two players in his sights, but gave it to Ella on the inside. Lynagh converted to make the count 24-12. It was the game-breaker, the final score being a massive 37 to 12. The Grand Slam was Australia's, and Mark Ella had scored in each of the tests.

Mark Ella had this to say of his final try in *Path to Victory*: "It was bad play on the Scottish five-eighth's part. He virtually stopped running when I went past him on the blind side after we'd pulled a set move, thinking that Roger was going to throw the ball wide. In fact, he could have let the pass go wide, but there was an opening on the inside and Roger gave me the ball, thank God. I looked at the line and there was nobody in front. I just couldn't believe it. When I scored the try I was ecstatic. When I was coming back, I was laughing. I was giggling. I couldn't stop myself."

The amazing part of it all was that as the Wallabies ran onto the field to start the game, "Mr Cool", Roger Gould, had said to Mark: "Stick with me, mate. I'll give you the try you need."

Mark was rightly lionised after the Grand

Slam tour, but retired, at 25 years of age, at the peak of a remarkable career. Perhaps he knew he could never attain such heights again, or perhaps he was more aware than others of the transience of sport. A.E. Housman had written a wonderful poem, *To An Athlete Dying Young*:

The time you won your town the race
We chaired you through the market-place,
Man and boy stood cheering by,
And home we brought you shoulder high.

Today, the road all runners come,
Shoulder-high we bring you home,
And sit you at your threshold down.
Townsman of a stiller town.

Smart lad, to slip betimes away
From fields where glory does not stay
And early though the laurel grows
It withers quicker than the rose.

Eyes the shady night has shut
Cannot see the record cut,
And silence sounds no worse than cheers
After earth has stopped the ears.

Now you will not swell the rout
Of lads that wore their honours out,
Runners whom renown outran
And the name died before the man.

So sit, before its echoes fade,
The fleet foot on the sill of shade,
And hold to the low lintel up
The still-defended challenge-cup.

And round that early-laureled head
Will flock to gaze the strengthless dead,
And find unwithered on its curls
The garland briefer than a girl's.

Though retired early, he was, perhaps,
"Smart lad, to slip betimes away
From fields where glory does not stay…"

In this case, because he retired, the glory has indeed stayed. He had already won the young Australian of the Year Award, in 1984 he was awarded the Order of Australia, and a host of other kudos.

The transition period from that of a player is always difficult for athletes, and Mark hit the so-called 'chicken circuit', speaking here, there and everywhere, commented for the ABC on rugby, made a comeback with Randwick, took an Aboriginal Cricket team to England, and coached in Milan. He now works for the ARFU.

There have been many rumours about the relationship between Ella and Jones, and surely the last word should be Mark's. In *Path to Victory* he states unequivocally: "For the sake of rugby, Jonesy and I try not to be enemies. We get along fairly well, but when we chat we don't talk about rugby. These days he never asks my opinion and I never offer one. I'd rather offer my opinion to the players.

"People say I'd still be playing if Bob Dwyer was Australian coach, but I'd always said I wanted to retire at 25. I hinted before we went to the British Isles that this could be my last tour, and everyone thought I was joking.

"I just kept my word." So there it is, the unsaid word, the mystery behind the meaning.

Terry Smith put it eloquently and yet colloquially when he said in *Path to Victory*: "Mark Ella, the only Aborigine to captain Australia in any sport. Gloriously instinctive. Sublime in handling and knowing where to be. Twenty-five caps…as indigenous to Australia as kangaroos, koala bears, Edna Everage, Paul Hogan and a Foster's tinny."

He turned his back on countless rugby league offers, a game in which he would have been sensational. Money did not drive him. There was the love of combat, the emotion of the contest, the challenge of the opponent, the unpredictability of the match, the feeling of the ball in his hands. He might possibly have been the greatest player who ever lived.

# Nick
# Farr-Jones

Australia has had some fantastic captains in its glorious rugby history, such as Tommy Lawton, Johnny Wallace, Trevor Allan, John Thornett, John Hipwell, Geoff Shaw, Mark Loane, Tony Shaw and Andrew Slack, but arguably the greatest has been Nick Farr-Jones. He was electric on the field, switching play from right to left like no other halfback in history, urging his forwards on, marshalling the backs, surging forward when the occasion demanded it, and cover-defending ferociously and with a natural fervour that simply cannot be taught.

It is always difficult to compare captains or halfbacks, as there have been periodic changes in the game, the most significant being that Australia in recent years has developed packs equal to any in the world. In the dim and distant past, Australian halfbacks worked off twenty to thirty percent possession from scrums and lineouts, and a different kind of halfback was required, one with unbelievable guts and the skills of a magician.

Farr-Jones could not sidestep with the audacity of a Cyril Burke, and lacked perhaps the elegance of Des Connor, the inspired running of Ken Catchpole or the marvellous cover defence of John Hipwell, but his all-round attributes were perfect for the modern game. Farr-Jones was an incomparable artist who covered the canvas with broad and confident strokes, not restricting his finished product to a particular school of artistry. Like Picasso and other greats, there was a variation

in his work over time. What he was at the conclusion of his career was not what he was at the start.

The authorised biography of Nick Farr-Jones, by his friend, fellow Wallaby tourist Peter FitzSimons, paints in our minds a picture of the youngster as he was growing up as undisciplined, over-competitive and with an explosive temper. Nick's father's philosophy of life that he imparted to his sons is told in his biography:

"Life is *about* winning. I wanted them to know that that's what counts - to be competitive, to get better, to succeed." In fairness to Nick he always gave the impression that he played the game to the ultimate maximum and yet could generally put any loss into the correct perspective.

There is no doubt that the family genes were right, mother and father being University blues and grandfather being a gifted athlete, and certainly there was massive encouragement to find sporting outlets for an obviously physically talented and hyperactive youngster. Soccer, swimming and surfing, athletics, golf and cricket, even skiing, were all an essential part of Nick's early life. He was fortunate to be born into a sports-mad family.

Interestingly enough, Newington's most famous rugby player never made the first XV at his school, a certain Murray McGavin being the choice of the coach. Perhaps it was a blessing in disguise, as Nick concentrated on his studies sufficiently to gain entrance to the alma mater of his parents, to do Law at Sydney University.

While at the Uni, Nick made the University Colts team, and in his second year boarded at St. Andrew's College. Sport provided him with a considerable outlet for his considerable energy, and when the Colts coach, Lindsay McCaughan, took over Sydney University's First Grade team, Nick found himself as the first team's scrumhalf.

Rugby politics and a disappointing start to the season by the firsts saw his coach displaced, first by Rupert Rosenblum and Johnny Rouen, and then by the one-and-only Dave Brockhoff. His own demise at halfback was only temporary, and was completely rejuvenated by 'Brock', a legend in coaching circles through his blood-and-guts approach and a conversation continually littered with extraordinary similes and metaphors. Chris Handy wrote of the infamous 'Brock' in *Well, I'll Be Ruggered*: "I found him to be different to say the least. His style could be described as bombastic buffoonery. He knew what he wanted, but he couldn't explain it in simple terms. It was disguised by flowery phraseology that had you smirking or giggling when all was meant to be deadly serious. You tended to laugh at Brock rather than laugh with him."

In 1984 Alan Jones, a virtual neophyte in coaching ranks, took over as national coach from Bob Dwyer. At the time Sydney University was relegated to the Sydney competition's Second Division. On the surface it appeared as if the career of Nick Farr-Jones was on a slide, but the selectors at Sydney figured the youngster had the makings of a test player, and selected him on a Sydney tour to Europe. As is often said, the rest is history.

Simon Poidevin was the Sydney captain on that fateful tour, and though he also recognised the latent talent of the University scrumhalf, he took it upon himself to talk to Nick about his undisciplined play, and off-the-field behaviour. And ever-watchful, in the background, was new coach Alan Jones, who had his own particular game plan in mind. Farr-Jones met most of the criteria. In a fairy-tale year, a Second Division player was selected on the Wallaby tour to Fiji as the number two scrumhalf to the diminutive Phillip Cox. Though he did not force his way into the single

test, he almost did, and created a most favourable impression.

Farr-Jones, like the other Wallabies, was enormously impressed with their new coach, and Jones, indulging in what is now referred to as 'Jones-Speak', continually exhorted all players to greater physical and mental challenges for the good of Australian Rugby. It was as if they were all caught up in a surging wave propelling them forward, this highly articulate man continually urging them to keep going. Chris Handy, in *Well I'll Be Ruggered*, wrote that what Alan Jones "brought into our rugby was a professionalism that it really needed…he sought from their players an ultimate commitment."

For the first All Black test that year, which Australia won 16 to 9, Farr-Jones was a reserve. A sensation occurred in Sydney as eight of the team, the test players, withdrew from Sydney's upcoming encounter with the All Blacks. The press, and Sydney coach Peter Fenton, were staggered at the Jones-led decision, but it was fortuitous as it gave Farr-Jones the opportunity to play for Sydney against the All Blacks. He was only a reserve, but he showed he could mix it with the very best in the game. Nick was solidifying his own future by his on-field magic. Despite his evident claims, Nick was not selected for the remaining two All Black tests. Australia narrowly lost the series 2 to 1.

In 1984 Farr-Jones was selected for the Wallaby tour to the UK, now known simply as the famous Grand Slam tour. Nick was now 22 years of age and was reaching his physical maturity. What was becoming obvious was that with him at halfback, it was tantamount to having a third breakaway on the field because of his size and strength. Farr-Jones had an early opportunity to impress on tour as the incumbent test halfback Phillip Cox had an injured shoulder, and Nick seized upon his unexpected good fortune in the first match against London Division, scoring a try and demonstrating his effectiveness with a fine, robust, all-round game.

Farr-Jones was never, in his career, averse to a little nocturnal activity, and after a night on the town in the UK he was summoned to coach Alan Jones' room and was subjected to a 20-minute tirade. The story is told in *Nick Farr-Jones*: "Who the HELL did Farr-Jones think he was, going out every night drinking? Did he think this was some two-bit Sydney University tour, where you could do whatever you liked? Did he think that a rugby tour was no more than just one big party? Did he want to be over here just as a back-up or did he have some ambition to play test rugby and, if so, didn't he think it could be a good idea to start focusing a bit more on football and a lot less on partying? Well, didn't he?" Nick had had his bum kicked, and thereafter concentrated on the task at hand.

To no-one's surprise after his continuing on-field performances, Nick Farr-Jones was selected for the first test in the UK, and his first for Australia, against England. When victory ensued, and his ability became obvious for all to see, there was no longer any question as to who should be the test scrumhalf, and he played in all the subsequent Grand Slam tests. His entry into the test arena was certainly aided by the mercurial play of partner Mark Ella, whose basic instructions to Farr-Jones were simply to throw the ball in his direction.

Mark Ella wrote about Farr-Jones in *Path To Victory*: "Playing the running game, all I wanted from a halfback was to give me the ball. Apart from his size and strength, Nick has a fantastic pass. To vary my game, I sometimes stood a little wide and Nick always found me."

Nick is also a very good runner with the ball.

There were significant attitudinal changes towards Farr-Jones after the Grand Slam, as was noted in *Nick Farr-Jones*: "While Farr-Jones had previously noticed the difference in the way people treated him as soon as he had become a Wallaby, it was a nothing compared to the way they now regarded him now that he was a fully fledged test player in a victorious team. The phone seemed never to stop ringing, there was a constant round of celebratory dinners to attend and people even held the lift for him."

Nick, on his return to Australia, took a job with the law firm where his grandfather had been a partner, and thereafter had the unenviable task of balancing his legal duties with his sporting commitment with his club, and the representative demands of Sydney, NSW and Australian teams. In 1985, there were two relatively easy tests against a weakened Canadian team, and a single test against the All Blacks, the latter a narrow loss through a simple manoeuvre called 'Shuckey' by the All Blacks

and 'Bombay Duck' by the Wallabies. The Wallabies seemed to lose concentration just once, and that was enough for the All Blacks, who took a quick tap and were over the Aussie line. The Fijians were next on the Wallaby calendar and two spiteful games were won by Australia. It was, in actuality, a rather uneventful year after the drama and emotion of the Grand Slam.

Though the world was seemingly Nick's oyster, there were some troublesome undercurrents in 1986 and 1987. One was a continuing vacillation in his relationship with coach Alan Jones, who was, after all, in the driver's seat and was continually curbing and correcting real and fancied indiscretions by Farr-Jones. Their temperaments were diametrically opposed, Jones demanding discipline, subservience and agreement and Farr-Jones exploring forever the limits of his own strong personality, in which freedom had been a prerequisite since childhood. Jones was most certainly a coach for the golden moment, and had resurrected Australia's flagging prestige, but was fading through excessive exhortations over the passage of time. Put another way, Jones was reaching his 'use-by' date.

As well as one-off tests against Italy and France and a two-test series against Argentina in 1986 there was also a three-test series against the All Blacks. Nick also played in the two games at Cardiff and Twickenham marking the centenary of rugby's controlling body, the IRB. The Wallabies had a glorious year, winning all the tests except one, and gaining the Bledisloe Cup in New Zealand. Nick's contribution in the victories was enormous, and Jones nominated him as the Player of the Tour in New Zealand.

The second undercurrent occurred in 1987, and was not of Nick's making but rather neophyte NSW coach Paul Dalton, who was convinced that Farr-Jones, and not the incumbent Simon Poidevin, was the captain required to lead the Blues on to bigger and better things under his tenancy. Such a move was against the wishes of the national coach Alan Jones, and caused a worsening of the relationship between the Jones boys. The move was also not a popular one from the viewpoint of many players. It was not that the NSW team disliked Farr-Jones in any sense, but rather that Poidevin was both popular and had proven his capabilities. Despite the apparent opposition, Farr-Jones was duly appointed to the captaincy.

It was the World Cup year in 1987, and particularly because of the Wallaby successes in 1986 there was an unduly high expectation that the Cup would be Australia's. It was all a tragic comedown as Australia was, early on, bundled out of contention, which then became virtual humiliation as they were beaten out of third place by lowly-regarded Wales in the isolated confines of Rotorua.

The bells then tolled inexorably for Alan Jones. Winners are grinners, 'tis often said, and all sport psychologists agree that victory rarely elicits recrimination, whereas defeat inevitably brings the rats down the drain-pipes. Defeat always requires explanation, and excuse, and much of the pent-up emotion and invective were directed at Alan Jones. The basic arguments were: Jones had required total commitment from his players, yet perplexed his team by continuing with his own radio show and subjecting his team to afternoon practices; the team was not supervised well enough through being in their own country; and Jones did not respond well after the defeat by France. The litany went on and on.

Then, after the World Cup, Jones alienated most of the players because of his changing position with respect to a South African tour by the Wallabies, and the harsh treatment which was allowed to be meted out by the ARFU to Andrew Slack and David Codey, who took it upon themselves to cement negotiations by flying to South Africa. Jones was seemingly inconsistent and ambivalent in the minds of many of the players.

When he took the Wallabies to Argentina and they emerged with but a draw and a loss, it was inevitable that Jones had reached the end of his tenure. His position was not enhanced by his selection of what players felt was the 'teacher's pet', Brian Smith, over Farr-Jones in the first test in Argentina. Smith was unduly and incessantly praised by Jones in the opinion of many senior players, and to demote Farr-Jones, slight knee injury or not, was deemed as inexcusable. Jones was 'rolled' on his return to Australia, and Bob Dwyer was back at the helm.

With Dwyer, it was 'different folks, different strokes', and there was a particularly important stroke in so far as Farr-Jones was concerned. Dwyer wanted Farr-Jones as captain, recognising the leadership potential of the scrappy scrum-half. It had been thought that Simon Poidevin would have been the automatic choice, particularly because Poidevin and Dwyer both had Randwick affiliations, but Dwyer shied off Poidevin either because of his support of Alan Jones or his fear after the Roger Gould-Paul McLean fiasco in his initial reign that once more he was being blinded by the green colours of Randwick and did not want to wear that accusation again. There was also Michael Lynagh looming in the wings with tons of captaincy potential. What did Farr-Jones care about the whys and wherefores? He was the captain. As the saying goes, 'ours is not to wonder why, ours is but to do and die.' And Farr-Jones, as always, would 'go into the valley of death' for the green and gold.

Under Farr-Jones and new coach Dwyer, the Wallabies prevailed in two tests against England, and Nick revelled in the different personality of the new man, his more consultative and laid-back coaching methods and his own overall role as his country's captain. The early success did not continue, however, in the annual clashes against that old nemesis New Zealand, the Wallabies recording a single draw against two heavy losses.

The subsequent Wallaby tour to England and Scotland started off in a devastating manner as England beat the visitors 28-19, but fortunately the Aussies got back on track with an axe job on Scotland to the tune of 32 to 13. The new coach and the new captain were not performing sensationally, but they were at least keeping their heads above water and combining well.

In 1989 the British Lions were on hand to test the mettle of the Wallabies. An easy 30 to 12 opener seemed to foreshadow a 3-0 pasting of the Lions, but they employed biff and bash tactics which unbalanced Australia in the second test, and the Wallabies went down 12 to 9. In the final game of the series Australia lost 18 to 19, after an extraordinary gaffe by David Campese when he ran the ball out of his in-goal area and gave a 'hail Mary' pass to Greg Martin which resulted in a Lions score. It was one of the classic foul-ups in modern rugby history and Campese and Martin were never allowed to forget it.

There were a few changes to the Wallaby team after that debacle. Simon Poidevin was brought back, and three virtual unknowns were then blooded against the All Blacks, Phil Kearns, Tony Daly and Tim Horan. Kearns was at the time playing second grade for Randwick, and Horan was not even in the Queensland 'A' side. The All Blacks won the single test at Auckland, but the new boys and the 'old' veteran performed admirably. However, the losses were mounting, and the critics were already taking aim at Bob Dwyer.

Dwyer was partially rescued by a tour of France in which Australia emerged as victors in the first test, only to go down in the next. However, it was up and down like a yo-yo for him, and Alan Jones on radio and many of the press called for the hangman's noose. Dwyer then barely survived a challenge for national coach against Alex Evans, the non-official assistant coach of the Grand Slam Wallabies.

A 2-1 series victory over France in 1990 in Australia temporarily restored Australia's rugby prestige, yet a 1-2 loss to the All Blacks in New Zealand sent them backwards again. One step forward, two steps backwards. Inexorably, however, Dwyer was putting the pieces together, marshalling the players and technical experts who could perform at his own level of expectation. Willie Ofahengaue, Phil Kearns, John Eales, Marty Roebuck, Tim Horan, Tony Daly and Jason Little were part of the master plan.

It all started to come together in 1991 with the arrival of the Welsh and English teams, and they were disposed of in a clinical manner. That it was all for real at last became clear when the All Blacks were taken apart at the Sydney Football Stadium by 21 to 10. Though the New Zealanders emerged as victors two weeks later in Auckland, the 3-6 scoreline emphasised that the difference between the two countries was minute. The All Blacks have ever been the ultimate test of Australia's strength. Dwyer and Farr-Jones were riding high.

The pinnacle of both careers was Australia winning the World Cup in 1991. The Wallabies were now atop the world, and every country fossicked around trying to find out how Australia did it. Sure, there were dietitians,

strength trainers, sport psychologists, assistant and assistant to the assistant coaches, biomechanists, coaching advisers, etc, etc. All the advice in the world is useless without the right player personnel. It was those on the actual paddock who counted.

As U.S. President Theodore Roosevelt put it: "It's not the critic that counts, not the man who points out how the strong man stumbled, or where the doer of deeds could have done them better. The credit belongs to the man who is actually in the arena; whose face is marred by dust and sweat and blood; who strives valiantly, who errs and comes short again and again; who knows the great enthusiasms, the great devotions, and spends himself in a worthy course; who, at the best, knows in the end the triumph of high achievement; and who, at the worst, if he fails, at best fails while daring greatly, so that his place will never be with those cold and timid souls who know neither victory nor defeat."

The leadership exerted by Nick Farr-Jones was crucial in the Wallabies' drive towards rugby immortality. Despite a narrow let-off as the captain reluctantly departed the field against Ireland and a brilliant Lynagh master-minded an incredible recovery, the indelible portrait of the World Cup, besides the genius of Campese, is of Farr-Jones, prodding, pushing, cajoling, reversing directions, kicking, running. He was the captain's captain. There had been times in his career where he was subjected to criticism for his off-field antics more than his on-field captaincy, but in the World Cup campaign he came into full maturity as a captain, a leader, a player and an inspiration, on and off the field.

Though being crowned world champions was the highlight of every Wallaby's career, there was in actuality a strange mix of feelings when the World Cup was all over and done with. These feelings are described in *Nick Farr-Jones*, and many athletes of the present day who have been subjected to modern multi-media hype will understand them: "You're happy, of course you are, basically. But really mixed up in the middle of it all is maybe the sense that in conventional terms a lot of people would regard this as probably the pinnacle of your life - and now it's fifteen minutes behind you and getting further away all the time."

Eventually the euphoria departs, to return

perhaps in later life with the onset of aching limbs and the realisation of one's mortality. Players come back to ground level again, and this occurred when the Wallabies went to South Africa in 1992.

This was a fantastic occasion in any rugby player's career. It had been a long time since a previous Wallaby visit. Like a visit to New Zealand, a South African tour was ever considered the supreme test of rugby manhood. This is not meant to denigrate the worth of other rugby-playing countries, but the All Blacks and the Springboks provided that extra measure of toughness, and a special breath of fanaticism. Wales used to be spoken of in the same manner, but with the closure of the coal mines, the Welsh have become mere mortals.

Author Bryce Courtney, quoted in *Nick Farr-Jones*: wrote: "To the Afrikaaner…rugby is not a game. It is a commitment, a chosen battlefield, a gesture of collective self-assertion against a hostile and unsympathetic world. It is a rally and call to arms. It is the initiation into manhood. It is a sacred covenant."

There were problems that surfaced in South Africa that were associated with their very rugby isolation and yet continuing fanaticism, even to the point that Australia actually and seriously considered abandoning their tour. Sanity fortunately prevailed, and the Wallabies thereafter overran the Springboks by their greatest defeat in 100 years, 26 to 3. For Farr-Jones, it was his 59th test, and time to retire. In the rugby sense, he had done it all. Now it was time to deal with the real world.

What was certain was that Nick Farr-Jones was now one of the game's immortals, and he could never escape the inevitability of his own enduring fame. He had come a long way from being a rather brash child, to being an unofficial ambassador for his country. Maybe he was not good enough to play in the first XV at Newington College, but he was sufficiently gifted to captain the Wallabies in glorious victories for the Bledisloe Cup and the William Webb Ellis trophy.

# Roger Gould

There have been many outstanding Wallaby fullbacks, starting with Queenslander Phil Carmichael, who scored 118 points on the 1908 tour, a record at the time. Then there was Dr Alex Ross, who played 29 of the team's 34 matches during the Waratah tour of the British Isles in 1927-28 and captained the Wallabies to South Africa in 1933.

Dr Brian Piper was the Wallabies' stalwart during the forties, and he was legendary under the high ball. Dr Dick Tooth and Terry Curley were others who performed herculean tasks for their country in the fifties, many considering Curley the equal of any, his career ending at 20 years of age when he retired to become a Marist brother.

Jim Lenehan was the giant of the sixties, though Arthur McGill, who played in the sixties and seventies, was a veritable match winner on his day. Laurie Monaghan was another brilliant custodian, who played 22 of the 26 games during the 1975-76 tour of the British Isles.

Arguably the best of them all was the long-striding, 193cm (6ft 4in) and 95kg (15st) Queenslander Roger Gould. He had it all: A towering punt that brought 'oohs' and 'aahs' from the spectators, unflinching courage under the high ball, safe hands, a crushing tackle, and an awesome and devastating burst when he elected to come in as the extra man.

Australia has been blessed throughout the years with stupendous fullbacks, halfbacks, five-eighths, wingers and breakaways, and it is interesting to speculate as to why. The simple fact is that Australia for many moons was outgunned in their 'tight five', and it put enormous pressure on certain positions. The breakaways had to negate superior possession by the opposition, and the scrum halves had to survive with disintegrating packs and required hearts like lions to withstand the endless pressure. Five-eighths also had to live with minimal good ball and were expected to attack as well as link. Wingers got the ball very few times and were forced to make the most of those limited opportunities. The fullback, the last line of defence, was harried from the word go, and was expected to break down opposition forays and at the same time turn defence into attack.

Roger Gould was Brisbane born and bred, his father a well-off hotel supplier, and his mother was related to Nev Broadfoot, one of the rugby league greats from Toowoomba's 'Galloping Clydesdales' in the twenties. He was a Kangaroo in the touring squad to Great Britain in 1921-22. His mother joked about young Roger: "He was eight pounds at birth, six pounds in the thighs."

From his early years Roger played for Wests in Brisbane, and attended Brisbane Boys' College, playing Australian Rules football as well as rugby union, until the BBC rugby coach put his foot down and his Aussies Rules days became a thing of the past. The vestiges of the latter experience remained with Roger, his phenomenal punting and safe hands in the air being such a testimony.

His Wallaby and Queensland colleague Dr Peter Horton said: "Indeed, he is the college's most decorated footballer and holds a mythical status at BBC along with such tremendous athletes as Kieren Perkins, Angus Waddell and, from a different era, the multi-talented Robin Shaw."

He was selected for the Queensland Under 19 team and in 1978, at 20 years of age, was selected for Queensland. It was at a time when Queensland's resurgence was complete, and there were some mighty names on the team: Mark Loane, Tony D'Arcy, Andrew Slack, Tony Shaw, Peter Horton, David Hillhouse, Peter and Paul McLean, Brendan Moon, Chris Handy, Stan Pilecki, Geoff Shaw and Greg Cornelsen being among them.

Under the able management of coach Bob Templeton and rugby devotee, manager John Ryan, the Queensland team went on a pre-season jaunt playing two games in Tokyo, one in Vancouver, two in San Francisco and one in Los Angeles, in the process winning five of the six. They lost the game in Vancouver 13 to 6, against British Columbia. This was heady stuff for the young Gould, who took to touring like a duck takes to water. He enjoyed the mateship and conviviality, and the new vistas that the game offered him.

Roger made his first appearance for Queensland in the British Columbia game, and though he impressed he played only once more, against UCLA at Los Angeles. Winger Brendan Moon was another newcomer who showed unbelievable promise, scoring 13 tries on that tour.

On its return to Queensland the state team faced a heavy itinerary, with many matches against New Zealand provincial teams. Graham Noon was Queensland's fullback against Counties and North Auckland, but then Gould played his first game for the state on the hallowed turf of Ballymore, against Victoria. Queensland won 76 to 0, Roger being injured in the match and replaced by Greg Moloney.

Graham Noon retained his position against Otago, but Roger was reinstated for the interstate match against NSW, which the Maroons won by 26 to 3, Gould kicking a penalty and a dropped goal.

Invaluable international experience was gained in Queensland colours in matches against Wales (24-31), and the Junior All Blacks (41-3 and 10-0). It was certainly some year for the youngster, as he gained selection for the Wallaby team to tour New Zealand. The No.1 fullback was Laurie Monaghan.

Despite the touring, which he enjoyed, it was a disastrous Wallaby initiation for Roger. What was thought at the time to be a torn hamstring limited his total New Zealand playing time to 17 minutes. In the post-tour pen sketches by veteran New Zealand writer Bob Howitt he wrote that it was ridiculous penning one of Gould because of his limited amount of playing time. Roger Gould never really forgave the writer for what he felt at the time was an indignity.

Laurie Monaghan broke his collarbone after the first test, and with Gould injured, Australia had to send for a replacement, Geoff Richards. New Zealand won the first test 13-12, and the second 22-6. Two weeks before the final test, Wallaby coach Daryl Haberecht had a heart attack, and captain Tony Shaw prepared the team. In one of the greatest upsets in Bledisloe Cup history, Australia won 30 to 16, Greg Cornelsen becoming only the second player in 53 years to score four tries in a test. It was the highest number of points ever scored against an All Black team in a test match. Roger had to watch, frustrated, from the stands.

1979 was Queensland's finest year, as the state side played 12 games against quality opposition and lost only once. Those which Roger played in were Australian Capital Territory, in which he scored two tries, kicked eight conversions and two penalty goals; Ireland; Wellington; NSW Country and NSW in Sydney.

In the sole test against New Zealand, Paul McLean was at fullback, in order to make way for the brilliant NSW five-eighth Tony Melrose. Australia won 12 to 6, for their second victory over the All Blacks in a row. Roger had missed his opportunity. He toured Argentina with the Wallabies in 1979, and though the only specialist fullback, injuries once more limited his appearances. He gave way in the tests to Paul McLean. Though he had physical problems, he was ever an enthusiastic tourist, falling in love with Argentina and its people.

Ex-Wallaby Dr Peter Horton noted: "He was a complete fullback yet, as legend has it, an injury ridden footballer. Mind you, he had a fantastic time all the same…! I will not bore you with a catalogue of his maladies and their physiological causes, perhaps they were social-psychological manifestations of his attitude to life and football. Hey, we did actually play for enjoyment in those distant days of the 1970s-1980s! Believe it or not. I can see no likelihood of such a cavalier emerging on the Australian scene for a while, more's the pity!"

There was no doubt as to who was Queensland's fullback in 1980, and Gould's supporters were in raptures as the young giant gave vent to his remarkable talents. Queensland was still dominant, beating Hawke's Bay, King Country, losing to Sydney 10-18, winning against Taranaki but losing to NSW in Sydney 36-20, then recording a fantastic victory over the All Blacks by 9 to 3. There was then a state tour to New Zealand, Queensland rolling by Manawatu, Thames Valley and North Auckland. It was a busy year, as back at Ballymore Queensland demonstrated its brilliance against Leicester, had a hiccup against Counties, then throttled NSW Country before beating the Blues in the return match 24 to 7.

It was some year, as the Maroons then toured England, Scotland, France and Italy in a post-season extravaganza, winning five games, losing one and drawing two. Queensland was put on the rugby world map in this era by far-sighted administrators, an excellent management team in John Ryan and Bob Templeton, and a group of talented individuals who were willing to absorb and learn from their various and demanding encounters. In the forties and fifties the state team would have been lucky if they played two matches in a year. In 1980, when Roger Gould became a fixture, the state team played an incredible 21 games. In a sense, it was a period when there was increased professionalisation of the amateur game. It was difficult to hold down any fulltime job or take a full course load at University. The players were not professionals with respect to money received, but they were indeed *time* professionals, with expectations high as to the amount of time they were required to put into the game.

The state commitments were only part of their involvement, as players had to balance their club alliances, as well as national responsibilities. Roger Gould was without question in 1980 Australia's leading fullback, and he was the automatic choice against the All Blacks in their three-test series in Australia.

In the first match, at the Sydney Cricket Ground, Australia prevailed in a hard-fought encounter by 13 to 9. It was the third straight victory for the Wallabies over the All Blacks.

New Zealand came back in the second test at Ballymore, squeaking home 12 to 9. This game was notorious as Wallaby second rower Steve Williams was forced to leave the field with a broken jaw. The culprit was breakaway Mark Shaw.

The third match at the Sydney Cricket Ground resulted in a 26 to 10 victory for Australia, and possession of the Bledisloe Cup, for only the fourth time in its history. Australian rugby had really turned the corner, and New Zealanders watched in shock and disbelief as the ecstatic Australians ran round the Oval brandishing the Cup. Roger Gould's contribution in the three test series was enormous, his kicks time and again sending the All Blacks scurrying back into their own half, and his thrusts into the backline sending alarm bells off in the New Zealand defence.

One of his personal ambitions was fulfilled in 1981-82 as he departed on a 23-match Wallaby tour of the British Isles under coach Bob Templeton. It was a highly talented team, and expectations were high in Australia as it departed that a Grand Slam might be in the offing. History was made when the three Ella brothers were selected. Other luminaries were John Hipwell, captain Tony Shaw, Michael O'Connor, Mark Loane and Paul McLean. Many held it was Australia's strongest team ever.

It was, however, not a successful tour. The team had 16 wins and a draw in 23 games, but surprisingly won only the initial international, against Ireland, by a narrow 16 to 12 score. Losses to Wales (13-18), Scotland (15-24) and England (11-15) followed.

There were many excuses advanced. The first was an horrendous run of injuries, starting with hooker Bruce Malouf breaking his leg a few days after arrival in England. At various times most of the team was sidelined, the most serious being John Hipwell, who had back and rib problems.

The second factor was that Paul McLean's kicking touch inexplicably deserted him in the tests. The greatest point scorer in Australian rugby history to this point had a form lapse, which all kickers do at some stage in their careers. This had an undeniable effect in the emotion-filled aura of test matches.

Then there was that element called luck. Nothing seemed to run the right way for the 1981-82 Wallabies. Perhaps being denied the last game on tour against the Barbarians typified their ill fortune. They were snowed in at Porthcawl and the game had to be cancelled. At least there was an amusing side to it, mainly because of streaker Erica Roe, who displayed an outrageous upper body development to a stunned international television audience during the English test. Instant fame came her way, and the team agreed that she could come to Porthcawl for publicity shots with them. A substantial sum went into the team fund. Erica was isolated with the Wallabies at their hotel during the snow-storm.

The magic of Mark Ella on the 1981-82 tour and the need to have Paul McLean in the team put undue pressure on Roger Gould, who had been widely heralded as the world's best fullback. Roger played against Ireland, Wales and Scotland, but the writing was on the wall in the Scottish test as Mark Ella was selected at five-eighth and Paul McLean was experimented with at inside centre. In the final game, against England, Paul McLean was selected at fullback, thus displacing Gould. In the game before that English test, against Combined Series, Gould was called on to kick, and made six from seven attempts.

An unusual incident occurred in the final test, as captain Tony Shaw was dropped, Mark Loane taking over the captaincy. A careless but obvious punch thrown in the open against Scotland by Shaw was generally held to be the reason for the relegation.

In 1982 the Wallabies had a new coach, Bob Dwyer, who made his reputation as mentor of the Randwick Club. His first major move was to axe Roger Gould and Paul McLean, absolute heroes in Queensland, and instead selected Randwick's Glen and Mark Ella. The game, against Scotland, was to be held at Ballymore,

of all places.

In an unprecedented display, Gould's replacement, Glen Ella, was subjected to merciless and unfair harassment from a biased Ballymore crowd. He coughed up the ball, and overall had an unfortunate game. Never before in living memory had an Australian crowd booed its own players. To rub it in, Scotland won the match 12 to 7.

The two Queensland icons were back for the second test in Sydney. Before the match, Paul McLean added drama to the proceedings by announcing that it would be his final international appearance.

Scotland was overrun by 33 to 9, and Queenslanders Roger Gould, Paul McLean and Michael O'Connor scored all of the points. Gould scored two devastating tries, the first time in history that two had been scored in an international by a Wallaby fullback. Paul McLean really turned the screws, scoring an Australian record 21 points, with five penalty goals and three conversions. The game was one of the most satisfying in Gould's illustrious career. "It was fun out there," he said.

The Wallabies toured New Zealand in 1982, Glen Ella and Gould being the two fullbacks. Ten of the Wallabies withdrew from the touring party: Paul McLean, Brendan Moon, Mark Loane, Tony Shaw, Peter McLean, Tony D'Arcy, Bill Ross, Stan Pilecki and Michael O'Connor, all from Queensland, and Gary Pearse from NSW.

The stated excuse of the players was that they had been playing too much rugby, but there was little doubt that in the main it was a player-revolt over the axing of popular father-figure and Queensland coach Bob Templeton as national coach. Bob Dwyer, in his book *Winning Way,* wrote that the players "assured him it had nothing to do with the coach, yet I remain to be convinced that this was the case generally". One player who would not have been selected but for the mass defection was 19-year-old David Campese, who was selected out of the Australian Colts team. As they say, the rest is history.

Gould is a laid-back character who loved travelling and playing, and did not allow himself to get caught up too much in the politics of the game, so he accompanied the team. Mark Ella was to say of him, in 1984: "Roger has been around and knows exactly what's going on with his life. Nothing worries him. Things can be falling apart around us, but Roger stays as cool as ever."

The Wallabies lost the first test in 1982 to New Zealand 23 to 16, Roger kicking eight of the team's points. In a stunning second test, the Australians reversed the result, winning 19 to 16, Roger scoring 11 of the points. There was tremendous interest in the third test, with some 52,000 in attendance. Australia were steam-rolled, losing 33 to 18, Roger, however, getting 15 of his team's 18 points, with a try, a conversion and three penalty goals.

In this final game there was an altercation between Gould and the irascible All Black Mark Shaw. Roger expressed his ideas about Shaw forcibly to the referee, and was penalised for his impertinence. Roger was never one to lie down when he felt he was in the right, and this included, throughout his career, Prime Ministers, coaches, referees and players. A shrinking violet he never was.

The year 1983 was a busy one internationally, with a single test against New Zealand (Roger being unable to play through injury), a tour by Argentina and a short tour to France. It was not one of Roger's great years, as he played only three of the five tests, but he played in Argentina, Italy and Hong Kong. He became a rugby troubadour, one of the first Australians who realised the potential rewards from the world of so-called amateur rugby. A car, apartment, meals and a generous allowance in Italy were all grist to the mill for this great player.

1984 was one of the greatest years in the game's history in Australia. It began with great drama, as Bob Dwyer was rolled as national coach in favour of the mercurial Alan Jones, coach of the 1983 Manly premiership team. He was Prime Minister Malcolm Fraser's speech writer in 1979, 1980 and 1981 and, though a school teacher originally, he became, in 1983, fulltime executive director of the NSW Employers' Federation.

Jones added a new dimension to Wallaby teams, being an amazingly verbose and articulate man, as well as a workaholic of gigantic dimensions. A master of the one-liner, and a superb psychologist, he once said of himself, with tongue-in-cheek: "I'm not outspoken, other people are silent."

Mark Ella and Terry Smith, writing in *Path To Victory*, stated: "As a man of words, an academic involved in a sport of harsh physical contact, Jones loves rugby because of the values it should embrace: 'Commitment, evaluation, sense of team loyalty, the unapologetic pursuit of victory.' If all of these things could be transmitted into the life of the nation, life would be successful. Too many of the values which are projected to young people are wet, weak and pathetic. There is no shame in ambition and no shame in pursuit of success."

The erudite Jones appealed to the imagination of the Wallabies and he immediately informed Gould of his place in the master plan. The All Blacks were the first supreme test for the neophyte coach, and in the three-test series, with Gould the fullback in each, the All Blacks barely won the Bledisloe Cup, with scores of 9-16, thus losing the first encounter, then the New Zealanders had a 19-15 win and a nail biting 25-24 victory in the final encounter. One minute from the finish in the final test Mark Ella tried a dropped goal, and it barely missed.

The subsequent tour to the UK is now part of the folk-lore of Australian rugby. The Eighth Wallabies of 1984 were the first team in Australian history to win the Grand Slam, beating, in turn, England, Ireland, Wales and Scotland. Roger played in each of the tests. Australia on tour scored 400 points to 232, which included 51 tries. This was certainly one of the pinnacles of Gould's career.

Mark Ella said of Gould in *Path To Victory*: "Not only is Roger Gould the biggest punter of a ball in world rugby, he's the best fullback I've ever seen. Roger is just dynamite. He's strong, safe and although he doesn't look that fast, his long, loping stride can be very deceptive when he gets steam up. Just having Roger there takes the pressure off you. He's a terrific defender, too. Because of his size, he crunches people."

It might have been the ideal time to retire after the Grand Slam victory, but the world was Roger Gould's oyster. Skiing in the Alps, travelling round the Greek Islands, and escorting a bevy of beautiful women became part of his image, a camel-hair coat and sun glasses being his trademarks. He always gave the impression that he knew where life was at, but underneath the play-boy image there lay a very competitive individual. He and the remarkable French player Serge Blanco were seen as the best in the world in their position. One could beat you with finesse, the other with sheer power.

Roger developed a particular love for Argentina following his first visit there in 1979. He loved the lifestyle in this exotic country, and the devotedness and friendship of the rugby fanatics there. A particular friend was the legendary Hugo Porta, and whenever Roger could he would schedule airline connections to visit Argentina. One time, coming back to Australia from a European jaunt via Buenos Aires, he rang Porta to tell him of his arrival. He was whisked off to Porta's home from the airport, to be met by virtually all of the Puma test team, who had come from all over the country to pay their respects. "That's what it's all about," Roger said, "the friendships that I have forged all over the world as a result of rugby. There's no game like it." Argentina has been like a second home to him. "Rugby," he went on, "is a game I play with and against my friends."

What was surprising was Roger's ability in seven-a-side rugby. It might have been thought that he would have lacked quickness, but it was not the case, and he proved a master player and tactician.

Roger hung on in the game as long as he could, his continual hamstring problems being traced finally to his back, and remedial exercises solved his major problems. He played his last test match against the All Blacks in 1985 in a one-off test won by the All Blacks 10 to 9. A crucial play in the game was Roger coming in to the backline to put James Black over, and Lynagh's conversion put the Wallabies ahead 9 to 6. An unexpected move called 'Shuckey' by the All Blacks and 'Bombay Duck' by the Wallabies put Craig Green over the line for the narrow victory.

His last appearances for Australia were against Italy in 1986 and South Korea in 1987, both at Ballymore, and against England in the World Cup in 1987. It is perhaps fitting that his exit was against teams from various corners of the globe.

Roger Gould put much back into the game, coaching his beloved Wests for three years and taking the Australian Barbarians on a tour to North America in 1995. He showed the same facility for coaching as for playing.

Unmarried, he runs a very successful hotel supply firm with over 40 employees, and indulges himself with polo. It seems to fit the image, and he is occasionally seen running from the polo to the rugby field. He remains his own man, imperturbable and unwavering in a righteous cause.

When questioned by the Prime Minister's office on his decision to tour South Africa, he countered by proffering a few suggestions to the Prime Minister on how to run the country. He was perhaps the first of the modern players, embracing all the world in his considerable grasp. Many were to endeavour to copy him, but they were pale images. There is only one Roger Gould, and he strode the rugby field in his time like a veritable colossus.

His team mate Dr Peter Horton had this to say of him: "In pure football terms Roger Gould was an exceptional talent and was a great - I was going to say 'servant' but Roger was never a servant of rugby, more the other way around - player, I suppose that sums it up. He loved to play and when he lost the passion he moved on. I certainly felt very secure knowing he was behind us taking those high balls and it was a sheer delight to know that his siege-gun punts would take us into the comfort zone of the opposition's 22. Roger could also chime into a backline incisively and for the big man he was, he was very fast and more than a handful to arrest. Having been without what one could consider a good fullback for the past decade Australia would love another BBC lad with Gouldy's talents to appear and I am sure so would Western Suburbs!"

# Jules Guerassimoff

**J**ulius Guerassimoff has changed remarkably little since his playing days in the sixties, his rugged countenance and lean body a ready reminder of what he was at the height of his career. A no-nonsense type player, he was possessed of superlative fitness, speed off the mark and a damaging tackle.

He and his erstwhile partner, the late Greg Davis, terrorised the inside backs of the world when they were at their peak. Davis, whose bald noggin seemed to be everywhere, was a New Zealander who rose to captaincy of the Wallabies. He was tough. Once he had his nose badly bent out of shape, but spurned medical advice and belted it back into something resembling its normal shape with a bottle. It was called the 'Greg Davis Cosmetic Surgery'.

It is often said that the greatest boxers of the world come from the slums and immigrant families, as they are imbued with that extra motivation to succeed. Lacking an education they relied on their fists to do the talking. Jules could lay no claim to a background of poverty, but he certainly had the immigrant ties, and this might have served him with that extra drive that was a feature of his play.

His grandparents were white Russians, and they left Siberia in the late twenties, using falsified documents. All they wanted to do was escape the oppression of the Communist government. They got on a Japanese ship, and bribed the sailors to let them ashore at Hokkaido. They eventually went on to Canada, then back to Japan, where his mother and father met and married.

Next step was Manchuria, and in 1940, with war overtaking the family once more, they got a ship from Shanghai to Cape York. Jules' father worked a share farming homestead at Thangool, south of Gladstone, and grew cotton. Then in 1944 they purchased a farm at Yarwin and farmed pawpaws and tomatoes. Jules, or Julius as they named him, was born on 28 June 1940, ten days after the family's arrival in Australia, and grew up on the farm, running around, as he put it, "like a junior Tarzan". It laid the foundation of his trade-mark, supreme fitness.

With his Russian background, it was almost inevitable that he would be tagged as 'Vodka', though the nickname 'Big Julie' came his way as well. 'Big Julie' was a larger-than-life character created by Broadway writer Damon Runyan, and immortalised in the musical comedy *Guys and Dolls*.

Jules attended nearby Yarwin State School, and then was sent to Rockhampton Grammar School as a boarder. There was no rugby union at the school, not that he cared, so he threw himself into rugby league. He had four years playing league, which suited his mobility, two in the school firsts, playing second row and lock. There were a few future rugby league notables in Rockhampton at the time, the most famous being future international Bobby Banks.

Always competent in his studies, he was

accepted at the University of Queensland on a Commonwealth Scholarship in 1958, doing his degree in Agricultural Science. He had never played rugby union to this point, but turned out for the university, playing for the seconds and occasionally the first team. He was also state javelin champion, winning the title in 1958, 1959 and 1960.

He can remember clearly his initial first grade encounter in 1958, against Souths, at Kalinga Park, Brisbane. Souths had a few wily veterans in their team such as Nev Cottrell and Neil Betts. He remarked: "I was kicked from pillar to post, but you know…I liked it! I thought you had to be tough enough to cop it!"

There were a few handy players around the University at the time, such as the great breakaway 'Chilla' Wilson, all-round back John O'Neill and five-eighth Ross Sheil.

The biggest influence on Jules' career was university coach Ashley Girle, who had been a fullback for Queensland, University and Australian Universities in the fifties. Until Ashley took over at the University there was no real training, and upon his arrival there was an emphasis on skills, game analysis and fitness preparation. 'Big Julie' revelled in it, accepting any personal criticisms that came his way and attempting to eradicate perceived faults in his game. Now he was a breakaway, and he enjoyed the relative freedom of the position.

One thing he remembered from Ashley Girle was his credo to "always take the goal", and throughout his career this belief was reinforced as countless times his team came from behind, after being in a seemingly hopeless position, courtesy of a few penalties.

In 1960, just when he had established himself as a regular first grader, he was sidelined with an acromio-clavicular dislocation. Nowadays this is not a serious injury, but then it was so considered, and the subsequent operation had him languishing on the sidelines for many months. He was admonished that he might never play again, and he certainly acquiesced for that season.

A turning point in his life was watching Queensland get absolutely demolished by NSW to the tune of forty to fifty points. He thought: "I can play better than that even with a broken shoulder."

He started training with a new fervour, and in 1961 started to make his presence felt. He represented Queensland for the first time in 1962. He was to play 79 games for his beloved state. In those days the interstate matches acted as Wallaby selection trials, so he had an opportunity to achieve higher honours. However he missed out playing against the New Zealanders that year and going on tour as well, Terry Reid, Ted Heinrich, John O'Gorman, Geoff Chapman and Peter Crittle being his principal rivals.

In 1963 he was back in the interstate trials, with a tour to South Africa in the offing. There was an opinion among Australian manager Bill McLaughlin and coach Alan Roper that Jules was a bit of a 'seagull', that is, a forward who did not get involved in the tough stuff but hung off the rucks to get the ball, but selectors Terry MacBride of 1947-48 Wallaby fame, and Joe French of Queensland, seemed to support his candidature.

After the interstate games there was a Possibles versus Probables game. His team was captained by rival breakaway Geoff Chapman, and to all appearances the final breakaway position was a toss-up between the two of them. During the match superlative five-eighth Rupert Rosenblum was badly concussed and had to leave the field. Chapman, as captain, moved Jules to five-eighth, in his mind finishing forever Jules' tour opportunities. As luck would have it, Guerassimoff scored two unbelievable tries in five minutes and that clinched his selection, Chapman missing out. As Jules said: "I had nothing to lose, so when I saw an opening I just pinned my ears back and went for it." It was his first Wallaby tour.

Prior to departure, there was a game against an England side captained by Mike Weston. The Australian breakaways were John O'Gorman and Ted Heinrich, and it did not augur well for Jules' future test possibilities when Australia prevailed at the Sydney Sports Ground by 18 points to 9.

His premonitions were reinforced on the South African trip, for he had the distinct feeling that coach Alan Roper did not like his style of play and felt he was lucky to get selected. He was given one game, against "the worst team in South Africa", North Eastern Districts, but before the game the Wallabies were treated to a day in the hot springs at Burgersdorp by the cunning locals, and all the players, including Guerassimoff, were zapped on the field of play the next day. They were lucky to emerge with a victory by 9 to 8. Jules, as well as the others, were not very impressive.

Guerassimoff was never one to sit back and accept defeat or mediocrity, and he quickly became disenchanted with his lot. By subterfuge he got hold of his return airline ticket, and confronted Wallaby coach Alan Roper. He said: "I didn't come to South Africa to be a tourist. I came to play, and if you don't play me I'd rather go home. I've got my ticket. I'll go home if I don't play."

Roper had to be bemused a bit by the confrontation, but admired 'Vodka's' guts and gave him some game opportunities. Jules took his chances in Rhodesia, the Wallabies first of all getting by a Rhodesian XV in a fine game of open rugby 22 to 11, and then playing against Rhodesia, which resulted in another win for the Aussies by 12 to 5. As Ian Diehm put it in *Giants in Green and Gold:* "It was a game in which the loose forwards excelled. Jules Guerassimoff had taken some time to settle into a team that was dominated by New South Wales players, but in this game he gave glimpses of just how great a breakaway he was to become. Ted Heinrich and David Shepherd also had good games, while flanker Piet Greyling was outstanding for Rhodesia."

It was against Rhodesia that the Wallabies came up against the might of prop Andy McDonald. The Wallabies could not understand why the Springboks did not appreciate his scrummaging ability. He was simply too strong for them. In later years they heard Andy had been hospitalised. He had been on his horse surveying his property and unknowingly was being stalked by a lion. The lion leapt on to his horse and knocked him off, so he fought the lion with his bare hands, strangling it to death. He finished up with 200 plus stitches, but understandably became a bit of a legend because of it, though the Wallabies had an inkling of his phenomenal strength well before this.

While in Rhodesia Guerassimoff, with the others, visited the famous falls, and the team was invited to view an enormous crocodile in an enclosure. Jules was first there, and prodded the creature with a stick. It slid off the riverbank

and into the water, never to be seen again, to the disgust of the tourists. 'Big Julie' was duly appointed as the 'duty boy' by manager McLaughlin over his misdemeanour.

Guerassimoff had, however, impressed on the playing field, but not enough to make the first test team, which Australia lost to South Africa by 3 to 14. Following the loss, Jules got runs against Border and Western Transvaal in the lead-up to the second test. They were both wins for the Wallabies. Against Border, Guerassimoff scored the first try and set up the second in a narrow 6 to 3 win. Against Western Transvaal, a 14 to 12 win, noted writer AC Parker observed that: "The Wallaby forwards, too, were unusually quicker to the tackled ball, and here the breakaway, Jules Guerassimoff, excelled." Parker also said Jules was "pugnaciously aggressive". He was now a test possibility.

It took a lot to upset the equilibrium of phlegmatic Wallaby manager Bill McLaughlin, but on the eve of the Western Transvaal match that certainly happened. He was taking a morning bath and in response to a knock shouted "come in!"

To his consternation a full-grown chimpanzee burst into the bathroom, a bottle of beer pressed to his mouth.

The chimpanzee, a tame one, was well known in Potchefstroom, and Jules had talked its trainer into participating in the gag, and herded the animal into the bathroom. Jules had enlightened the team as well, and they all walked into Bill's bathroom, laughing uproariously.

Jules' 'second string' status had made an astonishing turnaround through these two pre-test wins. Greg Davis, who was having a superlative tour, was one obvious test choice. Jules was up against the more experienced Dallas O'Neill and Ted Heinrich for the remaining slot.

When the final selection was made, the name of Guerassimoff was there. It was to be his first of 12 tests for Australia. There were seven changes in the team from the first test, many of them now Wallaby legends: Terry Casey, Jim Boyce, Beres Ellwood, Ian Moutray, Dick Marks, Phil Hawthorne; Ken Catchpole (vice-captain); Jon White, Peter Johnson and John Thornett (captain); Greg Davis, Rob Heming, Peter Crittle; Jules Guerassimoff and John

O'Gorman. Maxwell Price wrote at the time: "The most improved forward in the side is Jules Guerassimoff."

The test at Newlands resulted in a shock victory to Australia, by 9 to 5. It was the first defeat for South Africa in 16 tests. As well as Guerassimoff, the stars of the victory were the mercurial halfback Ken Catchpole, fellow breakaway Greg Davis, centre Beres Ellwood and front rower and magnificent captain John Thornett.

An Australian pressman had this to say:

"On his display in his test debut Guerassimoff can be certain of his place in the next two.

"The fierce tackling by Guerassimoff and breakaway Greg Davis was the decisive factor in Australia's win.

"After the match Davis said, 'I could not have played nearly as well without Jules.'

"'He was tremendous. I knew that if I went for a man or the ball and missed, Jules would be there to succeed.'"

This single match cemented his place in future Wallaby teams. Jules showed he could 'go up a gear' and not be overawed by the fervour and intensity of the international game. He and Davis had wreaked havoc among the Springbok inside backs, blotting out scrum half Piet Uys and five-eighth Keith Oxlee, and destroying the rhythm of their backs. A new halfback pairing, Nelie Smith and Norman Riley, was set up to blot out the effectiveness of the Wallaby breakaways.

The third test at Ellis Park provided another stunning win for the Wallabies by 11 to 9. Dr Danie Craven, the guru of South African rugby, said: "This is the best touring team to visit us since the 1955 British Lions. They thoroughly deserved their win. They were the better team, their handling and backing-up was superior to the Boks and I heartily congratulate them on this fine display."

Paul Irwin wrote, in the *Sunday Times:* "The Wallabies were brimming with enterprise, always looking for the opening and moving quickly to take it. And there linking up with the backs were Greg Davis, Jules Guerassimoff and John O'Gorman, the loose forward trio."

There were to be only four tests on the 1963 tour, and incredibly Australia was 2-1 up.

The Springboks stormed back to win the final encounter by 22 to 6 and square the series, but the game was one that left a sour taste in the mouths of many Wallabies. Nineteen of the Springbok points came after the 22nd minute of the second half. The Wallabies had been leading by 6-3, when 'Tiny' Naude kicked a penalty from 46 yards out to level the scores. Another penalty and a try made it 14 to 6, but the Wallabies were still in it, though they were disenchanted by the refereeing of Captain Piet Myburgh.

It was then that a sensation occurred. Schoeman, the Springbok flanker, was held up by the Wallaby defence, and dropped the ball. All of the Wallabies thought it was a knock-on, but when 'Tiny' Naude scooped it up and went over, a try was awarded. The non-whites, who traditionally supported touring teams, were seated at this particular end point of the stadium, and they erupted at the decision, swarming on to the field at Port Elizabeth. The game was stopped for several minutes as the police made a baton charge to clear the in-goal area. At one stage things got so bad that warning shots were fired into the air. The disturbances were the worst seen to this point at a rugby game in South Africa. This, and what appeared to be an error on the referee's part, clearly unsettled the Wallabies.

Still, in retrospect Jules thought it was a marvellous tour, and he personally had grown in stature as a player. The Guerassimoff-Davis combination was considered lethal.

In 1964, Jules was a certainty for the New Zealand tour, the Wallabies again being led by John Thornett. It was tough going up against former Wallaby and halfback Des Connor, who really came into his own behind the All Black pack. There were some mighty New Zealanders in action in those days, maybe the greatest forward of them all, Colin Meads, breakaways Kel Tremain and John Graham, front-rower Ken Gray and the unbelievable long-kicking fullback, Don Clarke. There was also lots of experience with the Wallabies, such as the 30-year old formidable front-rower Jon White, Beres Ellwood, Peter Johnson, Rob Heming, Ted Heinrich, 'Charlie' Crittle, Ken Catchpole, the Boyce twins and Phil Hawthorne.

It looked as if Australia had been let off the hook when the famous D.B. Clarke cried off with a knee injury, but his replacement, Mick

Williment, kicked eight points in a close 14-9 All Black victory in the first test. The Davis-Guerassimoff pairing stood for all three tests on the 1964 tour, and Jules played in seven of the eight games.

With Clarke back for the second test, the All Blacks won 18-3. 'The Boot', in scoring six points, brought his own personal tally to 205 points in 30 tests and put his aggregate in first class rugby to over 1800 points.

The Wallabies came storming back to win the third test by 20 points to five. It was the heaviest defeat ever inflicted upon an All Black team in a full-scale international. Bob Howitt wrote: "Guerassimoff was undoubtedly Australia's finest forward. His covering and crash tackles racked New Zealand time and again and he was also a driving force in broken play."

The president of the New Zealand Rugby Union, Tom Pearce, presented a tie to the 22-year-old Guerassimoff at the after-match dinner, and stated: "I understand you're a White Russian. A few years ago I presented a rugby ball to the crew of a Russian whaler. If the Red Russians ever learn to play rugby as well as you, then God help us."

In 1964, Guerassimoff was accorded a rare, perhaps unequalled, achievement, certainly for an Australian. He was selected as one of the greatest players of the year in the almanacs of New Zealand, South Africa and Australia.

In 1965, the Springboks came to Australia on their way to their much-heralded clash with the All Blacks for world rugby supremacy. Jules was unavailable for the first test through a knee injury, a game which the Wallabies won 18 to 11. The Springboks then vented their feelings with a 50 to 5 romp over Queensland, a game in which Guerassimoff scored Queensland's lone try and proved his leg could stand up to the pace of international rugby.

An injury to Greg Davis made Guerassimoff's selection for the second test in Brisbane a formality. In a dramatic game, the Wallabies triumphed again, 12 to 8, Peter Crittle and Jules Guerassimoff chairing their captain, John Thornett, off the field. It was his 34th test, breaking the previous record established by prop Tony Miller.

The British Lions came to Australia in 1966, and he and Davis linked up again, but after a

narrow loss by 11 to 8 at the Sydney Cricket Ground, the Wallabies were mauled in the final encounter at Brisbane's Lang Park by 0-31.

'Vodka' made the 1966-67 tour to the British Isles, France and Canada, Bill McLaughlin and Alan Roper being the management team, and John Thornett the captain. The team started poorly on tour, and was torn apart when hooker Ross Cullen was sent home for biting the ear of Oxford prop and Irish international Ollie Waldron. Waldron had been boring in on Cullen and as he was getting no help from his front row, he bit Waldron.

The ensuing furore was such that Cullen was sent home, and indeed did not have the opportunity to even say farewell to his compatriots. He was whisked away while the team was training. Guerassimoff was a sole witness as the sorry and depressed figure of Cullen left for the airport.

Never one to hide his true feelings, Jules openly expressed his anger to Thornett, saying that the discipline was excessive and he was disgusted at the lack of support of the captain and players. Fortified with a few drinks later on, he gave manager McLaughlin the same incisive message. It was a bad situation, and it was no wonder that Australia lost to Scotland, Ireland and France, beating only Wales and England on that tour. Guerassimoff played in three of the five tests, against England, France and Ireland.

This was the end of the international career of Guerassimoff, and though he personally has no ill feeling over what happened, he remains adamant that his own stance was correct, and that Cullen was unnecessarily pilloried. There will always remain the possibility that Guerassimoff was thereafter branded NTTA - 'Never To Tour Again'. If so, he would not be the first or last so dealt with by management.

Evan Whitton, in *The National Times*, said: "Guerassimoff was then, as perhaps the greatest breakaway in international rugby, at the height of his powers, but while we cannot say that his outspokenness necessarily had any effect on his career, it is a fact that, after that tour, he was never again invited to play for Australia."

Despite some of the political and personal animosities that permeated the 1966-67 tour, Jules considered it was the experience of a lifetime.

One incident he particularly recalled with amusement. John Thornett, as captain of the Wallabies, and the long-serving Peter Johnson, were invited to the royal yacht *Britannia* to meet the Queen and Prince Phillip. Thornett was a wonderful ambassador for Australia, and listened carefully to the protocol, which essentially was not to speak unless you were spoken to. He had this on his mind constantly, as he did not want to disgrace Australia. He climbed down the gang-plank to go to lunch, and unexpectedly came face-to-face with Prince Phillip. "Oh," stammered Thornett, "have you had a good day?"

Guerassimoff never complained after 1967, figuring correctly that one determines one's own destiny. He threw himself into his club rugby with University and his representative games for Queensland, playing for the state until 1973. As Max Hawkins wrote in *Maroon*, he "was the brains and moving force behind Queensland's onfield rugby when he was in his early 30s".

In one game against NSW, second rower Tony Abrahams went down, and the Maroons treated him like a doormat, raking his body furiously. Alex Evans, not noted for his delicate play, was late appearing on the scene, and had not even been in the ruck. But as Abrahams looked up he saw the menacing visage of Evans, and called him everything, even questioning his parentage in an unfeeling manner.

Evans looked at Abrahams and said: "It wasn't me, mate, look, I've got rubber tags!"

Another time prop David Dunworth was playing his first game for Queensland, and was very nervous, and the players told him that his opposite number in the Blues pack, Ross Turnbull, was the meanest animal seen on a rugby field, and was liable to tear him apart.

When the game started, Turnbull looked with disdain at the 'new boy', and gave him a none-too-gentle right to the chops. Nothing happened, and the Queensland team wondered whether they had taken a real pussy-cat on board. So at the next scrum Turnbull let him have one again.

Dunworth then leapt out of the scrum, his fists flying out at the erstwhile Turnbull, who was backing up furiously. In hasty retreat, he called out to referee Kevin Crowe: "Ref, ref, call him off, he's a madman!" Dunworth had

made the grade.

Another time the New Zealanders were playing a game against Queensland at Ballymore, and 'Fergie" McCormick, a tough fullback who was never a shrinking violet when action stations were called, shoved one of the Maroons, and Guerassimoff and a few of the boys gave him a vigorous massage with their cleats when the opportunity presented itself. It is called by the locals a 'Queensland hello'.

Years later Guerassimoff met 'Fergie' in a bar in New Zealand. 'Fergie' immediately said: "You bastard, Guerassimoff, you're the only bloke I never got back at!"

In 1974, pursuing his profession of agricultural science, he went with a German company to the Philippines, and soon got Saturday rugby games going there. When he was then sent to Hong Kong for three years, he played on, winning the Plate at the initial Hong Kong Sevens. He was back to Australia in 1977, moving to Canberra, and kept his hand in playing second grade, with an occasional game in the firsts.

In 1978 there was a testimonial match for Greg Davis, who tragically was dying of cancer at 39 years of age in New Zealand. Jules played in a backrow with the legendary All Black Ian Kirkpatrick and the brilliant Frenchman, Jean-Pierre Rives.

Evan Whitton wrote at the time: "While Kirkpatrick was the dominant figure and, indeed, virtually controlled the rather desultory match, Guerassimoff made it clear that he was not there just to make up the numbers. Playing against an international back row consisting of Cornelsen, Pearse and Battishall, he put Kirkpatrick in for a try, had a major hand in that scored by the other All Black, Norton, and scored two tries himself, one after an incredible piece of interpassing between Rives and Kirkpatrick.

"All of which, for those aware of the circumstance of his abrupt departure from the international scene 11 years ago, gave Guerassimoff something of the appearance of a skeleton at the feast: 'If he could play like this at 38, could his form have totally deteriorated at 27?'"

Jules was still playing after his fortieth birthday, but called it quits when he dislocated his shoulder playing in a Barbarians match at

Rockhampton. One of his last matches he remembers very fondly. Then over 40 years of age, playing for University against Easts, he got in a scuffle with one of the Easts players. Neil Betts, who was standing on the sideline, called out: "Why don't you pick on somebody your own age, Guerassimoff?"

One of the real characters of rugby, 'Big Julie' still looks to be the 5' 10", 14.5 stone tearaway that terrorised inside backs. You get the feeling with him that no matter how involved he gets in business, in marketing and development, that the smell of the liniment is what he misses most, the nervousness of the dressing room, the anticipation of the battle, and the drama and intensity of the contest. The rugby field was his stage, and he lit it up like few before or since.

A mustachioed 'Bunter' Shaw on the rampage.

Roger Gould in a typical charge, with Mark Ella in support.

**Greg Cornelsen training in the country with a real wallaby.**

The Wallabies of 1908 giving a war-cry.

The 1908 Wallabies on their way to England by boat.

Dr 'Paddy' Moran, the Wallaby captain of 1908.    A caricature of the young Graham Cooke in 1933.

The Gold Medal Certificate won by the Wallabies at the 1908 London Olympic Games

Some of the 1947-48 mob: Sir Nicholas Shehadie, Bob McMaster, Graham Cooke, Bill McLean and Cyril Burke.

Cyril Towers on the burst in 1928.

Cyril Burke showing his skill as a jockey in South Africa.

Breakaway Col Windon lining up All Black Wally Argus for a fend during the '46 Bledisloe Cup series.

Some of Australia's legendary heroes. Back row: Ron Walden and Bill Cerutti; front row: Dave Cowper, Sid Malcom and Eddie Bonis.

The most successful Wallaby team to tour South Africa, led by one of Australia's great captains, John Thornett.

Graham Cooke (head taped) shrugging off a tackler during the 1947-48 tour of the UK and France.

# Chris Handy

Chris Handy is known to the rugby fraternity as 'Buddha', and the nickname corresponds with his general appearance. It began when he was on an Australian Colts tour of Japan in 1972. There he was squatting cross-legged on a bed in a hotel room playing cards, his, even then, ample stomach disgorging from a kimono. He was at this auspicious moment tagged as 'Buddha', and 'Buddha' he remains affectionately to this day.

When the list of truly great Wallaby front rowers is drawn up Chris Handy's name may not immediately appear, instead those such as 'Wild Bill' Cerutti, 'Wallaby Bob' McMaster, Steve 'Sort-'em'-Out' Finnane, Ewen McKenzie, Tony Daly, Andy McIntyre and Enrique Rodriguez might be proffered. The simple fact is, however, that no front rower is better known nationally and internationally, and none has made a greater overall contribution to the game, as broadcaster, public speaker, personality and player.

When debates rage over heredity and environment and their relative influences on a particular individual, one is always left with a basic dilemma as to which is the primary influence. Most front rowers are type-cast, they seem to come out of a similar evolutionary mould. The physical build is rather obvious, you need to be a bit of a mutate, with a squat and solid body where the head and shoulders come together with no apparent neck, and turning one's head on normal occasions is at best done with difficulty.

But it is the personality of the prop that is the kicker. Generally they are fun loving, gregarious, of the 'hail fellow will met' variety, renowned for their drinking and after-match antics. Just like the heredity-environment argument, were they born this way or did playing in the unfriendly cauldron of the front row make them all like that?

The great Bob McMaster of 1947-48 Wallabies and then rugby league fame was typical of this strange break of mutants, and it is no accident that his son Danny is one of Australia's leading comedians. Bob was, in his playing days, first to the bar after a game - and sometimes before it - and last to leave, and in between gigantic and seemingly never-ending guzzles of beer would be regaling all and sundry with outrageous stories whose relationship to fact were never questioned through a fundamental trepidation in ever questioning the story-teller's veracity.

As an inexperienced youngster on the 1947-48 tour, the author would listen with wide-eyed disbelief as Bob would recount his war-time experiences. Confidence is ever part of the art form of the story-teller, and unabashedly Bob proclaimed one night that he single-handedly had won the war in New Guinea against the Japanese. The conversation went like this.

Max Howell (sheepish): "Oh, come on, Bob, that's a bit much."

Bob McMaster (indignant and assertive):

"You're not calling me a liar, are you, son?"

Max Howell (fearful): "I wouldn't do that, Bob!"

Bob McMaster (conciliatory): "I didn't think you would, son!"

Max Howell (compromising): "Then how did you win the war, Bob?"

Bob McMaster (confident and conspiratorial): "You've seen the Kokoda trail, haven't you, son?"

Max Howell (agreeably): "Well, at the pictures, Bob...I've seen it when I've gone to the pictures."

Bob McMaster (increasingly confident, having the youngster now on the hook and reeling him in): "And what did it look like, the Kokoda trail?"

Max Howell (completely trapped): "Well, it looked like a narrow, winding trail with jungle on either side."

Bob McMaster (gleefully): 'That's it, son, that's exactly it. Everyone was in single file, mate. Someone had to be in front, and I volunteered. Always in front, lad, always in front. They had to get by me, son, those Japanese, to get at the others. I fought 'em back, son, fought 'em back. As simple as that."

He thumped his glass down for emphasis, just to provide the story with that extra bit of finality. You had to agree, it made sense. But then there was another thing you instinctively knew when you were talking with front rowers, and they were telling stories and drinking heavily. You always agreed with them.

It was forty years afterwards that the author found out that McMaster had never been near the front line, the lying so-and-so. But if McMaster told him the story again today - though Bob's drinking capacity has changed - he just might agree with him again, if only for safety reasons.

Chris Handy is of the same ilk as McMaster and the countless others who have plied their trade in the engine room, staring with glazed and uncomprehending eyes across at equally ugly and distorted faces and playing games against equally smelly and sweaty counterparts. Handy endeavoured to describe himself in the book *Well, I'll Be Ruggered,* written with two other great characters of the game, Jeff Sayle and John Lambie: "I was a no-holds-barred, boots-and-all footballer, who loved the contest,

the competition, the physicality of the game, who happily accepted the pain of it. It was my drug. Scrummaging in a rugby test was getting the ultimate high in the most brutal way - without the need to pop pills. I reckon a lot of rugby players have a masochistic streak. They're always testing themselves for the bigger fight, the larger game. If you're not able to conquer yourself and your own inhibitions, abilities, fears and skills (or lack of them), you won't make it through to the end.

"Rugby and more pointedly the front row, epitomises contact sport. There is no place where you meet your opponent more often or more physically than in the front row of a scrum. You can't tell lies, and you can't hide."

This strange breed of man who gravitates to the front row reminds one in behaviour and appearance of the wrestling fraternity, who have that same unnatural urge to roll around in another person's body oils. Yet after a bloody encounter when deadly enemies have duelled at close contact it is invariably the front rowers who are arm-in-arm with their former antagonists, while the wingers and centres remain comparatively aloof, watching these childish antics with the disdain as befits the true aristocrats of the game.

Chris Handy learned early in life elemental survival skills, being the fifth son of Brisbane dentist Alex Handy and his wife Noel. Physically outgunned by his brothers, he learned quickly how to stake his own claim by digging in and demanding part of the territory, and in desperate situations filling the air with some rarefied expletives learned from his more worldly brothers and others patrolling the avenues of Kedron, Brisbane, where he was brought up.

Chris was a Terrace boy through and through, and that school has been a rugby nursery since the turn of the century. The Terrace and Catholic connection have been significant in Queensland's rugby heritage. When young he was athletic, though not tall, and broad-shouldered, being a butterfly swimmer of some note. Schoolboy coach Les Cricker earmarked him as a scrumhalf from grade five on. He thoroughly enjoyed the position, particularly cover defence, his particular love being the last ditch tackle. His heroes at the time were rugby union's legendary

Ken Catchpole and rugby league's tough Ron Coote.

Like many rugby luminaries Chris repeated his final year to get in an additional year of school rugby and raise his marks somewhat, and the first XV coach was Norbert Byrne, an ex-Terrace and University player who was to make an outstanding contribution to the Queensland Rugby Union and the ARFU in future years. Norbert co-opted the aggressive former Wallaby Jules Guerassimoff, and Chris was made into a number eight.

Chris was the only one of the Handy boys to continue with sport, and after high school graduation he gravitated to the home of the Queensland Catholic rugby mafia, Brothers Club. It was Dick McGruther who convinced him that Brothers club was where the game was really at. They were re-establishing themselves in the sixties, with such stalwarts as Dallas O'Neill, Adrian Hose, Mick Purcell, Peter Reilly and David Dunworth creating a winning ethic and a momentum within the club.

In 1969 he joined the Brothers Colts team which won the premiership that year, and captained the Queensland Under 19s. These were his formative years, and his appetite was slowly being whetted when he saw the Des Connor-coached Wallabies almost beat New Zealand in the famous penalty try test in which referee Kevin Crowe officiated. Then in 1971 he was enthralled as Queensland downed the Lions on their way to New Zealand, where they triumphed. And then later he read of the humiliation of the 1972 'Awful Aussies', and came to the realisation in so far as his own prospects were concerned that anything was possible.

After graduating from the Colts at Brothers, Handy found himself playing any position in the scrum - back row, second row or front row. His versatility and all round skills made him difficult to leave out, and the number of Brothers players representing Queensland and Australia meant someone had to fill the gaps.

In 1970 the Brothers team was replete with outstanding players of the calibre of Barry Honan, David Dunworth, Shane Sullivan, Mick Flynn, Rod Kellaher, Mick Barry, Alex Pope, Jeff McLean and David L'Estrange, and were coached by Jim ('Adolph') Kenny, who "had a fanatical approach to the forward-based style

of rugby of hitting, driving, and cleaning out." Despite their overall power, Brothers were thwarted in their drive to the Grand Final in 1970.

In 1971 Chris was firmly and irrevocably in the front row as Wallaby Shane Sullivan retired after 1970 to concentrate on medicine, one season after he toured South Africa. Brothers won the Grand Final against Easts that year in a tough contest, as Easts coach Ken Donald worked his over-matched team into a frenzy in an endeavour to equalise matters. The match had an unfortunate aspect to it as Ian McMillan, ex-Wallaby captain Bill McLean's son-in-law, had his neck broken packing down in the first scrum against hard-rock David Dunworth.

In 1972 Handy had a taste of rugby against and with the 'big boys' when he was picked on a Barbarians side with players such as All Blacks giant Kel Tremain and the late 'Slaggy' Miller, against the Junior All Blacks. His first representative selection for Queensland was against the California Bears, but he had to withdraw through injury. From that point on, except when he broke his ankle, he became a fixture in the teams forging a renaissance of Queensland rugby from 1972 to 1980. Queensland had a plethora of magnificent front rowers at the time such as Stan 'The Man' Pilecki, David Dunworth, Trevor Davies and Bruce Brown, and though there was a bench-warming exercise or two, he became a familiar figure to the knowledgeable Ballymore crowd. Gradually he found himself typecast, having to play the role of what he euphemistically calls 'the great distracter'. That is a nice modern term for what was described in the old days as 'the enforcer', or 'hit man'.

Chris is realistic as to his worthiness to be rated among the top echelon in this regard. In *Well I'll Be Ruggered*, he said: "I might have won something of a reputation as a hit man, but the real story was that I couldn't fight. I got belted all the time. I was the belted, not the belter. But the 'bloodied hero' photographs littered the pages of the sports dailies as we won game after game against them.

"The legend of the toughness and fighting abilities of the Buddha were created out of that time. It was all ridiculous, really. My mashed-up and multi-broken hand, and the blood all over my face, attested to the fact that, yes, I could certainly step forward - but that I was more stupid than capable as a pugilist."

His first overseas tour was in 1972 to Japan, as part of an Australian Colts team. The legendary Steve Finnane and Lars Hedberg were the other two props. Finnane's humour was at times questionable. Once in Hiroshima he asked why all the buildings looked so new. It was on this tour that he acquired his 'Buddha' nickname. It was a tour that he did not recall "with much pride or affection", as the tourists did not set an example when it came to utilisation of the boot when any Japanese player found himself on the ground.

A story is told that when Japan drew with the Australian Colts a local official lamented on Australia's misfortune. Handy looked him in the eye and said: "Ah yes, but we won the big one in 1945."

Chris had a set-back in 1973 as he broke his ankle in an 18-10 victory over Tonga. He remembers it all too clearly, as most front rowers do when they ever get the ball in hand. He had doubled around to take a pass from Jeff McLean and, while trying to stop, put his foot into touch, twisted and broke his ankle. This began a never-ending relationship with Dr Fergus Wilson, orthopaedic surgeon extraordinaire, who used then revolutionary pinning techniques which allowed Chris to continue his rugby career.

One game in 1975 had a detrimental effect on his budding career. It was Queensland against England, and they had an excellent front row, Mike Burton in particular causing Handy heaps of problems. The English props were far more upright, not as low as was the practice in Queensland, and Queensland found the only way to resist their superior push was, under orders, to collapse the scrum. He was not the only one in Australia to have problems with northern hemisphere front rowers who were trained to pack more upright because of the softness of their grounds. Australians more typically 'tent pegged' because of the hardness of the ground, and the 'Aussie style' traditionally consisted of getting the feet back and propping the hips up, the shoulders and hips in line, and driving through with the legs.

Selectors at times can have long memories, and the Australian selectors shunned him, rightfully or wrongly, after his performance against England. In some ways the enforced wait was good for his career, as the quality of Queensland rugby was spiralling upwards under the genial Bob Templeton. Welsh coaching director Ray Williams was brought over and infused new life into the Queensland ranks, and games against New Zealand teams such as the tough as teak Cantabrians, emerging powers like North Auckland, and those of the old school at Wellington, not only hardened Queensland's scrum but built confidence in their ability to handle New Zealand's finest.

One's rugby career often lies in the lap of the gods, and Handy got his chance when legendary hit man Steve Finnane did a Tyson-like job on the Welsh front rower Graham Price, shattering his jaw. Chris wrote in *Well I'll Be Ruggered* what happened next: "In 1978, the Australian Rugby Union hierarchy in their wisdom decided that it was appropriate for Steve not to tour New Zealand, despite his prominent role in the series win over Wales earlier in the season. Yet he was exactly what we needed, as he had proven in France and at other times when he had been called upon to stand his ground. Apart from his reputation as a hard man he was a bloody good prop and a damned good player."

Finnane's indiscretion opened up an opportunity at last for the 'Buddha'. He was the fourth front rower picked to tour New Zealand, and seemed destined for a 'Dirt-tracker' role, one of the 'Wednesday boys'. The other props were Rob Onus, Stan Pilecki and John Meadows. He did not care where he was in the pecking order, he was a Wallaby at last, and really found himself on tour. Bret Harris, in *The Marauding Maroons,* said of him: "Handy was a happy rugby troubadour. An enthusiastic singer and joke-teller, he was ideal company on the long bus trips representative touring teams must endure. Unlike most players who naturally shy away from the heavies, Handy delighted in chatting with local officials."

He was not the only 'new boy' on that fateful 1978 tour under manager Ross Turnbull and innovative coach Daryl Haberecht. The other neophytes were Peter ('Carso') Carson, Roger Gould, Martin Knight, Brendan ('Benny') Moon, Rob Onus, Stan ('The Man') Pilecki, Bill Ross and Andrew Slack, as well as what were to be replacements, Steve Streeter and Peter McLean. Tony ('Crazy Eyes') Shaw, a hard rock if ever there was one, was the Australian captain.

Australia lost the first and second tests, and a clean sweep seemed inevitable. The Aussies pulled themselves up by their boot-straps, a not unusual occurrence among Australian athletes, despite injuries to Laurie Monaghan, Mark Loane, Paul McLean and Roger Gould, and a near fatal heart attack suffered by the Aussie coach while the team was in Wanganui. Chris Handy was selected as prop. He was the team's lucky omen, as he had played, in all, seven tour games and Australia had won them all. He was 28 years of age, an experienced businessman and rugby player, but the night before the test he was a 'nervous wreck', 'shot to pieces'. A bottle of Kahlua and milk, not on the recommended pre-match list, provided him with a sound sleep.

The pre-match talk by Ross Turnbull informed all and sundry that this was an all-important game, the future of Australian rugby being dependent on it. After his talk, he sent the backs away, and spoke only to the forwards. International backs throughout the world now know what the 'pigs' really think about them, as Turnbull, a forward himself, said, as told for posterity in *Well I'll Be Ruggered:* "Look, these Phantom-comic-swappers and Mintie eaters, these blonde-headed flyweights (the backs!), are one thing, and we will need them after the hard work's done. But the real stuff's got to be done right here by you blokes."

It was decided that the 6'7", 17 stone giant All Black Andy Haden, the world's best lineout jumper, had to be 'attended to', as it is delicately put in Public School circles, and in his first test the squat Handy was given this assignation. He pushed, pulled, even belted Haden in the game, and received double measure in return. Handy is the last to claim that his was the vital role, a fellow called Greg Cornelsen playing the game of a lifetime and scoring four tries, but the simple fact is that Australia, in one of the upsets of the decade, rolled the All Blacks by 30 to 16.

He wrote of that "fairytale ending": "To stand arm in arm with those guys on that field that day, singing the national anthem, proved to me the importance of bonding. It can make a good team great. In that side we were able to smoothly integrate people who hadn't been

with us long. Yet this was a time when you couldn't contemplate going into battle against the All Blacks with your best players missing from the team."

This was certainly one of the highlights of Handy's rugby career, but, as is only too well known, one must always beware a wounded All Black. Rugby to them is more than a passion, it is life itself. In 1979 there was to be a single test at the Sydney Cricket Ground, and the betting was one-sided, the sceptics being only too well aware of All Black pride.

Dave Brockhoff was the Australian coach for the single test, an irrepressible type known "more for his style of coaching than for his capability", and he supplied the passion that perhaps the Wallabies needed. He was blood and gutsy, personal, and bumptious, but was probably the catalyst the team needed. He said: "It's up to our tight five. It'll be total war up front, and if our forwards hold them we'll be smelling like roses. But if they overrun us there, the test is theirs."

The Wallabies won 12-6 in a dull but fierce encounter, and Australia had the treasured Bledisloe Cup. New Zealander DJ Cameron wrote: "It will remain one of the vivid memories of sport - 15 jubilant Wallabies... hoisting the ungainly Bledisloe Cup aloft in triumph... and doing a lap of honour of the Sydney Cricket Ground." It was only the second time the Cup had been won by Australia in its 48-year history, and competition for the Cup has subsequently become a matter of national pride. The Wallabies who created history that day were Stan Pilecki, Peter Horton, Chris Handy, Greg Cornelsen, Peter McLean, Tony Shaw, Andy Stewart, Mark Loane (captain), Peter Carson, Tony Melrose, Andrew Slack, Geoff Shaw, Phil Crowe, Brendan Moon and Paul McLean.

Handy accompanied the Wallabies to Argentina that year, the Wallabies being astonished at the fierce scrummaging of the Pumas and the genius of their five-eighth, Hugo Porta. Among their forwards was 'Topo' Rodriguez, who would grace many Australian teams in the years to come, and a man called Carlos Sanz Trapaga, who was the toughest man he ever scrummaged against.

Phil Tressider quoted 'Buddha' in *Australian Sports:* "I scrummed against him and it was one of the few times when I felt my eyes were going to pop right out of my head...I could feel my piles exploding out of my backside due to the strain and weight coming through."

It is a delicate subject, but Handy has had trouble with his arse ever since.

In the second test, the Wallabies also got extra serious in their scrummaging. As he put it in *Well I'll Be Ruggered:* "Looking back, I think the moment we realised we had started to achieve our task was when we packed the scrum and the opposition hooker's mouthguard fell into the middle of the tunnel between us, with two of his teeth embedded in it. It was probably one of the most sensational, satisfying, exhilarating moments I have experienced - and I know Stan (Pilecki) and Bill (Ross) felt the same way."

The All Blacks were back in 1980 under captain David ('Trapper') Loveridge, once again thirsting for revenge and snorting fire. The Aussies had, incredibly, won two in a row over the All Blacks and were now a confident and well-rounded team. When the test teams were announced, the All Blacks had four 'new boys', Brett Codlin, Wayne Smith, 'Hika' Reid and one who would plague the Wallabies in future years, 'Cowboy' Shaw.

A story of Simon Poidevin's about Shaw is related in Trevor McKewen's *Real Men Wear Black:* "We were all having a few beers when suddenly Cowboy thumped the bar with his fist. We got a bit of a shock and said: 'Cowboy, what's wrong mate?' He looked at us and scowled: 'I'm pissed off, that's what's wrong!' 'Why?' we asked. 'Because I'm getting to like you Australian bastards.' The whole lot of us fell about the place laughing. It was classic Cowboy."

There were two of the greats making their initial test runs for Australia, Roger Gould and Mark Ella.

The final score was 13 to 9 for the Wallabies, for their third consecutive win over the All Blacks. The continuing confrontation between 'Buddha' and Andy Haden exploded in the match, Handy emerging with a badly gashed forehead. He had his head bandaged and played on, with blood streaming down his face. He looked like the American rendition of 'spirit of '76. This picture of 'Buddha' is the most lasting one of him in his various rugby encounters. As he put it: "Every Sydney daily the next day, with the win, carried my photograph - and I have been reminded of it often enough by the mothers of children who prevented their kids from playing rugby because they didn't want them to end up in such a rough game."

The All Blacks came back in the second test at Ballymore, emerging as 12 to 9 victors over the Wallabies. 'Hika' Reid sealed the match with a dream try.

In the third and deciding match Australia chose two new props, Declan ('Deckchair') Curran and Tony D'Arcy, and the Wallabies prevailed to the tune of 26-10. The All Blacks later claimed they were nobbled, a severe case of food poisoning debilitating the team. The second test, then, was to be Chris Handy's farewell to the test scene. It was a disappointment, but at least there was some consolation: 'When the team wins you simply dip your lid."

From then on it was the end of any serious rugby. He had not had a northern hemisphere tour with the Wallabies, though he had for Queensland, but he had a great run, and most of his goals were accomplished. One more disappointment lay in his way, and that was when he was invited to play with a World XV in South Africa in 1980. The manager of the QRU, John Ryan, and Norbert Byrne, the then chairman of the QRU, put tremendous pressure on him and the others not to go. Byrne threatened his own resignation, so 'Buddha' ultimately turned down the invitation. He put his feelings in *Well I'll Be Ruggered:* "So we (Loane and he) didn't go. Paddy Batch, Garrick Fay and Greg Cornelsen did, and had the time of their lives, forming great and lasting friendships. Missing that trip was probably the biggest disappointment of my career. It's not that I considered myself all that hot, but I thought that if the South Africans were any better that the Argentineans in the front row then I just had to experience it before I died - if just to be able to say I was or wasn't good enough."

Anyhow, he was getting on in years, and he had a young family to support, so he gradually weaned himself off top rugby, playing in the lower grades for Brothers and coaching them one year.

What really brought him back into the game was television, as the expert commentator, first with the ABC, then with Channel Ten. He was and is a genius with the mike, coming through as an honest man with a lot of rugby 'savvy', which he has. He is arguably Australia's most popular rugby presenter. A typical frontrow forward, he is loquacious and earthy, unpretentious and non-political. He has at times clashed with many of the so-called modern greats of the game, but he has never deviated from his basic principles. He has been reborn, rugby-wise, by his involvement in television.

As he put it himself: "I love television commentary, just as I love my other pursuits, as a publican and a great speaker. Given that my playing days are gone, I can think of no other role in life I would crave. The combination of commentator, publican and guest speaker are natural extensions of each other."

He now gets his 'jollies', as he puts it, from talking about what is going on rather than participating. He has no desire to play in the 'Golden Oldies', or 'Classic Wallabies', for his memory lingers on of the pain after giving his all for his country. In many ways he was the honest toiler, the tryer, the perfect tourist, proud to play for his country until he collapsed. The vision rugby aficionados have of him, with blood streaming down his face, was the real Chris Handy, for he would never take a backward step when playing for his beloved 'green and gold'.

His team mate Dr Peter Horton had this to say of him: "Chris really is a caricature of himself. He is a journalist's/rugby writer's dream...even to this day his immense size, broken hands, jowls and rasping commentary style characterise and perpetuate the myth of the 'prop-forward' - the legendary 'Buddha'. His increasing bulk, his enlistment to the ranks of firstly back row and then to prop make tremendous bar-side stories.

"Despite all of this legendary copy much of the substance of the myth is valid...he IS one of the most courageous, obdurate, awkward (in terms of scrummaging technique that is!), he WAS one of the most totally physically and mentally committed forwards to have played for Australia...and really by the standards of the modern era which our vintage immediately preceded he would be utterly undergunned to compete in the modern game...so what?

"When he played things happened and, as his short career at the international level demonstrates, he was a 'winner'...sometimes the effect of an ingredient in a team is not overt, yet take it away and the combination falters.

"Essentially, Chris played till he broke...he would never give in and always came back, and as a hooker they are the first qualities you want in your props. Chris was also a very skilful footballer, and amazingly agile and deft with the ball in his hands and always a tremendous team man off the track, an organiser of scams, a purloiner of tickets or lifts, parties whatever, a great rugby-networker, a great host and an absolute Australian, Queenslander and Brothers man."

# John Hipwell

*As a rugby player Hippy is I believe the best all-round halfback to have played for Australia in the last thirty years, particularly considering the really somewhat inferior forward packs he had to play behind from the Waratahs to Australia. It was only after the momentous series against the All Blacks in 1974 that Australian packs really started to be paid any real respect. However, John was invariably given poor ball from the scrums and lineouts but with his power and skill gave his backs an impeccable service. One of the classic images of world rugby, and remember John Hipwell is widely viewed as one of the world's greatest halves, is of Hippy making an electric blindside break from the scrum base with his low scuttling style. He possessed the most dynamic of tackles, an excellent rapid and uncomplicated service and a good tactical brain.*

*Hippy is a legend amongst his peers and when one reflects on the length of his service to Australian rugby football both as player and schoolboy coach at TAS and Churchie it's little wonder he has been given so many honours such as his OAM and the life membership of The Waratahs, Armidale City and NSW Country... it's only a pity to think that he could not have enjoyed with the rest of us old codgers some of the more tangible rewards available to today's players, yet perhaps he would not have been such an important figure if he had not had to overcome the deprivation and hardship that being an elite rugby union player meant at that time!*

*John Noel Brian Hipwell is one of the very few people I consider a true friend and I have been honoured to have known him and to have played with him.*

*— Dr Peter Horton, ex Wallaby*

It is generally held that the remarkable Queensland secondrower Graham Cooke played longer for Australia than any other. He played his first international against New Zealand in 1932, his last international against France in 1948. He was still in Wallaby colours when the 1947-48 mob played in Canada and the United States, and then ran on to the field when the triumphant Wallabies returned home and played matches in Queensland and NSW. In all, then, he played for 16 years.

John Hipwell, called 'Hippy' by all and sundry, went on the British Isles tour of 1966-67 and played against England on January 2, 1982. Hippy also had 16 years' service, so they both can claim the greatest longevity of any Wallaby in history. 'Hippy' did not play a test on his first tour, so, if one only considers continuous test representation, maybe Graham Cooke remains the victor.

What halfbacks Australia has produced over the years! So many can be considered legends of the game: Cyril Burke, Des Connor, Sid Malcolm, Ken Catchpole, Nick Farr-Jones and John Hipwell. Ask the players of their time period, and they will name the scrumhalf they played with as the greatest ever in the game. And so it goes with 'Hippy'. Anyone who played with him unreservedly picks him as 'Mr Big'.

Comparisons are difficult at the best of times, and we are always clouded with respect to our memories, ascribing to our personal heroes deeds that they may never have in actuality performed. The mind plays tricks, the runs and passes become longer over the passage of time, the tackles more devastating, the speed more blistering. Among all the super heroes that have worn the green and gold, 'Hippy' might just have been the best, for most of the time.

Like 'Burkie', he played behind losing packs, and despite that was heralded as a giant of the game.

One has to have been in the cauldron oneself to appreciate what it is like receiving the ball behind a scrum base when the scrum is going backwards, or getting the ball from a lineout when your opponents are moving through it like a sieve. The scrumhalf must have courage extraordinaire in these circumstances, and to survive one has to compensate by getting rid of the ball faster.

We all have our pet visions of players we admired. Mine is of watching the ball flashing along an opposing backline and, coming across in cover defence, to quell any breaks, keeping level with the ball, was this sturdy, tough little bloke. When asked who he was, a fellow Wallaby said: "John Hipwell". Whatever else he was, he was the greatest cover-defending halfback the game has ever known. Others might have been as effective in getting there, but no one could punish the ball carrier quite like 'Hippy'. He was tough, and could really bowl them over. It was like having an extra number eight or breakaway.

John was Newcastle born and bred, the second eldest of five boys and a girl. His father was of Irish descent, which he always deprecated until a relative came up to him on the Irish portion of a tour. Father tried his hand at a little boxing and weightlifting in his youth, but did not go on with them because of the demands of a growing family and his work as a carpenter. All the boys in the family played rugby for the Waratahs, though only he and his brother Ed played first grade for the team. Cyril Burke, who is a rare judge of talent, has often

said that given the breaks, and without injuries, Ed could also have gone all the way in the game.

Hipwell's first footballing experiences were with Waratah Primary School, and rugby league was the code played there. His father built a home at Wallsend, however, and the family had to move there. This interrupted his rugby career, so he and his brother started playing baseball. A friend of his father's and ex-Wallaby Cyril Burke, Sonny Payne, induced them to go to the Waratah Club, at Station Street, Waratah. He started in the under-14s, and Cyril Burke was the coach. Cyril was not only a devotee of the game, he stressed the fundamentals. Hipwell and the other youngsters revelled in the environment.

'Hippy' had two years with the under-16s, and then one year with the under-18s, winning the competition. Burke took most of them into first grade, and they won the Newcastle competition. He was captain from then on.

In 1966 'Hippy' was in the NSW Country side to play Sydney, the great Catchpole being in the Sydney side, and then played for NSW Country against the British Isles in Canberra. It was a pretty fair country side, with Phil Hawthorne at five-eighth and Beres Ellwood in the centres. It was a tough introduction to play against another country that day, as he had his two front teeth kicked in by one of the Lions' loose forwards. NSW Country lost the match, in the wet, by 9 to 3.

The same year he went on the five month, 1966-67 tour of the British Isles, France and Canada under captain John Thornett. He was 18 years of age and understudy to Ken Catchpole, but unfortunately was jumped on in a ruck during the tour, and the preliminary assessment was that he had a burst blood vessel. When he was unable to train he had X-rays taken, and it turned out he had a broken fibula. As a consequence he played only 13 matches on tour, and in France, in one game, breakaway Jules Guerassimoff had to play scrumhalf.

The tour was a disappointment, though they were the first Wallabies to beat Wales. They won only one other international, against England, but had their pride restored somewhat when the Barbarians were defeated in a memorable match. This was the tour during which the captain was dropped for all but one international, and hooker Ross Cullen was sent home after an ear-biting incident during the Oxford game. The latter was 'Hippy's' first game for Australia, his counterpart being the present BBC rugby announcer, Nigel Starmer-Smith.

It was on this trip that the author met John Hipwell for the first time. 'Hippy' sidled up and introduced himself, and said quietly: "Cyril said if ever I was to see you I should pass on his regards." That same message was passed on many times over the years, in Canada, South Africa and the United States.

'Hippy' achieved a rarity in playing for Australia before he had played for NSW, as 'Catchy' was the incumbent NSW scrumhalf.

Cyril Burke was the guiding force in 'Hippy's' career, and he followed his advice slavishly except in one instance. Cyril was one of the great teetotallers of all time, and early on he introduced 'Hippy' to his favourite drink, sarsaparilla and lemonade. The Wallabies on tour introduced him to something with a little more kick, and he found out he preferred that concoction to Cyril's sarsaparilla and lemonade.

Cyril emphasised the running game to young 'Hippy'. Every time he kicked the ball in a match he heard Cyril's unmistakable voice from the sidelines: "Cut your leg off!" Cyril was also fanatical about the importance of speed over the first five to ten yards, and made him do continual short sprints in training. This was supplemented by a sage piece of advice: "If you see a break, go for it!"

In 1967 he went to New Zealand for the single game celebrating the 75th Jubilee of the founding of the New Zealand Rugby Union. Some 19 Wallabies were sent, but only 15 played. The ones who did not were Bob Honan, John Hipwell, David Crombie and David Taylor. Ken Catchpole captained Australia that day. At least 'Hippy' got to study 'Catchy' once more. He said of Catchpole: "He was quick, and very much the general. And he had a great playing partner in Phil Hawthorne."

A turning point in 'Hippy's' life occurred when the 1968 New Zealand team, led by Brian Lochore, came to Australia. There were some very experienced players on that All Black squad: Colin Meads (31), Kel Tremain (30), Ken Gray (29), Bruce McLeod (28), Tony Steel (26), Earle Kirton (27), Brian Lochore (27) and 'Jazz' Muller (26).

Des Connor, who had played for the Wallabies and the All Blacks, was now home in Brisbane and was the Australian coach, and ex-All Black Fred Allen presided over the All Blacks.

The result of the first test was clearly in New Zealand's favour, 27 to 11, but the match was overshadowed by two incidents. The first, which provoked the New Zealanders to cry 'foul' and 'contrary to the spirit of the game', was the introduction by coach Des Connor of the short lineout, now acceptable but then a revolutionary concept.

The second, which absolutely shocked the sporting public, was the sight of Colin ('Pine Tree') Meads pulling on and twisting the leg of Ken Catchpole when he was trapped in a ruck. The injuries to Catchpole were so horrific that they ended his representative career.

Replacements were allowed in the game, and there were three. The All Black captain Lochore came off as a result of a broken thumb, to be replaced by Ian Kirkpatrick, John Brass damaged his shoulder and had to leave the field, Barry Honan going on in his stead and Catchpole came off, with Hipwell taking over at halfback for his first test.

The unfortunate injury to Catchpole made Hipwell an automatic choice for the second test. The Australian team, for 'Hippy's' first full test, was: Arthur McGill, Alan Cardy, Barry Honan, Phil Smith (replaced in the game by Alex Pope), John Cole, John Ballesty, John Hipwell; Hugh Rose, David Taylor, Greg Davis, Stuart Gregory, Norm Reilly, Jim Roxburgh (captain) and Roy Prosser.

'Hippy' soon made his presence felt in the match, as in the first ten minutes he went on the blindside, and in his parlance, scored Australia's only 'meat-pie' (try) of the match. The final score was 19 to 18 for the All Blacks, the New Zealanders winning by a stunning penalty try in the final few minutes awarded by referee Kevin Crowe.

Hipwell showed all the qualities in the game that were to make him the best halfback in the world in his era.

There was a short five-match tour to Ireland and Scotland that same year. Australia lost the two tests, to Scotland 3-9 and Ireland 3-10, but were competitive, and 'Hippy' played in both of them. An injury to Arthur McGill particularly affected the team's performance, as he was the only kicker of note on the tour and was unable to play after the third game. Though just 21 years of age, 'Hippy' had now been to the British Isles twice and once to New Zealand.

In 1969 he was with Greg Davis' side on their three month tour to South Africa. Davis was the only survivor from the highly successful Thornett-captained team of 1963. Ex-Wallaby Charlie Eastes was the popular manager, and dual international Des Connor the coach. The Wallabies had many fine players, but injuries to Rod Batterham, Dick Cocks, Phil Smith and Owen Butler weakened them. They lost all of the tests, 11-30, 9-16, 3-11 and 8-19, though they won 15 provincial games. The absence of veterans Peter Crittle and Jules Guerassimoff was sorely felt.

Ian Diehm said this about Hipwell in *Giants in Green and Gold:* "Whatever the shortcomings of the Wallabies, Hipwell was outstanding. He put every ounce of his powerful frame into his surging tackles, while his quick clearances with a mere flick of the wrists tidied up a lot of bad ball and, when he broke, it was as if he was jet-propelled."

Hipwell particularly enjoyed the South African tour. He said: "It's a great country to tour. It was magic, particularly after the UK."

The fact is, the Wallabies of 1969 were completely outgunned. Maxwell Price summed it up in *Wallabies Without Armour: Tour of South Africa 1969:* "While the Springboks had retained their great forward strength the Wallabies came with a largely inexperienced front and second row. They came as middleweights to take on the heavyweights. They lacked the massiveness and the strength.

"With the All Blacks in mind the Springboks were steadily building for the future. The Wallabies were a serious exercise, and, in fact, they served to show up some Springbok weaknesses. They beat the Springboks to the loose ball, exposed some lineout uncertainty, but they failed lamentably in those old and time-honoured essentials, the set scrum and driving play.

"They could not shove and batter through in the manner of the robust Springboks; they had no iron front, they lacked the reinforced steel and concrete of rugby where they needed it most.

"They sorely needed the heavy guns up front to pave the way for the excellent talent behind. They probed, they thrashed, they were driven to desperation in trying to find ways of eluding the Springbok might. But with the slender scrummaging resources they had, it would have required the biblical trumpeter of Jericho to bring down the solid Springbok wall."

It was apparent that the Wallabies were lacking somewhat in discipline, arriving late for buses, training and meetings. The author went to his old Wallaby teammate, manager Charlie Eastes, and expressed his fears that the team was getting out of hand, and that discipline was absolutely essential for a touring party.

Eastes, one of the nicest and kindest individuals ever to stride the globe, listened intently. "That's what you feel, Max?" he queried.

"Charlie," the author went on, "there'll be chaos if it keeps up. You've got to assert your authority. Remember Arnold Tancred managing us in 1947-48? He'd never let us get away with what these blokes are doing."

Charlie walked out of the room, and sent the word out to all and sundry that there would be a team meeting at 3pm. Charlie, who couldn't hurt a fly, as they say, and the team knew it, read the riot act to the team. He said that if anyone was late for anything in the future, or was not in official uniform at functions, he would be sent home on the next plane. Sputtering in his inimitable way, and red in the face with emotion, he said: "The honeymoon is over! Any transgression and you're on the next plane. From now on when I say nine o'clock I mean nine o'clock! There'll be no exceptions! We start tomorrow. Everyone has to be on the bus for 9am. 9am! Got it! 9am!"

He turned on his heels and walked out. The team sat there stunned. Charlie was such a nice bloke, everyone loved him. They couldn't believe the tirade, but they knew old Charlie meant business. The honeymoon was really over.

Next day, unbelievably, everyone was on the bus by 8.45am, 15 minutes early. Everyone, that is, except 'Chucker' Eastes.

Greg Davis was the first to say anything. "Where's bloody Charlie?" he spat out.

The team looked around, and Charlie was nowhere to be seen. Someone said: "It's okay,

Greg, it's not time yet."

The team sat fuming, and waited out the fifteen minutes. At exactly 9 o'clock, they looked up, and there was 'Chucker' walking down the stairway in the hotel, as relaxed as can be.

Davis turned to the driver and said: "Nine o'clock's bloody nine o'clock! Leave the silly bastard. Let's go!"

The driver shut the door, and started to drive off. It was about 9:01am, and Charlie was just coming out of the door. The team gave a few rude hand signals as the bus went by him. One of the funniest sights of all time was the new convert to authoritarianism, Charlie Eastes, running down the street after the bus, pleading for it to stop. The team was virtually on the floor of the bus, engulfed in paroxysms of laughter. Poor Charlie had to catch a taxi to get to the ground. So much for Charlie's discipline.

One of the highlights of the tour was the traditional three-day visit to Kruger National Park, where the team travelled around in four-wheel drives looking at animals in the wild. It was a rare experience. At night the team was bedded down in rondavels, the South African huts in the ground, in enclosures. However, wild game such as impala and wart hogs had come into the enclosure during the day when the gates were open and, at night, after a few drinks, the Wallabies took off after the impalas. They were darting in all directions, and that set off the wart hogs, who were also scattering around, their tails sticking up in the air like pipe-stems. In between them were Australia's finest, tripping, laughing, running. "It was a stupid thing to do," said 'Hippy', "but it was so bloody funny."

In 1970 NSW toured New Zealand and 'Hippy' was with the Blues, and then Scotland came out and were soundly beaten in a single test by 23 to 3, 'Hippy' scoring a fine try.

The Springboks came to Australia in 1971, and they won the three tests handily, 'Hippy' playing the first two tests and Mick Barry the third through an injury. The ugly anti-apartheid demonstrations seemed to unsettle the Australians, who did not play the quality of rugby of which they were capable. The Springboks won all of their thirteen matches in Australia that year.

The next overseas tour was to France and North America in 1971, and though John enjoyed seeing France in some depth, the language problem was considerable. He particularly appreciated the more urbane Peter Crittle looking after him, squiring him around on this trip and educating him about the history of France. In the eighties he was astonished to be at Notre Dame Cathedral and to see Crittle there, showing his daughter the sights, just as he had done many years previously for young 'Hippy'.

It was a rugged tour, as the Australians found themselves going from one tough Regional XV to another. There were two tests, the first of which Australia won 13 to 11, 'Hippy' and Russell Fairfax combining well in a memorable display. Australia lost the second by 18 to 9.

In 1971 'Hippy' was married, but like any devoted rugby player carefully fitted the marriage vows into his rugby schedule. The post-marital revelries were understandably put on hold as he listened to the announcement of the Australian team to tour New Zealand for two months, in which his name was included. He thereafter played for Newcastle against South West on the Saturday, and fronted up for a club game on Sunday, during which he dislocated his shoulder. Waratah medico Dr Kerridge put it back, but informed 'Hippy' that he would be unable to play for six weeks.

He immediately phoned Bob Templeton in Brisbane, and 'Hippy' could hear the sounds of a fair party going on in the background.

He said: "Tempo, I've done my shoulder in!"

"Yeah, yeah," replied Tempo, always on guard for the rugby prankster.

"'Tempo', I've really done my shoulder in," persisted 'Hippy'.

"Yeah, yeah," repeated Tempo.

It took a while, but Bob Templeton got the message, and Gary Grey went to New Zealand in his place.

Maybe it was a good tour to miss, as the Wallabies went down to three heavy test defeats, and were thereafter variously dubbed the 'Woeful Wallabies' and the 'Awful Aussies'.

There was a short eight-match tour of England and Wales in 1973, a "snatch and grab trip" as 'Hippy' described it. He was now completely recovered from his shoulder problem. Only two matches were won by the Aussies, against Metropolitan Counties (17-5) and West Wales (18-3). The Aussies were sent packing in the two tests, losing to Wales 0-24 and England 3-20.

Greg Davis dropped out of the scene in 1974, and the All Blacks came to Australia on tour. It was a high point of 'Hippy's' career, as he led Australia in the three tests. In the first test, played under atrocious conditions, the Australian team under his initial captaincy was: Laurie Monaghan, John Cole, David L'Estrange, Geoff Shaw, Jeff McLean, Paul McLean, John Hipwell; John Lambie, Mark Loane, Ray Price, Roger Davis, Garrick Fay, Stuart MacDougall, Peter Horton and John Meadows. They were all close encounters, New Zealand winning the first test at the SCG by 11 to 6, the second at Ballymore, a 16-all draw, and, the third at the SCG, another All Blacks victory by 16 to 6. It was a great comeback, however, after the debacle of 1972. 'Hippy' scored a try in the second test.

This was the year of the Daryl Haberecht-inspired 'up the jumper' trick, which was successfully used in the dying stages of the New South Wales Country versus Sydney game. NSW Country was behind 16-20 until the ploy was called by Haberecht. After they turned their rears to the opposition, there was a great run by Greg Cornelsen and then Geoff Shaw, for Brian Mansfield to go over for a try. Jim Hindmarsh kicked the goal. This provoked the famous after-match speech by Ron Graham, who stated: "Today we saw that ass beats class."

The 'up the jumper move' and 'the flying wedge', originally devised in American football and introduced to rugby by Haberecht, are now outlawed by the International Rugby Board as being not in the true spirit of the game. 'Hippy' feels that the rolling maul is a retrograde step, which has set rugby back many years. He feels it should similarly be designated as contrary to the spirit of the game.

'Hippy' was back to the British Isles on the 1975-76 tour, managed by Ross Turnbull and coached by Dave Brockhoff. The team won 19 of their 26 tour games, losing six and drawing one. They won only one of the four tests in the British Isles, against Ireland, and

won an unofficial test against the United States on the way home. It was a disappointing tour for the Wallabies, but more so for Hipwell, who damaged cruciate ligaments in his leg against Wales and had to be replaced by Rod Hauser. It was the end of the tour for 'Hippy'.

He made a comeback in 1978, and was impressive in all the games he played, but the ARFU felt he had played insufficient representative games and ruled him out of the 1978 tour of New Zealand, picking, instead, Peter Carson and Rod Hauser.

Because of a lingering injury to fullback Roger Gould, Australia asked for a replacement player, and instead of sending a fullback sent Hipwell, though the two Aussie halfbacks were uninjured. New Zealand sportswriter Bob Howitt called it an "Aussie con trick". Hauser had been good enough to be halfback in two stirring wins over Wales before the tour. 'Hippy' played all three New Zealand tests. New Zealand won the first two 13-12 and 22-6, but Australia romped home at Eden Park to the tune of 30 to 16. The latter was the highest number of points ever scored against New Zealand in a test match.

Although he did not play in the Bledisloe Cup winning matches in 1979 and 1980, 'Hippy' was back in the Australian team for the two tests against France in 1981, both won by the Wallabies. Because of his sterling performances he was selected for the 1981-82 tour, thus becoming the first Wallaby to make three long tours to the British Isles. There were some brilliant players on that team, such as Roger Gould, the three Ellas, Andrew Slack, Paul McLean, Mark Loane, Tony Shaw, Michael O'Connor, Greg Cornelsen, Simon Poidevin, Chris Roche, Chris Carbery, Tony D'Arcy and so on, and considering the talent, the results had to be viewed as disappointing. They won one test against Ireland, the first, and lost the other three, as the 1975-76 tourists had done.

For 'Hippy' it was a sad tour, as he had to leave the field with a rib injury and a torn hamstring against Wales. To his credit, he made it back for the international against England. This was to be his 35th, and last test, nine of them as his country's captain. He kept playing until 1986, when he eventually decided it was time to call it a day.

His was a career of great honour and

devotion. The players who toiled with him in the sweat-box swear by him, as well they should. He always played an honest, courageous game, but he also had remarkable strength, as would readily be attested to by players he grounded in cover defence. When he arrived for his first tour in South Africa and the airport was lined by eager fans catching their first glance at the Wallabies, one was heard to say: "Why, he's only a little one." Though only 5 foot 7 inches, he was a solid, compact 11 stone 7 pounds in his prime. And he had the heart of a lion.

His close friend Dr Peter Horton has this to say of him: "He is an icon, he is I believe the epitome of a real Australian and certainly embodies the essence of what we in the Country team like to call 'being Country', just as Queenslanders have that parochialism that imbues their sport/culture, etc. John is one of the few examples that confounds the post-modernists who criticise sport's potential as a vehicle for social advancement. He was an apprentice fitter and turner at BHP when I first knew him and by sheer talent and hard work, driven by his indomitable spirit and perseverance, he is now a Bachelor of Education, a leading teacher of Industrial Technology and Design, a dedicated boarding house master and sports coach, at the prestigious Anglican Church Grammar School in Brisbane…and of course has been honoured with the Order of Australia Medal (OAM) for his service to the game. Some cynics may suggest that he would have made more as a fitter and turner! However, the lives of many people, students at TAS and 'Churchie', would have been the poorer for it!"

# Tom Lawton Jr.

The Lawton family is one of the great families of Australian rugby, nowhere near the unbelievable McLean dynasty, but not one to be sneezed at. The McLeans were pretty straightforward with respect to their lives, whereas with the Lawtons there was a sense of drama about them. To write about the McLeans is to write an historical family biography, whereas the Lawton story reads more like a gripping novel.

Grandfather Tom Lawton was a unique character, a legend in his own time, a phenomenon. He is undoubtedly the greatest sportsman ever to attend Brisbane Grammar School. He entered BGS, Brisbane's senior and most elite private school, in 1913. He represented them in cricket for four years, captaining the school in 1916 and 1917, was adjudged best fieldsman in 1915 and 1916, and had the best batting average in 1917. His best scores included 176 not out against Armidale School and 137 against Toowong.

He rowed number two in the school crew for three years, and was a fine tennis player. Tom won the all-schools' open high jump with a leap of 5 foot 6 inches and was second in the 120 yards hurdles. He also gained his swimming colours in 1916 and 1917, won the breast-stroke and back-stroke race in 1917, and was school champion and school captain in that sport the same year.

However, it was at rugby union where he really made his mark, playing in the first team for three years and winning the award for best back in 1916 and 1917. The school magazine said of him, in his last year at school when he was playing mainly in the centre: "His rapidity in taking advantage of any opening offside, his ingenuity in originating passing rushes, his clever 'raking in' of wild passes, and his sure foot, combine to warrant him the position of in-centre of any team. Without in any way detracting from the merits of the other backs, he was undoubtedly superior to them all, and innumerable times he saved a dangerous situation so that in fact the others began to rely so much on his ability that far more than his portion of work was always thrust upon his willing shoulders. A splendid kick with both feet, he could find the line to a nicety."

His reputation was such that Tom was selected for interstate rugby in his last year at school, 1917, and was ultimately to play interstate matches in 1919, 1929, 1930 and 1932.

During the first World War he was a gunner in France with the 12th Field Artillery Brigade. On his return to Queensland he entered the University of Queensland where he played rugby league as it was the only available code in the state. In his first year there University won the competition. However, he did play for Queensland and Australia against the 1919 AIF team after its return to Australia at the end of World War I. He then went to Sydney to pursue a medical course at St. Andrew's College, Sydney, where he was until 1922. He played for Western Suburbs and Sydney University. In 1922 he began his studies at Oxford University as a Rhodes Scholar, residing at New College.

He, of all people, represented the scholar-athlete, and with his war-time service included, he was the perfect choice for the Rhodes honour. While at Oxford he won three Blues, a merit which is granted a player who plays in the Oxford versus Cambridge Game.

In 1921-22 he played 60 games, for Oxford, Blackheath, New College and the Barbarians. The year 1923 was a highly emotional one, as after a challenge he and two other Australians were suspended because they had played rugby league. The underlying reason was that a 'colonial', Lawton, had been elected as captain at Oxford. There was much drama involved, but finally the three Aussies played in the 1923 fixture. Tom also won an Athletics Blue in the shot put and represented the University at swimming and water polo.

He returned to Sydney and in 1925 played for NSW, captaining them to New Zealand. The NSW team had only two losses in 11 games, one of them against the All Backs.

Then he made the famous Waratahs team of 1927-28 to the British Isles, France and Canada. In the internationals - in recent years they have been accorded test status - the Waratahs beat Ireland, Wales and France, and lost to Scotland and England. It was a glorious tour, the Johnny Wallace-led team playing exciting, running football. The 'Waratah' style of play is still a major force in Australian rugby. The legacy carved out by Johnny Wallace, Tom Lawton, Cyril Towers, Syd Malcolm, Alex Ross and others has been significant. On the tour, Tom Lawton easily top-scored with 124 points.

*The Daily Express* had this to say of him: "In Lawton...we saw the player whom we remembered, right from the start of the tour at Devonport. If any change had come about, it was that Lawton played ever more unselfishly than had been his habit in Oxford and Blackheath days. Lawton is a deceptive stand-off half. With his long legs and his long stride, he seems slow to the casual spectator. And at times he does not appear to be doing much in what we may term a formal attack - the ball heeled out and passed to Lawton, who runs on a few yards and gives it to some one else.

"This is all. But watch Lawton closely, and you will see, as likely as not, that in those few yards he draws an unwary opponent, and so times his pass that the attack is likely to prosper. He scores few tries himself: but helps his comrades to many. He is always in the right place. His defence is excellent, his kicking well judged, and as a 'converter' he runs up the goal score within a pitiless accuracy equalled only, in another place, by that of a taximeter."

He scored only one try on tour, but the backs outside of him scored 40. As Johnny Wallace was to say: "Tommy smoothed the way for us."

As for his style, it was certainly deceptive. Tall and elegant, everything seemed to come easily to him. All Black captain Cliff Porter called him "the loping ghost".

He came back to Queensland when rugby resumed there in 1929, and captained Australia to an historic three-test victory over the All Blacks. These were pre-Bledisloe Cup days. The following year he led Australia to an exciting 6-5 victory over the British Lions.

In 1932 he again captained Australia in the first two tests against New Zealand. Australia won the first at the SCG 22 to 17, but lost the next in Brisbane 3-21. Inexplicably, he was dropped for the third test, thus ending a distinguished career of 13 tests.

Tom fathered a son, who in turn was to have two sons, Robert ('Rob') and Tom. Neither could be described as loping ghosts, unmistakably growing up with the physiques of frontrowers.

The youngest of the sons was Rob, and he was to play four tests for Australia as a prop. He is at present on a New Zealand Rugby Union contract and is playing for Otago.

Tom was born in Darwin in 1962. His father was a mining engineer, and the family moved between the Northern Territory and Malaysia from 1962 to 1968. They next moved to the Gold Coast for three years in 1969, and then to Brisbane.

Tom's first rugby experience was at the State School at Mount Gravatt, playing a season there of rugby league there. One teacher identified his latent ability, and told him to go to Souths Rugby Union, which he did, playing for the under 11s, and all the way in subsequent years to the under 16s. He came under the influence of long-serving coach Roy Elmer, and got a perfect grounding in the fundamentals from him.

He received a scholarship and departed to TSS, and played for the firsts in grades 11 and 12, and in a repeat Grade 12 year. Ex-Wallaby 'Jake' Howard had come up from St. Joseph's in Sydney, and really honed young Tom in with the do's and don'ts of scrummaging. 'Jake' is an assistant coach with the present Wallabies, the father of Wallaby Pat, and is considered to be one of the great thinkers in the modern game in Australia. Throughout his representative career, Tom would continually ring 'Jake' to exchange views.

Ex-Brisbane Grammar master Alex Evans was another who was to have a profound influence on him. When Tom was picked to go to the Schoolboy trials in 1980, Alex showed the youngster how to pack, saying: "Look, this bastard does it this way, Jake Howard does it another way, but every other bastard is going to do it my way."

Another to assist his early career was ex-Wallaby Bill Ross. Tom said: "It was a real eye-opener to see Bill's skill. It was the old dog teaching the young puppy a few tricks of the trade."

The presence of Queensland hooker Mark McBain was another factor that kept Tom on his toes. Mark Ella and Terry Smith said of him, in *Path to Victory*: "Mark McBain is one of those players whose commitment is such that admiring spectators begin wondering if they ought not to take off their coats and offer to help. Apart from his hooking skills, the gutsy Queenslander is virtually a third breakaway as he hunts for the loose ball. At times he's a human hurricane." It was McBain who kept Tom out of the Queensland team for some time. In fact Tom had played three tests before he represented his state.

Tom played for Queensland in the under 12s, 14s, and 16s, and in 1980 made both the Queensland Schoolboys and the Australian Schoolboys teams. In 1982 he played for Souths in the firsts, and for Queensland and Australia at the under 21 level, touring New Zealand with the 21s.

Luck enters the career of some players, and for Tom that luck came early in his career, as hookers Chris Carberry, Bill Ross and Lance Walker retired, and Bruce Malouf was married.

So he was selected, with McBain, to tour Italy and France with the Wallabies in 1983.

During the first test against France, which resulted in a 15-all draw, McBain incurred a life-threatening injury and Lawton came on in the 75th minute to replace him, and thereafter played the second test in Paris. In 1984 he toured Fiji, and played his third test, his two props being Enrique Rodriguez and Andy McIntyre. This trio changed the nature of Australian front row play. New coach Alan Jones quickly realised the necessity of such a platform if Australia was to reach new heights in the game.

New Zealand came to Australia for three tests, and it was this front row that fronted up against the experienced All Blacks, Gary Knight, Andy Dalton and John Ashworth.

By this time Tom had acquired his nickname of 'Turtle', given to him by fellow Souths player Andrew Slack, who said if Tom ever fell on his back, like a turtle, he wouldn't be able to get up. Slacky, however, got his come-uppance, as he was designated as 'Sugar Ray', after famous boxer 'Sugar Ray' Robinson, because he "couldn't fight his way out a paper bag".

The 1984 Wallabies in the British Isles were not over-impressive in their early games, drawing with South and South-West, and losing to Cardiff, but when the internationals came around they played with great intensity and control. England and then Ireland fell in turn.

Wales held a special significance for 'Turtle', for his grandfather had told him: "One of the best things to do is play Wales at Cardiff Arms Park. The only thing better is to beat the bastards." Though his grandfather died in 1977 and was not at the game, his mother was, which added to the emotion of the contest.

Before the test, a reporter asked him: "What do you want to achieve?"

He replied: "'I'd really like to score a try. If not, I'd like to score a pushover try.' And I ended up getting both. It was my biggest thrill, my greatest memory. We could have beaten anyone that day!"

The pushover try against Wales is one of the great moments of Australian rugby. The proud Welsh crowd sat stunned in disbelief at the turn of events. It had never happened to a Welsh pack in the history of their game.

After the try, Lawton ran towards the stands,

and looking at the Wallaby reserve bench, clenched his fist and punched the air. "You know," he reflected, "we were a team, we were close and respected each other, and I felt compelled to do it. Not being selected is tough on one's ego, it all comes down to one man's decision, and any of those players would have done the job. It was instinctive, it was for them what we had done.

"Australian teams train ruthlessly, because everyone is trying to make the test team," he went on. "Many spectators watching us train can't believe it. Prior to the test Stan Pilecki broke my nose with his elbow, not deliberately - he was in there proving he was good enough for the test. But once the team is selected Aussie teams all come together in a support mode. People like Chris Roche were terrific, despite their deep disappointment. They inspired the team."

The Wallabies had now come three parts of the way towards the 'Grand Slam'. Only Scotland remained, and it was tough coming back to earth after the Wales demolition job, but realising the enormity of their responsibility the team finally focused on the game. This is where Alan Jones' ability to mould the team really came to the fore.

After the pre-match talk in the dressing room, coach Alan Jones left the room early. Lawton said: "Jonesy left the room. I heard afterwards that he immediately rang London and told someone to put pounds on us to win, that he knew we would do it."

The match was extremely tough, particularly in the front row. For Tom it was a rare thrill to play against the great Scottish player Colin Deans. He said: "It was a real honour, as I watched him as a kid, little thinking that one day I would be playing against him. We had real trouble in the game with their tighthead prop, Iain Milne, a big, strong, tough man. At one stage Nick Farr-Jones couldn't put the ball in the scrum. I was stuck in there, hardly breathing, the pressure was so great, and I couldn't lift my foot off the ground. I was signalling 'Topo' to collapse the scrum, but he couldn't either.

Nick got the ball in, but it just stayed in the middle of the scrum. No-one could lift a foot, them or us. It was a very tough game."

So it was, but Australia won, to be forever part of the nation's rugby history by being the first Wallaby team to snare the Grand Slam. Everyone on that tour is now designated as a 'Grand Slam Wallaby'.

Mark Ella wrote of Tom in *Path to Victory*: "At one stage we weighed in and 'Turtle' was the heaviest man in the team at 111 kilos. Unbelievable. Having a huge hooker made our pack so big it wasn't funny. Lawton has all the skills, too. He can catch and pass and get round the field in a way that is amazing for such a big man. His ability to throw the ball right on to the man in the lineout was another big part of our play.

"Tom grew up very quickly on the tour. Of course, he got a lot of help from 'Topo' and Steve Williams. But once the pack went down, there was never any doubt that 'Turtle' was master of the scrum. Although he was the youngest, he wasn't shy about ripping into that part of the tour. 'Turtle' is an hilarious guy, one of the funniest on the tour, playing his guitar, singing songs, telling some of the best jokes ever."

What he was also good at, as mentioned, was his pin-point lineout throwing. He worked constantly on this part of his game. No one was better than him in this department.

After the Grand Slam, matches against Canada and Fiji in 1985 were low-key, though Tom was surprised at the ability of the Canadians, particularly in their set plays. The late Kerry Fitzgerald was the referee in the second test, and penalised the Canadians near their line. Australian teams are taught to accept decisions without comment, and Tom has never forgotten the Canadian response, with their North American accents: "Jeez, ref, shiiitt, ref."

There was a one-off test against New Zealand that year, which New Zealand won 10 to 9 through a simple surprise move in the final minutes. It was a rehearsed tap penalty move 60m out from the tryline, which winger Craig Green scored from. Many of the Grand Slam players had retired or were unavailable for that game, such as Andrew Slack, Mark Ella, Michael Hawker, Brendan Moon, and Chris Roche, who had gone to rugby league.

In 1986 there was a single test against France at the SCG which Australia won by 27 to 14, and then the Wallabies went to New Zealand for a three-test series. Australia won the first test at Athletic Park, Wellington, 13-12, lost the second 12-13 at Carisbrook, Dunedin, and raced home winners by 22 to 9 at Eden Park, Auckland.

The first test was played without the rebel Cavaliers, who had gone to South Africa, but after the All Black loss they were quickly recalled. The Bledisloe Cup was to be Australia's that year.

Greg Campbell wrote, in the *Sydney Telegraph*: "The victory surpasses the historic Grand Slam achieved by the Wallabies in 1984 and now elevates Australia to the pinnacle of world rugby, with only the isolation of the South African Springboks casting a slight shadow over the claim.

"Unlike the 1949 Wallabies, when the bulk of New Zealand's leading players were touring South Africa, yesterday's victory was against the best the Kiwis could muster."

Coach Alan Jones put it into his own personal perspective when he proclaimed: "This is bigger than Quo Vadis. This is bigger than anything."

Long-time Wallaby breakaway Simon Poidevin said, simply: "Now I can live in peace."

The tour to Argentina followed in 1987, and it was about this time that the wheels started to fall off for Alan Jones, despite his excellent record. Perhaps he had reached his 'use-by' date, perhaps it was time for a change, perhaps many of the players had lost their motivation or were simply not good enough any longer.

Whatever the reasons, the Wallabies did not perform up to expectations in the 1987 World Cup. In Lawton's words: "Jones is a great coach and motivator. But I believe we overtrained for the World Cup. We trained in Sydney, it was hot as hell, and we went at it 3-4 hours daily. It was not the same build-up as in the British Isles. We played some good games in the World Cup, but against France in the semi-final we were exhausted, zapped, ambushed."

New Zealand flogged France to win the World Cup, while the Wallabies lost ignominiously to Wales in Rotorua for third place. It was a sad ending to their World Cup campaign. A month after the World Cup the Wallabies had their chance to rectify matters at Concord Oval against the 'world champions', but were soundly beaten by 16-30. Lawton said:

"In my opinion that all Black side was the best New Zealand team I played against."

Alan Jones was deposed as Australian coach in February 1988, and Bob Dwyer took over. The All Blacks made a sojourn to Australia, Tom playing the three tests, two of which were won decisively by New Zealand. The other, at Ballymore, was drawn. It was a tough 'hello' for the new coach.

Then followed a short tour of England, Scotland and Italy. The Wallabies lost to England 19-28, before defeating Scotland (32-13) and Italy (55-6), Tom playing in all the internationals. A big personal thrill was playing with his brother in the Murrayfield test. They were to play three tests together in their careers.

The British Lions came to Australia in 1989, but the games were very disappointing, Australia winning only the first of three tests. Tom was still the number one hooker. The games were the catalyst for Dwyer to make sweeping changes to the Wallaby team. Tom, who had played 41 tests for Australia and was considered among the finest in his position in the world, was devastated when dropped in favour of Phil Kearns, who at that time was playing second grade for Randwick. Tony Daly was also brought in, and he had not played a senior representative game in his life. As it turned out, the players were to go on to outstanding careers playing for Australia, but it was an enormous shock to Lawton.

Tom never felt close to Bob Dwyer from the start, and he never did get an explanation concerning his action. He did receive a call from Dwyer, just as he was going into a meeting. Dwyer said: "I'm terribly sorry, but that's it!"

Tom thought to himself: "What can you say, what can you do?" He hung up.

It was no easy matter for him to reconcile himself over what had happened. As he said: "I'm not the first or the last to be dropped, but it's a shit-house feeling all the same. You can't change what's happened, but it's tough to be objective. It took time to recover, for you know in your heart it's just one bloke's opinion."

Positive responses from others, people who knew what his contribution to the game had been, aided his recovery. He was selected for a World XV to play in South Africa shortly after he was dropped, and that aided the restoration of his self-image.

He went to a bar to watch the Wallabies play New Zealand, and a fellow, also watching, turned towards him with shock on his face. Then the fellow looked at the TV and shook his head, as if to say to Tom: "Why aren't you there?" Somehow he felt better. But, as he said: "It's very difficult to leave when it is not on your own terms."

Ex-Wallaby Dick Cocks came to Australia on a holiday about this time, and he suggested that Tom go to Durban and play. He did that in 1990 and 1991, and one of the great thrills in his life was playing for Natal and unexpectedly winning the Currie Cup. He said: "It was quite a cultural shock. Maybe I should have been born there, as they love their rugby. Actually, they love their rugby, cricket and beer."

Tom did play for Queensland after his South African venture. John Connolly was the coach, and Tom got a little more than normal satisfaction when Queensland defeated NSW.

He retired in 1992, after Souths had won the Grand Final. He had played 41 tests for Australia and 41 games for Queensland. He coached Norths in the Brisbane competition in 1993, and in 1994 Souths. Now he is Coaching Director of the Queensland Rugby Union.

He has successfully made the transition from the playing ranks, but thoroughly enjoys fulltime coaching, having that urge of the true competitor to see how far he can progress.

Rugby has been one of the greatest things in his life. As he put it: "I have a million bucks worth of memories. I can go anywhere in the world and I will have friends there. The Wallaby network is amazing."

Money has never been his principal motivation in life. When in 1983 he was selected to go to Fiji, he was working in a hardware store. The manager read of his selection and pulled him aside, saying, "Mate, you've got to make a decision between your sport and your job. If you go to Fiji I'll have to sack you."

Tom quite enjoyed his job, and had little money, but had no hesitation in saying: "Then sack me now!"

The papers got hold of the story, and eventually he was offered his job back. Just at that time he got a call from Sydney, from the head of TNT, Ross Cribb, who offered him a job in Brisbane, which he took.

As he summed it up: "Hell, I was making about $10,000 a year more than anyone else my age. I went from the shit-house to the pent-house."

They even paid him when he went away. Support from the TNT company was vital to his having the chance to play international rugby.

Tom Lawton was arguably the greatest Australian hooker since the 'prince of hookers', Eddie Bonis, a Queenslander playing in the pre-Second World War period. His size and strength in the front row changed the nature of hooking in the modern game. He not only was effective in the tight, he was faster than he appeared and effective in the loose.

The ardent spectator will never forget France scoring the final try in the corner in the 1987 World Cup semi-final. The one who made a glorious run in cover defence in a desperate bid to tackle Serge Blanco was none other than the hooker, Tom Lawton. The backrow was nowhere to be seen. It was typical of the effort he put into the game. His grandfather would have been proud of him, but more so if he had seen him at Wales in 1984 kissing the hallowed turf after the Welsh had been beaten.

# Mark Loane

**M**ark Loane is arguably the greatest player ever to wear a Maroon jersey. The super-charged number eight was once described as being like a train without a station; his driving leadership inspired Queensland to so many of their victories. Blessed with amazing speed for a man his size, Loane's thundering bursts from the scrum base and bone shattering tackling have become legendary. He is the closest thing to a folk hero Queensland has ever produced... Loane was both the saviour of Queensland rugby and the avenger of past defeat.
- **Bret Harris. The Marauding Maroons.**

Mark Loane was born in Ipswich on July 11 1954, his father a magistrate who moved throughout Queensland in the course of his duties. In those days it was a common procedure for public servants - school teachers and clerks, railway workers as well as magistrates - to accept appointments in various country towns mainly for purposes of promotion. 'Country service' it was called by the school teachers, and they were required to do two years if they had received their education on a government scholarship.

Mark's was a rugby league family, and father played lock, as Mark was to do. If it had not been for the war his father might have played for Australia. He was one of the many thousands deprived of the opportunity to go on in the game because of the hostilities. After coming back from service he was sandwiched in a concussive tackle and in the aftermath Mark's mother put her foot down and that was the end of Dad's frolicking on the rugby field. His mother represented Queensland in athletics at 16 years of age and her father was a well-known sprinter.

Six months after Mark's birth the family was off to Sarina, a small country town near Mackay, one of the resident constables there at the time being the future Labor guru and Governor-General, Bill Hayden. The family covered some territory over the years - Ipswich, Sarina, Cooktown, Ingham, Gympie, Kingaroy, Roma and Mackay. They did not settle down until they arrived at Rockhampton.

Mark had two elder brothers, Michael and Paul, both highly talented in sport. Michael was an outstanding athlete, being the state champion, and Paul, though lacking somewhat in motivation as regards sport, was the Wide Bay sprint champion. They were both Wide Bay rugby league stars.

There was little rugby union outside of Brisbane in those days, rugby league being the game of the people. What experiences Mark did have were in league, though they were quite limited. He did not show particular promise when he did play, and in fact played mainly hockey. If he had stuck with it, it would have been an awesome sight, the mighty Loane on the dribble, with a hockey stick as an extra weapon.

Michael and Mark attended Gympie

Christian Brothers school in grades 6, 7 and 8, and then the family moved on to Kingaroy. Mark came back to do a year's boarding school there, but his brother Michael was on the verge of being thrown out of the school for taking a girl out of the school dance. He was seen kissing her. "That was enough in those days, particularly in the Queensland countryside," said Mark, "for the Christian Brothers to seek expulsion."

Dad hurriedly arrived on the scene and transported both boys to Roma and the next school term to Nudgee Christian Brothers in Brisbane, one of the great nurseries in Australia for rugby union talent. Michael spent one year there, and Mark three. It has been said there are two religions at Nudgee, one Catholicism, celebrated on a Sunday, and the other Rugby, worshipped on a Saturday.

Michael captained the athletics team, ran 10.8 in the 100, won the 200 and the 400, the latter in a time that stood for approximately 15 years, was third in the long jump, won the school tennis championship and broke the record for the greatest number of tries scored in a season in GPS. Despite having unlimited potential, he had no desire to continue in sport after high school and, athletically speaking, dropped away from the scene.

Even to this day Michael and Mark are confused. One time Mark was assisting Dr Tony Blue, Queensland's athletics Olympian, in surgery, and he said: "Mark, that 400m run of yours was the greatest schoolboy athletic feat I have ever seen!" Mark immediately said it was not him, though Tony appeared unconvinced, thinking that Mark was just being unduly modest.

Rugby league was held to be the man's game in country circles, and rugby union a game for the weak. After a few months at Nudgee, however, Mark became a complete convert, at 14 years of age, though he had never played rugby union before. There are flats at Nudgee, where there are numerous rugby fields, and Mark presented himself for the school trials, and made the Under 15 Bs at first, but after one trial against Churchie he was in the Under 15 As.

Mark had an enjoyable time that initial year, his choice of position being lock. When asked why he gravitated to that particular position, he said: "I was naturally attracted to it. I don't really know why. I liked the very name 'lock'. It sounded different. While at Sarina in the 4st 7lb rugby league team a fellow said he thought I should play lock, and I asked him why. He said it was because you lock the scrum. I knew about front rowers and second rowers, and I liked the idea and the sound of being the lock. There was an attraction about it, and I would often reflect on it, even the sound - lock."

It was a big thing to be playing at Nudgee, more so because Mark played in boots for the first time, and he actually had to order some. "Playing in boots for the first team was a big deal," said Mark.

There was this fanaticism about the game at Nudgee that similarly enthralled the young Mark, and even in the off season the boys would gather on the flats at the school and play the game of 'tackle' for hours on end. They would line up against one another and just tackle and tackle. It was done for fun, at every available opportunity. Mark loved it.

About Grade 10 he started to sprout. In Grade 11 he was captain of the 16 As, and in Grade 12 was in the first XV. Paul McLean was also in the first XV that season, repeating his final year, and was a sensation. Nudgee won the competition undefeated, beating State High in the final, scoring a try under the posts for victory after the final bell had gone, to the consternation of the opposition.

After leaving Nudgee there was a dilemma as to who he should play for, Brothers or University. Despite the natural drift of the Catholic fraternity to Brothers, including Paul McLean, Mark decided on University. He was influenced by two other outstanding Nudgee players who also elected to play for University the previous year, Steve Cerutti and John Henderson. "I thought it was a wider world offering at the University," Mark said.

Mark came under the tutelage of Dr 'Chilla' Wilson, former Wallaby captain and manager extraordinaire. 'Chilla' was the Under 19 coach. "The team were mystics, like the coach," quipped Mark, "the maximum making an appearance at training any one night being ten or eleven." Sometimes people had to be rounded up from the sidelines to make up the fifteen. They lost in the Grand Final to Brothers that year.

Mark made the Queensland Under 19 team

in his first season, alongside very talented players such as Tony Shaw, Paul McLean and Greg Shambrook. It was after one of the Under 19 representative games that he saw the Queensland senior team being demolished by NSW by about forty points, Russell Fairfax being the principal architect of the devastation. Mark thought, at the time: "Surely anyone can do better than that. They looked so pathetic. It used to be, in those days, that the efforts of the Queensland team lasted about the same time as the psych-up talk. If you missed the first five minutes you missed the game."

There was, however, something in the air then in Queensland, and the administrators of rugby in the northern state were working hard to develop junior rugby. "You either breed them or buy them," laughed Mark, "and we were breeding them at that juncture."

Before the final match of the Under 19s, Mark explained to Paul Mooney that he would be unavailable, as his brother was driving home to Mackay. The coach informed him that he could not go, and Mark protested that it was his only way of getting home. The coach then said that they would fly Mark to Mackay. This quite nonplussed Mark, who found it hard to believe that they would want him enough to pay his way, or that anybody thought that the game they were going to play was that important. He stayed and they beat the NSW Under 19s in the game.

The following year, still 18, Mark could have played Under 19s again, but senior University coach and former great Wallaby breakaway Jules Guerassimoff felt that Mark was ready for the big time. After three games, Mark was flabbergasted when informed he was selected in a Possibles v Probables game for possible Queensland senior team selection and, following a fine performance, made the state team. As Mark saw it, he was having a "magical spell".

Queensland then played against Sydney, a game which featured the 'human tank' Paddy Batch scoring four tries. Then followed a close match with NSW, which the Maroons won. Mark was so impressive in these encounters that he was picked to play for Australia against Tonga. He was still 18 years of age, the youngest to represent Australia since the legendary Bill Cerutti in 1921.

Australia won the first test in Sydney, and Mark was an automatic selection for the second match at Ballymore. In a lack-lustre performance, the Wallabies lost, and some of the blame was apportioned to the youngster.

He had been told by coach Bob Templeton that, as eighth man, he should remain binding the scrum and pushing. Two tries were scored on the blind, and Mark was adjudged culprit.

As he now says, after years of reflection on the humiliation: "It was the last time in my life I would listen to anyone else as to how to play my position. Both tries were my responsibility. I had been selected because of my tackling ability, and stupidly I had listened to this push, push, push credo when I should have been breaking when the ball was lost." It was 'Tempo's' nascent belief that Australia should start to consider the scrum, and as Mark states he was absolutely correct in his interpretation.

The defeat against lowly-ranked Tonga was a low point of Australian rugby, and neither Templeton nor Loane was picked for the 1973 short tour of England and Wales. A scathing report in the *Sydney Morning Herald* served as his temporary obituary, declaring Mark should hang on to his Australian rugby jersey as it would be the last he would ever get.

The person selected in his stead was Ken McCurrach, a former Scottish schoolboy international, who did not have a successful tour and faded away from the rugby scene. The Wallabies lost to both England and Wales. Even to this day Mark may be walking down the street, and one of his close mates, like Chris Handy, will jokingly call out after him: "Remember Ken McCurrach!" "They never forget," said Mark laughing, "they never forget!"

At University, he had not quite found himself. "The trick is, you had to succeed at University and yet give the appearance that you weren't really trying. There was nothing worse in those days than appearing to be conscientious. There was nothing worse than being called a 'conch'. What you learned at school, however, carried you through your first year, like a bow wave."

In his second year Mark, now considered by many of his friends to be the world's No 1 super-achiever, almost gave up going to lectures. Towards the end he realised his dilemma, and that all might be lost. There were three big subjects, Anatomy, Physiology and Biochemistry, and Mark decided to forget Anatomy and concentrate on the other two subjects, figuring if he passed them he would get a 'supp' in the third.

His calculations were correct, but it was the only time he ever failed a subject in his life. Mark is simply not the failing kind. He had recurring dreams at the time of the slack kids at school, dreaming away in a non-caring manner during examinations while good students like Mark were reeling off pages of answers. He learned his lesson.

Mark came back to the Australian side in 1974, balancing his rugby and his studies in a manner rarely equalled in the modern era. The All Blacks were on a three-test tour, and it was a 'new-look' team for them, with an incredible 15 debutants. The incumbent skipper Ian Kirkpatrick was deposed in favour of Andy Leslie, and perennials like 'Grizz' Wyllie, Alan Sutherland, Sam Strahan and Super Sid Going were among those axed. It was Paul McLean's first test, along with Ray Price, John Lambie, Roger Davis, Peter Horton and 'Twinkletoes' Meadows.

The conditions were horrendous for the match, the SCG being under water. During the game Mark came across in cover defence and had Duncan Robertson all lined up for a tackle, but Robertson brought his elbow up to fend Mark away and he suffered a cracked cheek-bone. The Wallabies lost a close match 6 to 11. Mark consequently could not be considered for the next two tests, his position being taken by John Lambie.

In 1975 it was Australia versus England, and Mark was in the two tests, won gloriously by Australia. Japan then was on deck for two tests, and Mark played only the first one, as he was inadvertently kneed in the kidney in the first. It required an operation ten years later, but Mark soldiered on despite a massive haematoma which had him 'peeing blood'. The injury was eventually to develop into a fibrosis.

The British Isles tour occurred in 1975-76, fulfilling one of any rugby player's dreams. Mark played only two internationals as in the fifth game, against Leicester, on a very cold night, he tore a hamstring and broke his hand. The tests he played in were against England and

Ireland. In the last game of the tour he was injured again, damaging his shoulder. "I was injured many times playing for Australia," reflected Mark, "and yet never for my club or Queensland."

The next three internationals were against Fiji in 1976, and then there was an inglorious short tour to France. "We were slaughtered," said Mark of the second test there. In retrospect the Aussies, Mark felt, were not strong enough, short of scrummaging power and lineout ability. A narrow win over Italy on the way home added further humiliation to the tourists.

Coach Bob Templeton was at the end of his tether before the Italy test, proclaiming to his team: "If you lose this match it is highly likely that I will never again coach Australia. But if you lose and I am coaching, I will personally see to it that none of you plays for Australia again." These were tough words from rugby's popular and genial 'Friar Tuck'.

1977 was Mark's final year of medicine, and there were no internationals that year, which was a welcome relief. Queensland, in the preceding years, had become a world rugby power, proving clearly it was no longer the whipping boy of the southern state. Under Loane's captaincy in 1976, for example, the Maroons defeated New England, Sydney, NSW (42 to 4), Fiji and Canterbury. On a state tour of New Zealand they edged Waikato, Bay of Plenty, Southern Sub-Unions and Northern Sub-Unions, losing only to Counties (13 to 9) and North Auckland (15 to 12). Many Wallaby teams have had worse records. They rounded off the 1976 season with a resounding 60 to 3 victory over Combined Services.

The pattern was repeated in 1977, with victories over New Zealand Barbarians and New England, before another state tour of New Zealand. Otago took the Maroons' scalp to lead off their excursion, but they bounced back to beat Mid-Canterbury and Canterbury. Their return to the mainland heralded victories over NSW Country, NSW twice, Australian Combined Services and the Rest of Australia. The only losses Queensland suffered that year were against Otago (7-19), Sydney (9-10) and ACT (25-27).

There were some household names in those glorious times among the Maroons, captained in the main by Loane: Graham Noon, Andrew

Slack, Greg Cornelsen, David Hillhouse, Peter McLean, Stan Pilecki, Bill Ross, Peter Horton, Chris Handy, Paul McLean, Roger Gould, Tony Shaw and Geoff Shaw, to mention the principals.

Now a graduate in medicine, Mark Loane led the Queenslanders to Japan, British Columbia and California, losing one of the six games, against British Columbia, a veritable graveyard for touring teams. Another international scalp was added to the Queenslanders' ever-growing, impressive list, when they defeated All Japan 42 to 6.

On their return to the sunshine state, Queensland continued on its winning way, defeating Counties, North Auckland, Victoria, Otago and NSW. This was followed by successive defeats against Canterbury (0-25) and the touring Welsh international side (24-31).

Everyone was keen to play against the Welsh that year because of the 'bath' they had received in 1975-76, and it was therefore a highly motivated Wallaby team that defeated Wales in two hard-fought tests (18 to 8 and 19 to 17). The games were like a re-enactment of World War II, the final ignominy being Welsh front rower Malcolm Price leaving the field in the first five minutes with a broken jaw. Steve ('Sort 'em Out') Finnane was the aggressor.

A sensation occurred when the Wallaby teams against Wales were selected, Mark Loane being relieved of the captaincy in favour of his Queensland teammate, that no-nonsense hard-rock Tony Shaw.

When the 1978 tourists to New Zealand were announced, Shaw held his captaincy. It was a pivotal tour by the Aussies, as their last tour, in 1972, had been dubbed as a national disgrace, the 1972 team being dubbed the 'Awful Aussies'. It had even been suggested that regular fixtures between Australia and New Zealand should be dropped in favour of liaisons with such countries as the USA. Fortunately, sanity prevailed, but players and administrators alike from that time onwards felt the pressure of restoring the game's honour and good name in Australia.

The withdrawal of some players from consideration was a blow to the tourists, the controversial Steve Finnane and lineout sensation David Hillhouse being the main

losses. A hamstring injury to fullback Roger Gould was also a concern on departure, as was the inexplicable omission of the legendary scrumhalf John Hipwell. There were many new Wallabies: Gould, Peter Carson, Chris Handy, Martin Knight, Brendan Moon, Rob Onus, Stan Pilecki, Bill Ross, Andrew Slack, Steve Streeter and Peter McLean.

Mark Loane did not fly in with the team. He arrived late and left early through injury and was not able to play in any of the tests. This was the fateful tour when Australia went down 12-13 and 6-22 in the first two tests, but regrouped after innovative coach Daryl Haberecht had a heart attack, and stormed back with an historic 30 to 16 win at Eden Park, which resolved forever any questions about the fragility of the Wallabies.

A torn hamstring sealed Mark's doom on that tour, as it did Roger Gould's, who was only to play 17 minutes in total. "I came back to Australia," said Mark, "because I spent five weeks recuperating after an injury in the British Isles, and it was just terrible, wandering around and going to different physiotherapists. You simply cannot contribute in these circumstances. There were no physios in those days travelling with the team, and you would just go from town to town. One person thought you needed heat, the next ice, and so on. I just couldn't bear the idea of doing all that again. So I came back."

In 1979, the Wallabies lost both tests against Ireland, which resulted in the sacking of Tony Shaw as captain and the restoration of Mark in that slot. There was then a one-off test against New Zealand for the Bledisloe Cup, and Australia won a rugged test 12 to 6. No try was scored in the match. Australia had now won an unprecedented two tests in a row over New Zealand, and New Zealand fans watched in horror from a distance as the Aussies ran round the Sydney Cricket Ground brandishing the Cup. From that point on possession of the Cup gained greater significance. Brilliantly led by the redoubtable Mark Loane, blood-and-thunder coach Dave Brockhoff summed up the occasion when he said: "They took New Zealand on at their own game and outrucked them. They were under them all day." Mark then went on to captain Australia on its first tour of Argentina, the Wallabies winning and losing a test.

At the end of 1979 Mark started to get a little restless. He had, after all, experienced heavy commitments at the club, state and international level since 1973. He had previously harboured the idea that he might accept another physical challenge and play rugby league, but after a long discussion with rugby league scout and former international Bill Tyquin, he convinced Mark he should stay with union. But that was after he had been dropped following the Tonga game.

So instead off he went to South Africa, where he felt he could broaden his medical, even more than his rugby, education. He had been preceded there by such as Dick Cocks and Gary Pearse. He did 10 months' trauma and 4.5 months' obstetrics training. "It convinced me," he stated, "that I should do something more genteel like ophthalmology."

Rugby-wise, it was a great experience, and while in South Africa he allied with Natal, which finished third in the standings. He became captain of Natal against Zimbabwe, and beat Northern Transvaal at Loftus Verveldt for the first time since 1938. He played breakaway that season, though he was back at number 8 and captain of the South African Barbarians who did well against the British Lions, and then was picked in his favourite position for the Junior Springboks, a rare honour for an expatriate.

He was then selected as one of thirty players under consideration to tour with the Springboks, which would have been a rugby first, but he withdrew because of a work undertaking and a desire to return to Australia.

Mark came back to Australia in 1981. Two tests against France were on the ledger, and Australia was victorious, Tony Shaw understandably hanging on to the captaincy. Then came the tour of the British Isles 1981-82, and by this time Australia had finally developed a strong scrum as well as lineout offensive and defensive patterns, but they had still not learned how to win consistently away from home, and their losses continued on that tour. Three of the four internationals were lost. Near the end of the tour, in a rugby rarity, Australia's captain, Tony Shaw, was dropped, and Mark was once again captain. This event had been precipitated by Tony swinging a haymaker at a Scottish forward at a crucial time

in the international. Australia outscored other teams on the tour in tries scored, but were let down in their kicking. Paul McLean, for once in his career, lost his touch, which could possibly have been because he was carrying most of the pressure for the rest of the team.

The year 1982 saw the Scottish team in Australia, and the Wallabies had a new coach, Bob Dwyer. He committed the unpardonable sin of dropping two of Queensland's folk heroes, Roger Gould and Paul McLean, in favour of two Randwick-ites, Glen and Mark Ella. It was the only time in Wallaby history that its team was booed by its own supporters. Glen had a nightmare of a game and Australia lost 7 to 12.

For the second test, Australia's favourite sons were restored, Gould and McLean scoring all but three of Australia's points in a devastating 33-9 victory. Some of the giants of the game retired: Paul McLean, Mark Loane, Duncan Hall, Chris Roche and Peter McLean.

Mark said frankly: "I had, simply, had enough. I have always thought New Zealanders the best rugby players generally in the world. The further south you go, the better they are. After all they did invent the ruck in Dunedin. They are a generous and hospitable people but I had had enough."

Mark had always heard a different drummer throughout his rugby career. A man of unyielding commitment, he set goals and achieved them. When he went on tour, he would make lists of things to do, and would tick them off in his notebook when achieved. If there were 800 steps in the leaning tower of Pisa, Mark would reportedly walk them off while counting, and then methodically draw a stroke through that assignment.

Wallaby touring teams had a Culture Club in those days, though the roll-call was ever self-limiting. They would arrange excursions to the ballet, opera, museums, etc. Mark Loane, Tony D'Arcy and Chris Carberry were the principal advocates.

In 1983 Mark rafted the Franklin River in Tasmania, did a locum and studied towards a specialty in ophthalmology, hitting the books in his normal Type-A personality manner up to twelve hours a day. He did the first exams in 1984, topping the field in Australia. He was awarded the Cowen medal for his achievement.

The rigorous requirement for ophthalmology then in force was six years of medicine, four years in general training, then one year of full-time study for the first part. Then there were another four years on top of that for the second part.

After finishing this second examination Mark worked in Adelaide for 1.5 years, and then 14 months in San Diego. He completed two Fellowships, one in corneal transplantation and one in glaucoma, a rarity in ophthalmology. In 1990 he returned home to set up his own specialty practice.

The highlights of his career were winning a premiership against Brothers in a 200-minute match. "Amazing game," he said. "Near the end, Tony Shaw, who was captain of Brothers, had a scrum about five yards out, and it was a perfect position for Paul McLean to take a dropped kick, which would have tied the game. They went for the try instead."

After the match Mark said to his opposite number, "Why didn't you go for the drop goal, Tony?"

Shaw replied: "I was sick and tired of it. I wanted a result, win or lose."

His second highlight was the 42-4 win against NSW at Ballymore in 1976. The third was the victory in 1979 in the one-off test against the All Blacks, and the fourth a win in the second test against Argentina.

"In the latter match," Mark said, "we were ahead by one point, the game was almost over, Argentina had the scrum feed, and Hugo Porta was drooling at the mouth as he readied for a dropped goal, and he had radar control in those days. Billy Ross won the scrum against the feed. It was the best strike for the ball I have ever seen."

Beating Ireland in 1975 in Ireland was another high point, as was beating France in two internationals in Australia.

Asked what his main attributes were, Mark said: "I had the weaknesses of my strengths. My strength psychologically might have done good for some people around me, though at the end it might have been a defect. I always had great certainty that we could win. I never went on the field thinking that we might possibly lose. I had this enormous belief that we could win, and that was important in those early days."

He went on: "I had a mono-maniacal desire to win. Tony Shaw and Paul McLean had it too. By the time we retired we were winning at home and had the concepts of the scrum, lineout and defence almost worked out. The next generation improved on all those concepts and started not only winning at home but away as well. I had no physical fear about anything that might happen on the field. I also do think I had the ability to anticipate play. I could almost always walk to the danger or advantage points. At eighth man you almost have this Buddhism-like symmetry. You have seven people in front of you, and seven people behind you, and you have both sides of the field of play available to you, involving all aspects of play. You are in the middle of the game. Breakaways are often there before the play has evolved, whereas the No.8 has half a second to think and anticipate play. As an intellectual pursuit No.8 play is incomparable. It's perfect, it's the thinking man's position."

"Only once did anyone say this is the way I should play. I did it by deduction. One time I was on a plane to Bermuda with All Black Murray Mexted, and we compared notes. I had arrived at the same conclusions as this almost canon of eighth man play. I also had the ability to accelerate quickly over ten metres. I worked a great deal on my upper body strength, so that I would not be pushed back by anyone in the world. My defensive play and my support for the breakaways at the breakdown were also important factors.

"My main disadvantage was when I had the ball in hand I got so excited that maybe I did not pass it off as often as I should. That is also part of my character. When I had the ball in hand I wanted to protect it. I felt always I could get further and further, and in so doing I could get isolated. The down side is that I may not have been as creative as I might have been. Also, in the lineout I could have been better. Tony Shaw and I would disturb our opponents and destroy their ball. We did pretty well, however, Corney, Shawie and myself. We were a good combination at the back."

As for captaincy, Mark felt that "there is some necessity to lead by example. You had to be brave enough to fall on difficult balls, to make the tackle, and the rest follows. You could not have the command or respect of the players without these things. You can never in a game situation ask a player to do something you are not prepared to do yourself. Most captaining is done off the field. If you run into big problems on the field your preparation hasn't been good enough."

In retrospect, Mark played because he enjoyed it, and only later on realised that what he was a part of was so important. And, he noted, like being called the Father in the Holy Trinity, with Tony Shaw the Son and Paul McLean the Holy Ghost, these occurrences and incidents in which he was involved were all embellished over the years, like most rugby stories, which depart from fact when the story can be improved. As Zane Grey said to his journalists when he sent them out looking for Wild West stories: "If there is a difference between the legend and the facts, print the legend."

The fact is, Mark Loane was a pivotal figure in the resurgence of Queensland and, indeed, Australian rugby. For whatever reason, a core of players emerged like Mark and coaches and managers like Bob Templeton and John Ryan, who were determined to win. It was a long road, but ultimately the battle for the restoration of Australia's rugby prestige was successful.

In all, Mark played 28 tests for Australia, seven as captain. An introspective, scholarly and thoughtful man, he never succumbed to ribald behaviour but always maintained a certain aloofness, bred of intense self-discipline. He was never a loner, but was always content in his own company, ever educating himself in the world at large.

Andrew Slack composed a limerick about the man called the 'dogmatic doctor' by Bob Templeton:

*Our leader's name was Loane,*
*rather than smile he'd groan*
*his idea of debauchery*
*was to visit a mauchery*
*or Igguassu Falls on his own.*

Mark Loane is devoted to medicine and his specialty ophthalmology, and is understandably concentrating on his work after long years of rugby and medical education. He has stated, however, that one of these days he might like to coach, when he is 50 or 60, when he has more time. Such statements from Mark Loane are not met with hilarity, for those who know

his single-minded nature realise that if he sets his mind to it he would do just that, and be highly successful as well. He is just that kind of man.

Dr Peter Horton, the no-nonsense, combative hooker, now sport historian-sociologist, who played with Mark, had some succinct points to make about the 'big fellow': "The Mark Loane you read about, the colossus, the nordic-like behemoth, the 'super-charged No.8' is of course but a fraction of the real person (As indeed all athletes are of course! A point sometimes forgotten). And strangely it is more for my off-field relationship that I so fondly remember him. However, in footballing terms it was his awesome power-running and ability to break the gain line that will always remain upper-most in my memory. Not the silky ball distribution skills or gazelle-like lineout jumping which of course, however, were by the standards of us mere mortals, exceptional, it was the man's power that could in a single charge both rejuvenate his own team's flagging spirits and at the same time completely demoralise even the most eminent of opposition: Queensland's victory against Canterbury in 1977 when he tore holes in their defence and utterly marginalised the 'Grizz' immediately comes to mind.

"I had and still have the greatest respect for Mark - I suppose like many of life's ironies it is hard to understand. I think essentially we recognised each other's personal qualities and understood and accepted each other's idiosyncrasies - which many of the more conventional types could not and why should they? No big deal - no deep and meaningful friendship but by the same token no bullshit and we were/are doers. I feel the game will not see many more such characters with its turn to professionalism! I hope I am proven incorrect, however."

Yes, the bumping, charging runs that Loane made were his public persona, but the private Mark Loane is entirely different. Just recently, when interviewing Loane, Dr Xie expressed surprise that his hands were so big, and suggested that he must have difficulty in delicate eye surgery. He looked at her calmly and said: "Do not confuse size with delicacy!"

The author knows another side of Mark Loane. He and his late wife Reet were doing research in early Indian cultures in what is called the Four Corners region of the United States, the territory encompassing parts of Utah, Colorado, Arizona and New Mexico. Mark was doing a Fellowship in San Diego, and they invited him to Arizona for a weekend. They took him on a tour of the archaeological sites comprising the Anasazi, Hohokam and Sinagua cultures, and when he left said, simply: "That was one of the most educational and wonderful weekends I have ever had."

Some years later, Reet Howell was suddenly and unexpectedly struck down with cancer while she was lecturing overseas, and when she was opened up in Toronto the doctor said all that could be done was to take her home to die. This beautiful and vital woman was riddled with cancer.

The author got her back to Sydney, and she was operated on at the Royal Hospital for Women. It was touch and go whether she would survive the operation, and the emotional strain was understandably enormous. They had been so busy fighting for her life they had told virtually no one of the desperate plight they were in. The telephone range in Reet's room, and the author answered it. It was Mark Loane, ringing from Brisbane.

He said, "It's Mark. I just heard about Reet. How is it?"

"It's all unbelievable, Mark, but we're going to fight it out. We feel we can make it."

Reet, was nearby, and did not wish her husband to state the reality, that she was really dying.

"I've spoken to the medical staff there, Mark said, "and I know the situation. Don't say anymore. I'm flying down to see Reet. I'll be there in two days. Tell her we'll have a party."

"What, Mark, you can't be serious. There's no need, Mark, you don't have to."

"I'll be there. Mate, that is what life is all about. When there's a real crisis you have to close ranks. That's what real friendship is all about. I'll be there."

Reet brightened up unbelievably at the news, as she loved Mark very much. It gave her something to think about, to get her mind off her pain and her problems, and his visit worked wonders.

She eventually got home to Brisbane where something burst inside of her and she had only a few hours to live. The author had no idea how Mark found out, but he was at her bedside those last hours. It was about midnight when the author said, "I think she should get some rest."

She smiled wanly and said: "Don't stop talking, fellows, I like to hear your voices." They were virtually her last words.

Peter Horton was right. The athletic part of Mark Loane was but a small part of Loane the man. He was and is an exceptional human being, one to depend on in a crisis, willing to take that extra step to demonstrate the importance of values in our modern world. He is, indeed, a man for all seasons.

# Andy McIntyre

*A*ndy Mac is one of the quiet achievers in a team full of star players. He's so willing to get in there and do the hard work. The forwards won us the Grand Slam, and without Mac and Topo, we wouldn't have got the ball.

*The big thing about Macca is his sheer strength. On the tours we made together in New Zealand, France and the British Isles, he'd do weights every chance he got. If there was a weight gym where we were staying, Mac would be there. He works out all the time.*

*Macca isn't one of those gifted footballers to whom the game comes easily. He became Australia's tighthead prop largely with his enormous strength and hard work. Yet he's not a big man. Look at Andy in a suit, and most people wouldn't pick him as a prop. Sure, he's thick, but he's no giant.*

*– Mark Ella, in Path to Victory*

So what is a tighthead prop, the neophyte invariably asks? Peter FitzSimons, in his amusing book *Rugby Stories*, puts it quite simply: "The tighthead: the right-hand side of the scrum. The way to remember this is that 'tight' rhymes with 'right'. So there it is, as simple as that."

Andy hears a different drummer to most frontrowers. He could party with the best of them when the occasion presented itself, but he rarely reached the outrageousness of some of his colleagues. He was his own man, but always seemed more contained and reserved socially, displaying an inner strength which indeed he did have. He was quieter, more gentlemanly and dignified, which description would undoubtedly have him wincing.

Terry Smith, in *Path to Victory*, put it this way: "A man of action, not words…his rugby drips with blood." And against the Barbarians, the last game of the 1984 Grand Slam tour, he was chosen ahead of the great 'Topo' Rodriguez. Coach Alan Jones said: "I thought it the most appropriate way to thank a man who does his work silently and unspectacularly."

That was the role he played, toiling in the engine room without ostentation, an unsung hero. He was not of the garrulous, extroverted mode of most frontrowers. He would never match players such as Bob McMaster and Chris Handy in terms of behaviour. He always seemed reasonably under control.

He was born in Toowoomba, his mother an ex-school teacher and father a farmer, the crops being principally wheat and maize. The farm was about half-way between Cecil Plains and Toowoomba, on the Darling Downs.

There were six children in the family, and he was sent to Bongeen State School, which had only about 70 students. He found schoolwork rather easy, which allowed him to pursue his passion for sport.

"We played rugby league at school," he said, "and sometimes we'd play other schools, sometimes having to combine with another local school to get a team. I loved rugby league, and would watch it on TV whenever I could. I also loved anything to do with the Olympics. To me there was a certain mystique about it all." He then digressed: "Many things in rugby are foreign to me at the moment. Players are looking at rugby as a job, whereas we looked at it as enjoyment and adventure. I hope what we had isn't lost, because it will be extremely difficult to bring it back."

He was sent to Brisbane Grammar School as a boarder, his eldest brother preceding him there, being quite good at cricket and tennis. It did not take him long to switch his allegiance from rugby league to rugby union, and after a selection process which entailed nothing more than putting his hand up, found himself in the F team for the under 13s, playing in the second row. However if any of the teams was short of players he would volunteer for double duty. He loved his sport.

When he got to the under-15 As, he gravitated to breakaway, which he found took the pressure off his lineout ability. The following season he was captain of the Under-16 As.

After that, he was in the firsts, and came under the tutelage of Brian Short and Alex Evans, who provided him with the foundation in skills that lasted him throughout his football career. They won the GPS premiership that year, with 'Andy Mac' still on the side of the scrum.

History master and rugby fanatic Brian Short was also coaching GPS at the time, and Andy took very little persuasion to play for their under-19s when he left school. There were many Australian Schoolboys on that team, such as David Hillhouse. Andy had always enjoyed training, and still does, and was on weights even in this period of his life. He started to fill out, became bigger and stronger, and moved in to the front row. In that first year out of school they lost the under-19 competition to Souths. The captain of Souths was Andrew Slack, of whom Andy said: "He was the best captain I ever played under."

At this stage of his life he was almost lost to rugby, having commenced a Bachelor of Surveying degree at the University of Queensland and spending much of his spare time surfing, to the detriment of his studies.

The only rugby played during this first year at University was GPS thirds, until a less than planned trip to Sydney on an Inter-University campaign with some less than serious fellow students introduced him to the University style of less than organised rugby.

Wallabies Bill Ross and Bruce Brown (who used to complain that he was too fit to play for University), convinced him he should trial seriously at the University of Queensland, where he made the 'A' Grade side almost immediately. Mark Loane and 'Paddy' Batch were two of the most endearing of the University players at the time.

'Paddy' took his rugby seriously, and consistently inspired his teammates with his dedication to training and his meticulous preparation before games. An unlikely-looking winger at 17 stone, he loved to eat, and it was a personal tragedy for him when he broke his jaw and was put on a liquid diet, his only culinary pleasure being toasted sandwiches prepared in a blender.

Mark Loane was something else again. Whilst 'Paddy' Batch tended to restrict the amount of running he did in a game, Mark preferred to involve himself more heavily by proclaiming 'My Ball' at every opportunity. Having secured the ball, it was invariably tucked under the left arm, where it would stay until Mark emerged from the bottom of a ruck, asking 'Where was the support?'

In 1977, Andy was paying his dues, patiently learning his trade, including how to pass the ball by Mark Loane, and the intricacies and skullduggery of front row play. He played for Queensland Under-23s and Australian Universities between motor cycle accidents, finally surrendering to a broken collar-bone towards the end of the season.

His initial breakthrough to the 'big time' came in 1980 when he was selected for the Queensland tour of New Zealand and later to England, Scotland, France and Italy. Queensland was blessed with outstanding front rowers at the time - Stan Pilecki, Tony D'Arcy and Chris Handy being his main rivals. His first full game for Queensland was early in the 1980 season against Thames Valley in New Zealand. He also played against Bristol, and Beges at Bordeaux.

After the European tour he went off to the

United States for six months, playing half a season of rugby at New Orleans followed by a non-affluent vacation in the ski fields of Colorado. His world-view was expanding, as on his return he was off to Japan with the Australian Universities team, which included Simon Poidevin, Roger Davis and Tony Parker. The competition for the Queensland side was simply too rugged in 1981, Tony D'Arcy and Stan Pilecki being 'untouchables'. He was, at this stage of his career, still a 'dirt-tracker' when it came to international rugby.

The year 1982 changed all that, as Bob Templeton was bounced as Australian coach and Bob Dwyer was at the helm. Nine Wallabies decided not to tour New Zealand, among them Tony D'Arcy and Stan Pilecki. 'Stan the Man' actually flew over later as a replacement. Because of this exodus, Andy obtained his chance at last at the national level. Thirty-four-year-old John Griffiths was chosen for the tour as a tighthead prop as well, and he had difficulty with the demands of the tour, presenting Andy with the opportunity to play the first five games straight, which seriously affected his recreational activities.

The props chosen were John Coolican, John Griffiths, Andy McIntyre and John Meadows. There was little doubt that Andy would not have made the tour but for the defections, but neither would have Steve Cutler or David Campese. As the saying goes: "Opportunity never knocks. You will wait a lifetime waiting for a knock. **You** open the door."

'Macca', like the others, was progressing up the ladder of success, working on his strength and fitness, and Australian representation was inevitable. He seized upon the opportunity when it presented itself and made every post a winner.

Andy made the first test side, for his initial foray into the 'big time'. The Australian team on that day at Lancaster Park, Christchurch, was: Roger Gould, David Campese, Michael Hawker, Gary Ella, Peter Grigg, Mark Ella (capt.), Phil Cox; John Coolican, Bruce Malouf, Andy McIntyre, Simon Poidevin, Steve Williams, Duncan Hall, Chris Roche and Peter Lucas.

The opposite front row comprised the fearsome 'Geriatrics', the much-experienced Gary Knight, Andy Dalton and John Ashworth, considered to be the toughest in the world at the time. They were a fearsome-looking lot, these All Blacks, captained by Graham Mourie, with other formidable characters like Andy Haden, Murray Mexted and Mark Shaw, lightning-fast backs like Stu Wilson and Bernie Fraser, and a great goalkicker in Allan Hewson.

Contrary to expectations, the Wallabies were not rolled, though they eventually went down 16-23. The 'new boys' showed they could handle the 'big time'.

Bob Dwyer, in *The Winning Way* had this to say: "Our other tighthead prop, Andy McIntyre, went on to become a fixture in the Australian front row in the 1980s. When we chose McIntyre for the tour he was not even first choice for Queensland. In fact, McIntyre played quite a few tests before he became Queensland's first choice in the position."

With 'Macca' having proven himself, he remained in the front row for the remaining two tests, though John Meadows replaced Coolican and Lance Walker replaced Bruce Malouf. Stan Pilecki, the leading Queensland front rower, who had flown over prior to the first test, could not displace McIntyre. The Wallabies shocked the All Blacks by winning the second test 19 to 16, second rower Duncan Hall being injured early on in the game, but were soundly beaten 16 to 33 in the third.

One of McIntyre's indelible memories is of the Wallaby try at the start of the third test, a move that was planned by Bob Dwyer. Instead of playing conservatively, the Wallabies attacked and scored, utilising a double cut-out play. The ball went from scrum half Phil Cox to Mark Ella, who cut out inside centre Michael Hawker, the ball going to Andrew Slack. He cut out fullback Roger Gould, who was into the backline, the ball instead going to the winger, with Gould doubling around to get the ball. He scored in the corner. It was a sensational start. Stan Pilecki, who was on the bench, turned to Bob Dwyer and said: "What did you say to do next?"

There were few opportunities in 1983 for 'Macca', as he could not break into the Queensland lineup and hence could not dent the test lineup. Stan Pilecki was back, Declan Curran had shown his wares and John Meadows was still a force, though Tony D'Arcy was now out of contention as he had turned to rugby league. The Argentineans came to Australia in 1983 and Pilecki was played at loosehead against Enrique ('Topo') Rodriguez, and had a losing battle with him. He was happy to go back to tighthead. 'Topo', of course, was to be playing for Australia the following year. There were three front rowers used by Australia against Argentina, Pilecki, Curran and Meadows.

There was a single test against the All Blacks in August, Meadows and Pilecki getting the nod.

'Macca' was in the tour to France and Italy in November of that year, with newcomers to test rugby such as Tommy Lawton and Steve Tuynman, and Jeff Miller and Michael Lynagh making their first tours. The manager was one of rugby's beloved characters, ex-Wallaby captain 'Chilla' Wilson, and Bob Dwyer was still coach, though the knives were being sharpened in Australia in his absence. As the saying goes: "When the cat's away the mice will play."

France has always been a difficult opponent for Australia, much of it having to do with variations in tempo and rhythm when playing against them after combating New Zealand and northern hemisphere teams.

The French tend to be more explosive and unpredictable, and in the case of 1983, a lot dirtier. When France toured Australia in 1981 it had been a bloodbath, particularly against Queensland, and the French scrumhalf had to be sent home because of a wound in his head that required fifty-odd stitches, and six to eight Maroons had to get repair jobs after a violent game.

The Gallic flair gave way to Gallic revenge in the first game, the cry of 'Queensland, Queensland' reverberating through their scrum.

The Aussies found themselves against Selection XV after Selection XV, their opponents hard-rock customers interested only in mayhem and setting the record straight. The Wallabies were losing players with almost every encounter. Andy said: "I think they got some of them from the Bastille. The Battle of Strasbourg, we called one game."

One of the worst offenders was a certain No. 8, who had a long memory from that 1981 tour and was doing all he could to right what he considered to be past wrongs. Fortunately he broke his hand against the head of mild-mannered second rower Nigel Holt and was not seen again for the duration of the tour.

Steve Tuynman was belted and knocked out, and while lying on the ground, unconscious, the ruck went clean over him, twice. Chris Roche, a combative and gutsy player who would put his life on the line every game, came up and yelled at Tuynman: "You'll never be any good the rest of your life if you don't get up, you'll be a weak prick." Tuynman got to his feet, and played a blinder. No one ever doubted 'The Bird's' intestinal fortitude after France.

Everything seemed to be done to put the Aussies at a disadvantage on that French tour. Everything and everybody was late, the hotels were mediocre, and so on. On the morning of the first test, they were served raw steaks as only the French can cook them and chips for breakfast, and beer and wine to wash them down, which is no longer considered or recommended as a pre-game repast.

The first test, with Andy and John Coolican in the front row, upped the stakes in the ferocity game. Hooker Mark McBain was savagely kicked in the head, to be replaced by Tom Lawton. Not only did McBain get his skull fractured, but the cerebral fluid leaked into his mouth for a certain period afterwards. As only Aussies can, they saw the humorous side to it all, not that there really was any, and nicknamed him 'The Leak'.

Not wishing to appear soft on his charges, captain of the tour, Mark Ella, was seen dispatching a string of fire crackers into a toilet which McBain was temporarily occupying soon after his release from hospital.

When the second test came around, the front row was Coolican, Lawton and McIntyre. "The French were so worked up," said 'Macca', "that when they threw the coin up they lost it. They were really out for some fun that day."

Andy was kicked in the chin, receiving ten stitches, but was more fortunate than Tuynman, who was heeled out of a ruck with his ear hanging from his head. He was taped up and continued on. When the tape was taken off after the game a piece of the ear came off in the tape. He had plastic surgery when he returned to Australia. The first test was drawn, 15-15, and

France won the second, 15 to 6.

It had been a tough tour, to put it mildly, but McIntyre feels that the team spirit for 1984 was forged on this trip. The lads learned to stick together in tough times, like the old Digger spirit that made Australian soldiers famous.

Alan Jones emerged as Australian coach in 1984, an erudite man, highly professional, who took Australian rugby to new heights over the next few years. Above all things Jones did his homework, and had his own agenda in mind. There were some players vital in his vision, and history has shown him to be correct in his judgment. He wanted to win the lineout, so he got Steve Cutler.

He wanted a front row of strength and power as the basis of the scrum, and he got that in Andy McIntyre, Tom Lawton and Enrique Rodriguez. He wanted breakaways who could get to the breakdown first so as to get the ball, and he found them in Simon Poidevin and Chris Roche.

When it came to the backs, he had his eye on Nick Farr-Jones, but for a time he felt Phil Cox could handle the position. As for the rest, there was genius at every turn - Mark Ella, David Campese, Michael Hawker and Roger Gould, and a captain everyone respected in Andrew Slack.

There was a short tour to Fiji, and then New Zealand came to Australia in 1984. There certainly was not much in it, Australia winning the first test 16 to 9, then losing the next two 15-9 and 24-25. In the three tests, Australia scored 55 points to New Zealand's 53. Jones and the boys were on course for a history-making tour of the British Isles.

The 1984 tour of Britain and Ireland is now known simply as 'The Grand Slam Tour'. The only previous team to the United Kingdom that could be compared with them is the 1947-48 team, which won 25 of 30 games in the British Isles for an 83 per cent average. The 1984 team's average was 72 per cent, winning 13 of 18 with one draw. In points scored, the 1947-48 team averaged 14.3, and against 6.5. Taking into account the difference in points for tries, the 1984 team scored 19.3 points a game and had 12.8 points against them.

It is an interesting comparison, as on the surface it would show that the 1947-48 team had a better winning percentage, and a better defensive record. The '84 team was better on attack. The fundamental difference is that the 1984 Wallabies won all the 'home' internationals, whereas the 1947-48 Wallabies lost one to Wales, by two penalty goals. However the 1947-48 team created a record no one has equalled, in that it did not have its line crossed in a 'home' international.

But nothing can detract from the performance of the 1984 Wallabies, for it was a remarkable feat, unparalleled in Australian rugby history. Each of the players, and the management team of 'Chilla' Wilson and Alan Jones, and assistant coach Alex Evans, will have a unique position in Australian rugby history. The players on that historic tour were Roger Gould, David Campese, Andrew Slack (capt.), Matt Burke, Peter Grigg, Ross Hanley, Michael Hawker, Tim Lane, Brendan Moon, Ian Williams (replacement), James Black, Michael Lynagh, Phil Cox, Nick Farr-Jones, Bill Calcraft, David Codey, Simon Poidevin, Ross Reynolds, Chris Roche, Steve Tuynman, Bill Campbell, Steve Cutler, Nigel Holt, Steve Williams (vice-capt.), Cameron Lillicrap, Andy McIntyre, Stan Pilecki, Mark McBain, Tom Lawton, Enrique Rodriguez and Greg Burrow (replacement). The "dirt-trackers", or the "Green Machine' as the '84 Wallabies called them, were vital to the success of the team.

Mark Ella and Terry Smith offer their comments in *Path to Victory*: "Alan Jones reminded the British media (after the Scotland win that sealed the Grand Slam) that the glittering show had come about only through months of slogging practice. Hour upon hour on windswept paddocks. Try, try and trying again to perfect a single move. Jones said: 'I take the Gucci view about hard work on the practice field - long after you've paid the price, the quality remains. Lots of times when it's cold and dark and wet, you feel like packing it in and going under a hot shower. But we stuck it out.'"

And so they did, leaving a legacy for all the Wallabies that preceded them and for all the Wallabies who will follow. They, indeed, showed the Gucci factor.

One of the great characters of the tour was the manager, Dr Charles Wilson. 'Chilla' Wilson, let it be said, is the perfect manager, and beloved by all, because of his impeccable nature and his total lack of discipline. Described in a nice way as "a boy who never grew up", 'Chilla' is at perfect peace when touring with the boys, and was the perfect foil for the intense Jones. He was also the custodian of the team's liquor supply, and of course this was only too well known to the insomniacs in the team.

'Swill' Williams was one who really responded to the challenge of the 1984 tour. He had two broken jaws in his career, and really came into his own as a pack leader. He was a "great player", according to McIntyre.

Prior to the England test, 'Swill' addressed the pack: "These guys (the English) are nothing but a bunch of pricks," he said, "They were trying to shoot the mates of this guy (Rodriguez) a couple of years ago." The reference to the Falklands War to stir the team up had the opposite effect, the team bursting out in laughter, just as the ball was to be kicked off.

The victories against all the home countries are all now treasured memories, but the pushover try against Wales was something special. "We would have beaten anyone that day," said McIntyre. It was quite a sight to see many of the Welsh crowd leaving in disgust and disbelief before the game ended, and to know that the Welsh were singing no more.

The Scotland game topped it all off, they had achieved the seemingly impossible, the Grand Slam. At the black-tie dinner after the game, a glorious affair, Alex Evans, Andy McIntyre, Bill Campbell, Mark McBain, Steve Tuynman and Nick Farr-Jones dressed in kilts, and in a never-to-be-forgotton episode stood on their chairs singing 'Auld Lang Syne'.

The end of the 1984 tour was delayed by one last stop in Europe by the frontrow combination of Lillicrap, Lawton and McIntyre. Unfortunately, their skiing skills did not match their rugby skills and one small but well-known Austrian town will no doubt not be erecting a monument to their visit.

It was tough to come back to earth after the tour, as all the Wallabies received a hero's welcome in a sport-mad country. The New Zealanders, as always, were waiting in the wings, ready to show the upstart Aussies who really was king. There was a southern hemisphere single match shoot-out, but Mark

Ella, that genius who had done what no one else in rugby history had done, and scored tries against England, Ireland, Scotland and Wales, had announced his retirement, at 26 years of age. The captain Andrew Slack, was also unavailable, David Campese and Brendan Moon were injured, Michael Hawker had retired, and Chris Riche had gone to league. Still, it was a pretty fair Wallaby side, though not good enough on the day to beat the All Blacks, losing a close contest 9-10. Andy, Lawton and Rodriguez were the Aussie front rowers.

The following season some revenge for the series loss to France was forthcoming in the one-off test match in Sydney.

'Macca' did not go to New Zealand in 1986 because of work commitments, but was back into action for the World Cup in 1987. It was generally thought that the World Cup would be a show-down between Australia and New Zealand. It did not work out that way.

The Wallabies looked supreme in beating England 19-6, then defeated the United States 47-12 and Japan 42-23, and next Ireland 33-15 in the quarter final. That most unpredictable rugby-playing nation, France, ended Australia's hopes in the semi-final, as the home team lost 24-30 on the final bell. It was tough to wear on home soil, and a psychologically-down Wallaby team then lost to Wales 21-22, at Rotorua, in a play-off for third place after breakaway David Codey was sent off in the first five minutes of the game.

A month after the World Cup, Australia had a chance to restore its flagging prestige with a one-off test against the 'world champion' All Blacks at Concord Oval, but they went down to a heavy defeat 16-30.

The knives were now flashing for Australia's hero of yesteryear, Alan Jones, and his doom was sealed when on a subsequent tour to Argentina, in late 1987, Australia drew the first test 19-all and was outgunned 19-27 in the second. Andy was unable to play in the first test. Bob Dwyer was, thereafter, re-installed as Australian coach.

There was a short tour of Scotland, England and Italy in 1988 under captain Nick Farr-Jones, and the team started badly, losing four of its first seven games. It was an unbalanced Wallaby team, and the loss to England 19-28 was a severe setback to the campaign. The Wallabies rallied to win their next eight games, including tests against Scotland and Italy.

'Macca' was also back against the All Blacks on their tour to Australia in 1988 and played the three tests, then finished his test career against them in 1989 in the single test. Tony Daly was brought into the team as the other prop that year with Phil Kearns. It was time for the changing of the guard.

Andy had always felt a great responsibility towards his work, but was very tempted to accept an invitation to play in a World XV in South Africa. However, after considering his work situation and the political problems it was causing his employer he retired. Missing the opportunity to tour South Africa due to the pressure of minority and self-interest groups who insist on using sport for political gains was

difficult for him to accept and left a lasting void in his career. He had played 38 tests for Australia. The front row combination of 'Topo' Rodriguez, Tom Lawton and Andy McIntyre was the finest that Australia had produced to this point in its rugby history, rivalled perhaps only by John Thornett, Peter Johnson and Jon White. They provided the platform on which Australia's success was built, and gave respectability to Australia's scrum.

Andy McIntyre was not the archetypical frontrower. He could party with the best of them when required, but he was quieter than the normal mutant that occupies his position. He was solid and dependable, a person you knew would never give up amidst adversity, a player who did the hard slogging with little praise and publicity. That was the very nature of Andy McIntyre.

Cyril Burke . . . took his share of batterings behind the struggling Wallaby packs in the 1940s and 1950s.

**Andy McIntyre** . . . one of Australian rugby's quiet achievers.

**John Hipwell . . . a halfback with "the heart of a lion".**

Mark Ella, who scored a try in every test of the Grand Slam achievement of 1984.

Simon Poidevin pounces on a loose ball against England during the World Cup grand final at Twickenham in 1991.

**Andrew Slack . . . awarded the Order of Australia in recognition of his services to rugby.**

Nick Farr-Jones ... inspirational captain of the World Cup winning Wallabies in 1991.

**Wallaby captain Andrew Slack holds the Bledisloe Cup aloft following his team's stunning victory against the All Blacks at Eden Park in 1986.**

# Paul McLean

Australia has been blessed with some outstanding five-eighths in its rugby history. If they ever shone in this position they were brilliance personified, as they invariably played behind losing packs. Some of the truly greats among the Wallabies at five-eighth were Tom Lawton sen, Arthur Summons, Phil Hawthorne, Mark Ella, and, of course, Michael Lynagh.

Paul McLean rewrote the record books and many consider him the finest five-eighth ever to don the green and gold. A lot depends, however, on which side of the border you live, Queensland supporters opting usually for Paul McLean or Michael Lynagh, and NSW rugby fanatics throwing in their lot with the mercurial and gifted Mark Ella, or Phil Hawthorne or Arthur Simmons. Rugby pundits have been known to come to blows over this one. It seems to be able to raise unprecedented passions and destroy life-long friendships.

In some ways it can be considered a question of style. Lynagh and McLean were often perceived as being overly conservative in their approaches, relying on the boot for position and opposition errors in their own half for victory. Ella was heralded as an attacking genius, acting instinctively and throwing game plans out of the window as opportunities presented themselves.

This analysis is all too over-simplistic, emotion spilling over equally in the breasts of Lynagh and McLean as well, with individual brilliance not only residing in the Ella camp.

Who will ever forget Paul McLean's farewell to the test arena in 1982? Paul was 28 years of age, and though he was playing a more orchestrated, predictable type of game in his later years, his brilliance showed in two victories over NSW in the annual interstate series, by scores of 23-16 and 41-7, and an 18-7 victory over Scotland.

New national coach Bob Dwyer dropped a bombshell of near-atomic proportions when the Wallaby team to play Scotland in the first test was announced in 1982. Not only Paul McLean, but Roger Gould was dropped, and Queensland supporters and writers were incensed, mortified and horrified. Glen Ella was selected as the new fullback, with Mark Ella at five-eighth. With the Ellas stars at Randwick, and Dwyer the long-serving custodian of that club, the crowd at Ballymore, of all places, jeered Glen hoping he would drop the ball following a Scotland up-and-under. Australia lost 7-12, and the two Queenslanders were recalled for the second test in Sydney. Before the match, the prideful McLean announced that the match would be his last in the international arena.

Australia won the game 33-9, and McLean was masterful, kicking eight goals from nine attempts. He scored 21 of the 33 points, a new record for Australia in an international match. Roger Gould was equally effective, scoring two tries, a record for an Australian fullback. Between them, they scored the first 27 of

Australia's points. Paul demonstrated to all what a rare champion he was. Bret Harris, in *The Marauding Maroons: The Rise of Queensland Rugby,* called him "a rugby thoroughbred".

Hugh Lunn, noted Brisbane author and journalist, wrote in the *Australian:* "Paul McLean played thirty-one test matches for Australia, and one hundred games for Queensland. He won the Rugby Premiership for his school (St Joseph's College, Nudgee) with a fifty-five-metre penalty kick; Brothers club lost only one of eight grand finals in which he played; he brought up his one thousandth point for Queensland in his one-hundredth match in the last match of the Queensland Rugby's Centenary year; he kicked fourteen consecutive goals against Wales on their Australian tour; he holds the individual Australian point scoring record for a test match of twenty-one points, against Scotland in Sydney; and he is the greatest point scorer in the history of Australian Rugby Union."

Paul McLean was immortalised as one of Queensland's Holy Trinity by David Dunworth. God the Father was Mark Loane, the Son was Tony Shaw and the Holy Spirit was Paul McLean.

There is an excellent biography written about this Queenslander by Malcolm McGregor entitled *Paul McLean.* In it, he wrote that: "There is a certain irony in the fact that someone of Paul McLean's self-effacing nature should have been one of Australian sport's most controversial figures." McGregor likened his lack of adulation to that of Sir Donald Bradman, as both were clinical in their efficiency and perfectionism, and seemingly remote in their relationship with the crowd.

Paul McLean had it all. He was a brilliant tactician with an apparently ice-cool demeanour; he had impeccable hands; he could sift through his opponents when it suited him; his touch-finding ranked with the best in the world; his place kicking was also world class; and in the words of the captain of the 1984 Grand Slam Wallabies, Andrew Slack: "As a player's man, Paul McLean has no peer."

Paul certainly had the right pedigree. It all started with one Doug McLean. Born on 15 April 1880, Doug had been an outstanding athlete in the western districts of Queensland.

A sprinter of considerable repute, he once defeated world champions Arthur Postle and Jack Donaldson at Brisbane's famous 'Gabba stadium. Doug began his football career in the Queensland country town of Roma, but gravitated to Brisbane and was picked on the wing for Australia against Great Britain in 1904. He toured with the Australian team to New Zealand in 1905, scored the first try for Australia on New Zealand soil and played 21 games for Queensland. When rugby league started in Australia he was one of the first three Queenslanders to switch, playing against New Zealand in 1907.

A rugby dynasty began when Doug McLean married the daughter of one Jack Wieneke. This was no ordinary marriage, as Jack Wieneke was a legendary all-round Queensland athlete, who performed outstanding feats throughout Queensland, including standing high and long jumps, sprints, hurdles, hop, step and jumps, and pole vaults. So it was a pretty fair mixing of athletic genes when a Wieneke and a McLean got together.

They produced four sons, Doug, Bill, Jack and Bob who, with the exception of Bob, all played rugby union for Australia. However, Bob was the father of the illustrious Paul, who was to play 31 tests for Australia, and Jeff McLean, who played 13 tests. The family consider Bob the most talented rugby player of all the boys.

Bill McLean, Paul's uncle, was captain of Australia in 1946 in New Zealand and again during the 1947-48 Wallaby tour of the British Isles, France, Canada and the United States. Bill's son Peter was the seventh McLean to play for Australia.

Born at Ipswich in 1953, Paul was a bit of a loner, though like many a young athlete past and present, he could hardly wait to get a bat or any kind of a ball in his hands. He learned his basic skills naturally, though his kicking was honed by an Ipswich rugby league player named Mick Cannon.

His secondary schooling was at St Edmund's in Ipswich, but he attended the famous rugby nursery, St. Joseph's Christian Brothers school, Nudgee College, as a boarder for one year, repeating his senior year. Mark Loane was also at Nudgee at that time. Paul was a primary reason Nudgee won the GPS competition that year, a last-minute long pressure kick by him sealing the match against Brisbane Grammar. Paul received the James Baxter Memorial Prize as the most outstanding cricketer, student and footballer in the school.

Despite attending the University of Queensland, Paul went to play for that haven of the Catholics, Brothers Rugby Club, in 1972, and the under-19 team of which he and Tony Shaw were members easily won the competition and was undefeated.

The year Paul started with the Brothers Club in Brisbane coincided with one of the low-points of Wallaby rugby. On their tour of New Zealand, the Wallabies were overrun by scores of 29-6, 30-17 and 38-3. There were six tries to none in the final test, and they were tagged the 'Awful Aussies'. It was even expounded that New Zealand should dump the Aussies from their regular itinerary, and seek more tours from other countries, including the USA.

A committee in Australia under John Howard addressed the problems facing Australian rugby and drew up a list of recommendations. Inadequate coaching methods were fundamental in the brief, and a National Director of Coaching, ex-Wallaby Dick Marks, was appointed in 1974.

Crucial to Australia's revival as a rugby power was a resurgence of the game in Queensland. A multiplicity of factors aided the Queensland cause. One was a plethora of outstanding young players imbued with a missionary zeal, such as Tony Shaw, Mark Loane, Jeff and Paul McLean, Chris Handy, David Dunworth and Stan Pilecki. They were determined to restore Queensland and Australian rugby prowess.

Another vital element was the emergence of a super-coach, the genial and much-beloved Bob Templeton. He was an eager student of the game, and he was not too proud to learn at the feet of the masters, such as Welsh coaching guru Ray Williams, and key All Black coaches and players. He bled them dry in his thirst for rugby knowledge, and passed on what he had learned to these youngsters eager to show themselves on the game's wider stage.

By 1973 Paul McLean was a state reserve, vying for the five-eighth position with talented Geoff Richardson, who was to become a rare dual international in the two rugby codes.

However, Queensland centre Jim Creagh was injured, and Paul McLean was picked as five-eighth and Richardson moved to inside centre to combat a very powerful North Auckland side. Many felt that the young McLean was being fed to the lions.

In one of the greatest games seen at Ballymore, the Maroons came back from a 0-20 deficit to draw the match 24-24, with McLean kicking a dropped goal with a few minutes to go. He also kicked four goals from six attempts. He had served notice of his coolness under pressure and his enormous footballing talents. A broken jaw at the tail end of the season in a club game, however, provided an unfortunate end to a year that was fundamental to his future.

Luck turned in his favour in the 1974 season as two of his main rivals, Geoff Richardson and Russell Fairfax, signed with the professional code. At 20 years of age, Paul was selected for Australia against the redoubtable All Blacks in Sydney. Though the New Zealand team was considered 'green' by their standards, as usual they were a mighty conglomerate, with full-back Joe Karam, wingers Bryan Williams and Grant Batty, captain Andy Leslie, breakaway Ian Kirkpatrick, hooker Tane Norton and second-rower Peter Whiting being among their most notable performers.

Paul lined up against Otago's Duncan Robertson that day. Australia's hopes rested on the lineout work of Garrick Fay, the tenacity of breakaway Ray Price and the power of eighth man Mark Loane, Paul's schoolboy associate. Australia's captain was the great scrumhalf John Hipwell, while Geoff Shaw, as solid a player as ever to don the green and gold, was in the centre. Paul's brother Jeff was also in the team that day. Australia fielded five new test players. Paul's first test was Jeff's last. Jeff was not selected for the second test, then broke his leg soon afterwards and never played again.

The field was a quagmire, and only 11,000 turned out for the match. At one stage the All Blacks' captain Andy Leslie was down on his haunches sweeping water away with his arm so fullback Joe Karam could kick at goal. The final score was 11-6 in New Zealand's favour. Grant Batty was to say, after the game, that the conditions were "the worst I have ever experienced. The only time I was colder in my life was when I worked in the cold store at the freezing works during the school holidays once."

In the second test, at Ballymore, the bearded Greg Cornelsen came into the Wallaby team for his first test when it was revealed that Mark Loane had a hairline fracture of the jaw. The result of the game was a 16-all draw. Paul McLean kicked two penalties and a conversion. With seven minutes left in the game, McLean kicked ahead and fullback Laurie Monaghan kept the ball at his feet and dropped on it as it passed over the line. Paul's conversion missed the left goalpost by twelve inches, otherwise Australia would have won.

The Sydney Cricket Ground was still heavy for the decider. Australia lost 16-6, Paul McLean scoring all the points. What had been demonstrated clearly was that Australia was once again competitive. The 'Awful Aussies' tag was no longer heard. The Wallaby revival had begun, and Paul was a vital cog in that rehabilitation.

Malcolm McGregor wrote, in his biography: "By the end of 1974 Paul McLean was the toast of Queensland rugby. His playing exploits were recruiting an army of followers from a sporting public which had not had many home grown idols to fete. And they loved the aesthetic, slender twenty-year-old."

Despite such adoration in his home state, he was not selected for the 1975 home series against England, young Randwick star Ken Wright getting the nod. It is a strange fact that although he was one of the most gifted players to don the green and gold, he was forever, throughout his career, being challenged by others, universal acceptance ever elusive in his case, Ken Wright, Tony Melrose and Mark Ella in turn being selected at times ahead of him. He was often selected at fullback because of these challenges.

Paul was recalled as fullback in 1975 against Japan, and he scored a then record 21 points. In the second test he was back at five-eighth as Ken Wright was injured. It was another 18 points for Paul.

It was one of his rugby ambitions to tour the British Isles. His uncle Bill was captain of the legendary 1947-48 Wallabies. In 1975 he was selected as a member of the Sixth Wallabies. The genial Ross Turnbull was the manager and the 'blood and thunder' Dave Brockhoff the coach,

and mainly utilised Paul mainly as a fullback.

It was not a successful tour, the Wallabies being particularly outgunned in the 'tight five'. Only Ireland was defeated by the Wallabies in the internationals, Scotland, Wales and England prevailing over them. Injuries to Mark Loane, Ray Price and John Hipwell certainly did not aid their cause.

Malcolm McGregor summed up Paul's contribution: "For Paul McLean the tour marked his emergence as a player of world class. In eighteen matches he scored 154 points, the greatest ever contribution by a Wallaby tourist. His general play was consistently excellent and on some occasions, inspirational. The realisation that he was the only reliable goal kicker, and the only available fullback, placed him under intense pressure, but he handled it with a coolness and aplomb that endeared him to team mates and spectators alike. His eighteen appearances in twenty-four games afforded him almost no rest, especially as two of the games he missed were the final two. But he proved that he was both resilient and unflappable. The more demanded of him, the more he produced. That tour was the crucible in which Paul McLean's talents took positive shape. The earmarks of his game were impeccable handling, perfectly judged kicking, and an accurate football intellect."

The year 1976 saw Queensland, led by stalwarts such as Paul, Tony Shaw, Mark Loane, David Hillhouse, Andrew Slack, Paddy Batch, Stan Pilecki, Bill Ross, Chris Handy and Jim Miller, gain a clear ascendance over their southern rivals after almost 90 years of being overwhelmed themselves. The highlight for Queensland was a 42-4 victory at Ballymore over the Blues, when Paul McLean, instead of kicking penalties, put up two soaring up-and-unders which resulted in Queensland tries.

New South Wales and ACT players migrated north, and this aided the Maroon strength in Queensland's glory years. Expatriates Michael O'Connor, Geoff Shaw, Peter Horton, Greg Cornelsen and Chris Carberry were to make the greatest impact.

1976 saw the Wallabies on a difficult short tour to France and Italy, and though Paul McLean was their most consistent back the momentum of the Wallabies towards international respectability was temporarily lost through the energy-draining, overly physical games they were confronted with. The first test was narrowly lost by 18-15, but Australia was overrun in the second by 34 to 6. Bob Templeton found himself no longer Australian coach after the tour.

There was no international rugby in 1977, but McLean was honoured as the sole Australian invited to play for a World XV in South Africa. Despite unbelievable and continuous pressure from the highest levels of government in Australia, McLean went. He believed that apartheid was a social problem rather than a sporting one, and he felt sport could promote goodwill among people. He never regretted his decision. The *Australian* newspaper in 1977 declared him to be rugby union's Player of the Year.

Wales came to Australia in 1978, and there remained, among the Aussies, players still haunted by their 3-28 loss to them at Cardiff Arms Park in 1975. A new coach was appointed, Daryl Haberecht, arguably the most thoroughly prepared coach to this point in Australia's history, and he saw Tony Shaw, Paul McLean and Mark Loane as the corner-stone of his tactics, with Tony Shaw rather than Queensland captain Mark Loane as leader.

Barely recovered from a fractured thumb, Paul took his place in the first test side, despite calls from southern critics for the inclusion of Ken Wright and newcomer Tony Melrose. Paul could never shake off a bevy of aspirants from the south. Whereas the genius of cricket's Donald Bradman was never questioned when it came to selection, rugby's Bradman of the time, Paul McLean, never gained universal acceptance. He continually had to prove himself. Perhaps it was because he never courted adulation, and had a detached manner and perhaps an over-clinical approach. In some ways he represented the typical Queenslander, or even the state of Queensland, seemingly denied their dues by southern interests. There could even have been a deep religious aspect to it all, the dominant Catholicism of northern rugby on a collision course with the rampant Protestantism of the south.

Anyhow, against Wales, short of match fitness because of his injury, Paul McLean once more showed his deep competitive drive by scoring 14 of Australia's points in a bitter 18-8

victory. It was a magnificent team effort by the Wallabies, though accusations of biased refereeing and overly-jealous physicality were hurled at the Aussies.

The second test will live forever in the memory of those who personally witnessed it and countless thousands who saw the newspaper evidence, when the Welsh front rower Graham Price was forced off the field near the commencement of the match with a badly broken jaw. Steve Finnane ('The Gunfighter') was the culprit. Australia won the encounter, Paul McLean again making a magnificent contribution.

The 1978 New Zealand tour had great meaning for Australian rugby, as they were still endeavouring to remove the 'Awful Aussies' designation from the minds of fervent and patriotic All Black supporters. It was an unhappy tour for Paul personally, as in the fifth match against Manawatu he severely injured the medial ligaments of his knee. He could not take his place in the first test, his position being occupied by Ken Wright, who missed a critical last-minute kick which would have won the match for the Wallabies.

Injuries to fullback Laurie Monaghan and Roger Gould forced the selectors to rush Paul McLean into the second test, but he was merely a shadow of his normal self and was replaced after 30 minutes by Geoff Richards, and New Zealand ran out a comparatively easy winner, 22-6.

The test results were a great disappointment to the highly successful management team of Ross Turnbull and Daryl Haberecht, and Australia's difficulties seem to have been compounded by the coach's heart attack a fortnight before the final test, and Paul's inability to play. In one of the most amazing comebacks in Wallaby history, the Wallabies were triumphant by 30 to 16.

Though carrying a serious injury, McLean delayed the operation on his return to Brisbane in order to lead his beloved Brothers against Easts so that they could progress to the Grand Final. He scored a try, kicked a dropped goal, a penalty and two conversions in Brothers' 26-12 victory. He was also dominant in the Grand Final win against the Mark Loane-led University team.

In 1979 Ken Wright turned professional, but

that left Tony Melrose and an-up-and-coming genius called Mark Ella as his rivals, and McLean quickly showed where he stood in the conflict, scoring a try, five conversions and two penalty goals in a 48-10 slaughter of the Blues at Ballymore. He was, understandably, selected for the first test against Ireland. The Irish took the Aussies apart 27-12, and in the second test eked out a 9-3 victory, with Paul for once having an off day.

However, in the single test against New Zealand in 1979, Paul was selected at fullback, Tony Melrose gaining the five-eighth slot. The All Blacks had not lost a single test in Australia since 1934, a game in which his uncle Doug McLean had participated. The Wallabies won the single test 12-6. There were no tries in the game, Paul kicking nine of Australia's 12 points. The Bledisloe Cup was, thus, won by Australia for the second time in its 48-year history. The other win was in New Zealand in 1949, with 30 of New Zealand's best players in South Africa.

Who can ever forget this moment of triumph, as 15 frenetic Wallabies did a lap of honour around the Sydney Cricket Ground brandishing the Bledisloe Cup for all the world to see. It was another milestone to add to the legend surrounding Paul McLean.

The year was not over, however, as the Wallabies, led by Mark Loane, flew off on a tour of Argentina. Despite a dislocated scaphoid bone in his wrist McLean played in the tests, though Australia was outgunned in the first. He kicked a 45 metre penalty goal to assure a Wallaby victory in the second.

With Tony Melrose's defection to league, it appeared as if 1980 would be the climax of Paul's career. It *was* in one sense, as he was elevated to the Queensland and Australian captaincy, taking the Wallabies to Fiji for a successful four-match tour, including one test. However, the Ella boys were the rage of Sydney. Michael Hawker was, despite this, selected as five-eighth, and even Paul's position at fullback was under threat from Glen Ella. Mark Ella rode the bench during this time.

Paul's captaincy was short-lived, as he injured his left knee in a club game, and was unable to play against the All Blacks in their three-test tour. At 26 years of age it appeared as if his test run might be over, though he was

a key figure in Queensland's defeat of the All Blacks by 9 to 3. It was sufficient for him to force his way on to the Wallaby bench for the third test, but that was as far as he got in reinstating his claims to international representation. The year ended with major surgery to his knee.

Paul refused to give up despite the adversities that had come his way, and was back at it in 1981 testing out his leg. Victories over Sydney and NSW reinforced his claims and he was selected as five-eighth against France. He left his kicking shoes at home in the first test, goaling only once in seven attempts at, of all places, Ballymore, the scene of so many of his triumphs. In a career rarity, he was replaced as kicker during the game by Geoff Richards.

Australia won the first test narrowly, 17 to 15, but with Paul as fullback and his boot behaving normally, Australia romped home 24-14 in the second test. Paul's contribution was 16 of the 24 points.

When the Wallaby team departed for the UK in 1981-1982, the pundits felt that it was the best team to leave Australian shores, and a Grand Slam was even predicted. It was not to be. Though he topped the scoring with 118 points, Paul's kicking prowess deserted him in the four tests. Inexplicably, he kicked only seven goals in 23 attempts. He was selected as five-eighth ahead of Mark Ella against Ireland and Wales, inside centre against Scotland and fullback against England. The Wallabies' only victory was against Ireland. It was a shattering experience for Paul, whose kicking touch deserted him. There was also undue pressure put on him by pressmen such as Evan Whitton and David Lord, and adding fuel to the fire was the old chestnut of Queensland-NSW rivalries splitting the team.

It has been said that it is no disgrace to fall down, but it is if you stay down. Paul McLean, for the umpteenth time in his career, came back in 1982. Queensland recorded two great wins against New South Wales, with Paul McLean masterminding the victories.

As mentioned earlier, he and Roger Gould were dropped from the first test against Scotland at Ballymore by new national coach Bob Dwyer. His reinstatement in the second test, his announced retirement before the test, and his fantastic farewell performance will ever be the stuff that legends are made of.

Paul McLean, one of the greatest players ever to don the green and gold, displayed for all to see that he was a thoroughbred all the way. Often maligned, he overcame shocking injuries and divided support throughout his career to always give his all for his country. His remarkable hands, his unerring boot and his remarkable courage, pride and personal standards set standards rarely achieved in the long history of Australian rugby.

Bret Harris said of him in *The Marauding Maroons: The Rise of Queensland Rugby*: "Of all the Maroons, McLean was the most naturally gifted. His powers were subtle and precise. He controlled a football with the same magical expertise a Harlem Globetrotter manipulates a basketball. He can receive the most untidy service from his halfback and, without even rearranging the ball's position in his hands, stitch the sideline with uncanny accuracy. McLean is unflappable under pressure. His icy-cool exterior is legendary and he rarely makes a mistake. He possesses a ruthless eye for opposition weaknesses and is able to read a game better than any of his contemporaries."

# Herbert H. Moran

**P**addy Moran was the captain of the Wallabies in 1908, the first team to leave Australian shores to tour the British Isles. They were called the First Wallabies, and the custom until recent years was that you were not a Wallaby until you made a trip "home", as it was affectionately called.

Twenty-nine players embarked on that historic sea voyage, but severe injuries forced Australia to send two replacements. The mystery of the appellation the "Wallabies" is explained in Moran's partial autobiography, *Viewless Minds*: "When we arrived in Plymouth a pack of journalists fell upon us. They were very anxious to give us some distinctive name, but their first suggestion of Rabbits we indignantly rejected. It really was going a little bit too far to palm off on us the name of a pest their ancestors had foisted on our country! Ultimately we became the Wallabies, although we wore for an emblem on our jerseys not the figure of this marsupial but the floral design of a waratah. Our new name some of the local Devon people could not pronounce correctly, but then around Newton Abbot, which we made our headquarters, there were local inhabitants who were frankly surprised to find that we were white and that we spoke a colourable imitation of the King's (East End) speech!"

Future generations of Wallabies must breathe a sigh of relief that the Rabbits nickname never stuck. Apart from the fact that it was an important pest, its sexual proclivity is well known, and would have been hard even for rugby tourists to live up to.

As a medico, Dr Moran gave his charges two lectures on the way over on the dangers of venereal disease, and at a crucial time produced some very chilling photographs from Fournier's work on syphilis. Moran was pleased to report that his warning was heeded, as not one of the 31 players contracted VD, whereas to his knowledge there were other "touring sides which have had to lament, in private, their venereal losses."

What has passed into history is the fact that the Australian Rugby Union instructed the team, for box-office purposes, to give a war-cry before each game. It was similar to the New Zealand haka.

The following presents for the first time that infamous haka. It has never to this point been published.

War Cry taken from La Perouse Camp - the Native greeting to strangers in peace.

Gau-Gau x (     ) Wir-r-r
Win-nang-a-lang-nur
Mui-an-yal-ling,
Bu-rang-a-lang-yang,
Yai! Yah! Gun-Yib lang-yang, Yai!
x (     ) <u>Name of club or team playing</u>
against to be given.

**Definitions:**
Gau     -'Hullo' or form of salutation.

Wir-r-r    - A sign of defiance.
Second line - You are great men.
Third line  - We are glad to meet you.
Fourth line - Come on, and may the big or
                 better man win.
Fifth line   - Come!

**Instructions:**
1. Slapping the thigh three times to begin together.
2. Putting left foot forward and throwing out left hand, holding right by side.
3. Hands at breast and at the word (Gau) hands to be stretched palms down.
4. Hands up at full extent.
5. Hands in front at full extent, and at the word (Yang) dropped to side with force.
6. Left hand at full extent raised from front to right rear over shoulder finishing at the word (Yah) facing your right then from a stooping attitude one long sustained "Coo-ee" sustained whilst making a complete circle from left to right.

Moran thought the whole thing was an indignity. His views were forcefully put: "I refused to lead the wretched caricature of a native corroboree, and regularly hid myself among the team, a conscientious objector. None of the men liked it. The average Australian has a keen sense of the ridiculous and dislikes acting in a burlesque or wearing any strange regalia. They might just as reasonably have expected us to wear the broad arrow on our left arms as a respectful tribute to our first families. As it was, we performed shamefacedly some grotesque antics before crowds that were patently not interested in the indifferent show."

Fortunately the war-cry custom did not prevail, though many players feel the New Zealand haka puts them at a definite psychological advantage.

Paddy came from very modest circumstances. His mother was Annie Quain of Irish parents from Limerick. She was deeply religious, and died quite young in 1890, leaving four children, Paddy being the third. His father was born at Ballinahown near Athlone, Ireland, in 1856, and came to Sydney when 20 years of age. He began work in a bakery business, which was ultimately very successful.

Paddy attended, first of all, Darlington Superior Public School. All pupils had to pay threepence a week in fees, and each Monday morning the roll was called and each young lad had to dutifully produce the money or publicly state why. It was a school world which the young Paddy did not enjoy, with filthy expressions and low conversation the order of the day.

He went to St. Aloysius' School in Surrey Hills, another rough Sydney area, where there were street gangs aplenty. Alcoholism, violence and abject poverty were common. Catholics, in particular, were disdained.

There was no opportunity to play organised sport at school, so when he went to University at 15 years of age he had not played a formal game of cricket and only two at rugby. It was not until his third year at University that this introspective young man was niggled into playing a nondescript game for the Rosebay Football club. He hastily made cut-down trousers and his own boots, hammering in bars at the front and sprigs at the back of an old pair. Training was a preliminary run down the field before the game began.

He ended his first year by being awarded a special honour cap for forward play. His laconic father - were all fathers like this in the old days? - remarked simply on hearing the news that the others must have been a 'damn poor lot'.

Next year he was invited to play for the University second team, and he was chosen as a front row forward in a representative team to tour the lower Northern Rivers in NSW. He was 19 at the time, and one incident in particular amused him.

One of his team mates, Bill, always drank five or six pints of beer before playing, believing that it improved his vigour and speed, and during a ruck emerged with the ball and ran eighty yards before diving across the goal-line for a glorious try - over his *own* line!

At the post-mortem, poor Bill justified his mistake by saying "the jerseys of the two sides were very alike", but this did not fully explain Bill ignoring the frantic calls of his fullback, "Billy, you silly b—!" Perhaps the five or six pints taken before his game might have been offered as an excuse, but this was never considered by the aforementioned Bill.

At the next country town the Mayor addressed the team. After the normal bonds of

Empire speech and reference to the town's performance at the last Butter Show, he went on eloquently: "'You may beat us', he said, in an eloquent and moving peroration, 'you may beat our country lads *tomorrow* '(and he emphasised *tomorrow* (cheers)' but from what I hears of your doin's down at Taree, the day will come when on this ground, and beside this river, we'll be beatin' you city fellows with your own prodigy' (prolonged applause). Clayton (one of the players), who as befits a lawyer could always interpret the mind of a deponent, said that he meant this last word for progeny."

The next year he was in the University first team and won his 'blue'. Moran observed that at this higher level none of the refinements of sportsmanship was followed but the game was not without its chivalries. There were, he stressed, two absolute commandments on which players were judged and condemned: "Thou shalt not squib it," and "Thou shalt not squeal."

In 1906 he was selected in the NSW team to play Queensland - he was now a breakaway or eighth man. There were three games, and he had his nose broken in the second encounter.

Upon graduation from University he took up an appointment at a hospital in Newcastle. The hospital refused to release him to tour Queensland with the state team, but he captained a Newcastle side in 1908 which beat a strong Metropolitan side at the Sydney Cricket Ground. This doubtless vaulted him into the Australian captaincy for the 1908 tour, at a mere 23 years of age.

These were the days of real amateurs, and the players on tour received three shillings a day. It was called 'wine money'. Forty years later, in 1947-48, the Wallabies received five shillings a day, with millions of pounds profit being made. Scotland and Ireland, in 1908, refused to give the Wallabies games, feeling that the acceptance of three shillings a day was evidence of professionalism. How the game has changed, and how limited was the vision of those in executive positions in the early years.

The team in England was subjected to a merciless press which complained continually about the rough play of the Australians, many asserting in public and private that their conduct was related to their convict ancestry. The patriotism of the team lessened under the continuing barrage, and it is of interest that only seven of the thirty-one players took part in the First World War.

The simple fact, however, is that this first Australian team was not primarily comprised of private-school types or university men, but rather they were in the main men of the working class who saw hard play as the basis of the game. They were all tough men, many the products of the slums of Sydney, where a knuckleduster boosted inadequate courage and yet 'king hits' were frowned upon. For most of the Wallabies the credo was 'take no prisoners,' the playing field most certainly being a battle ground where superior intestinal fortitude won the day.

The Wallabies of 1908 had a mascot, which the great all-round athlete Bob ('Boneta') Craig smuggled into England: a carpet snake nicknamed 'Bertie'. It died on the day of the Wallabies' first match of the tour against Devon. Peter Flanagan opined that it caught a cold from an Irish breeze. Many thought its death was a bad omen, as Peter Burge broke his leg in the match. There were no substitutes in those days, and the Wallabies won despite playing with only fourteen players.

Then in the third match the Queenslander Flanagan, who was acting as a linesman, had his leg broken when the great Wallaby winger 'Boxer' Russell crashed into him. Cec Murnin had caught a severe chill in the Red Sea on the way over and he had been sent home from Naples. So the team was three short, and two replacements had to be sent from Australia, forwards 'Son' Burge and Ken Gavin.

Another kind of misfortune followed them, in that the robust play that it was alleged they were engaged in resulted in three of the team getting their marching orders, a rarity in this time period. Sid Middleton was ordered off for striking a player in the Oxford match; A.B. Burge was sent off at Cardiff for deliberately kicking a player, and was hooted all the way to the dressing room; and Tom Griffin was dismissed against Swansea for a repetition of rough play.

Hamish Stuart, writing for the *Daily Chronicle*, exemplified those who put a literary boot into the Wallabies, and it is no wonder that the Australians were incensed: "The fact that the Australian player suffers alike from the lack of a conscientious education and the debasing effect of an unconscionable [sic] system of tuition, must make one lenient towards his failings, which are not those of nature but have been acquired in a bad school." Such arrogance was continued, stating that "custom and the national idea have so blunted their moral sense that they are sublimely unconscious of their delinquencies, and are sincerely surprised when accused of unfair practices."

When the team played their first match against Wales, Moran noted: "In the front row was Barnett of English ancestry, then Griffin of Welsh-Irish and Hammond of Scottish origin. In the second rank, there were Burge of Anglo-German stock and Pat McCue, Irish of the Irish. In the last row there were Craig, proud of his Caledonian forbears [sic], Richards of Welsh blood, and myself who locked them was of Irish descent. We all felt a sentimental attachment for the lands of our fathers, but none thought of himself as anything but Australian."

The general feeling among the Wallabies was that an Englishman loves winning, but was "petulant in defeat", and the Australians were no better or worse in their behaviour than their opponents.

It is of considerable relevance that the professional Kangaroos were in England at the same time as the Wallabies, and their tour was a complete disaster. They played 46 games, losing 22, drawing 6 and winning a mere 18. This was in stark contrast to the Wallabies, who played 31 games, winning 25, drawing one and losing only five. They scored 633 points to their opponents' 164. In the two internationals played they beat England 9-3 but lost to Wales 6-9.

The Kangaroos lost money on their tour, while the Wallabies did not. Professional rugby was in 1908 in a tenuous state, with spectator support dwindling. At the end of the 1909 season, fourteen of the 1908 team defected to rugby league and, from that moment on, rugby union lost in the popularity stakes. The heart of the Wallaby team was ripped from its body. The defectors were most of the outstanding players: Bill Dix, 'Boxer' Russell, 'Macker' McCabe, Eddie Mandible, Chris McKivatt, 'Daisy' McIntyre, Jack Barnett, Paddy McCue, Peter Burge, Bob ('Boneta') Craig, Charlie McMurtrie, 'Darb' Hickey, Ken Gavin, and 'Son' Burge.

The loss was even greater as the captain stayed in Scotland to take up a Fellowship, and Australia's most brilliant forward, Tom ('Rusty') Richards, went back to mining, and then in 1910 went to South Africa.

One highlight of the Wallaby tour of 1908 was winning the gold medal at the 1908 London Olympic Games. Rugby was introduced to the Olympic Games in Paris in 1900, and France was victorious over Germany 25-16. In 1904, there was no rugby at the Olympics, but it returned on the Olympic calendar in 1908. However, there were only two teams, Australia and England, and in actuality England was represented by a club team, Cornwall, the previous year's county champion. The Wallabies had already defeated Cornwall 18 to 5, and won the gold medal 32 to 3.

The fifteen gold medallists were Jack Barnett, Phil Carmichael, Bob Craig, Dan Carroll, Tom Griffin, 'Darb' Hickey, Malcolm McArther, 'Macker' McCabe, 'Paddy' McCue, Chris McKivatt, Charlie McMurtrie, Syd Middleton, 'Rusty' Richards, 'Boxer' Russell and Frank Bede Smith. Neither the captain, Moran, who was injured, nor Fred Wood, the vice-captain, played in the match.

Paddy Moran did not look very much like a rugby player, rather he resembled an Oxford don. Scholarly and reflective, he put sport into a perspective that few famous players do. As he said himself, he "disliked getting too far involved in a life of athleticism", and he declined to play after the tour. He deliberately went to Edinburgh instead of London for his Fellowship, so that he would not be beguiled by sporting attractions.

He was a fierce tackler and an aggressive player, but above all a leader of men and an idealistic sportsman. During his career he played only one test for Australia against Wales. He badly wanted to play against England, but withdrew of his own volition as he was having problems with his Achilles tendon. That was the kind of man he was. In fact, though captain, he always left the selection room when his own name was discussed.

Though he turned his back on the game to concentrate on medicine, he recognised its value and nostalgia: "For Rugby is a great game, not ending with the blown whistle. Years after we see again the rift in the opposing defences. We get ready to break through with a sudden flash of speed. Long after the events we still stretch ourselves full length barely to reach the heels of a flying threequarter, drag them to ourselves and him to the ground. We leap once more, higher than the others on a long lineout, gather the ball on our finger-tips, marvellously, and head the rush onward. We sink at the feet of dribbling forwards and gather the ball as the attacking force tumbles pell-mell upon us; the situation is saved! We feel the joyous rapture of massed forwards taking it on in a fierce irruption, or of centre-threes swerving through and just reaching the white line as they hit the green turf. The earth trembles, but a try has been scored."

Moran wrote three books and numerous medical articles, cancer being his specialty. His first book was *Viewless Winds*, which is autobiographical and deals with his early years, and rugby is but one of nine chapters: *Beyond The Hill Lies China*, which is a fictionalised biography; and *In My Fashion*, which deals with his last ten years.

The books reveal an introspective, well-read man. After obtaining his fellowship at Edinburgh he went to the London Hospital for post-graduate work, and returned to Sydney at the end of 1910. He worked at the only teaching hospital, Prince Alfred, and set up his first private practice in an industrial, working class suburb. The practice started slowly but soon built up, but the intervention of the First World War had him sailing to London to offer his services, and soon he was a lieutenant in the RAMC at Aldershot. Boredom became action as he was sent to Gallipoli and surrounding areas to succour the injured. Amoebic dysentery followed, but after recovery he was off to Mesopotamia, and with further illness there he was repatriated to India, and thence to Australia.

More and more he became interested in cancer, and three years after the war, went to Paris to study the use of radium, and went from there to the United States, searching for the latest on the dreaded disease. He was not your normal surgeon, or normal man. He was a true pioneer. He was the first medical practitioner in Australia to use radium needles or radium tubes in the treatment of cancer. He went to France again in 1926 working at the Cancer Clinic at Villejeuf. His persistence and stubbornness accelerated the adoption of new techniques in Australia.

Perhaps too introverted and intellectual for his own good, he retired in 1935 from medical practice, a mere 50 years of age. He had become disillusioned with many in his profession, inertia in his own country, anti-Irish sentiment, and inroads into standards within Catholicism. He said, simply: "I could not find peace."

He turned once more to Europe, searching for a new vision, where there was hope for mankind. He roamed through France, Italy, Germany and England, pursued by phantoms within his own mind. He had a premonition of impending doom and was of course correct, as the Second World War engulfed everyone.

He came under the spell of Italy and became fluent in the language, and in fact had done much to initiate the teaching of Italian in Australia at the University level. He had four audiences with Mussolini, and for a time might have been under his influence. He acted as a one-man legation to England to argue for continued good relations between the two countries, despite the invasion of Abyssinia. Moran even got permission to go to Abyssinia in 1936 as a freelance doctor.

Eventually he became disillusioned with Rome and went to live elsewhere in Europe, staying there for a year to learn German. So this was certainly an uncommon rugby player, fluent in French, Italian and German.

He went back to Australia in November 1937, arriving the day of the Melbourne Cup, and when he stated the world would be at war again he was ignored.

He returned to Rome, then went to Paris, and was at Antwerp when war broke out. He immediately went to England to volunteer his services, and again became a medical officer with the rank of full lieutenant in the British Forces, but was transferred at his own request to the Australian Military Forces. He became a lieutenant-colonel; but he never lost his hyper-critical manner, being a "traditionalist, by temperament and faith", and his three books reinforce his belief in the fallibility of members of his own profession.

In February 1945 he noticed the deteriorating irregular shape of a mole on his own stomach, and decided to have the growth excised. Like so many cases he treated in his own lifetime, he also was doomed, and in the last pages of his third book, *In My Fashion*, he details his last days. Despite all his knowledge, he decided: "There was nothing to do but carry on."

He was released from the Army on April 14, 1945, now being racked with pain. In May 1945 the war in Europe ended. He died on November 20,1945, in the Hope House Nursing Home, Cambridge.

His last words are a reflection of the man: "But the call has sounded and I must go. I must go forth after the long wander of my faith, into the darkness. Into the darkness and beyond, hesitant still a little.

"Suddenly a road pierces the dark uncertainty of my doubt; and I see the way bright and clear before me. The air is gentle to the listening trees which bird-song perfumes. And so, with joyous step, submissive to the Will, I take the road."

# Stan Pilecki

*S tan Pilecki was the most typical Queenslander in the state team. Pilecki was hard and tough. Straightforward both on and off the field, there was nothing pretentious about Pilecki's character. He was the salt of the earth. Easy going and casual, nothing ruffled Pilecki's feathers.*
**– Bret Harris, The Marauding Maroons.**

Stan Pilecki is the stuff of which legends are made, and the difficulty in summarising his life and rugby career is to separate the myth from the reality. Players actually and continually elucidate different versions of the same event, all with verve and confidence. Wingers can recall exactly what Stan said as he packed down against the Welsh front row, though Stan himself in unclear about what actually happened. As in Boswell's diary of Samuel Johnson, the Pilecki scribes have recorded his heroics with equally loving pens.

He is a man universally beloved. Much has to do with his own personality, where he is perceived as honest and unpretentious, but it has also to do with the way he played. He somehow epitomised the average player, though he was obviously more than that. He was unspectacular, a vital cog in the engine room, unsung and unheralded. He was the stoker, the toiler, the labourer, the man who dirtied his hands while many of the others pranced and danced. To many he represents the rock on which the very game is built.

In his testimonial in 1995 before 300 supplicants, superlative MC and ex-Wallaby Dick Marks said that everyone could go home and say with complete honesty they were not the ugliest man in the room, an amusing aside related to Stan's rugged visage. One time, when the Wallabies were at Fisherman's Wharf in San Francisco, they went into a novelty store, where there were false noses, moustaches, beards and so on. As they were leaving the store, a sales lady ran up to Stan and exclaimed: "You've got to pay for those ears, sir!"

Known as 'the Pole' because of his Polish heritage, Stanislaus Pilecki was born in Augustdorf, Germany, in 1947, the eldest of three children. Part of his mythology is that he was actually quarried and not born normally, and second that he was 38 pounds at birth. Trying to survive as a Pole in post-war Germany was not easy, and the family migrated happily to Queensland when he was three years of age.

Before the mythology overtakes the reality, a few facts need to be presented as a framework and to put a proper perspective to this biography. First, Stan was the first of Polish descent to play rugby union for Australia. Second, in an era when some of Australia's greatest players were at the forefront, he was the first Queenslander in the state's history to attain 100 state caps, and in total achieved 122. Third, he played 221 A grade games for Wests, and was the first Wallaby ever from that club, as well as the first from his school, Marist Brothers College at Rosalie. Fourth, he played 18 tests for his adopted country.

His first contact with his beloved Wests was in 1961 when he was on the Under 15 Rosalie Marist Brothers team, and international Paul Mooney recounted that the game could not be started because of the absence of one of the Rosalie front rowers, Stanislaus Pilecki, who arrived later on a bike, smoking a cigarette. When the coach objected to this new arrival smoking, one of the players allegedly said: "That's all right. It's Stan. He was engaged when he was six."

Still a youngster, though well in advance of his age group, he was reportedly at a function at Lane Cove National Park, and he and his life-long friend Bill Cusack were seen sitting on a log sobbing. One player came up and said: "What's wrong, Stan?"

"Ah," he replied, "they told us to piss off from behind the bar."

In 1956 at 18 years of age he joined Wests, his school days forever behind him, and played a game against Toowoomba. He drew plaudits because though the battle was lost, the war was won. Then began one of the most enduring legends about 'Stan the Man'. He received a very severe cut to the head, and it was long and vicious. To the astonishment of all, there was no blood, just some white material oozing from his head. This oddity was reported on by many believers during his career, including that worthy medico and opthalmologist, Dr Mark Loane. He did not bleed like a normal human being, it was held.

Stan then worked on the oil rigs, a vocation that toughened up an already hardened body.

Stan was in second grade in 1966, and first grade in 1967, his initial entry into the 'big-time' in firsts being on 27 May 1967. The front row consisted of Stan and John Ryan as props, and Lyn Crowley as hooker. Each was to make a significant contribution to Queensland rugby. Lyn Crowley was a selector who rose to the highly successful management committee of the QRU in 1975, his aggressive management and marketing style being in the 'take no prisoners' mould. He became locally famous for his newspaper inserts, such as 'Come to Ballymore and Boo a Blue'. According to Crowley, Stan was "the definitive front row forward". Ryan,

whose father was a distinguished rugby league international, became the long-serving and highly respected manager of Queensland teams during the hey-days of their renaissance.

It was difficult to maintain club morale in those days, when rugby was absolutely and emphatically dominated by two clubs, Brothers and University, with all others well distant also-rans. Rugby owed much to the Crowleys and Ryans, and more particularly Stan, who chose non-fashionable clubs and were their rallying points.

Stan played on for Wests until 1986, and thereafter served various functions in the club, including coaching the lower grades.

He departed for Rockhampton in 1973-74, working as Central Queensland Building estimator for K.D. Morris and Sons. While in 'Rocky' he played for the Pioneers. He had in actuality given up on playing for Queensland again, as he had made the Queensland team in 1970 and was only a reserve in 1971. He got a new lease of life after playing country rugby, and on his return played with Wests again. He was awarded a Life Membership at Wests in 1978.

Stan's first State game was on 10 June 1970, versus Mid-Canterbury. It is interesting to view the Maroon players that day: Lloyd Graham, Jeff McLean, Ken Donald, Alex Pope, Peter Lewis, Rob Mackay; Mick Barry (v.c.), Bob Wood, Jules Guerassimoff (c), Stewart Gregory, Keith Bell, Stan Pilecki, Mick Freney, Bruce Brown.

As Bret Harris put it, Stan became "the reluctant enforcer". Andrew Slack, with tongue in cheek, said he was "a fringe dweller, quintessential rank and file". His ambling and fearful visage, his drooping moustache and ears like dinner plates, endeared him to Ballymore fans. He resembled one of the 'old school' players, not one of the private school types. He was a man's man all the way.

His first test was a long time in coming, against Wales in the first test in 1978. He was 29 years of age. The Wallaby team was: Laurie Monaghan; Phil Crowe; Andrew Slack; Martin Knight; Paddy Batch; Paul McLean (v.c.); Rod Hauser; Mark Loane; Tony Shaw (c); Greg Cornelsen; Garrick Fay; David Hillhouse; Stan Pilecki; Peter Horton; Steve Finnane.

Stan was up against one of the best in the

world in his baptism by fire, the renowned Graham Price, who would talk incessantly throughout a game. Tony Shaw said that "Stan saw parts of his anatomy he didn't realise he had that day". Price was not going to give 'the Pole' an easy time, and said cheekily to him: "How's that snow on your backside?" As 'Stan the Man' caught on to Price's tactics, captain Shaw said to Price: "The snow's starting to melt."

For all that, after the game he was asked by fellow prop Roy Prosser how he played, and Stan said: "Under an assumed name." The fact is, however, he was selected for the second test.

Stan's partner in the front row was the notorious Steve ('Sort 'em Out') Finnane, a barrister who believed in equal rights, an eye for an eye and a tooth for a tooth. He was also called 'the Gunfighter', as every time he knocked someone out he added a notch to his belt. In one game he threw his lethal right at Stan, who did not even blink, and in fact said laconically: "You've got to do better than that, son."

Anyhow, in the second test, the loquacious Welshman, Price, said to Steve: "It's going to be a long day for you, Finnane."

'The Gunfighter' replied: "Not for you, mate." In the first five minutes of the game Price left the field with a badly smashed jaw. It may have created a rugby story for later generations to recall, but it was an unhappy day for Australian rugby.

Stan Pilecki's first overseas rugby trip was with Queensland to New Zealand in 1970. It remains his favourite country to tour, Stan feeling an affinity for the New Zealand forwards who likewise toiled away in the engine room. Stan was a typical front rower, always critical of backs, terms such as "useless", "hopeless", "always dropping the bloody ball" and so on emanating from his lips. In reflection, however, he said: "I must however admit I didn't see much of what they were doing because I always had my head up somebody's bum!"

He and coach Bob Templeton, the 'Friar Tuck' of Australian Rugby, were soul mates. It was alleged by one Wallaby that it was because "they were both such ugly pricks", though it is reportedly a fact that Tempo would look at Stan, laugh and then cry. It has been said that this abnormality has been reciprocated.

These Queensland ventures into the daunting hell-fire of New Zealand rugby did much to strengthen the capabilities and resolve of the Maroons, and were repeated by Stan in 1976, 1977, 1979, 1980 and 1981. On the 1980 visit the three horse lovers, Andrew Slack, Paul McLean and Stan, went along to a stud farm. They were accompanied by an unnamed (female) member of the Royal Family, who insisted that she witness a mating scene, though it was not the 'season'.

The stallion took up a certain erotic stance, and the Royal asked: "Why is he doing that?"

The studmaster replied patiently: "He is demonstrating his masculinity."

Then the mare was teased, and the Royal queried again: "Why are they doing that?"

"The mare needs to be stimulated, ma'am."

Then the stallion sniffed the mare's vital parts.

The inevitable question came: "Why is he doing that?"

This was too much for the Queenslanders, and an unnamed guttural voice exclaimed: "Because he hasn't got any fingers, you stupid bitch!"

One of the finest and most ambitious of the Queensland junkets was to Japan, British Columbia and California in 1978. In the first game, against Japan B at Chichibu Stadium, Stan had to be taken off with a medial ligament injury through a 'kamikaze tackle' and did not play again on tour. Mark Loane, the resident medico, called the 'kiss of death' by his team mates because he always had them go off after his examination, told Stan that he should retire, as he would be putting his team in a quandary. Despite Mark asserting that Stan thought a quandary was where you cooked potatoes, Stan left the field.

They decided to send Stan to an acupuncturist, who declared that Stan's leg was calling out in pain. "In Japanese or English?" asked Stan. Originally they tried to put the acupuncture needles in his ears, but gave up on that.

His first rugby tour overseas with the Wallabies was to New Zealand, in 1978. There were some illustrious 'new boys' in the team as well as Stan: Peter McLean, Steve Streeter, Peter Carson, Roger Gould, Chris Handy, Martin

Knight, Brendan Moon, Rob Onus, Bill Ross and Andrew Slack. It was the first tour since the 1972 mob had been tagged as the 'Awful Aussies'. The manager of the team was Ross Turnbull and the coach Daryl Haberecht.

Stan's idea of coaching and that of the various coaches who have endeavoured to fit him into the normal mould have at times been in conflict. Haberecht was considered way ahead of his time in his business-like and analytical approach to the game, and was an advocate, with 'Tempo', of the three P's: Position, Possession and Pace. It is said Stan had a different advocacy: Piss, Physios and Parties.

The legend of Stan the roommate originated on this tour. Stan was a prolific smoker, a poor sleeper and renowned snorer, and team mates would wait with bated breath as room assignments were made, all hoping upon hope that they would not be landed with 'the Pole'. He would be scratching around at night lighting fags and polluting the air, and would be up walking around incessantly. He was way ahead in the voting for the 'Worst Wallaby roommate in history'.

Stan played the first two tests on tour, lining up with John Meadows and that aggressive expatriate Peter Horton. His antagonists were among the all-time greats of New Zealand rugby, Gary Knight, Andy Dalton and John Ashworth. In the first test it must be said that 'Stan the Man' threw a haymaker in the lineout in the second half after taking an elbow from 'Filthy Frank' Oliver, and the resultant kick made it 13-12 for the All Blacks. It was the last scoring in the match, though Ken Wright could have won it but his last-minute penalty was wide of the posts. The second test was a clear-cut All Black victory by a score of 22-6.

Chris Handy replaced Stan in the final match. This was the match won by Australia 30 to 16, in an astonishing form reversal. If it were horse racing the stewards would have called for the swab. It was doubly sensational as coach Haberecht was in hospital with a heart attack, and the team coached itself.

Stan, Peter Horton and Chris Handy were in the engine room against Gary Knight, John Black and Billy Bush for the next year's one-off test in Sydney, won gloriously by the Wallabies 12 to 6. This victory gave Australia the Bledisloe Cup, for only the second time in its history, the previous time being 1949, with 30 of New Zealand's best players touring South Africa. The nature of the Bledisloe Cup changed as an international television audience watched as the 'Upstart Aussies' ran around the Sydney Cricket Ground with the Cup in hand.

In 1978 Australia went on their first tour of Argentina, and Stan was selected as a reserve No.8, of all things, for a match against a Mendoza XV. It was certainly not a game of any consequence, but the thing about legends is they do not discriminate with respect to time or place, and another 'Stan the Man' legend was in the making. There was no dressing shed at the ground, and the team changed in the bus.

During the game our unlikely reserve No.8 was sitting on the Wallaby bench, smoking a fag in his irrepressible way. Mark Loane went down and explained to all and sundry that he had torn his adductor muscle and would have to go off. Though no one on the team had ever heard of an adductor muscle, they realised the seriousness of the matter.

Distraught coach Bob Templeton ran towards the bench and signalled Stan to get on the field.

"I'll be on when I'm ready," said Stan.

"Well at least bloody well warm up," growled Tempo.

"What do you think this is?" replied Stan, talking a quick pull of his cig.

There is even a version of this anecdote that has Stan putting the lit cigarette in the pocket of his shorts as he ran on the field. The cigarette incident is one of the classic Pilecki stories.

In 1980 the All Blacks were back in Australia for a three-test series. Stan played the first two tests. Incredibly Australia won the initial match 13 to 9, which meant the Wallabies had won three in a row over the vaunted All Blacks.

It was a fiery clash, and Stu Wilson reflected on his own poor choice in *Ebony and Ivory:* "If we're going to talk about Aussies, let's get it straight. Stan Pilecki is a prop built, as they say, like a concrete crapper. His head does not, as normal heads do, sit on a neck. It squats between his shoulder blades. Normally I would not hit Stan Pilecki if he was bound in chains, hoisted 10 feet into the air and he had a spiked sledge hammer in my hands. That's the way I feel about Stan the Man.

"It was sheer irrational patriotism and unbridled insanity which led me to whack him at the Sydney Cricket Ground on June 21, 1980. Young Hika Reid, a delicate boy, and Stan were having an exchange of pleasantries, very physical pleasantries, and I sensed Stan was rather overdoing it. As he was engaged and not especially interested in my movements I thought I was safe to strike a blow for Maoridom. So with my famous quickness off the mark I was at his side with the speed of light.

"I swung the big one, just as Stan turned his back on me. It was a poor punch, anyway. My fist was loose and wrist was limp. The back of Stan's head was cast iron. I felt the finger snap. It put me out of the Australian tour except for a humiliating comeback against Queensland."

The second test was narrowly won by the All Blacks, who are merciless on the enemy after a defeat. A fantastic Hika Reid try sealed the Aussies' doom. Two youngsters were picked for the final test in the front row, Declan ('Deckchair') Curran and the 19-year-old Tony D'Arcy. Influenced perhaps by a debilitating bout of food poisoning on the eve of the all-important test, the All Blacks lost 10-26, and Australia had its second Bledisloe Cup in a row.

In 1981-82 the Wallabies, under captain Tony Shaw and coach Bob Templeton, went to the British Isles. It was not a successful tour in terms of international successes, only Ireland succumbing to the Aussies.

While in London the team went for a run from their headquarters, the Britain Hotel, and Stan, not noted among the world's best trainers, indeed generally held to be among the world's worst, slipped further and further behind. The team arrived back at the hotel, minus 'Stan the Man'.

After the team had changed, a taxi drove up, and there was Stan in the back, smoking a cigarette. He had got lost, prevailed upon a taxi driver to take him to the hotel, and on the way bummed money off him to buy a packet of cigs.

During the tour it was suggested that Stan go to the West End to see some theatre. Stan rather indignantly declined: "I've got no interest in seeing 'My Fair F- Lady!'" That ended the discussion.

In 1982 Bob Dwyer displaced the amiable Templeton as Wallaby coach, and ten of the Wallabies, nine from Queensland, withdrew from consideration from the New Zealand touring party. Though players are tight-lipped as to their real reasons, Dwyer believes to this day that dropping Paul McLean and Roger Gould from the first test against Scotland was the crucial factor. Stan, however, did tour as a replacement player, though he played no tests.

His last test was in 1983, when he was recalled for the single test against the All Blacks. It was the 'battle of the geriatrics', with John Meadows and Stan going against All Black veterans Gary Knight and John Ashworth. His last test was an 8-18 loss, though the Wallabies scored two ties to one, the boot of Allan Hewson doing the damage.

Incredibly, Stan won his way back in 1984 as a member of the Grand Slam team. Enrique Rodriguez, Cameron Lillicrap and Andy McIntyre were his principal rivals for a test position, and he resigned himself towards playing for the 'dirt-tacklers', or 'dirties', as the midweek, non-test team is colloquially called. It is tough being a real team man in such circumstances, it takes a special form of courage and commitment, and Stan played his part dutifully, being a veritable father figure among the Wallaby contingent.

Mark Ella and Terry Smith, in *Path To Victory:* said: "When Stan Pilecki was picked for his sixth Wallaby tour at the venerable age of 37, he remarked with touching grace: 'I didn't know the selectors had that many brains.' His young team mates benefited from the Queenslander's dry, cynical wisdom, while they in turn made old Stan feel as young as a merino lamb gambolling in the paddock. Not once did he let the Wallabies down as he grafted away in the tight for the Green Machine. 'Exercise removes fat, Stanley', Alan Jones shouted one day at training. 'Yeah', Pilecki shot back. 'You're living proof. No double chin!'"

He and Wallaby coach Alan Jones were miles apart in many things, but Stan played his part well. Only once did he let fly at schoolmasterish Jones, and that was after an unbelievable long and arduous work-out at Swansea. The test team were rested, but the 'dirt-trackers' were put through their paces in a manner that only Jones could do. The weather was deplorable, the players slipping in the mud and being inundated by the rain, while the loquacious Jones kept up a continuous tirade. It was 2.5 hours before Jones gave up, and the team was absolutely exhausted. Stan let fly: "I hope you're bloody hoarse, you bastard, because I'm bloody deaf."

It was said on the tour that Stan, when shown Stonehenge, asked why they built it so close to the highway.

An inveterate gambler, Stan, when at Porthcawl, heard of a certainty, and prevailed upon the Wallabies to pool their resources for a major plunge. When he got to the betting shop, he found to his horror that the horse had been scratched, but like any good gambler, felt he should not waste his visit. He turned to some half-stoushed Welshman and asked him which he thought would win. The man told him, and he put on all of the Wallaby pool. The nag came home at about 100 to 1, and the players were enriched in the team fund by about five hundred dollars a head. It broke the betting shop.

The stories go on and on, the legend becoming the truth in the constant regurgitation. Dick Marks jokingly said that when Stan saw ballet participants for the first time dancing on their tip-toes he wondered why they just didn't get taller dancers. Also, that his favourite dish was seconds, and that once when he was asked to send an SOS from his boat he asked how to spell it. It is also held that he noticed one young lad kept asking for his autograph, and Stan asked him why. The reply was: "If I can get ten of yours I can trade them for one of Mark Ella."

Ex-Wallaby Dr Peter Horton offers a few remarks on 'the Pole': "I read with a deal of humour some rather shallow descriptions of this tremendous personality. How anybody (Bret Harris included) can consider Stan Pilecki to be the most typical Queenslander in the team…one thing Stan 'ain't' is typical! He is however as Harris tagged him 'the salt of the earth'…the best kind of person. There will never be another Stan Pilecki, he is unique, he is a contradiction, he is a paradox. Stan has, conservatively speaking, lived about four lifetimes! He has experienced so many swings of fortune and the absolute range of experiences in his life it would be inept to attempt to describe them. Suffice to say he came from war-torn Europe, survived the Marist Brothers at Rosalie, a few All Black front rows, a career as a greyhound and indifferent race horse owner, the slump in the building trade and innumerable deep sea fishing trips with yours truly! (We have still to do the big one yet, the legendary Swaines Reef!).

"As a footballer he was sheer guts and resolve. As a prop forward he broached the eras of the minimalist scrummagers, like Roy Prosser who spent most of his time striking for the ball and trying to contort opposition front rows, and the total scrummaging props and hookers of today. His technique as a prop and his levels of fitness developed through sheer obstinacy and a complete denial of the laws of mechanics and principles of exercise physiology! But if I borrow the 'Boy's Own' cliche there would be no one else you would choose to go over the top with. In my last test which was against Argentina in 1979, in Buenos Aires, the front row was Stan Pilecki, Chris Handy and myself…think about it, I was the best looking one out of that lot! Mind you, after we lost I was the one to get dropped!

"If you say anything about Stan, say that he is not only one of the toughest, irrepressible characters ever to have graced a football field, he is also one of the most generous men I have known, but a shocking fisherman! But really his absolute claim to fame is his ability to keep an entire team awake with his bloody snoring! In this he is only matched by John Hipwell."

The truth and the legend merge with one Stanislaus Pilecki. They, however, should never detract from the fact that 'Stan the Man' was a remarkable rugby player, who started international rugby at 29 and was still a force at 37 years of age. He was the footballer's footballer, who never took a backward step unless he was reaching for a cigarette. A monumental character, he always gives more than he takes, is genuine, universally beloved, and is generous and honest. If we could all have a similar epitaph!

# Simon Poidevin

Simon Poidevin grew up on the family farm called 'Braemar', a 360 hectare property outside of Goulburn, where fat lambs and cattle were raised. Generations of his family came from the region, the original settler to Australia being one Pierre Le Poidevin, a French soldier who took an Irish wife. So Simon's shock of curly red hair, pale skin, quick temper, love of good wine and travel appear to have generational roots.

There was the occasional athlete cropping up in the family, the most famous being Dr Leslie Oswald ('LOS') Poidevin, an allrounder who played cricket for New South Wales, the Poidevin-Gray Shield for inter-club cricket in Sydney being named after him. He also represented Australia in the Davis Cup in 1906, no mean feat, partnering the dashing New Zealander Tony Wilding.

Simon would have to be classified as a country boy, but he has little of the air of the farm lad about him, except perhaps a genuineness and openness that has never deserted him despite considerable world-wide fame. Whereas a Wallaby like Greg Cornelsen has remained essentially a country boy through and through, and has changed little with the passing of the years, Simon leaves an impression of sophistication and urbaneness, and is as much at home on the ski slopes of Europe as on the various rugby fields of the world. He more resembles a Roger Gould than any other player in recent times. Somehow you expect to see

Simon arm in arm with a gorgeous model stepping out of a jet plane in Cannes or Monaco. His quiet manner and matinee idol looks were fortunately never unduly damaged by the occasional blood-letting ritual after copping one at the bottom of a rugby ruck from some malevolent opponent.

For a country boy, it can be said that Simon did all right. He broke the record for the greatest number of rugby union tests for a breakaway in Australia, an incredible 51, which speaks well for not only his longevity but for what was his trademark, supreme fitness. Now a stockbroker by profession and an occasional articulate television commentator, the world seemingly became the Goulburn boy's oyster. That gifted and controversial Wallaby coach Alan Jones used to speak constantly of the 'Gucci factor' - "Long after you've paid the price the quality remains..."

That was Simon. He paid the price by placing inordinately high expectations and standards on himself, and was almost fanatical and obsessive in his drive for the superior fitness demanded of his playing position, that of breakaway. One can picture him now, astonishing fellow players and followers alike with non-ending one-armed push-ups while the majority had already called it quits through physical exhaustion. Always, with him, the quality remained.

And my, did the redhead see the world like few other rugby players before or since: New

Zealand, the British Isles, the United States, Canada, Argentina, Hong Kong, Paraguay, France, Monaco and Italy. Times had certainly changed since the 'good old days', when tours to New Zealand were every two years and those to the British Isles every ten years, and an international was considered a phenomenon if he played about 20 times for his country.

Australia has been blessed with great breakaways, from another country boy, Tom Richards, in 1908, to Wylie Breckenridge in the twenties, Keith Windon in the thirties and his brother Col in the forties and fifties, New Zealand born Greg Davis in the sixties, Greg Cornelsen and Tony Shaw in the seventies, and players like Simon, Chris Roche and Willie Ofahengaue in the eighties and nineties. Of them all, arguably Col Windon and Simon Poidevin were the seers. Col was a great ball handler who could mesmerise his opponents when on the run, whereas Simon was the indefatigable ferret, ever first to the ball and a tower of strength in support play. They portrayed different styles, Windon and Poidevin, but they were equally effective. What a combination they would have been.

The foundation for Simon's rugged constitution lay undoubtedly in his early life on the family property, running as free as a breeze, in wild abandon. Maybe there is a special flavour to the air round Goulburn way, as close to the family farm a few other Wallabies of high repute have graduated: Jim Roxburgh, John Klem, Barry McDonald, Jimmy Hindmarsh and Alan Cardy. One more Wallaby nearby and they could have fielded a pretty fair seven-a-side squad.

Simon's first formal schooling was at Our Lady of Mary preparatory school in Goulburn. They had two under-6 rugby league teams, but they were not overly observant when it came to identifying rugby talent and missed such future league and union notables as Simon, Gavin and Bruce Miller, and Paul Feeney. Perhaps someone up there was looking after them, as a third team was formed, which provided adequate opportunities for a little action for these hyper-charged youngsters. Primary school was at St. Patrick's Primary, and some kind of a record was established as Simon was sent off the field after a scuffle with a player from the South Goulburn Public School. This indignity occurred in the under-10s, of all things. Maybe it was a blessing in disguise, as such an early exit was never duplicated in future forays.

When Simon entered senior school at St Patrick's, there was an enforced departure from league to rugby union, and like every other kid in school there was also a fervent desire to make the first fifteen. He was to make Brother Powell's team the final two years of high school, and was elevated to the vice-captaincy in his final year. He also made the Australian schoolboys team that year, though unfortunately there was no overseas tour to look forward to.

A surprising decision was to forego university for a year after graduation, though a year with the pick and shovel might have aided in putting a little extra muscle onto an already sturdy and rugged frame. He did not pass up his rugby, however, playing for the Goulburn club. He made the Southern Tablelands representative team for Country Week, barely lost the Sydney seven-a-side final against Randwick, and won the Grand Final with Goulburn. It was a great introduction to his career with the 'big boys'.

After his years among the blue-collar workers Simon was off to the University of New South Wales to pursue a degree in agricultural science, and played for them for two years in the first division, soon making the first team. He came under the notice of representative selector Maurice Goldberg, who recognised his raw potential, and in his second season made the 'big time' by his selection in the NSW Under 23 and Australian Universities teams.

In August of 1979 he was picked for NSW against Queensland. It was a formidable Queensland team that accorded him his baptism by fire: Roger Gould, Peter Grigg, Andrew Slack, Geoff Shaw, Brendan Moon, Paul McLean, Duncan Hall, Chris Handy, Peter Horton and Stan Pilecki. Each was a Wallaby stalwart, and they had already demolished the Blues 48-10 in their initial Ballymore encounter.

Jim Webster wrote of Poidevin's first match with NSW in *For Love Not Money:* "They (Queensland) won by 24-3, scoring four tries to nil. After the final whistle, as we were walking off, I felt like I'd just spent 80 minutes in a medical torture chamber, either being stretched on the rack or dangling from the wall in chains. Hardly a bone in my entire body wasn't aching and I was bleeding from a dozen scrapes and cuts. Then I caught sight of my socks. The tops of them were intact and the binding I used to keep them up was in place, but the rest of them, from the tops of my calves virtually to my ankles, had been ripped to pieces. I'd been to war."

There was a certain masochism in the redhead throughout his career, an idiocy inexplicable to the non-contact athlete, for he concluded that "I really enjoyed it".

In 1980 he went on his first of many overseas junkets, an odyssey with the University of NSW against teams from the west coast of the United States. On his return he received notice that he was in the Sydney representative squad, and came for the first time under the coaching expertise of one of the great devotees of the game they play in heaven, Peter Crittle.

In *For Love Not Money* Poidevin spoke of this rugby eccentric: "Crittle's one of the great characters of rugby. He has a brilliant and perceptive mind, which he deploys so effectively these days at the NSW Bar, and by all accounts was an hilarious character to have in any team. I gather that he used to keep his teammates constantly laughing with his witticisms and his antics. He also liked the unusual. During his career, which included four Wallaby tours, and his subsequent wanderings to the far-flung corners of the earth, he behaved like a bowerbird, collecting the largest and weirdest objects to take home for souvenirs. Nowadays, he's surrounded in his chambers by hand-crafted masks from south-east Asia, a mountain tiger's head, a python skin and an elephant's foot, which is used as an ash tray."

Crittle was a demanding coach and took the Sydney team for a short and successful tour of New Zealand. There were players on the team such as Glen and Mark Ella, Michael Hawker, Steve Williams, the Cox brothers, Phillip and Mitchell, and Bruce Malouf. The Sydney team prospered under Crittle's tough regime in the ensuing years.

Simon made his first Wallaby tour in 1980, to Fiji. Twelve of that Sydney team were among the Wallaby selections. He played his first test at Suva, a 22-9 victory, and returned to Australia

to face the dreaded All Blacks. He had his share of the New Zealanders that year, going against them six times, in the three tests, for Australian Universities, Sydney and NSW. The Sydney team eked out a 13-all draw, and Australia won the first test, but Australia came back to reality at Ballymore when Steve Williams had his jaw broken by an errant punch from the one-and-only 'Cowboy' Shaw.

In an episode now part of Australian rugby folk-lore, the Wallabies emerged as 26-10 victors in the SCG show-down. It was the first time Australia had defeated the All Blacks in a home series for the Bledisloe Cup since 1934, except for the one-off win in 1979. Simon Poidevin had certainly made an impact in his first year of top rugby.

The euphoria was short-lived, though his future world traveller image was being formulated by a short tour by Australian Universities to Japan. A 16-all draw by the Sydney team against a World XV was then followed by a 30-4 thrashing from Queensland, who rolled easily over the Blues. A 7-6 victory over the Maroons in the return match boosted morale, but then there were blood-baths against France, for Sydney, NSW and then Australia, after the French had been subjected to similar severe blood-letting against Queensland.

The first test against France at Ballymore marked Mark Loane's return to Australia after a rugby medical experience in South Africa. The young Simon held Mark in a special kind of reverence, as he stated in *For Love Not Money*: "In my eyes he was something of a god, and I guess my feeling was the same as a young actor getting a bit part in a movie with Dustin Hoffman".

Simon scored a try in the test after tailing the dynamic Loane on one of his dinosaur-like bursts, and Australia squeaked home 17 to 15. France was also defeated in the return fixture at Sydney, and this match featured the return into the French lineup of their dashing and gutsy captain Jean-Pierre Rives, a player who would cross swords with Simon many times in the years to come. Rives and Queensland's indefatigable Chris Roche were players always much admired by Poidevin.

Selection in Tony Shaw's Wallaby team for the British Isles in 1981-82 fulfilled one of Simon's rugby goals, and the team was heralded before departure as the finest to ever leave Australian shores. Players from the highly successful Australian Schoolboys team of 1977-78 were reaching maturity, and rugby appeared on the upsurge in the Antipodes, with players like the three Ellas, Michael Hawker, Steve Williams and Roger Gould ready to place their marks in the game's history books. With already established giants like Paul McLean, Greg Cornelsen, Tony Shaw and Mark Loane, it appeared as if Australian rugby would attain dazzling new heights.

It was a disappointing tour, as Paul McLean inexplicably lost kicking touch for once in his illustrious career, and the Wallaby scrum generally, except for the backrowers, lacked the fire-power, scrummaging and lineout ability of the top British teams in this particular era. Despite many gallant performances and often out-scoring the opposition when it came to crossing the line, the Wallabies returned to Australia with their tails between their legs, losing the internationals to Wales (13-18), Scotland (15-24) and England (11-15). Only Ireland succumbed to the highly talented Wallaby tourists (16-12).

There was a dramatic change to Simon Poidevin's career on his return to Australia as he switched from playing club rugby with the University of NSW and threw in his lot with Australia's glamour club, Randwick. Simon's non-stop play was ideally suited to the open style advocated by the Flying Greens since the days of Waratah scrumhalf Wally Meagher. Other changes were Peter Fenton taking over from Peter Crittle as Sydney's coach. Crittle was now NSW coach, and the NSW manager, Alan Jones, was a voluble non-rugby type who was to exert considerable influence over Simon in future years. Crittle and Jones formed a very effective partnership on a short of New Zealand tour by the Blues.

Despite a fine buildup by NSW that season, the Queenslanders celebrated their centenary rugby year with 23-16 and 41-7 victories over the Blues. New South Wales was strong in 1982, but Queensland was just that much stronger, and when Scotland came to Australia, Simon lost his test spot to Chris Roche, which represented a down-turn in his career after four tests on the British Isles tour. It was Bob Dwyer's first test as the new Wallaby coach, and

though Simon's omission was glaring, that of Roger Gould and Paul McLean was hailed by all and sundry as the rugby disaster of the ages in the northland.

Simon's observation that he would "never leave him (Gould) out of any side for which he was available" was an opinion shared by almost every rugby devotee in Australia other than Bob Dwyer and the two national selectors, John Bain and Bob Templeton. A Scotland victory by 12-7 reinforced the selectors' stupidity.

Sanity prevailed for the second test, which saw the return of the prodigal sons, Paul McLean and Roger Gould, and a lop-sided 33-9 Wallaby win. Paul McLean scored a record 21 points and retired, and Gould became the first Australian fullback to score two tries in a test.

The Scotland tour to Australia was a humbling one for Simon as he missed out in both internationals, and he also found out in near-record time that yesterday's hero can be today's nonentity when, after ten consecutive tests, he was not even provided with a complimentary ticket to the games by the ARFU.

The season witnessed a mini-revolt by Queensland players, sparked particularly by excessive time demands on amateur players in the increasing professionalisation of the code and by the accession to the crown of the Australian coaching position of Bob Dwyer over the 'Friar Tuck' of Queensland rugby, the likeable and popular Bob Templeton. Tony D'Arcy, Mark Loane, Tony Shaw, Peter and Paul McLean, Stan Pilecki, Bill Ross, Michael O'Connor and Brendan Moon withdrew their names from the upcoming New Zealand tour. Only one NSW player withdrew from consideration, breakaway Gary Pearse.

Mark Ella was selected as captain for that New Zealand tour, which had the popular 'Chilla' Wilson and Bob Dwyer as manager and coach, respectively. Many new players came into consideration through this mass defection, and, as so often happens, the extra motivation provided by inexperienced players determined to do their all for the Green and Gold can occasion unexpected results. Though the Wallabies lost the first test 16-23, they stormed back with a courageous victory in the second test at Wellington. The Wallabies suddenly had a shot at the Bledisloe Cup, and though they lost in the showdown 18-33, the players had covered themselves with glory, and Poidevin was back in the fold as the country's premier breakaway.

There was a disturbing start to the 1983 season, as David Lord was openly promoting a professional rugby venture, a harbinger of things to come. Twelve years later the plan would come to fruition with the professionalisation of the higher echelons of the sport. Lord was simply ahead of his time. Like most of the top players, Poidevin was interested in involving himself in whatever was to be the top-level competition. It is the nature of man to respond to a challenge, and if a professional game had been the ultimate, players would have joined its ranks. The scheme lacked a Murdoch or Packer to act as guarantor, otherwise it would have taken off.

The American Eagles toured Australia in 1983 and they exceded expectations in all games except the test, in which Australia triumphed by 49 to 3. The other tourists were the Argentinians, who always seemed to cause Australia trouble, particularly in the set scrums. The Pumas introduced a front rower who would have a considerable influence on Australia's future success in international rugby, Enrique Rodriguez, who was to be called 'Topo' or the 'Mole', the latter terminology relating to how he dug in for stability when he scrummaged.

The Argentine scrum completely devastated Australia in the first test at Ballymore, and the Pumas ran out victors by 18 to 3. The return match at the Sydney Cricket Ground was won by Australia 29-13. The match featured the most amazing penalty try in living memory, awarded by the posturing Welsh referee Clive Norling, who always gave spectators the impression that his own presence was more important than that of any of the players. His egoism could affect the course of a game. The fact is, however, that Australia had improved its scrummaging technique and its superior backs won the day.

There was also a one-off test against New Zealand in 1983, but the All Blacks were simply too strong, and emerged victorious by 18 to 8. A surprising end to the season was Randwick's defeat, after five successive premiership grand finals, by Manly. Manly's coach was one Alan Jones.

A Wallaby tour to Italy and France followed. After a 29-7 win over a committed but inadequate Italy, the Wallabies ventured into France, where they were rushed headlong into masochistic matches against various French selections, all determined to avenge the harsh treatment the French team had suffered in their previous tour of Australia in 1981. The call of 'Queensland…Queensland' signified the intentions of the locals, who rushed headlong into the fray endeavouring to square accounts.

The first test was a draw, 15-all, and its low point was the deliberate kick to the head that felled Wallaby hooker Mark McBain, which many Wallabies thought might result in his demise. He not only suffered a fractured skull, but the release of cerebral fluid into the back of his mouth.

It was Simon Poidevin and Steve Tuynman's turn in the second test, lost by 6-15. Tuynman not only had his nose broken, but one ear was virtually hanging off. Poidevin was also kicked in the head and was in a daze. The French players were not unscathed either, the French prop Michal Cromaschi, who had been responsible for McBain's injury, leaving the field to have his head stitched. Players are not averse to meting out a little justice on their own.

Bob Dwyer was rolled as Wallaby coach in 1984 by a Ross Turnbull faction, and Alan Jones emerged, after little experience in the coaching ranks. Poidevin's support lay with Dwyer. As he said in *For Love Not Money*, "Dwyer did not deserve to lose his job. He had been a courageous coach, certainly deserving of another season". His opinions were ignored, and to give Jones his due, he immediately summoned Poidevin and had it out with him. The presence of Manly breakaway Bill Calcraft had Poidevin somewhat tremulous about his future in the game under Jones.

Simon's concerns were temporarily alleviated as he went on a six-match tour of Italy, France, England, Wales and Ireland as captain of the Sydney team, under manager Andy Conway and coach 'Fab' Fenton. In reflection, Poidevin felt that he did not give the captaincy the attention it deserved, and this might have dented his future aspirations at the national level.

Meanwhile, in Australia, Jones, in his meticulous and single-minded manner, had been doing his homework, and was busily filling the gaps in what he perceived as weaknesses in the Wallaby team. He sought height in the lineout to ensure possession, and he got that in Queensland's Bill Campbell and the Blues' towering Steve Cutler. Andy McIntyre and 'Topo' Rodriguez fitted his requirements for the front row, and Nick Farr-Jones afforded a number of variations in scrumhalf play that were absent. What Jones was good at, as well as identifying talent to fit his own master plan, was in utilising others uniquely qualified to provide the assistance his own coaching and knowledge might have lacked. As a consequence individuals like Alex Evans, Dick Marks, David Clark and Arthur McGill were pressed into service when a national training squad of almost sixty was created.

He spoke about the Jones influence in *For Love Not Money*: "Layers of confidence soon started to develop around Jones and his grand vision. He obviously knew precisely what he was doing in terms of our national rugby team, and he was going about it in a more professional manner than any sporting coach in this country had ever done before."

A three-match Wallaby tour of Fiji was but a preamble to the visit to the British Isles, though an All Blacks three-test tour was slotted in beforehand to examine the credentials and guts of the players marked by Jones as necessary for Australia's rugby future. The Wallabies survived the All Blacks' ordeal by fire, winning the first test 16-9, losing the second 15-9 and the third, a narrow but brave loss, 24-25.

The British Isles tour of 1984 was history-making for Australian rugby, in that it was the first time in its illustrious history that Australia won the Grand Slam. Poidevin played in every one of the Grand Slam internationals.

Mark Ella, in *Path To Victory* said of Poidevin: "Simon is such a perfectionist, it's almost a disease. Not only is he the best rugby player in Australia, he's the most determined. He wants to win. He wants to go forward. He hates missing tackles or doing anything wrong. He hates losing. Simon just wants to be the perfect rugby player.

"You need players like that to drive you and the team. Watch Simon's performance and physical aggression and you are inspired by it. Because he wants to play the game to the limit, for the whole eighty minutes, he works harder than anyone I've seen at being superfit. He actually enjoys the physical work and exertion of training."

The secret of the Wallaby success in 1984 was the highly professional manner in which the team was prepared, and credit for this has to go to Alan Jones and Alex Evans. Then there was the manager, 'Chilla' Wilson, a man's man and a player's manager who would invariably take pressure off the team when required. Then there was the total balance in the team, in both teams, in fact, as the 'dirt trackers' were all quality players who could be depended on in every situation. And this team had a goalkicker, in the unflappable Michael Lynagh.

The Canadians were led to the slaughter in two tests in 1985, due to an incredible run of injuries which decimated the team. Then it was off to New Zealand for a single test, won 10 to 9 by the All Blacks 10-9. One-point games between the All Blacks and the Wallabies were becoming the order of the day in these years, certainly pointing to the closing of the gap between the two countries with respect to the rugby code. Mark Ella and Andrew Slack had retired by this time, so the narrow loss was a respectable showing, though there are no prizes for second place in the Bledisloe Cup.

The Fijians then came for two tests, won easily by the remnants of the Grand Slam Wallabies, and Simon still retains a souvenir of the conflict in the form of a substantial scar on his face.

In 1986 there were no overseas tours by the Wallabies except to New Zealand, but there was an invitation to the UK, with other Australian players - Cutler, Slack, Rodriguez, Lawton, Gould, Farr-Jones, Tuynman and Lynagh - for the matches in celebration of the centenary of the IRB. At the end of these games the New Zealand Cavaliers departed to South Africa, to the surprise of all, including Poidevin. Internationals against Italy, France and Argentina were all on the plate of the Australian team and then it was off again to the land of the long white cloud. Despite the absence of thirty-one of its best players, New Zealand displayed its unbelievable reservoir of talent by narrowly going down 13 to 12. There is nothing that disturbs New Zealanders more than losing in their national obsession, and the 'bounced' Cavaliers were recalled to show the Wallabies a thing or two in the second encounter. Australia lost by the identical score of the first test, 12-13.

In a rare and historic win on their home soil, the Wallabies then won the Bledisloe Cup with a stirring 22-9 victory. As Poidevin put it in *For Love Not Money:* "They are the greatest team in the world, and to beat the All Blacks in New Zealand in a series as we did in 1986 is the ultimate in Rugby."

A severe disappointment in 1987 was Poidevin's surprising replacement as NSW captain by Nick Farr-Jones, a reminder that the world of rugby had its cruel as well as its glorious side. New coach Paul Dalton was not among Poidevin's favourite people, then or since.

1987 was World Cup year, and Australia failed badly. Excuses are always easy to come by, but the main obvious ones were:

1.  Australia's lack of preparation. There was only one prepatory test, a romp over non-rugby power Korea.

2.  The selection of Concord Oval over the Sydney Cricket Ground as the venue for the Cup, a change in tradition that alienated the players.

3.  The widening gap between the players and coach Alan Jones who, like all coaches, ultimately reached and then passed his time of real effectiveness.

Unconvincing victories over England, the United States and Japan in the World Cup did not augur well for the Wallabies, but they seemed to find themselves at last against Ireland. However, Australia's farewell was against the unpredictable French. Australia went down 24 to 26. The Wallabies were disinterested against Wales at Rotorua in the show-down for third place, and showed it by going down to them in a humiliating though close 21-22 loss. New Zealand prevailed over France that year to become world champions.

Alan Jones next dropped both Australia's captain Andrew Slack and its vice-captain Poidevin, for the one-off test against New Zealand, and the All Blacks rolled the Wallabies 16 to 30. It was at this point that the tenure of

Jones as national coach was no longer secure, and his position worsened over his vacillating and what appeared to some to be his contradictory role over a projected Australian tour to South Africa. Bans on Andrew Slack and David Codey by the ARFU did not sit well with the players either.

Poidevin was selected as Wallaby captain in 1987 for the tour of Argentina and Paraguay, at a critical period in Australia's rugby history through the World Cup losses and turmoil over the South African fiasco. The first test against Argentina was a 19-19 draw, and in the final stages Poidevin received a fracture of his wrist, which meant he could not play in the final test, lost 27-19 by Australia.

On the team's return to Australia there was obsessive reporting about Alan Jones, and the final outcome was that Bob Dwyer was asked to be coach. As Poidevin had rallied behind Jones in his bid to retain his position, Simon had misgivings about Bob Dwyer's support of him, and this appeared to have been substantiated when Nick Farr-Jones was appointed as Australian captain. After 47 tests for Australia, Simon decided to call international rugby quits after a match against a World XV, and announced his decision to the Australian press. He kept playing for Randwick and captained NSW, and watched with some misgivings as Australia downed England without him. He really relished, however, a 'first' as his glamour club Randwick did battle against the ever-awesome All Blacks.

Poidevin's retirement was short-lived, however, as Jeff Miller and Steve Lindbury were injured. He readily agreed to front up in the first test against the All Blacks. Though the contest was a one-sided 7-32 loss, he was at breakaway again for the second test at Ballymore, which was a face-saving 19-all draw. The All Blacks rounded off the series with a convincing 30 to 9 victory. He had played 50 tests for Australia and was now 30 years of age.

The taste of the big stuff still lingered in his mouth, and though he did not make himself available for the Wallaby tour of England, Scotland and Italy in 1988, he did decide that he would play only for Randwick and Australia. His love of rugby overcame any such firm resolves, and he actually did play for Sydney and NSW that season when he was requested, but he was not selected for the series against the Lions, which Australia lost 2 to 1.

The press argued for Poidevin's inclusion for the one-off test against the All Blacks, and he was included. It was a 24 to 12 loss, and his 51st test, and ran down the curtain on his illustrious international career.

Simon Poidevin, a red haired, good looking country lad, left his mark on the game like few others in Australian rugby before or since. He was the personification of fitness, and the aspiring breakaway's role model. He never admitted defeat in his life, and never backed away when the going got rough. Visions will hopefully ever remain of his eager, intense, desperate and committed visage, his body surging forward, always doing his best for his beloved green and gold.

# Tom Richards

*If ever the Earth had to select a team to play Mars, Tom Richards would be the first player chosen.*

*– London Times, 1908*

Nothing perturbs a modern player more than listening to the old adage that they don't make sportsmen any more like they used to. In the case of Tom Richards, they may be just right.

Tom Richards was indeed a product of his times, an unlikely aspirant to international fame. Yet, through the sport of rugby, he was provided with a window to the world.

His record is second to none. He played for: Charters Towers, Queensland; the Mines Club in Johannesburg and represented that city, and Transvaal, in the Currie Cup; Bristol, England, and represented Gloucestershire; the Wallabies of 1908, and became, with Phil Carmichael, the first Queenslander to receive a gold medal in the Olympic Games, by being a member of the Wallaby team that defeated Cornwall in the 1908 Olympic Games rugby tournament; the British Lions in South Africa, thus becoming the only player to represent Australia and the British Lions; Manly Club in Sydney; the 1912 Wallabies on their tour of the United States and Canada; and Toulouse France, winning the club championship of France. He was Australia's first rugby troubadour, to be followed by Cyril Towers in the '20s, and modern entrepreneurs such as Roger Gould, David Campese and Michael Lynagh.

Tom Richards' story is an incredible one, and can only be appreciated by an understanding of the social and economic changes that rocked Australia before he was born and during his formative years.

Gold was discovered in Australia by a shepherd in 1823, but the gold rush really commenced when Edmund Hargraves came up with his find in 1851. In the following decade the Australian population virtually doubled, gold seekers coming from all over the world, including over 18,000 Americans and 40,000 Chinese.

The Victorian finds preceded those in NSW, and led to the opening up of Queensland as diggers leapfrogged over one another in their trek northward.

There were 23,520 people in Queensland in 1859, and ten years later, in 1869, there were 109,161.

The beginnings of many Queensland coastal and inland towns can be traced to the gold discoveries. The ports of Rockhampton, Townsville, Cooktown and Port Douglas served as outlets and receiving centres for the gold and the resultant trade, while the towns of Gympie, Mayfield, Palmerville, Croydon, Ravenswood, Mount Morgan and Charters Towers came into existence with such finds. Gold infrequently brought the first white people into these areas. They were mining frontiers. The most enduring of the finds were at Charters Towers and Mount Morgan.

Gold was discovered in what was later called Charters Towers in December 1871, though the claim was not registered until late January 1872. The name originally given to the field was "Charters Tors" - Charters for the first Gold Commissioner and Tors for the tower-like hills surrounding the site. The name was quickly bastardised and became known as Charters Towers. The influx of gold seekers was rapid, and by the end of the first year there were 3000 diggers in the area. They came by horse, via bullock teams, and by foot.

Charters Towers became one of Australia's greatest gold producers and was rivalled in gold production only by Mount Morgan and much later Kalgoorlie, Western Australia. Although it was not until the 1880s that it achieved world-wide recognition, the settlement was declared a town in 1877 when its population reached 10,000. In 1909, the city of Charters Towers was proclaimed, the population at that time reaching 30,000. It had in this short time become Queensland's second largest city.

In its heyday, Charters Towers was simply referred to as 'The World'. The residents, never reticent in their praise, claimed that their town was superior in wealth, culture and refinement to comparable European cities. It was said: "If you haven't been to Charters Towers you haven't been anywhere." Incredibly, there were 70 pubs in Charters Towers in those years.

A poem by J Coward, entitled "Good Old Towers", and sung to the tune of "Old Black Joe", summed it up:

*These are the days to renew old friendships o'er,*
*These are the days forgetting strife and war;*
*These are the days to review the days of yore*
*Still travelling, onward, upward to a golden shore.*

Chorus:

*I love it, you love it,*
*And our love is here unfurled;*
*There's not a greater place on Earth,*
*It is - "The World".*

On the gold fields there was an obliteration of class barriers, and sport offered a welcome respite to the confinements of the miners in particular, and an opportunity for them to display their physical prowess. The half-day holiday emerged at this time, and this was significant for the proliferation and popularisation of sport among the miners.

The game that captured the imagination of everyone at the Towers was rugby football. Outstanding state and national players emerged from the mining town. It was considered a rugby stronghold for a 20-year period, from 1890 to 1910.

It was often held that the players trained on beer, being as full as frogs on a Saturday night and playing like champions on the Sunday. When they travelled they carried their own 'Towers Brew' with them, refrigerating the casks with onion skins.

Though the standard of their play was high, the ground they played on was held by one to be the world's worst. The field was built on a reef which protruded in places like chisel edges.

One poem by an unknown author called "Football Days" described the football fervour in the town:

*They were vintage years round nineteen-eight,*
*When Sundays seemed a month between, so slowly passed a week;*
*There was football talked in home at night, there was football talked in schools.*
*And there was little that we didn't know, about the football rules;*
*There was football talked in hotel bars, and up on the cabby's rank;*
*By old men too, with delivery vans, in Deane Street by the bank.*
*In the dust of the Victory's levels, in the hell of the Brilliant Deeps.*
*Down the bowels of the Great Extended, and on the big mullock heaps;*
*But it's no wonder that we talked so much, or lauded those who played,*
*For the team we sent away that year - mark the record that it made;*
*It swept the State from end to end, then trounced the rest combined,*
*While we at home had a good team still, with the men who stayed behind.*

Tom Richard's father was a poor miner, living in a humpy at a nondescript mining settlement at Vegetable Creek, NSW. Forever lured onwards by the dream of the precious metal, he followed the rush to the Towers. Tom's mother followed later, bringing their five boys and meagre possessions over daunting country tracks a distance over 1450 km (900 miles). They certainly did breed them tough in those days.

Two of the Richards boys achieved everlasting rugby fame by the fortuitous circumstance of coming to the Towers at crucial periods of their upbringing. 'Billy' Richards was born in 1878, and Tom in 1887, so 'Billy' preceded his younger brother and doubtless served as a role model for him.

'Billy' Richards, like the rest of the family, gravitated to the mines, an arduous and dangerous occupation in those days. They banked on their physical strength in the congestion and heat of the mines, unaware that the 'miner's disease' would ultimately take its toll regardless of fitness.

'Billy' was a second row forward who played for the Towers representative team from 1900 to 1905, and for Queensland from 1903 to 1905 and again in 1907, for a total of 17 caps. He captained his state against New Zealand in 1907.

He played four tests for Australia, two against Great Britain in 1904 and two against New Zealand in 1905 and 1907. The 1905 New Zealand game was played at Dunedin, and there were some famous players on the Wallaby team: Alex Burdon, who was a prime mover in forming rugby league after he broke his collarbone in a union match and could not gain compensation; 'George' Anlezark, who was also an early defector to league and was on Australia's first 1908-09 professional rugby league tour; winger and centre Stan Wickham, who was to be assistant manager of the 1908 Wallabies; Mick Dore, another early leaguer, along with Doug McLean, the first Queenslander to play professional rugby and a scion of the famous McLean dynasty.

In 1907, in his last international game, Bill Richards played at number eight, and the immortal 'Dally' Messenger was on the wing. Many of the 1908 Wallabies were in the team, so the momentum of his career slowed down a year too early, though he was now 31 years of age. He was to die of 'miner's disease' at 50 years of age and is buried in the Manly Cemetery alongside his brother Tom.

Thomas ('Rusty') Richards worked first of all as a farmer's assistant for 7/6 a week, then for a coach-builder for 17/6, and in the mines for 2 pounds a week. He was understandably influenced by his brother's exploits, but a visit of a NSW team to Charters Towers in 1897, when he was only 10 years of age, captured his young imagination, and he resolved to do everything to make his mark in the game. His father forbade him to attend this particular match because it was played on a Sunday, an issue that divided the town in those days, but he and his brother surreptitiously attended. His own story was told in the *Sydney Mail*: "I learned, that memorable afternoon, that force alone cannot prevail over concentration and well timed movements. I trained every day and ran miles to achieve the honour of representing Charters Towers against Townsville and Ravenswood. In 1903, I was chosen for North Queensland during Country Week in Brisbane ('Billy' was also on that team and Tom was just 16 years of age).

"Brother Bill played splendidly and followed up his selection for Combined Country by playing for Queensland against NSW. Perhaps I was envious, but I was still overjoyed that at least one member of the family had reached such a high level in rugby. My determination to succeed wiped out my disappointment in not being selected with Bill. I went and watched the New Zealanders in Sydney and learned a lot of football lore. Back in Charters Towers, my training methods became far more intensive, from using diagrams of positions, field tactics, and scoring moves, to making my younger brother strengthen my abdomen and solar plexus with swinging punches."

He was, later, picked for the Queensland second XV against a NSW second XV, and learned a lesson or two in the game as he was beaten badly by two very experienced Wallabies, back Stan Wickham and outstanding forward Harold Judd. They carved up the young country boy, but he was intelligent enough to take stock.

"Close consideration showed that dodgy runners mislead tacklers by feinting to move left or right. To meet this ruse whereby they change direction and suddenly charge to the open side, I had to draw on my own patience when a man was coming at me, and not be led astray by preliminary drawing attempts. Then I found that my tackling was much simplified. I practised by catching fowls, but not rushing up to them, waiting patiently until they came within grabbing distance."

The careers of the Richards boys in Australia was put on hold as his father decided to go mining in South Africa, and Bill and Tom accompanied him and also worked in the mines there. Both brothers elected to play for the Miners Club in Johannesburg and for the first time in the history of the Club they won the premiership. They were both picked for the trials to select the Transvaal team for the Currie Cup competition, but Bill was unwell and indeed went back to Australia in order to regain his health. It worked, as he made the Australian team in 1907.

Tom played for Transvaal in the Currie Cup, but was frustrated when he was declared ineligible for the South African team to tour Great Britain in 1906 because of a six-year residential requirement. He decided to go to England himself, and played club rugby for Bristol and representative rugby for Gloucestershire, Middlesex and Midland Counties, even managing a game against the touring Springboks.

In 1908, yearning for the country of his birth, he went back to Charters Towers, now a mature and versatile player, 6ft in height and weighing 13 stone 1 lb. His goals were clearly put: "I set myself to develop a versatile, conspicuous, and yet safe, hard and effective style, and to fit myself to fill any emergency position on the field. It seemed to me that the loose forward game, attractive and spectacular, offered immense possibilities for development; so I concentrated my studies on an individual style that fitted my team's needs, learning to regulate my ideas according to my own lights and to cultivate 'attraction', so that wherever I might roam, I would command immediate notice. I aimed at travelling to distant lands, using rugby as my passport and my ability as an introduction."

This is a remarkable statement by a phenomenal athlete and person. The last two sentences could have been written by quite a few 'amateur' rugby players in recent times who have plied their trade in foreign lands.

Tom was quick to make his mark on his return to the Towers, playing for North Queensland in Country Week and against NSW. He was an automatic selection in the

Wallaby team to tour Great Britain and America in 1908-09 under fellow flanker 'Paddy' Moran. Scotland and Ireland refused to play against these first Wallabies, the main issues being that the invitation to tour came from England alone rather than a conjoint board of four unions, but also there was displeasure that in an amateur sport the Wallabies were provided three shillings a day out-of-pocket expenses.

There were other problems on tour. Captain Moran spoke about one of them in *Viewless Winds*: "There were little crowds gathering. Our methods had been subjected to some criticism in the England press. There was considerable disapproval of our breakaways (that is, Moran and Richards principally). Now in Australia referees gave these men considerable latitude. They were the lineal descendants of the old wing-forwards who in the good old days used to carry on a sort of personal vendetta at the bases of the scrum. In my time we were taught that we could - indeed should - swing out to block the men coming round, and that it was legal so long as we remained attached to the scrum. This, however, was considered obstruction in England. Further, the practice of following the ball through the scrum, keeping just behind it, always aroused the fury of a crowd who were unable to see that the player was still on-side.

Gallagher of the All Blacks had been the perfect exponent of this plan for keeping just within the law. The onlookers for some reason regarded it as a slim and unsporting practice."

Despite the continual carping over the Wallabies' methods of play, Richards as an individual was acclaimed. The *South Wales Echo* said: "He is looked upon as the finest of the Wallabies' side. He is unquestionably the best of the forwards." The *Daily Telegraph*, after the Swansea match, said that "individually, Richards, the Australian, was once again quite the cleverest forward on the field. He is generally at his best when his comrades are in difficulties, and yesterday he played better and better in proportion as the Welsh pack established their superiority."

The London *Daily Mail* said: "The greatest forward seen this season was Tom Richards. His pace, tackling and resourcefulness stamp him as one of the finest forwards who ever pulled on football boots."

The *Yorkshire Evening Post* wrote: "Tom Richards is a big and fast man, and he knows how to scrummage. In lineout and open play, he has no equal."

The London *Daily Telegraph*, ever praising his play, simply said: "He is the cleverest forward in the world."

There were only two internationals on the 1908 tour. Wales narrowly beat the Wallabies by 9 to 6, Richards scoring one of the two Australian tries, and 'Boxer' Russell the other. The Wallabies came back in the test against England in January 1909, winning 9 to 3. Richards was at number eight in the game, Norm Row and Ken Gavin playing at breakaway as the captain, 'Paddy' Moran, was injured.

Richards achieved immortality, however, not by his participation in the test matches, but in another game which was not held by the Wallabies to be one of any great consequence. It was for an Olympic gold medal, and the only one that Australia received in 1908.

Rugby was introduced to the Olympic Games in 1900 in Paris, when the host country defeated Germany by a score of 25-16, and except for 1908, was not held again until 1920 in Antwerp. Here the US team upset the pundits by defeating France 8-0, and proved four years later that it was no fluke by again defeating France, 17-3. The USA remain the rugby Olympic champions, as the sport was dropped from the Olympic programme.

On the itinerary of the 1908-09 Wallabies was a match on October 26, 1908, at Shepherd's Bush Stadium - the Olympic rugby tournament. Scotland, Ireland and Wales ignored the tournament, and New Zealand and South Africa, which had sent teams to England in previous years, elected not to participate. In actual fact this non-participation was indicative of the low status the rugby unions in those countries accorded the Olympic Games.

A week prior to the tournament, France withdrew as it was unable to raise a representative team, reducing the tournament to one match - Australia versus England. Cornwall, as the previous year's county champion, had the honour of representing the host nation.

Confidence was high among the Wallabies, who had comfortably won seven of the eight games they had played, the only loss coming in front of the highly partisan crowd at Llanelli. They had already defeated Cornwall at Camborne, by 18 to 5. It was thought, however, that the return of two internationals to the Cornwall team, halfback J Davey, and fullback EJ Jackett, would make a considerable difference. The slippery nature of the turf and ball was also likely to be more upsetting to the tourists than to the home side.

Neither the captain, 'Paddy' Moran, who had strained his shoulder in the previous game against London at Richmond, nor the vice-captain, Fred ('Possum') Wood, played in the match. They missed their appointments with destiny.

More than one thousand Cornish supporters travelled to London to support their side, only to see an overwhelming 32-3 win by the Wallabies.

The *Cornish Telegraph* recounted how the Australians 'easily worsted the Cornish fifteen'.

"The Australians displayed better form than they have as yet shown, except perhaps at Cardiff against Glamorgan, and the result was the biggest margin of the tour to date - 32 points to 3. The afternoon, without being associated with rain, was damp and cheerless, and the attendance at the Shepherd's Bush enclosure fell short of 3,000, though Lord Desborough and other prominent Olympic authorities were present.

"The Wallabies, who treated the company to their war cry before the start, lacked for the first time the services of their captain, Dr. Moran, who strained a shoulder in the game at Richmond on Saturday, and Wood was also rested at half. The Duchy team was as announced, except that Bennetts is hors de combat, and had to stand out of the three-quarter line. This added to the weakness of the Westerners, who were beaten, and beaten well, in everything, except the rushes. The game certainly had the effect of adding to the reputations of McKavitt*[sic]* and Carroll, and gave McGabe*[sic]* a chance of distinguishing himself which he utilised to the full. The Colonials were still rather too eager to kick up the field instead of going on, and another fault was that of "feet up" in the scrummage, for which they were several times penalised. It was barely five minutes after the start of the game - the kick-off was ten minutes late - when Hickey, after a feinting run, opened up the Wallabies' account, Cornwall easily converting. Each in turn had to touch down. Mid-walk through the first half McGabe cleverly scored and Cornwall landed a fine goal. Before halftime he also increased the Australians' advantage with a brilliant penalty goal from a few yards short of the centre line, and the Cornishmen found themselves on the change of ends in a minority of 13 points. For the first few minutes after resuming Cornwall attacked with vigour, and all but gave over. Hickey, however, bore away, and passing to Carroll, the latter wound up with a brilliant unconverted try. A few minutes later McGabe made an opening, and Richards, gaining the ball in clever fashion from the former's kick, ran right in between the posts. Cornwall placed a goal. Next came an unconverted try as the outcome of a movement in which McKavitt, Hickey, Bede Smith and Carroll in turn figured, followed by the only item of the day to the home side, for whom Jackett, now at threequarter, had previously failed badly with a penalty.

This item was initiated by Davey, and completed by Bert Solomon, whose brother failed with the place. In the last few minutes a try was accrued by McKavitt, on which Carmichael improved, and a final try by McGabe the place-kick failing. Result: Australia 4 goals, 1 penalty goal, 3 tries (32 points), United Kingdom, 1 try (3 points)."

The Wallabies did not treat the Olympic tournament as a momentous occasion, being much more concerned with the internationals against England and Wales. The Olympic victory receives only a brief mention in Moran's *Viewless Winds*, and even then only to record another accusation of unfair play that was levied against the Wallabies. During the game, a Cornish official had the effrontery to suggest that the Aussies were using running spikes on their football boots. Moran insisted on an inspection of his players at the conclusion of the game, and yet when they were cleared did not receive an apology.

One match Tom particularly remembered, as did the 1947-48 Wallabies many moons later, was their loss to the fanatical Welsh club Llanelli.

"I never imagined that men could stand up and kick so viciously at one another. I saw one of our men give a Welshman an unmerciful kick. The referee blew his whistle and asked him why he had kicked the man, to which he replied: "He kicked one of our fellows just now." That was the position; everybody was kicking each other. Our men, perhaps, kicked straight ahead more successfully than the opponents, but the Welshmen were superior at kicking from angles."

On his return to Australia, Tom went back to Charters Towers and mining, and though he played for Queensland in 1909, there was no international rugby where he could display his skills. He was offered a position in charge of black labour in Johannesburg mines, and went there in 1910.

The British, under captain Tommy Smyth, were touring South Africa at the time, and their team was decimated by injuries. Because of his appearances in the British Isles for county teams, and a Welsh heritage, he was prevailed upon to play. In all, he was in 13 matches, including three tests. So a Wallaby tourist and Olympic gold medallist became a British Lion as well.

Once more in 1912 he returned to Australia, this time to Sydney, and played a few club games for Manly. He showed enough form that he was selected as vice-captain for the first-ever Wallaby tour of the United States and Canada. The Wallabies scored 301 points on tour to the opposition's 94, but won only 11 of 16 matches, going down to Stanford University and the University of California at Berkeley, and all matches in Canada, to Vancouver, British Columbia and Victoria.

He did not return to Australia immediately after the tour. Australia's first rugby globe-trotter went to Bristol, and then on to the south of France, playing for Toulouse, and due in no small measure to his own efforts and experience, they won the club championship of France in 1913.

In 1914 he was back in South Africa, playing for Transvaal, before coming back to Manly.

When war broke out he immediately

volunteered in the AIF, and was one of the first to land at Gallipoli and one of the last to leave. He was awarded the Military Cross in France and was promoted to lieutenant.

He was severely gassed there, and was repatriated back to Australia, his football days sadly over. He later became a journalist on the *Sydney Mail*, a now defunct newspaper. His writings were keenly followed. He died in 1935, a mere 48 years of age, and was buried beside his brother.

Tom Richards was a legend in his own time, an international rugby troubadour before such ventures were popularised. Born in a humpy on a mine-field, he was an unlikely candidate for world fame, which he bore with modesty and humility. He was truly one of the greats of Australian rugby.

# Geoff Shaw

They called him 'Bunter', not because of the bunting and bruising style of play that he made famous, but because he was overweight when he joined the NSW Country team in his early years. Wallaby Dick Cocks wryly noticed his resemblance at the time to a legendary English schoolboy called 'Billy Bunter'. Billy, a fat pre-adolescent, was invariably depicted in the literature gluttonously diving into a huge plate of mashed potatoes with sausages sticking out of the spuds. So 'Bunter' he became for life, with the Aussie penchant for nick-names.

Geoff Shaw revolutionised back play in Australia, utilising a tactic that he views with some disdain today. Certainly he would not be its advocate for any young player. Because of 'Bunter's' size - he was close to 15 stone - his sturdiness and squatness, he was utilised as the pivot for 'second phase' play. He did not invent the tactic, and in fact Australia was slow if anything in learning the technique, All Black Ian MacRae being its main proponent many years beforehand.

MacRae, when interviewed, felt that he got type-cast through using the procedure, when in actuality he was a clever back with a variety of attacking skills. The tactic was to run straight down the middle of the field, parallel to the sidelines, forcing the tackle and drawing opponents in and stabilising and securing the ball for the ensuing ruck which essentially, then, was 'second-phase play'.

MacRae also revealed that the approach probably shortened his career, as it was one that produced injuries through the impact of people coming into him at various angles. Though Shaw did not have the same injury rate, he also suffered in that he too became type-cast, when he was also a centre of varied talents.

'Bunter' was a country boy, and still retains a certain idealism, almost innocence, that can only come from being brought up in a small town where everybody knows everybody and basic values have, somehow, deeper meaning and significance. His eyes glisten as he speaks of his rugby days, and his voice chokes as he speaks of old friends that nurtured him on the way or of the environment that he has left behind. When he played his first test he was understandably nervous, but chills ran up and down his spine as he heard the cry of 'Up the Blowhole', which was a call from his mates in reference to the area he came from. Geoff has never shaken off his roots, and is stirred with pride when thinking of those who helped and supported him over the years.

His father was a product of the depression years, and in the struggle for survival had little opportunity for sport. His main sporting interest in later years was lining up with millions of other Australians in the fine old art of fishing. Maybe Geoff's athletic genes came from his mother's side of the family, where a grandfather was a state baseball and Australian Rules player, and mother herself was Victorian champion in tennis. She would occasionally practise with her cousin, one of Australia's greatest-ever tennis champions, Frank Sedgman. Both parents influenced him. Father, though a plumber by trade, became the secretary-manager of the local Returned Soldiers' League, and always brought Geoff back to reality on his play. He was very astute, and taught him that no matter who he was playing for, to play to the best of his ability. Mother Shirl perhaps supplied him with his academic incentive, as she possessed two degrees and taught at St. Mary's College, Wollongong.

He was brought up in the country at Oak Flats, near Kiama, which was then a rugby league centre, and started off in that code at St Joseph's Primary school in the 4st 7lb team. He made the Illawarra representative team when he graduated to the 5st 7lb mob.

They had no electricity for two years at Oak Flats. His father worked at the power station, and because of the isolation it took five years to finish their home. They might have been considered quite poor, but for a youngster it was somewhat of an idyllic existence. Geoff was always good at school, and went off after primary school to Edmund Rice College at Wollongong, a Christian Brothers' school. The journey would take about an hour by train each day.

He was solid for his age, and enjoyed playing number eight, which gave him a fair bit of action and a lot of freedom. For the first four years it was all rugby league, but with the arrival of Principal Jim Brosnan, a man Geoff remains indebted to, the boys voted to play rugby union, and he moved to five-eighth.

There were a few rather handy youngsters also cavorting on the pitch at Edmund Rice College during his tenure there, two of whom played for Australia, centre Mick Cronin, and fullback Brian Weir, as well as state representative winger Brian Lachlan. The local clubs were highly involved in the coaching and the competition, and 'Bunter' blossomed under the tutelage.

The boys took to rugby union like ducks to water, and in twelve months at the code they turned around and beat power-house St Pat's from Waverley.

He was not too popular locally when he and many others from his school turned their backs on rugby league, the code of the battlers in his area, in favour of rugby union, but at Kiama he went from third to first grade at 16 years of age, already being between 13.5 and 14 stone. Ex-international back Bryan Palmer predicted even at that age he would play for Australia.

At 17 and 18 years of age he went to the Country Championships, and was picked on the NSW Country team. He replaced Beres Ellwood, who had retired. There were some legends on the Country team, such as John Hipwell, Jim Lenehan, Jim Miller and Ross Turnbull, and this provided him with an enormous learning opportunity.

In 1967 he was selected as a reserve for the state, and went on his first rugby tour with Country on a 13-match tour of New Zealand. Because of his age he had to obtain his parent's permission to leave the country, and the manager had to be his guardian, with promises to protect him from women and alcohol. The team was equally determined to break down such barriers. They certainly inveigled him into a drinking bout, so much so that he never had another drink until he was 21.

It was in New Zealand on this trip, at Hawke's Bay, that the management decided that he was ideally suited to play the All Blacks' 'second-phase' style. He lost a few teeth in the learning stages, as back-rowers and opponents came flying in from variable angles, and heads and elbows would often appear in the wrong place.

There were many offers to turn to rugby league at this stage, as his play was drawing attention and favourable comment. Peter Moore was the local Penfolds rep, and Johnny Raper the slot-machine man, and they tried to draw him away. 'Bunter' worked out with the local rugby league teams as part of his pre-season training, and actually felt his game was more suited to the league code. He turned down, however, all offers. Essentially he did not want to be owned. He wanted to hold on to his independence, and thoroughly enjoyed the rugby union game.

He worked for BHP in the late sixties, being well aware of the old adage, 'as goes BHP so goes Australia'. He was an electrical engineer trainee, and they gave him time off for rugby and his university studies at Wollongong. A slight hiccup in his studies in 1967 made him realise that he had to balance better his rugby and studies, so he took six months off to hit the books, lessening his rugby commitments. He never looked back after that, academically speaking, eventually completing his degree.

'Bunter' remembers playing against Queensland for NSW Country in this period, his weight being over 16 stone. The Queensland centres were Alex Pope and Barry Honan, and they had a good laugh when the fat one ran on to the field. The smiles did not last too long as NSW Country hammered Queensland to the tune of 25 to 11.

Geoff's appearance was always deceptive, in that he loved training, being a fair cross country runner at school. While at home he would run, once a week, a 20 mile course utilised by long distance champion Dave Power, which was a rugged, mountainous terrain. He would do medium runs in between.

With Geoff and his schoolmates rounding out the team, Kiama won the premiership in 1967 and 1968. Future Wallaby Peter Carson was scrum half at the time. In the 13 years 'Bunter' played for Kiama, they won 11 premierships.

The year 1969 was the real starting point of Geoff's representative career. He was 19 years of age. It was also the start of the Country era, which was a boon to Australian rugby, reaching its zenith in 1974, when eleven Country players were selected for Australia.

In 1969 the NSW-Queensland matches were Wallaby trials, and 'Shawie' was selected to go to South Africa. He was the 'baby' of the team. Before the tour there was a one-off hit-out against Wales, and Barry Honan was injured, so he went into his first test with Randwick's Phil Smith. A first test is never forgotten by a rugby player, and it holds a special memory for 'Bunter'. He still recalls his friends on the hill, and, as mentioned, the call 'Up the Blowhole'. "Never forget your grass roots," Geoff said.

The Wallaby team on that auspicious day was: Arthur McGill, Terry Forman, Geoff Shaw, Phil Smith, John Cole, John Ballesty and John Hipwell; Alan Skinner, Hugh Rose, Greg Davis, Tony Abrahams, Peter Reilly, Roy Prosser, Dr Paul Darveniza and Jim Roxborough. Wales had a few great ones, such as scrumhalf Gareth Edwards, fullback J P R Williams, and five-eighth Barry John. Wales won the encounter 19 to 16, but Geoff showed

that, at 19 years of age, he would be a bulwark for Australia for many years to come.

The tour to South Africa was a great learning experience for 'Bunter'. There were many innovations introduced to his armoury, particularly left-footed kicking. Ex-Wallaby winger Charlie Eastes was the manager, ex-scrum half Des Connor the coach, and breakaway Greg Davis the captain. As always, there were glaring omissions when the team was announced, the most serious being those of Peter Crittle and Jules Guerassimoff.

Geoff was a 'dirt-tracker' on his first Wallaby tour, that is a midweek or non-test player. As the song goes:
*We are the Dirt Tracker Riders,*
*Just for emergency,*
*We train all day but never play,*
*What blinking use are we?*

Geoff played only in one test, and that was a one-sided South African victory by 30 to 11. Phil Smith was injured so badly it meant the end of the tour for him, and 'Bunter' came in as a replacement. He was a vital non-test player on this tour, playing 18 of the 26 matches, proving for all to see his amazing durability. It was South Africa that ensured his future.

There were a number of retirements and defections to rugby league following the South African trip, and his position became more secure. In 1970 he went on a tour of New Zealand with NSW, then was picked out of the country area for NSW and on to the test against Scotland. In the test he partnered Steve Knight. For his state and his country, Shaw was dominant, victories coming in both games, to the tune of 28-14 and 23-3. A great honour was being selected as vice-captain of Australia, and he was still 20 years of age.

The British Lions came to Australia on their way to New Zealand in 1971, and after losing to Queensland, who were beginning their renaissance, they narrowly defeated NSW by 14 to 12. This was a considerable achievement, as this British side was considered one of the greatest to tour Antipodean shores, winning 22 of their 24 matches in New Zealand. Australian teams had out-scored them, 27 to 25, and broke even in matches. Shaw's reputation was enhanced by his display for the Blues.

There was enormous upheaval in rugby that year when South Africa played. There were 600 police endeavouring to handle over 10,000 demonstrators. Both teams were under a high level of security, Geoff received death threats and the ARFU even had sessions with the players on what to say and how to behave. It was all very distracting when a test had to be played. At least the South Africans were used to it, but the Australians were certainly not. The Springboks won all of their thirteen games, and scored 76 tries against 11 by various teams in Australia. The tests were 19-11, 14-6 and 18-6. It was all very unsettling for the Aussies. As Geoff said: "I felt that people had the right to demonstrate, but equally I had the right to play."

'Bunter' was off to France that year for another two tests, one won and the other lost, and in 1972 he got married. He has advice for all married couples, given to him by one of his best friends, who presented him with a big snoopy dog.

"Whenever you get mad at your wife", he was told, "just go and talk to the dog, he'll never answer back and it will smooth over all your problems." He has followed that sage advice ever since.

He had made so many great friends in South Africa that he decided he would take his wife, Lindy, there. Geoff wasn't too meticulous over what should he packed for a long trip and what should not, but there was never any question when it came to certain items. His rugby strip always went with him. He loved rugby with a passion, and took little inducing to 'have a go' no matter where he roamed. His overall plan was to go to South Africa for four months and then make Munich to see the 1972 Olympics.

The young marrieds loved South Africa, so they stayed longer than planned, Geoff making the Eastern Province team and being selected to play for the Junior Springboks, a rare honour. He was actually on the list for Springbok selection to go to Argentina, but he had to promise he would stay and play in South Africa the following year, an assurance he could not in all conscience give.

He and his wife then went off to London, and one of the first things he did was to ring up to get a game. He arranged to play for Richmond, and went to Athletic Park, but made a mistake with respect to the time of the match. He ran into the London Scottish captain of the tenth team, who did not know who he was, and when offered a game settled in for an afternoon of coarse rugby. Geoff didn't care, and certainly didn't want to pull rank, and had an enjoyable afternoon.

He went out to practice the following week, not saying who he was, but was recognised by the Scottish backline coach, who passed the word on to their eccentric coach, Gordon McDonald, who would appear at practices in a pin-striped suit and bowler hat. So Geoff went from the tenth team to the firsts in one week, somewhat of a record.

Their first game was, of all things, against Richmond, and they were more than slightly miffed that the Wallaby had eluded their grasp. It was the local derby, and London Scottish "were really hammered".

He played with London Scottish for three months, and was then off to see the sights of Europe, his boots an ever essential part of his baggage. He picked up games in France and Italy, and in between took in every tourist sight possible. They had little money, and wore out a few pairs of shoes as they hit the pavement.

He was back in Australia in June 1973, and the Wallabies were still reeling from their much criticised performances in New Zealand in 1972. The day he got back there was another ignominy, as the Wallabies lost to Tonga. Rugby was at one of its lowest ebbs. As can be so important in life, he was in the right place at the right time.

Ironically, Daryl Haberecht would not pick Geoff in the NSW Country team, as he had selected players who would play the style of rugby he wanted, and 'Bunter' did not fit the pattern. Non-representation in the Country team meant he could not break into the NSW team, but fortunately Australian coach Bob Templeton put on a Possibles versus Probables game for Wallaby selection. He may have been lucky that there were a few injuries, but great people make their own luck, and Geoff was back in the Wallaby team.

New Zealand was back touring in 1974, and Geoff played in three tests alongside Queensland's David L' Estrange. Australia had come a long way since the 1972 debacle, due in no small measure to the standard of NSW Country and Queensland rugby. Daryl Haberecht and Bob Templeton were two of the driving forces behind the revival, one of their ploys being constant tours of New Zealand to familiarise the players with the standard of play there. 'Tempo' made famous his 'Six Ps Principle' - 'Proper Preparation Prevents Piss-Poor Performance'.

The Wallabies lost to the All Blacks in 1974, but the scores were 11-6, a draw at Ballymore 16-all, and 16 to 6 at Sydney. The Wallabies were competitive again, though still a shade behind. According to Geoff, Australia should have won the second test. In the first half, he went over the line and referee Bob Burnett ruled a double movement. "It was a completely fair try," Geoff said matter-of-factly.

One of the ambitions of his life was realised when he was selected for the 1975-76 tour of the British Isles. John Hipwell was the captain, and Ross Turnbull and Dave Brockhoff the manager and coach, respectively.

The Wallabies were successful off-the-field under the astute management of Ross Turnbull, but were plagued with injuries to key players which reduced their effectiveness, John Hipwell, Mark Loane, Ray Price and Mike Fitzgerald succumbing at various times. They lost three of the four international matches. One honour came Geoff's way, however. When John Hipwell had to leave the field injured against Wales, Geoff was the captain.

Fiji was in Australia in 1976, and Geoff was in all three tests, each won by Australia. The third match was a particularly spiteful encounter, during which prop forward Josateki Sovau was sent off the field by referee Warwick Cooney for allegedly kicking an Australian on the ground.

The Fijians actually walked off the field in protest and the match stopped for 10 minutes. They were finally prevailed upon to continue, being advised that such a breach of international etiquette might result in their never playing international rugby again. Geoff received a fractured cheek-bone in the encounter, and had to leave the field.

On the tour to France in 1976 Geoff was the Australian captain. It was a very demanding tour, the team finding itself up against selection teams which levelled the Aussies with indiscriminate kicking and rough, dirty play. The first test was reasonably close, but they were demolished in the Paris test by 34 to 6.

There was little enjoyment on the tour, and when they got to Italy for the single test there, the weather conditions were atrocious, and Australia barely won the encounter. The results in France and Italy signalled the departure of Bob Templeton as Australian coach.

'Bunter' had always held a great respect for 'Tempo', and while in the southern state he increasingly found travelling throughout NSW difficult. Queensland offered an opportunity for him to extend his representative career, so he came north, and from 1977 to 1980 had 47 games for Queensland, touring with the Maroons to New Zealand in 1977, Japan, British Columbia and the United States in 1978 and the United Kingdom, France and Italy in 1980.

It was a great wind-down to an illustrious career, playing club rugby for University and state representation for Queensland. He was the vital cog in the Queensland backline, and passed on much of his knowledge to the young players around him. When Michael O'Connor came on to the scene in 1981, he called it quits. When Geoff originally came north, he said: "Everyone wanted to know whether I was receiving a block of flats in Tasmania or a yacht for playing in Queensland."

Bret Harris wrote of Geoff in *Marauding Maroons*: "Shaw was first selected to play for Australia on the Wallaby tour of South Africa in 1969 and became the permanent test captain in 1976 when Hipwell was injured in Britain. Shaw was a fine tactician and totally reliable under pressure. A big, burly centre, he was punishing in both attack and defence. He was also a skilled ball-handler and played the game with unusual finesse for a man of his bulk. Shaw provided the Queensland backline with authority and relieved the pressure which had been mounting on Paul McLean's young shoulders. All of the Maroons drew confidence from Shaw's presence on the field.

"The Queensland backline developed an understanding with Shaw which formed the basis of the Maroons' second-phase play. The sight of Shaw tucking the ball under his arm and charging up-field with his loose forwards in support became a feature of Queensland's game.

"The second-phase strategy may not have been spectacular but it was effective, and Queensland's wingers never complained while

Shaw was distributing the ball so assiduously."

An unexpected grand finale to his career came when he was asked by Bob Templeton to make himself available for the one-off test against the All Blacks for the Bledisloe Cup in 1979. What a team it was: Stan Pilecki, Peter Horton, Chris Handy, Greg Cornelsen, Peter McLean, Tony Shaw, Andy Stewart, Mark Loane (captain), Paul McLean, Phil Crowe, Andrew Slack, Geoff Shaw, Brendan Moon, Tony Melrose and Peter Carson.

Coached by Dave Brockhoff, the Wallabies won the single test in a dour struggle in which neither side scored a try. The victory was a glorious moment in Australian rugby, and only the second time the Bledisloe Cup had been won in Australia to this point in its 48-year history. No greater farewell to test rugby could be scripted, and 'Bunter' thereafter declined an invitation to go to the Argentine. He retired from test rugby, happy and proud. He had achieved 28 tests, and had captained Australia nine times.

He is now rugby football manager of the Queensland Rugby Union, and in that capacity will have an influential control on the game in the north. The game could not be in better hands, as Geoff has a deep understanding of the ethos and camaraderie of the code and hopefully will be able to assist in the maintenance of such past morality with the increased professionalisation of the game, with 48 Queenslanders presently on contract.

A deep, intelligent, committed, emotional and thoughtful man, he said: "You know, every time I come to work at Ballymore and see the oval, the hairs on the back of my neck stand up. When stressed, I go over and sit by the ground, recalling the ghosts of the past, and it aids in bringing everything back into focus."

Sport historian/sociologist and former Country, Queensland and Wallaby representative, Dr Peter Horton, endeavoured to sum up Geoff Shaw the man: "I first played with Geoff in 1972 and I think we played our last test in Australia together against the All Blacks in 1979.

"One of my earliest memories and surely one of the biggest rugby collisions ever recorded on the Richter scale was when he and Stephen Knight impacted, (to say 'collided' could never do it justice), in a training accident before we were to play Queensland! Both lads were in excess of 100kgs I would say, and upon seeing them run into each other in trying to catch a high ball I vowed never to play in the centres.

"Geoff had a fabulous career, I think he first played for NSW in 1967 and finished with Queensland in 1980...a great trot. He was also one of the first to travel the world as an individual player and even though being a graduate electrical engineer it was obvious his life was rugby and after heading the Queensland coaching staff he is now 'head rugby heavy' in the state and he loves it.

"'Bunter' came on the scene as a big hit-up type centre but gradually became an accomplished backline organiser, and he could also punt the ball a country mile from the inside centre spot. In fact, I will long remember the extemporised kicking games he and one of his centre off-siders would have at the end of training. David L'Estrange and Andrew Slack spring to mind as players in the contrived games of kicking tennis or 'forcey-backs'. Talking of Andrew Slack. I am certain considerable quantities of Geoff's implicit mentoring assisted Andrew's development into the class act he became both as a player and as a captain.

"Geoff always loved a debate and would often hold court, cigarette in hand, on topics from football to politics. He also had his own brand of wit which at times was acidic, at times subtle - he coined Tempo's real nickname of "Elmer Fudd"! And of course their friendship/ partnership is legend. Tempo loved the banter of 'Bunter', it seemed to invigorate him! Geoff Shaw is a total rugby man, someone who has been able to make his passion his career, though he always kept things in perspective with his family coming first. I wonder if the demands of corporate rugby allow him this luxury today?"

# Tony Shaw

Bret Harris had this to say of Tony Shaw in *The Marauding Maroons: The Rise of Queensland Rugby:* "Tony Shaw is that rare blend of toughness and technical brilliance which separates a good player from a great player. He was probably the most completely equipped forward in Australian rugby during the past decade. A hard-driving forward in the best All Black tradition, Shaw was an outstanding rucker and mauler. His forte was protecting his team's possession but he could spoil the opposition's ball with equal effectiveness. In the short lineout Shaw was second to none as he outwitted taller and more spring-heeled opponents. Shaw was a cunning lineout technician and the majority of Queensland's and Australia's variations can be attributed to him. Shaw was not as naturally talented as Loane or McLean, but he shared their fanaticism for physical fitness."

He was a tough one, was Tony, and he could easily have fitted into an All Black or Springbok pack. He was of that mould, a no-nonsense, hard-rucking and aggressive forward who never considered defeat. He married Judy McLean, the daughter of Bill McLean, who led the Wallabies to New Zealand in 1946 and the British Isles, France, Canada and the United States in 1947-48. Tony was in many respects, on the playing field, more like Bill McLean that Bill McLean himself. One shudders at the possibilities of the progeny of the Shaw-McLean match-up.

He was called occasionally 'Crazy Eyes', which came from his water polo days, a sport he relished in the off-season. He was good enough to represent the state in 1974. As for the eyes, there was a steely glaze that seemed to come over them when he was in the throes of combat. He was of the 'take no prisoners' school, uncompromising in his approach to the game.

The Shaw-Cornelsen-Loane back-of-the-scrum triumvirate was the most effective in Australia's rugby history. When looking at individuals to replace any one of them the names of Simon Poidevin, Jack Ford, Greg Davis, Keith and Col Windon, Jeff Miller, Chris Roche and Owen Bridle would be considered, but this Queensland trio was amazingly effective. They understood each other's game perfectly, and complemented each other, providing a balance that has never been equalled.

His parents owned a dry cleaning business in Hervey Bay, ran the Metropolitan Hotel in Bundaberg and moved to Brisbane in 1964 where they owned and ran two blocks of flats.

Mother had no particular known athletic ability, but father played what could be the toughest rugby league in the world, that in the small country towns. The grounds were like rock and the teams were made up of some very tough men. They would scramble onto the ute to get to the field and play for the sheer love of body contact. His father's smashed nose was a constant reminder of the fierceness of the contests. His father, at one time, was the youngest to be awarded a pub licence in Queensland.

Bundaberg is a great sporting town, and has produced some worthy champions over the years in a wide range of sports, and it was in this ideal atmosphere that the 9-year-old Shaw got his initiation into rugby league, at the Christian Brothers' School.

In 1974 the family moved back to Brisbane, and Tony went to St Joseph's College, Gregory Terrace, a famous nursery for rugby union, where Norbert Byrne was the head coach when Tony was in the firsts. As well as rugby at school, he played Brothers rugby league on a Saturday, which he also enjoyed. He was playing then in the centres and the front row, but found himself wanting to get where the main action was, in the forwards.

Eventually he could not keep up with the two codes, and concentrated on rugby union. In 1969 he made the first team at Terrace at 16 years of age, playing in the second row. In his early teenage years at Terrace, Tony was tall, and wore shoulder pads. As he put it: "I looked like a bloody tank".

His game was pretty immature at this stage, he was certainly raw-boned and lacking finesse, but even then he 'gave it a go'. He had no idea that he was even being considered, but he barely missed selection in the Australian Schoolboys team to South Africa. He had previously captained the Under-16 Queensland team for the Australian championships, and toured New Zealand with them later in the year.

Like Paul McLean and Chris Handy before him, he repeated his senior year. He said: "It was a lack of genuine scholastic ability rather than love of first XV rugby." He captained Terrace's first fifteen in the second row in that final year.

In 1971 Tony went to Brothers' Rugby Union Club, where Roy Hose as coach, fastidious in his methods, had a profound impact on Tony's game. After two years in the under 19s, with potential stars like Terry Burkett and Paul McLean, who was one year younger, he went straight to first grade. Brothers won the premiership in 1973, 1974 and 1975. Tony and Paul were the youngsters of the team. Brothers had some mighty players at that

time: Jeff McLean, David L'Estrange, Dick Cocks, Alex Pope, David Dunworth, 'Mick' Freeney and 'Mick' Flynn among them.

Tony's parents Harry and Cynthia were two of his greatest supporters. They were always at his games, and Harry was often there many hours prior to see the lower grades play. They frequently followed Tony's overseas tours but never imposed on Tony's time or that of the team.

Harry was a confidant to many of Tony's touring party and to many of the officials. The hill at Brothers' home ground, Crosby Park, is named 'The Harry Shaw Hill'.

Dallas O'Neill was at the time the head coach at Brothers. He was very fond of 'taking the mickey' out of the young tyro Shaw. He had a style of coaching Tony was not accustomed to. A really hard, uncompromising taskmaster, he was one who often gave overall direction, but left it to the experienced players to implement his vision at training. Dallas allowed the players considerable input but was never too distant to come down hard when necessary (many times from the bar). University and GPS were the main rivals in those days in the Brisbane competition.

In his first season out of junior ranks his potential was soon realised, and in 1973 at the age of 20 he made not only the Queensland team in the second row, but also the Australian team that year for a short six week tour of England and Wales. Though chosen in the second row, he played both tests as a lock.

Jim Kenny was the coach of Queensland at this point, and Tony said: "He was dictatorial, and looked a bit like Adolph Hitler with his hair down over his forehead and furrowed brow. He was always at you."

He found that he had to pass the same initiation rites meted out to other fledglings of the world and, when training, fellow second rower Dave Woods was deliberately throwing passes at his toes or away from him, and Tony would be diving in desperation trying to take them. Always, there would be Kenny's voice: "If you can't catch it Shaw, you shouldn't be here, how can you expect to play?" To Tony, he was just paying his dues as a neophyte.

He remembers with great fondness some of those early games. One was against North Auckland in 1974, where Queensland was down 20 points at halftime, and surged back to draw 24-24. The Queensland team was coming of age.

Then there was also a NSW versus Queensland game, and war-horse Alex Evans, who had been the heart and soul of the Queensland pack before retiring, was brought back because of an injury. Alex changed for the match and put on a swim cap.

"What's that for?" asked young Tony.

Alex glanced at Tony and said: "So I can head butt and I won't split my skull!"

"Shit!" thought Tony. "This guy means business!"

Alex went on. "I'll head butt (Ron) Graham, but I want you to come up from the second row and hit him."

"Okay, Mr Evans," said Tony, who had always been somewhat in awe of him.

So at the very first scrum Alex and his swim cap went at Ron Graham, and Tony did his part. "I gave Graham a limp tap," he said. "Fact is, I didn't know how to do it."

Understandably, a brawl broke out between Evans and Graham, the pair rolling around the ground. "It was a bit of a blue, I can tell you, but I bolted as it was one of my first games for Queensland and I was more interested in following the play, which didn't please Alex too much." He added, in reflection, "He was a fantastic competitor, that Alex Evans, and I had a huge respect for him as a result of not only the way he played but for his coaching of the Queensland pack."

After the short tour to England, Wales and Italy during which he played two tests, he came to the conclusion that at 15st 4lb and over 6 foot 2 inches, though he was strong enough, he needed more height and bulk to hold his position there. The experiment with the number eight position was reasonably successful, but there was one Mark Loane cavorting around in Australia, and it was not very logical that he would find a lasting future there.

So he decided breakaway was his best position, though Brothers was loaded in the backrow, with Dick Cocks, 'Mick' Flynn and Ron Price. So he was back in the second row with his club.

In 1974 the momentum of his career took a nose-dive, as he did not get a run in the two tests played by the touring All Blacks. John Lambie, Mark Loane and Ray Price were the back row in the first test, and Greg Cornelsen, Lambie and Price in the second.

An additional shock awaited him that year as coach Dallas O'Neill dropped him as he felt he was taking it easy in club games to conserve his energy for representative games. It was an appropriate and timely lesson. As he put it: "I suddenly realised an injury could end my career at any time and the thought of finishing my playing days in reserve grade changed my attitude to the game completely."

An interesting fact about Shaw was that he was always in the thick of it in any match, and could only be classified as a hard-contact player throughout his career, yet he never did sustain a major physical set-back apart from a broken jaw sustained halfway through the 1980 Grand Final against University. Tony finished the game and it was not until an excited supporter grabbed him by the cheeks in the dressing room that he realised he might have more than a few broken teeth.

As Bret Harris wrote in *Maroon:* "As a player, Shaw displays strength, fitness and durability. He seems almost indestructible. He has never suffered a serious injury and has missed only a handful of games through minor mishaps.

"As either a breakaway or a second rower he has always been noted for vigorous mauling, hard driving and determined rucking. In the short lineout he has been second to none as he continually outfoxed his opponents."

He was back in favour in 1975, and was put in his preferred position as breakaway against the English tourists. It was a series where Paul McLean was dropped, incredibly. So Mark Loane served his banishment period in 1973, Tony Shaw in 1974 and Paul McLean in 1975. England lost the two tests, 16-9 and 30-21. The second test at Ballymore was a violent encounter which had serious ramifications, as a future Wallaby tour to the UK was threatened because of the alleged mayhem. The match was dubbed by the media as the 'Battle of Ballymore'.

Malcolm McGregor wrote about the controversial match in *Paul McLean:* "Australia's firebrand coach, Dave Brockhoff, questioned about the violence in the Ballymore test, was unrepentant and replied, 'Australia has been on the receiving end for a long time. I told the players before they ran on not to accept a thing which would make them take a step backwards. They were magnificent.' Brockhoff's rendition of his pre-match introduction was a trifle euphemistic. As McLean remembers, 'While Brock didn't specifically tell us to go out and kick everything in sight, that conclusion was there to be drawn if you wanted to.'"

The three and a half month tour did go on in 1975-76, with Ross Turnbull as manager and a muzzled Dave Brockhoff as coach. John Hipwell started as the captain, but after he was injured the mantle was thrown to Geoff Shaw. The back rowers were Loane, Cornelsen, Shaw and Gary Pearse. The back rowers were very effective on tour, Tony playing on either side of the scrum. In those days breakaways usually played left and right depending on the preference of the player, but would shift sometimes during a match to effect a better balance if the scrum was off kilter. "It was wherever you wanted, the coaches didn't mind in those days," Tony said. His own preference was to be left breakaway, but he was always willing to play wherever he was required. Tony was the only back rower to play all four tests, and only one player took the field in more games than he.

There is no one quite like Dave Brockhoff, and Tony reflected on him in *Paul McLean*: "With hindsight, Brock was a good coach," Tony Shaw remembers. "He really drilled the basics into us. But he was so bloody monotonous. Loaney still has nightmares about Brock chasing us up and down the tram tracks. On that '75 tour we eventually decided to mutiny on Brock. We appointed Carbs (Chris Carberry) as shop steward, and he presented our log of claims. We asked for a bit more variety in our training sessions. We could tell that Brock was starting to come around to our way of thinking when, be buggered, if Reggy Smith doesn't stand up and in that drawl of his say: 'Come on fellas, we need the hard work.' Brock was beaming but the rest of us could have killed Reggy."

In 1976 the shift of rugby power in Australia from New South Wales to Queensland was complete, a 42-4 thrashing of the Blues now being part of Queensland folklore. However,

the tour to France that same year seemed to halt the progress of the national game, and heralded the death-knell of Bob Templeton's run as national coach. It was a hard tour. The first test loss was respectable, Australia going down 15-18, but it was a humiliating defeat in the second by 6 to 34. Tony played in both tests.

1978 marked a significant point in Shaw's career, as innovative coach Daryl Haberecht took over the national coaching reins. He recognised that Shaw was the forceful leader needed to bring Australian rugby to greater heights, and he brought Paul McLean as well as Shaw to Sydney for almost two days of discussions. Tony was impressed with the thoroughness of Haberecht's preparation. He had dossiers on every Welsh player and videos of Welsh games which they analysed day and night. Not only was Haberecht meticulous in his analysis, but highly innovative. Though Shaw was not even captain of his club team at Brothers, Haberecht chose him to lead Australia, over Mark Loane.

The Welsh were Five Nations champions, and perhaps expected easy games. Instead they met aggressive Australian teams that met fire with fire. "Look", said Tony, "we weren't lily-white, but the Welsh were blatant with the boot, and we retaliated with the fist. They were dirty games, to be sure. Even 'Paddy' Batch got kicked by J.J. Williams. You don't expect that from backs."

Malcolm McGregor wrote in *Paul McLean*: "Throughout the struggle one man had stood out above all - Tony Shaw. Urging his men on in the manner of some primitive warrior chieftain, he personified Australia's unflinching resolve that day. To a man, his team responded, with a performance of heroic quality. Australia has played more brilliantly but never more courageously. The Australian pack - Loane, Shaw, Fay, Hillhouse, Cornelsen, Pilecki, Horton and Finnane - withstood the pressure. In those twenty agonising minutes (in the second half of the first encounter) Australian rugby came of age."

Shaw's undoubted success led to his captaincy of the 1978 Wallaby tour of New Zealand. It had been six years since a Wallaby team had gone there, and that 1972 expedition had been rightly deemed a disaster.

The loss of Steve Finnane, David Hillhouse

and Phil Crowe, and a lingering injury to Roger Gould, weakened the 1978 team, but they fought on bravely, going down 12-13 and 6-22 in the first two tests. The Aussies felt they should have won the first test, a crucial lineout penalty near the finish, which could conceivably have been kicked, being awarded at the wrong spot.

The heroics of the third test have been told and re-told. Coach Haberecht was hospitalised in Wanganui with a heart attack. He sent them a telegram from the hospital, though he was forbidden to watch the match: "Good luck. Will miss being with you to celebrate victory."

The Wallabies came together as the crisis sank in. Shaw said: "We had nothing to lose."

Tony was influenced by a training visit from ex-All Black coach J.J. Stewart, then well on in his fifties. Stewart faced the Wallabies and said: "I can beat you all over ten yards!" Tony thought, "You old bastard! What are you talking about?"

Stewart went on: "I'll beat you, even at my age, no doubt about it. But on the signal to go you first of all have to take a step backwards. Can you see the connection between what I say and your rugby? You're taking a step back, in scrums, rucks and mauls. You have to set the platform and go forward."

It was a good lesson. "It made the penny drop," said Tony.

The match resulted in one of the most astonishing reversals in Australia's rugby history. New Zealand writer Bob Howitt wrote: "Stewards order swabs at racetracks for the sort of form reversal that saw the Wallabies go from 6-22 down in Christchurch to 30-16 up in Auckland.

"But blood samples weren't needed to establish the cause of this dramatic turnaround. It could be described in one word…motivation.

"The Aussies had it, the All Blacks didn't.

"The All Blacks had the series won, the Aussies had to win to avert a whitewash.

"The All Blacks had something to play for; the Wallabies had everything to play for."

When the game got to the crucial point, the All Blacks taking the score from 18 to 9 to 18-13, Shaw acted swiftly. Adrian McGregor wrote about what happened next:

"Captain Shaw knew…he gathered the team together, his face angry, and told them (major epithets deleted) that they'd bloody well lose unless they got committed again.

"We haven't come this far to throw it away, have we?" he asked. "Look around you. Look at each of us. Look at your mates. You'd do anything for them, wouldn't you? Well, do it now. Give me your guts."

It was his 'into the valley of death' speech, the Gallipoli and Tobruk spirit that was appealed to, and there was no better one than 'Crazy Eyes' to sound the battle call. It worked. The final score of 30 to 16 was the highest number of points scored against an All Black team in a test match, and a much-needed boost for Australian rugby.

In 1979 there was a change in the coaching ranks, Dave Brockhoff taking over again, and, as the saying goes, 'different strokes, different folks'. There were two games against Ireland, with Tony as captain, and when Australia tumbled to consecutive defeats, 12-27 and 3-9, Mark Loane was back as captain in the single test against New Zealand and for the tour of the Argentine.

New Zealand had not lost a single test in Australia since 1934, but the Australian team of 1979 comprised many well-blooded veterans with a sprinkle of youngsters. The Australian team was: Paul McLean, Phil Crowe, Andrew Slack, Geoff Shaw, Brendan Moon, Tony Melrose, Peter Carson; Mark Loane, Greg Cornelsen, Andy Stewart, Peter McLean, Tony Shaw, Stan Pilecki, Peter Horton, Chris Handy.

In an incredible game, Australia won 12 to 6. It was only the second win in the Bledisloe Cup in Australia in its 48-year-old history. The Aussies ran joyously around the field brandishing the Cup.

As D.J. Cameron wrote: "It will remain one of the vivid memories of sport - 15 jubilant Wallabies hoisting the ungainly Bledisloe Cup aloft in triumph."

Mark Loane departed for South Africa in 1980, Tony Shaw was back as captain, and Bob Templeton the Wallaby coach. Incredibly, Australia defeated New Zealand 13 to 9 at the Sydney Cricket Ground, for the All Blacks' third defeat in a row by Australia. After losing the second test 9-12, the Wallabies stormed back at the SCG to roll the All Blacks 26 to 10. The All Blacks had lost the Bledisloe Cup in consecutive years, proving that Australian rugby had attained dizzy heights. "It was," said Tony, "an exceptional period of time. Our team was young, aggressive, good at the breakdown, and we had the best backs and committed forwards. Above all, we knew we could win. We believed in ourselves."

In 1981-82 manager Sir Nicholas Shehadie and coach Bob Templeton took the team to the United Kingdom. Tony Shaw was the captain, thus being the first Queenslander to take the Wallabies there since his father-in-law Bill McLean in 1947-48. It was a disappointing tour, as the Wallabies won only 16 of 23 games and lost all the internationals except against Ireland.

When the Wallabies played in the north of Scotland, Shaw had an altercation with the captain of the representative team, Bill Cuthbertson, and a few words were spoken. When the international came around, they found themselves facing one another again, with no quarter asked, and none given.

During the game, it was frustrating for Shaw, because although Australia had scored three tries to one Andy Irvine kept Scotland in the match with his penalty kicks, which eventually won the test. The referee kept penalising the Aussies. The Scotland backline was way off-side according to Tony, moving up fast to nullify the superior Australian back line. It caused Mark Ella to fumble. The referee blew his whistle and ordered a scrum down, with Scotland putting the ball in.

Tony, as captain, appealed to the referee. "They were yards offside," he remonstrated.

As he argued with the referee Cuthbertson came up behind him. Tony recounts what happened next: "I was trying to talk to the referee, and Cuthbertson kept up his niggle, niggle, niggle behind me, with references to whinging Aussies." Tony admits he "lost it". He turned, threw a punch that whistled past referee Roger Quittenton's nose, hit Cuthbertson squarely on the jaw and knocked him off his feet. "He hit the deck in front of 60,000 spectators and God knows how many in the television audience, and I heard the Scots telling Bill, 'Stay down, stay down'. I figured I would be sent off, but it was a penalty. Afterwards, I apologised to the whole nation."

When it came to the next test against England, Shaw, the tour captain, was dropped after leading Australia in 15 tests. Mark Loane

was his replacement as captain. Shehadie and Templeton voted him out. It was an understandable shock, and to this day he has never discussed it with the other principals. He said: "I live with it. Tempo tried to talk to me about it once, and I told him I didn't want to know about it."

He was back in the game in 1982, and of all the teams it was Scotland on tour, under new coach Bob Dwyer. He played both tests. Cuthbertson came up to him at the bar after the match at Ballymore and Tony introduced him to his wife Judy.

Cuthbertson said: "He introduces me to beautiful girls all over the world, Judy, and I'm pleased to say you're no exception."

At that, he excused himself as Judy smiled politely at him, hiding her obvious displeasure at Tony. After a very quick explanation that it was an attempt to 'get square', Judy relaxed and exclaimed: "The bastard!"

After the Scotland games, ten of the Wallabies withdrew from the tour of New Zealand that year. Nine were Queenslanders. Although Dwyer still perceives the action as a mini-revolt over his ascendancy to the national coaching position over Queensland's favourite son Bob Templeton, Tony avers that this was not so. Had these players toured New Zealand, the state and national commitments would have meant six months off work in twelve months. With Tony already having to agree to a moratorium with the bank on his home loan for the three-and-a-half-month UK tour, another trip away was not possible.

In 1983 Shaw was dropped against the United States, as Dwyer wanted to play a more Randwick-style game, and players like Simon Poidevin and Chris Roche better fitted the bill. He thought to himself: "There's no point in sitting on the bench at this stage of my career. If Bob Dwyer doesn't want me and I'm playing well, I'm out. The reserve spot will be better filled by some up-and-comer who would benefit from the exposure."

And that is what he did. Dwyer sounded him out later about playing against the All Blacks, but Shaw felt if Dwyer considered he wasn't good enough to play against the United States, why should he suddenly be good enough to play against the All Blacks? Alan Jones also discussed the possibility of a comeback, but

Shaw stuck by his decision, though he kept playing for Queensland.

In 1985 he was captain-coach of his beloved Brothers, with whom he had eight Grand Final wins.

In all, he played thirty-six tests for Australia, and 15 of those were as captain. There were also 112 games for Queensland.

Throughout his career his main rival for the captaincy of the Wallabies was Mark Loane. Theirs had been an interesting relationship. Both are highly competitive. Shaw enjoyed the bar after the game and a night out more than Loane. Loane was more intellectual, Shaw a constant stirrer and niggler, revelling in confrontation with players and referees.

He said, with utter frankness: "Loaney could never understand me. My attitude was that your opponent was your enemy, and you could love that attitude or hate it. Mark's wife couldn't even talk to me. When Brothers played University, the local derby, Brothers had more mongrel. Anyhow, Mark understands the beast better now. We talk more now, and are good friends. He's a great thinker on the game."

Throughout his life Shaw was always a great club man, and even though he played for Australia on a Saturday he would turn out for Brothers on a Sunday. Playing for the Brothers Club, to Tony, was equally as important as playing for Australia.

Tony Shaw always led from the front. He was unflinching when the going got tough, an example for lesser mortals to follow. If you had to pick one person to be with when you were fighting for your life, a good choice would be Tony Shaw. He was a throw-back to the old days, a tough character of the old school. He had unbelievable determination, and never asked anyone to do something he wouldn't do himself. He always gave loyalty to his teammates, and expected and got the same in return.

He was a fierce opponent on the field of play, and it was the likes of him that brought Australian rugby back from the ashes to respectability. He was a man's man all the way.

His Wallabies team mate Dr Peter Horton had this to say of him: "…one of the most complete back rowers ever, not just in terms of Australia but world-wide. A.A. Shaw, Tony, also emerged a little prematurely in terms of senior representation and was I feel wrongly cast in the mould of the Reg Smith type second-rower and I even think his first cap as No. 8 was to be proven as a misguided selection, for his niche for us was the now much-vaunted blindside flanker role…though that is not to say he could not play openside.

"It is with pride, though, that I remember one of his early games for Queensland. It was against NSW Country at Scone in 1972 or 1973, when the young tyro, playing second row I seem to remember, was confronted by my very wily, grizzly and fairly 'direct' NSW Country pack, and ended up on the end of a very convincing thrashing.

"Tony was a tremendous competitor and very skilled ball player and of course he is renowned for his mauling and rucking which always had that Brothers' flavour about it! Though his ability to get a game of touch going, with the words, 'game of touch?' will long live in my memory and, by the way, he was a master of it!

"Really, how lucky was anybody to be in a team with these three great back rowers, Cornelsen, Shaw and Loane? They complemented each other so well and with Gary Pearse as a replacement the Australian back row of the mid-70s was close to being without peer in world rugby."

# Sir Nicholas Shehadie

Familiarly known as 'Nick', or 'Black Nick', this Lebanese-Australian is arguably the most beloved of any Wallaby in history. Only Bill Cerutti could rival 'Nick'. They both had the common touch, and wherever they went people instinctively knew that they had hearts of gold, were men's men who were as honest as the day is long, and wanted to talk to them.

'Nick' has had more international presence than Bill, combining his rugby with broader sporting interests, as well as being a media magnate, though he would recoil at the very words, and at the same time, a consummate, natural politician. Fundamentally 'Nick' is just a 'bloody good bloke', who, despite all the honours, is as down-to-earth now as he was in his early days. This is remarkable when you realise that he was knighted on January 1, 1976 for his contribution to local politics and sport and received an OBE mainly for his sporting exploits in 1969 and an AC in 1989 for his services to the media. His friends call him, familiarly, not 'Sir Nicholas' but 'Sir Nick'. It somehow fits better. Then there are a few little assignments like Chairman of SBS, Chairman of TAFE, Chairman of the Sydney Cricket and Sports Ground Trust, member of the Museum Board of Australia, etc.

His wife Marie is Clinical Professor of Psychiatry at the University of Sydney, and her contributions in her field of expertise are equally impressive. One month she may be in the centre of Australia working with aboriginal children, the next giving workshops in Victoria or Vietnam. Her social commitment, like Nick's, is incredible, and she too is universally beloved. They are in many ways different types, but are perfectly matched, both being able to handle busy and at times turbulent lives with grace and love. They have three children, and now three grand-children, Nick saying: "At last we have a Shehadie with blue eyes."

The author Max Howell was overseas for 33 years after the 1947-48 tour, and upon his return to Australia, contacted Nick, who came to pick him up at Ebley Street, Bondi Junction, where he was staying with his mother.

The author was waiting on the footpath outside his mother's apartment when Nick drove up. After the usual back-slapping, a remarkably unchanged Nick said: "And how's your Mum?"

"She's just fine, Nick."

"Haven't seen her in thirty years. Is she upstairs? I'd like to say hello."

Nick clambered up the stairs and greeted the author's mother with a big hug.

"It's good to see you again, Mum."

Mum was absolutely delighted that the then Lord Mayor of Sydney would remember her, and with such affection. But that is Nick, as natural as always, with a rare human touch.

Afterwards Nick took the author to the Rosehill Races, where he was a member of the board, and after a glorious race lunch, they

The remarkable Ella brothers, Gary, Mark and Glen getting a little instruction from their father.

The incomparable Mark Ella, with Simon Poidevin and Andrew Slack backing him up.

**Dr Mark Loane...when he got the ball he wanted to protect it.**

**Scrum-capped centre Trevor Allan scoring for the 1947-48 Wallabies.**

'Stan the Man' Pilecki having a rumble with some Wellington 'mates' at Ballymore in 1981 – from left, Steve Hinds, Scott Crichton, Paul Quinn (6) and Brendon Gard'ner.

The 1949 Bledisloe Cup-winning Wallabies, captained by 'Tubby' Allen.

Tom Lawton, a veritable giant among the hooking fraternity.

Tony Shaw, one of the most wily lineout tacticians in the business.

Andrew Slack...always looking for support.

An ecstatic Wallaby coach Dave Brockhoff shows off the Bledisloe Cup after his team's 12-6 victory in Sydney in 1979. All Blacks are Bevan Wilson, Andy Haden and Gary Seear. At left is the Wallaby captain Mark Loane.

Jules Guerassimoff, who also happened to be the Queensland champion with the javelin.

Peter Horton acknowledging Greg Cornelsen's remarkable four-try haul at Eden Park in 1978.

**Nick Farr-Jones showing his super-active follow-through, with Sean Fitzpatrick watching in admiration.**

moved to the paddock. He walked around, and it really was something to see.

"Hey, Big Nick! 'Ow ya goin', mate?" asked one punter.

"Fine, Charlie, how's your brother. Is he off the grog yet?" And on and on it went, Nick enjoying the repartee. While the other members of the Board were in their leather seats overlooking the finish line or holding up the bar, Nick was with the people he loves the most and who put him where he is today, the average Aussie.

Nicholas Shehadie is not the first Wallaby to be knighted. The honour goes to Sir Ernest ('Weary') Dunlop, a doctor who became a legend for his humanitarian work in Japanese POW camps in the Second World War. A Victorian, he was nowhere near the dominant rugby player Nick was, but he certainly played for Australia and, like Nick, made a significant contribution to Australian life.

Nick was the first son of a migrant family from Lebanon. They came from a long line of clergy, which seemingly ended with him. His father and grandfather were men of the cloth, highly respected by the community they represented. Nick's father, because of the reverence with which he was held, was more or less recognised as the unofficial Lebanese Ambassador in Australia during Nick's childhood.

Nick went to school first at Cleveland Street and then Crown Street, and anyone being brought up in that period knew they were pretty rough areas. You learned to look after yourself in that environment, Nick fortunately being large for his age and obviously not one to tangle with.

He had no experience with any of the rugby codes during his school life, but enjoyed athletics and cricket. A Lebanese minister did not make much money, so Nick felt obliged to leave school when he was still fourteen years of age because of the family's economic situation. A self-made man, that is what Sir Nicholas Shehadie is without question.

There were some abortive attempts at jobs, first with Fox Movietone News, which lasted about three weeks, and then a Biscuit Company, which between the scorching ovens and loading trucks simply did not appeal to his young imagination. The Lebanese have always been traders and shop-keepers, and Nick began to find himself when he started off with a men's wear shop, first at Peter's Corner, Randwick, and then a dry cleaning shop at Redfern. As he would say: "Drop your tweeds at Nick's."

A childhood friend of Nick's, Col Thornley, convinced Nick he should join the Coogee Surf Club, which he did, and before he knew it Nick had agreed to a try-out for the Randwick Rugby Union Club. It is hard to believe that a svelte young Shehadie started his career at inside centre, his protestations that "I had pretty good pace" reaching deaf ears or poorly restrained laughter among his friends.

He was in fourth grade in 1943, but as so often happens someone was injured in the game at the next oval in reserve grade, and Nick was called upon. So he jumped the fence and received a pretty rapid promotion. The next week he was picked in the second team, again there was an injury and Nick got a run with the firsts. He was all of sixteen years of age at the time. What amazed him that day was the amount of talking going on in the field of play, Randwick's Mal Murray, among others, keeping up a continual chatter.

In 1944 he was in first grade, as a breakaway, doubtless because of his avowed blinding pace, but when Keith Windon came home on leave from the Air Force, Nick moved down to the seconds. Keith Windon, the elder brother of Col Windon, was a Wallaby from the thirties, and one of the greatest to don the green and gold. As Nick says with due modesty: "I was replaced by an international."

In that same year he was selected in a rep team to play Army, with such pre-war immortals as Tom Pauling and Aub Hodgson gracing the paddock.

His first real breakthrough came in 1946 when he made the NSW team to go to Queensland. In those days the team went by train and played on the concrete dust-bowl at Toowoomba, which humbled many a great player over the years. Nick was then a 'dirt tracker', and though he did not play against the northern state he logged in some invaluable experience. Fullback Ron Rankin was the NSW captain.

In 1946 he was on the NSW second team, but when it came to making the Wallaby team to New Zealand, Australia's first post-war rugby tour, he unluckily missed selection. The captain Bill McLean was also a breakaway, and then there were the dynamos, Keith and Col Windon, and Alan Livermore from Queensland, who could place-kick from prodigious distances.

The All Blacks came to Australia in 1947, and this was a turning point in Nick's life. As was to be the custom for a number of years, the All Blacks were quartered at the Coogee Bay Hotel. The manager of the team was the famous Norman McKenzie, who was the sole selector of the New Zealand team, and his opinion on the game was rarely challenged.

The All Blacks had just arrived and went to watch Randwick play Gordon, and McKenzie watched the young Shehadie strutting his stuff. When the game was over, McKenzie went up to the Australian selectors and said: "There's a boy today I saw who should be playing for Australia - Shehadie!" Nick suddenly found himself on the NSW training squad.

Nick had never seen an international match to this point in his life, and could not believe how big and rugged the All Blacks looked when they went up against NSW. Though he was a spectator, he was thrilled when 'Mick' Cremin, Charlie Eastes, Col Windon and the others pulled off a stunning upset.

He was not in the first test at Brisbane, but got his first hit-out in a test at the Sydney Cricket Ground in the second encounter. This was the final match before the Wallaby team to the British Isles, France, Canada and the United States was to be announced. He had six stitches in his finger that day, but there was no way he would have cried off. It was the opportunity of a lifetime.

He can still recall the genial Bob McMaster continually talking in the dressing room, while the remainder were tense and nervous in expectation. The team ran out on the field, lined up, gave three cheers for their opponents, shook hands, and then kicked off.

Shehadie received the initial kick-off, and charged straight ahead. Despite monsters like 'Iron Man' Simpson coming at him like maniacs, Shehadie made over thirty yards, All Blacks bumping off him. "I did it out of sheer fright," reflected Nick. Australia lost the match, but the young Shehadie, now a second rower, impressed with his display.

On the Monday, the day the team was due to be announced, Nick, hooker Don Furness and breakaway Col Windon were with the All Blacks at the Coogee Bay Hotel. Justice Herron, who was the President of the Australian Rugby Union, asked Nick if he would drive Australian coach Johnny Wallace, who had had a few drinks too many, to Sydney. He winked at Nick and said: "I asked you because I know you will be able to drive in London."

When the team was announced by the ABC at 2 pm, Nick's heart sank when they announced four second rowers and his name was not among them. Then came "utility forward, N. Shehadie." When his name was read out his family, not overly interested in sport, broke out in cheers. A big personal thrill for him was a farewell in his honour at Redfern Town Hall, Redfern being mainly a rugby league area.

The 1947-48 team left from the number seven wharf, Woolloomooloo, and was farewelled by a thousand spectators, with coloured streamers stretched from shore to liner. It was very moving as they proceeded out of the Sydney Heads on their nine-month adventure, a group of youngsters, Nick Shehadie, Max Howell, Trevor Allan and Terry MacBride, with a core of hardened veterans, such as captain Bill McLean, Bob McMaster and Graham Cooke.

Nick said, however, that he must have got the "short straw", as his room-mate was the one-and-only Bob McMaster. Whereas most of the team travelled with a huge cabin trunk, Bob went on tour for nine months with a small globite case. "You only need another shirt and a pair of socks and an extra pair of dags," opined Bob.

"But what about the tuxedos we were all required to bring?" asked Nick.

"The blazer's good enough for me," said Bob. And that was that.

Bob McMaster, the father of present-day comedian Danny McMaster, was a handful in those days. He had been in the war, and this was heaven for him - tranquillity after horror. He was a natural comedian, surely the funniest man ever to tour, could toss the suds down equal to any in the world, was completely irreverent, as any good Army private completely disdained authority, and had a never-ending source of dirty songs that would burn the ears off the average person.

'Young Nick' was housed with this worldly veteran, and it took little time before they became the best of friends, keeping the team laughing throughout the tour. Bob was the one who called him 'Black Nick'.

"You black bastard," he would say, "What do you think you are up to now?" They were a rare combination. They could have been on the stage.

The cabin next to theirs was occupied by Canon Hammond, a religious friend of his father's, who must have been shocked beyond recall at the antics in the Shehadie-McMaster cabin. It became the place to go for a laugh and a yarn.

The tour was a resounding success, the Wallabies creating a record by not having their line crossed in a home international. It is a record that conceivably might be equalled, but never bettered. Despite injuries to captain Bill McLean and star winger Charlie Eastes which decimated the team, the players found an inner strength and did not ask for replacements. Nick dislocated his collar-bone against Cardiff, but fought his way back to make the last home test against England.

The balance of the team had much to do with their success, a combination of youngsters and veterans, as well as a strict manager, Arnold Tancred, and a 'soft' assistant manager, Jeff Noseda. As Nick says: "All the team are my closest friends. We have mateship forever. And I made so many friends overseas, people I still see today."

Everywhere Nick went in the British Isles the Lebanese community came out in force and were intent on giving him presents, shirts and other cotton goods being the most frequent. One time they delivered to his room a large chocolate cake, which was quite a delicacy, as in post-war England everyone still had ration cards. Sugar, flour, steaks and so on were unavailable. Many a time the Wallabies dined on whale steak and horse meat during their tour.

Anyhow, suddenly Nick had this glorious chocolate cake in his possession, so he took his room-mate, Col Windon, into his confidence: "Col, we've got this cake, and it would be completely wasted if we gave it to the boys. Can

you keep a secret? Let's keep it for ourselves! Agreed?"

Col agreed, and resolved to tell no one. Nick had to leave the room, and about two minutes later Arch Winning knocked on the door and came in. "Nick told me I could have some of his cake," he said. So he cut off a piece and devoured it. Another Wallaby came in, then another and another, until Nick arrived, and there was none left. Nick could never keep a secret. He didn't even get any of his own cake.

The Barbarians game was not on the original schedule of the Wallabies, and was put on for financial reasons after negotiation by manager Arnold Tancred so that the Wallabies could come home via Canada and the United States. Since then, touring teams have always played against the Barbarians.

The Wallabies had to get specific vaccination shots in London to go on the North American route, and dutifully lined up for their needles. The author was in line, after Shehadie, who was getting more agitated as he observed the needles going into his compatriots. When Nick's turn came, he changed colour and fainted. It was like watching a great whale being harpooned.

One story Colin Windon told was when the Wallabies were travelling across the Atlantic from England in the *Queen Mary* and the sea was horrendous. The majority of the supposedly tough footballers were either feeding the fishes with regularity or were very close to it, 'green to the gills', as they say.

'Black Nick' changed colour somewhat, and turned to his Randwick mate Col Windon, who himself was nauseous but had not as yet turned the dreaded corner.

"Big Nick sick, Col, big Nick sick," Shehadie lamented, rolling his eyes and holding his stomach. "Big Nick sick, Col, big Nick sick."

Just then one of the team said, "Look, fellas, I'm going up to the canteen, anyone want anything?"

Nick looked up and said: "Just bring me back a big box of chocolates."

Wallabies ran in all directions. The very thought of the chocolates started off a stampede to the ship's railing.

When the Wallabies got off the boat in New York they were all worried about the customs, as they had acquired numerous gifts and weren't anxious about paying duty in the United States as everything was being taken back to Australia. Nick in particular was vulnerable, as he was loaded with gifts from his Lebanese friends, his green Wallaby kit-bag being completely full of such presents.

The worst fears of the Wallabies were soon realised when a mean-looking customs officer decided to give the Wallabies a going over and, as fate would have it, decided to start his inquisition with Nick's kit-bag. The Wallabies all gulped. The customs officer thrust his hand into the bag, and then let out a blood-curdling yell and ran from the scene clutching his hand, with blood flying everywhere. Nick had inadvertently left his razor open at the top of the bag, and this unfortunate customs officer almost had his finger severed. That was the end of the customs inspection. Nick had saved the day again!

In 1949 there were tests against the Maoris, and then the tour to New Zealand, Nick's first visit to that country. The 'Tubby' Allan-led tour was in some ways reminiscent of the 1947-48 tour, as again there was a fine balance of the young and the old. The management team of Ron Walden and Bill Cerutti was magnificent, two old front rowers effecting a rare blend of discipline and enjoyment.

Though thirty New Zealanders were playing in South Africa at the same time, the strong Maori contingent had been left home because of apartheid and the games were highly competitive and close, but Australia won. The players did not worry about the critics, they at last had the Bledisloe Cup in their hands.

When in New Zealand, Nick injured his hip, and was in considerable pain, and felt he could not go to Feilding that day with the team. He asked the management whether he could stay in bed in his hotel to recover. Assistant manager Bill Cerutti offered to stay with him.

The team departed, and former All Black Mark Nicholls came in and said there was a party at a nearby hotel. Cerutti said it would be good for Nick so he carried Nick on his back, no mean feat in itself, to where the action was. They got back feeling none the worse for wear about 5am, Nick again being carried by Cerutti. The team had meanwhile returned from their excursion and the manager, Ron Walden, had gone to check on his sick charge.

He shook his head. He should have known better, with Cerutti and Shehadie stuck together.

The next big tour was to South Africa in 1953, and this was, for Nick, a great experience and an enormous challenge going against the likes of Jaap Bekker. Wherever he went he was asked whether he and the Italian-Australian Bill Cerutti were related. Nick would say: "He's my uncle!"

Nick actually went away as a second rower, but in the first test Bob Davidson and Jack Carroll found difficulty in handling the South African front row, Bekker in particular causing the Aussies trouble. Bekker was enormously strong, and reputedly broke a goalpost by pushing against it, and actually broke English forward Harry Walker's neck in one game. As part of his regular training he would put a chain around his neck attached to a huge rock, which he would lift off the ground.

So Nick was brought up from the second row to handle Bekker, which he did successfully. He counteracted the pressure by having his head between Bekker's head and shoulder. Both in South Africa and Australia in 1956 Shehadie marked Bekker effectively.

Nick, who during his career proved to be a tremendous tourist, an extraordinary team man, was always willing to play wherever the selectors wanted him, and never once let his country down. He played front row, second row, lock and breakaway, though his best position was probably front row.

He was the only one of the 1947-48 Wallabies to tour the British Isles a second time in 1957-58, ten years on. The Bob Davidson-led team seemed to lose spirit and confidence, though they had some outstanding players aboard, notably John Thornett, Jim Phipps, Jim Lenehan, Alan Cameron, Tony Miller, Des Connor and Arthur Summons. It might have been a sad end to an illustrious career, but it was capped off when Nick was asked to play for the Barbarians against his own team. He and New Zealand's Ian Clarke were the first to be so honoured.

In all, Nick played over 100 matches for Australia, 30 of these being tests. He broke the record set by Eddie Bonis and then Cyril Burke. He captained Australia in South Africa in the Port Elizabeth test in 1953, and at home in

Australia in 1954. He was later to manage the 1981 Wallabies on their UK tour, which team had aspiring greats like the Ellas, Simon Poidevin and Michael O'Connor.

He even became a referee after his retirement, though he failed his first examination. When asked what he would do if a player did such-and-such in a game, Nick replied: "I'd bloody well shoot him." As a referee he said he got to know Sydney rather well, adjudicating in isolated fields from one end of the city to another.

One day, after refereeing a third grade game, he retired to the bar to have a few drinks, and then some. This continued throughout the second grade match, and into the firsts. He was feeling no pain, when someone rushed in and said Nick had to go on in the first grade game, as the referee had pulled a muscle. Nick pulled himself together, changed back into his togs, and ran out onto the field. Who should be playing that day but two of his Wallaby colleagues and great referee-baiters, St George's Alan Cameron and Eddie Stapleton.

At the very first play Nick blew his whistle and penalised St George.

Cameron and Stapleton looked at Nick in astonishment and asked: "Why was that, Mr Referee?"

"Just to let you know I'm here and I'm boss, that's why!" said Nick, who had no trouble from then on.

Nick became vice-president, then president of the Australian Rugby Football Union for eight years, and perhaps his major contribution to the game was being the prime mover and advocate for the first World Cup in 1987. It was not easy to sell the idea, and eventually New Zealand and Australia came together in a co-chairing capacity.

The case had to be argued with each of the home countries, which was not easy. Shehadie received a lot of flak from a lot of people, and when it came to the crucial meeting with the International Rugby Board he was particularly castigated over Australia paying its players up front at a sevens tournament, which was held to be contrary to the strict laws of amateurism at the time. Everything looked hopeless, until one of the Board slipped him a note.

Nick then said: "Look, I'm really sorry, maybe in reflection we did do the wrong thing. But we knew England did it in the Argentine so we thought it must have been all right." There was some restrained laughter, and Australia and New Zealand received the World Cup. He was ever grateful for the note which told him of England's misdemeanour.

Though there were no ground rules, and most of the organisational assistance was voluntary, the World Cup was proven to be a master stroke, and of course has been a continuing success. Nick had banked a $2.6 million profit before the first game. The World Cup today remains as his rugby epitaph.

Nick was successful in business, going from the dry-cleaning shop to working with Wormald to an Engineering business with his brother.

It is said that something from Nick's engineering firm was in the capsule at the first moon landing. Rumours that it was his dry cleaning business have no foundation in fact.

A popular personality, Nick entered local politics, rising to Deputy Mayor of the City of Sydney and then Lord Mayor in 1973, 1974 and 1975. He retired in 1976, but was brought back in 1987 as one of a three-man committee to run the city. During his tenure as Lord Mayor great changes took place. Many streets were expanded, Martin Place was resurrected, the Festival of Sydney was begun, and of course the Opera House was opened. The plaque at the Opera House tells it all: "Opened by Her Majesty Queen Elizabeth in the presence of N. Shehadie, Lord Mayor."

Nick maintains that rugby changed his life, that he owes everything to the game. The principles he uses in business are those he gained on the playing fields of the world. Maybe all that is so, but Nick always had the personality to be successful, and the motivation. He has still retained that certain ingenuousness he had from his youth. Though he is now a man of business who makes decisions involving millions of dollars, the reality is that he is a man of high principles and complete honesty. That, and his highly developed sense of humour, is why he is the most popular rugby figure in Australian rugby history.

# Andrew Slack

There was a movie years ago called *The Quiet Man*. It was arguably the greatest movie John Wayne made, and should have won him the Academy Award, but it did not. *True Grit* won it for him later on for a rather nondescript performance. *The Quiet Man* told the story of a Yank making his pilgrimage back to Ireland, where his forefathers had lived. He falls in love with the beautiful Maureen O'Hara who, to put the discussion back to a slightly more modern perspective, was the mother of Mia Farrow, whose claim to fame was making *The Great Gatsby* and some arty movies, being married to Frank Sinatra for a few horrible months, and then going to a real loser, Woody Allen, until he seduced their adopted daughter. Maureen's father in the movie was Victor McLaughlin, who incidentally won an Academy Award himself but also fought the immortal Jack Johnson for the heavyweight boxing crown.

We could go on and on, but the quick summary is McLaughlin resisted the marriage, and the Yank, the 'Quiet Man', spent a lot of the movie restraining his temper despite extreme provocation. Of course, the 'Quiet Man' got the girl in the end.

Andrew Slack is no John Wayne in appearance. Wayne was a football line backer, Andrew would have trouble running around with the full American football uniform. But Andrew is a quiet and modest person, something like big John, and he also had a love affair with Ireland.

And he got the big one in the end, captaining Australia to its first-ever Grand Slam rugby win in 1984.

Andrew Slack was a different type of captain, and it really makes one think what captaincy, and leadership, is all about. Chris Handy said of Slack in *Well, I'll Be Ruggered*: "Andrew Slack, who had always preferred to follow rather than lead, who was always happy to be there with the Paul McLeans the Geoff Shaws, the Tony Shaws and the Mark Loanes, was chosen to lead the team. It was a joy to see how Andrew led the team. From being the humble but clever playmaker, he became a captain who inspired in his team a new respect. That respect had grown up under the tutelage of Geoff Shaw, Slack's Queensland team mate, and Michael O'Connor, who he had played with under Paul McLean. A great student of people and of the game, Slack had watched and taken all of it in and had developed himself along the way. So Jones had a great ally on the field. He was astute enough to know that he had chosen a leader the team would follow."

Andrew Slack is and always has been a leader of men. It is just that there are many ways to skin a cat with respect to leadership and he was not a traditionalist in his approach. Bill McLean was of the blood and guts variety, and the 9 st 13 lb Max Howell on his first Wallaby tour remembers McLean's opening diatribe only too well: "You're playing for Australia, for your country - you play to the death. If anyone takes a backward step he'll cop one from me. To the death, do you understand?"

Howell understood all right, but thought even at his young age there were tactical limitations to the message. Tony Shaw was another of the 'into the valley of death mode', and it's perhaps no wonder he married Bill McLean's daughter. The father and son-in-law were essentially of the same hell and brimstone mould.

There have been swearing captains, religious captains, 'I won't pass the ball captains' who tried to demonstrate that leadership was running straight ahead, 'have a drink with me' captains', and occasional philosopher captains. Two types had never emerged: homosexual and quiet captains. With the advent of Andrew Slack, at least one of these has appeared, and only history can tell us whether the former will ever emerge.

The simple fact is that teams can be successful under any form of leadership style. It helps when you have a good team, and that team wins.

The innovative style utilised by Andrew Slack was of the non-Ian Chappell mode, whose basic credo was that the world consists of only black and white. Slack would argue that there are times when grey is an acceptable colour, that leadership requires a certain flexibility, though that flexibility needs to be coupled with strength of character. Andrew had that, and the Wallabies knew it. They had seen him on the field of combat, and in all kinds of social situations. He had their trust, and there were times one could sense that the Wallabies were playing for their country, and themselves, but also Andrew himself…they did not want to let him down.

Andrew Slack instinctively knew that it was necessary to understand the players involved, their strengths and weaknesses, their idiosyncrasies, and he was superb in getting to know what made his players tick. He did not feel that a captain's role was tactical, rather he felt that this should be the role of the coach and the players themselves once the plan had been formalised.

He knew that being a captain did not mean you had to do everything yourself, that you had to keep your own ego in perspective and learn to delegate, for each team was made up of strong people of immense capabilities. A captain had most certainly to win the respect of his team on the field, but it was equally important to earn that respect off the field.

He learned through experience that captaincy is important at crucial times, for example when motivation and/or concentration flag. Then the captain has to be decisive, not in a vociferous manner, but in getting the minds of the team in focus.

Mark Ella summed him up in *Path To Victory* after the 1984 Grand Slam feat: "Slacky probably was the only person who could have handled the captaincy in the British Isles. He was fantastic. Every team needs a cornerstone, and Slacky was it. We all had lots of respect for him. He's been around for a long while, but he's not really that old.

"With players like Gould, Campese, Moon, Lynagh, Farr-Jones and myself, we had a backline full of exciting individuals. I'm not saying Slacky lacked initiative and flair, but his role was to settle the play down. Be the link man. Not be happy-go-lucky or adventurous. Slacky did it to perfection and always seemed to be there when he was wanted.

"Although he's a quiet person, Slacky is a great communicator. Because he had the respect of the team he could come up and say, 'I don't think you're doing this right,' or 'Why don't you try this?' Slacky didn't have to get up and rant and rave. He preferred to listen to people and do things in a quiet sort of way. Because of his experience, he could analyse things and understand how people are feeling."

Andrew was born in Brisbane and lived in the suburb of Mount Gravatt. His father came from a line of butchers, but he went into the wine trade and then hotels, taking over the Mount Gravatt Hotel.

The hotel was remodelled in July 1957, but tragedy struck when his father found out he had cancer in August, and died in December. Andrew was two years of age at the time, his sister Jane was three and a brother Michael six.

Mother continued on in the hotel before retiring in 1986, a sister, Mary Healy, coming to assist her during this time. It was tough going for the young family, but somehow they managed, his mother encouraging his participation in sport and driving young Andrew all over the place whenever it was necessary.

His early rugby was at Villanova College, starting off in 1964 briefly as a hooker, before moving to halfback, and to five-eighth in his last two years. He made the first XV in his last year, but his talents went relatively unrecognised as no representative opportunities came his way. He was interested in all sports as a youngster, but cricket was his number one priority and favourite sport.

He took a year off after high school and worked before enrolling at Mount Gravatt Teachers' College in order to become a primary school teacher. After being influenced by John Kelly and then Greg Moloney to go to Southern Districts for rugby, he played for Souths.

They were low in talent these years, so he quickly went from the Under-19s to the A Grade, still playing five-eighth. There happened to be a certain Paul McLean in the Queensland pivot spot about that time, so there was certainly no great optimism in representative rugby in that direction.

However, in 1975 he got his first breakthrough and state cap as five-eighth against Australian Combined Services, and was a reserve against New South Wales. The retirement of Wallaby centre David L' Estrange after the 1975-76 tour of the British Isles, France and America, caused the Queensland selectors, Bob Templeton in particular, to shift him to outside centre, which caused some degree of scepticism early but turned out to be a stroke of genius. In 1976 he became a Maroon fixture. It is of interest to view the Queensland team for its first match of the 1976 season, against New England: Graham Noon, Paddy Batch, Andrew Slack, Jeff Weeks, Paul McLean, Rod Hauser (replaced by Paul Smith), Mark Loane, Tony Shaw, Jim Miller, David Hillhouse, Peter McLean, Stan Pilecki, Bill Ross, and David Dunworth. Queensland was on the upsurge, and Slackie was a vital cog in its well-oiled machine.

Bret Harris, in *The Marauding Maroons*, said of him: "Andrew Slack was the most underrated player to represent Australia during the past decade. Slack was unfashionable in an era which produced brilliant attacking three-quarters such as Bill McKid, Michael O'Connor and Michael Hawker. But Slack was the best team player on the Queensland side. He was always conscious of his supports. He would have been just as happy to deliver the pass which led to a try as score the try himself. He was totally unselfish and served his wingers splendidly. Slack timed his passes to perfection and was never

guilty of selling a team mate the dump."

Slack was a bit of a throw-back to the old days, when all centres were taught how to 'set up' for the wings. Increasingly, it has become a lost art, and great players like Cyril Towers and All Black Johnny Smith would be turning over in their graves witnessing the demise of that art.

In 1976 Queensland toured New Zealand, part of the QRU's Master Plan to learn everything possible from the power-house of the rugby game. A broken jaw ruled out any possibility of a tour to France that year, so Andrew took six months off doing very unglamorous but toughening work for the Main Roads for six months.

In 1977 he finished his teaching certificate and went to his alma mater, Villanova College, where he taught and coached.

Andrew's first test was at Ballymore on 17 June 1978, against Wales, which Australia won by 18 to 8. The Welsh centres were Ray Gravell and Steve Fenwick, while he partnered Martin Knight in his debut. The Australian team was: Laurie Monaghan, Phil Crowe, Martin Knight, Andrew Slack, Paddy Batch, Paul McLean, Rod Hauser, Mark Loane, Tony Shaw, Garrick Fay, David Hillhouse, Greg Cornelsen, Stan Pilecki, Peter Horton and Steve Finnane.

In the second test at the Sydney Cricket Ground Australia triumphed again, this time by a 19 to 17 count, the game becoming part of the game's folklore as Welsh prop Graham Price had to leave the field after five minutes after being delivered the *coup-de-grace* by Steve Finnane.

His first overseas tour with the Wallabies was in 1978 to New Zealand. It was a 'nervous' expedition in so far as the ARFU was concerned, as it was the first time that the Wallabies had visited there since the disastrous 1972 'Woeful Wallabies' tour. There were many 'new boys' aboard as well as Slack: Roger Gould, Peter Carson, Chris Handy, Martin Knight, Brendan Moon, Rob Onus, Stan Pilecki, Bill Ross, Steve Streeter and Peter McLean.

Andrew made the first two tests, the All Blacks prevailing by scores of 13 to 12 and 22 to 6. The arrival of the brilliant 19-year-old Tony Melrose the week before the final test made him an automatic selection, and this forced Ken Wright into the centres, Andrew Slack missing out in the process. This was the Haberecht 'heart attack game', and against all odds Australia bounced back to win 30 to 16, Greg Cornelsen going into the game's history books by scoring a fabulous four tries.

When the 1979 All Blacks toured Australia for the one-off Bledisloe Cup contest, Andrew was back at outside centre, with the redoubtable Geoff Shaw inside him. Slacky has the utmost respect for Shaw, who had come north to add experience and know-how to the Queensland backline. Not only did he nurture Slack when he had an injury, as he did in the Canterbury game, but he gave him added confidence and broadened his skills. In the test, Australia won a tough struggle 12 to 6, to have the Bledisloe Cup in its possession at last.

Andrew and Geoff Shaw were particular friends of All Black winger and character Stu Wilson, and Wilson learned that one of the idiosyncrasies of these two Aussies was that despite the seriousness of a match they were always on the lookout for money or other valuable objects on the field of play.

Wilson became quite intrigued as he saw his Wallaby mates looking around and could not restrain himself. "Have you found anything yet?" he inquired.

Geoff Shaw put his hand in his pocket and pulled out an object. "Just a chicken bone," he said, "want it?"

Andrew loved touring, his life seemingly in suspension between one tour and the next. When he was young, he loved music, and his mother allowed him to take guitar lessons. At the same time he discovered basketball, and his appearance at lessons became more and more infrequent. As he put it, his basketball shooting improved, but not his ability with the guitar. Fortunately he had a good ear and he gained a little extra practice at parties. As Bret Harris put it: "Always mindful to pack his guitar on tour, Slack was a great source of entertainment to his team mates. A deeper thinker than most rugby players, Slack was the Maroons' resident poet and philosopher. He delighted in seeking out subterranean cafes in foreign cities and playing to unknown audiences through smoky hazes and dim lights. If a Welshman could sing and play rugby as well as Slack, a statue of him would be standing in Cardiff Square."

The Wallaby tour to the Argentine was a fabulous experience for all the players, the tour epitomising what rugby was all about, love of the game for the game's sake being evident despite certain refereeing and touch-judge eccentricities.

An incident in the first test in 1979 against Argentina is remembered by all participants. Peter Horton, a very aggressive character, was the Australian hooker, and of course in the modern game had the task of throwing the ball into the lineout. There was a very narrow distance between the touchline and the fence, and Horton scraped the line-judge - it has been said deliberately - as he threw the ball in. The touch-judge responded by hitting Horton on the head repeatedly with his touch-flag and chasing him onto the field. Though somewhat stunned at the time, the Wallaby players now regard the incident with great mirth, Horton's aggression having finally met its match.

Another amusing incident occurred after the fabulous Hugo Porta had devastated the Wallabies with three quite remarkable dropped goals, during the course of which he had left the Australian defences floundering. That evening, ·Phillip Cox, with more than a few drinks aboard, saw Porta, and took a run at him, driving him into the wall. "Got you at last, you bastard!" he said with a big grin on his face.

There was a short tour of Fiji in 1980, and Queensland toured New Zealand, then late in the year England, France and Italy. One sour note occurred in the season as Slacky was made vice-captain for the first test against the All Blacks, but had to withdraw with a shoulder injury. As so often happens, the players who came in were sensational, Michael ('Day Late') O'Connor and Michael ('Lord') Hawker. They were two of the best centres ever to appear in the green and gold, and Andrew then found himself on the reserves bench. It was a considerable disappointment, as he was fully aware of the honour of the vice-captaincy, and sometimes such an opportunity never occurs again.

Maybe Andrew read US author Maxwell Maltz, who wrote: "We must stop teaching that opportunity knocks. It never knocks. You can listen at the door for ten lifetimes, but you won't hear it knocking. 'You' are the opportunity. You open the door." Slacky always seemed to have the resilience to bounce back from adversity, the sign of a good athlete. As has also been said, it doesn't matter if you fall down, it does if you stay down.

Andrew went off to Ireland in the summer of 1980-81, playing for the Wanderers Club in Dublin. There was something about the green and emerald land that refreshed him. He has a particular affinity with the Irish. He worked on a building site while he was there. He also made the World XV for the centenary game in 1981.

When he returned, he worked at his mother's pub and did a little teaching, with the Wallaby tour of 1981-82 clearly in his sights. Though his name seemed to be absent in team pre-selections, he made the tour and played in four tests, his own game assuming new heights, though the tour as a whole was not successful.

The Wallabies did not have the muscle or height to match the British packs, Tony Shaw being out of place in the second row and Peter ('Spider') McLean, despite great all-round ability, not having the robustness to do it all alone. One story is that Mark Loane asked McLean to change in another room as he broke the team's morale when they saw him stripping with his light body build. Despite the unexpected losses suffered by the Wallabies, the team were close to one another, the experience fantastic, and Slacky was acknowledged as one of the 'form' players on the tour.

Poor Bob Templeton 'got the flick', as they say, after the tour and Bob Dwyer was now at the coaching helm. It was obvious Dwyer wanted the three Ellas in his test team, but Slack was selected as a compromise candidate when Glen and Mark Ella were picked, and Roger Gould and Paul McLean dropped, in one of the worst selections in Australian rugby history. Hawker, a natural inside centre, was placed on the wing. The loss at Ballymore to Scotland occasioned Peter Grigg's return on the wing, and Slacky was replaced, O'Connor and Hawker occupying the centre positions.

There were a number of withdrawals, mainly Queenslanders, from the 1982 Australian tour of New Zealand, and though Dwyer himself believes it was occasioned by the sacking of 'Tempo' and his dropping of Gould and McLean, Slacky believes the fundamental reason was that most of the players were 27-ish, and they had simply had too much rugby. Gary Ella occupied his position in the first and second tests, but he bounced back for the decider, which New Zealand won handily, 33 to 18.

1983 was an up-and-down year for Slacky.

He made the single test for the Bledisloe Cup, which was lost by Australia 18 to 8, and was in a single test against the United States and two against Argentina. Though he went to France that year, he did not play in the two tests, which was a major disappointment.

Alan Jones took over as coach in 1984, and he made it clear that whichever state was dominant he would support the captain of that state as Australian captain. Slacky became Queensland captain, and Queensland did its part by showing its superiority once more over the Blues. He was however surprised - and deeply honoured - when he received the captaincy in the three tests against the All Blacks on their 1984 tour of Australia. The first test was won by Australia 16 to 9, and then the All Blacks evened matters by winning 19 to 15. New Zealand won the series in a remarkable game, 25 to 24.

Though he felt he made some captaincy errors against the All Blacks, Slack learned from his mistakes, and was overjoyed to lead the Wallabies on their history-making Grand Slam tour of the British Isles. He was now 29 years of age, and mature beyond his years. As was stated in *Path To Victory*: "…Slack proved a remarkably popular captain of the Grand Slam Wallabies. Whether leading the players in song as he played his guitar or providing a steadying influence on and off the field, this engaging chap unquestionably was in charge. Slack had style, he had sincerity, he set the example."

This was the pinnacle of every player's career, captaining Australia in a Grand Slam, often envisaged but never realised by Wallaby teams over the years. He quit rugby in 1984, and began what he thought would be a career in journalism with the *Courier Mail*, but like teaching and stock-broking, his other career ventures, he felt "it wasn't me". He got married in 1985, to an English girl, but the lure of the pig-skin remained, and it took little persuasion to inveigle him back.

In 1986 he was back as captain of the Wallabies on their tour of New Zealand and there were, in reflection, signs that Alan Jones was missing the plot. This is certainly not meant to denigrate his contribution, but as the Americans have demonstrated over the years, coaching is one of the most fickle of the professions. Australia won the first test 13-12 and New Zealand the second by the identical score.

Jones did not take the latter loss lightly, and indeed said to the other players, while David Campese (the fullback that day) was in the shower: "Anyway, don't worry men. You played without a fullback today."

He also lost his temper with Nick Farr-Jones after a loss. A certain disenchantment was creeping in. Fortunately the Wallabies won the final test 22-9 and with it the Bledisloe Cup. It was the first time this had happened since 1980 and the first time in New Zealand since 1949. It was after this victory that Alan Jones came up with one of his most quoted remarks: "This is bigger than Quo Vadis. This is bigger than anything."

In 1986 Slack was honoured to be selected for World XV games, the Southern versus the Northern hemisphere, and also captained the Rest of the World against the Lions.

1987 was World Cup year, with sixteen of the top rugby nations of the world involved, though South Africa was notably missing. Australia beat England 19 to 6, the United States 47-12 and Japan 42-23 before thrashing Ireland in the quarter final by 35 to 15. Then the Wallabies came crashing to earth with a devastating 24 to 30 loss to France. There was a play-off against Wales for third place at Rotorua, and the pundits could not believe it when the Aussies went down 21 to 22.

There were explanations aplenty in the cold hard light of day. Principal among the arguments was that Jones had lost the plot, expecting the Wallaby contingent to make sacrifices that he himself was not prepared to make. He maintained his radio job, yet the players divorced themselves from their vocations. They trained in the late afternoon because of Jones' radio commitments, and this was resented by many of the team. On the other side of the coin there were perhaps a few players who were past it and held on solely for the World Cup, and lacked the enthusiasm evident at previous forays. The Rotorua match was Slacky's last test. He was dropped as captain for David Codey in the 1987 Bledisloe Cup test one month after the World Cup.

The South African spectre was ever present after the World Cup, and Slack got heavily involved in its advocacy. It was Alan Jones himself who got the ball rolling at Rotorua, and

the enthusiasm spilled over to many of the players. Slack felt and feels that as an amateur he had the democratic right as an individual to play in South Africa, but in so doing went against the might of the federal government and the ARFU. Jones, in the meantime, for whatever reason, had cooled on the matter, and it was left to David Codey and Slack to argue the case with the players. They flew to South Africa to assist the cause.

Their world came crashing down on them as the ARFU banned both players for 12 months, the present Wallaby captain and the past one, with wins in the Grand Slam and Bledisloe Cup as examples of Slack's leadership. Slack concedes that perhaps they were naive, and that maybe they had done the right thing the wrong way, but it was tough to wear the suspension after what these players had done for their country. Fortunately, player antagonism forced the rescinding of the ban, but it was a disappointing finale to a distinguished career.

They say you should quit while at the top, but Andrew notes with amusement that in his final year he was dropped from the Australian team, Queensland lost to NSW in the interstate game, and Souths lost the Grand Final. So much for quitting at the top.

Andrew stayed away from the game in 1988 and 1989, but is now back as an assistant coach for Queensland, and really found himself in television, rising in rapid order to Sports Editor for Channel 9.

Andrew Slack is one of the greatest captains Australia has ever had, and his record speaks for itself. He was deservedly awarded the Order of Australia in recognition of his services to the game.

Because he was not a flashy player, his ability on the field can be underrated. Australian wingers in his time period were universally happy that he was inside them, for he was an impeccable team player who played to his wings. He had good hands, could read the play well, was efficient at kicking and catching and was solid in defence. He chased harder than any centre in living memory - at kick-offs and kick throughs. The basic honesty of Slacky as an individual was mirrored in his basic honesty when he played. He was the player's player and the captain's captain.

# John Thornett

This massive figure ambled towards us, a little heavier than the old days, but still with the same blond, unkempt hair and rugged visage. There were the unmistakable signs of the long-time rugby player, as he had the scars of the trade, two great cauliflower ears. He could never have been a doctor, he couldn't have fitted the stethoscope into his ears! He was rolling slightly, the tangible evidence of two hip replacements, but otherwise he was the same formidable character, though now in his sixties.

Then he spoke. It was the same calm, quiet, gentlemanly voice. For he really was one of rugby's grand gentlemen. A man's man all the way, but a man of unusual honesty and high principles. He is possibly the greatest captain Australia ever had. He was a leader of men, and yet the epitome of the modest Aussie. He has the air of the country boy about him, and though he lives in the country now, he was a city boy born and bred.

He is modest and self-effacing, and is not the slightest bit affected. There never was affectation in this outstanding person. When asked what his main qualities were in rugby, he replied: "You know, I don't think I was a very good rugby player." That is just the way John Thornett is. The fact is, he was a good handler of the ball for a forward, was almost second to none in tidying up play, was a constructive tight forward, could 'read' a game well, had excellent concentration and played his best under pressure. He was a very, very good rugby player.

After 'Paddy' Moran, the Wallaby captain in 1908, the Wallabies were a surprisingly non-literate lot. A few wrote for newspapers and magazines, like Sid King, Cyril Towers and Tom Richards, but there was a hiatus when it came to books by Aussies. Then came *This World of Rugby* in 1967, by John Thornett, which is now virtually a collector's item. It is marked 'Approved by the Australian Rugby Football Union'.

Everything John did lined up with the requirements of the amateur code. It is in the main an instructional book, but there is much in it that provides the reader with insights into John Thornett the man. When he speaks of the game he loves so much, he provides much food for thought about the direction of the game today, though he certainly could not have perceived the extent of the changes.

He said: "Rugby, I believe, played correctly, is unique as a character-building game, and as an outlet for energy in this materialistic world, where financial gain and an easy, soft life are becoming objectives for which many strive. To survive, rugby cannot be compromised. It must stand for the highest values, for this is its real strength."

The type of player Thornett was is unveiled in his book: "Above all, rugby is an amateur game played by men who should always stand for the highest standards of sportsmanship. By amateur I do not only mean that Rugby players are not paid for playing the game. There is far more in being an amateur than the money factor. The amateur spirit to me is a state of mind about how you approach a match on the field, how you go into every ruck and tackle. It means that you play the game hard but for the fullest possible enjoyment, not just for yourself but for all the players on the field, and always with the highest ethical standards. There should never be the slightest thought of deliberately maiming an opponent. Any coach who encourages this does the game a disservice. On the other hand it is fair to upset an opponent with a hard legitimate tackle so that his concentration is upset, he becomes nervous, and starts dropping the ball. This is a tough game, which teaches how to take it as well as give it. Whatever the standard of rugby in which you are involved, however, the pursuit of the game should always remain secondary to your vocation. Football may sometimes overshadow all else, but it is unhealthy if it does so for a prolonged period."

It is interesting to read this viewpoint in the modern day, where crass commercialisation is the order of the day and professionalism has overtaken the code. His may be considered an old-world viewpoint, and it was not even supported by his siblings.

There were three Thornetts, all mighty athletes. John, the eldest, was born in 1930, Ken in 1937 and Dick in 1940. Ken and Dick played their senior rugby at Randwick, while John played for University and then Northern Suburbs.

Ken did not play rugby union for Australia. He turned professional, playing rugby league for Leeds, before he had the opportunity to play a rugby test, which would have come his way. When he came back to Australia, he went to Parramatta, and was so popular that he was called the 'Mayor of Parramatta', and after retirement a grandstand at the stadium was dedicated to him.

In all, Ken played 138 games for Parramatta (1962-68 and 1971) and 12 tests for Australia (1963-64). A fullback, he made his test debut against New Zealand in 1963. He was on the Kangaroo tour of 1963-64, and played in all six tests. He was a dangerous attacking player and completely safe under pressure.

Dick Thornett was also a remarkable athlete,

as he was one of a very select band of Australian triple internationals. He represented Australia in rugby union, rugby league and water polo, going to the 1960 Rome Olympics. Dick played rugby union tests with brother John against New Zealand, South Africa and the Fijians, before turning professional. He was with his brother Ken on the 1963-64 Kangaroo tour to England and France. Dick played 60 first grade games for Randwick at rugby union from 1958 to 1962, then played rugby league for Parramatta with Ken. He was to play 167 first grade games for them. Despite his size, he was always an extremely mobile forward, a clever ball handler and a prodigious punter of the ball. He was later elected to the NSW Sporting Hall of Fame.

So John, with his strict views on amateurism, had little influence on his younger brothers, who became rugby league greats.

Their grandfather migrated to Australia from England to Griffith on a new MIA irrigation area. John's father, a fitter and turner and draftsman by profession, went to Sydney to do his apprenticeship, and the family went to live at Bronte when John was five years old. Father had played a little cricket and was a capable breast-stroke swimmer, whereas their mother was born in the country and contracted polio when she was fifteen.

Bronte was an ideal area to be brought up in for the three boys, who gloried in the aquatic sports - surfing, swimming and later water polo completely dominating their attention. They were all successful swimmers, their home base being Bronte Swimming Club.

Ken, who John says was the most naturally gifted of the brothers, athletically speaking, was the first of them to play rugby at primary school, the code being rugby league. John had only one game at the Woollahra Opportunity School, a school for intellectually gifted youngsters.

John went to Sydney High School, Ken to Paddington Junior Technical School and Dick to Randwick High School. At first, John was placed on the wing in a class team for the 'also rans', being too heavy for the various teams in his early years. In John's third year of high school he made the fourth grade team, and in the final year captained the first XV and made the Combined GPS firsts. He was also elected captain of the school, thus demonstrating his popularity and leadership capacity. He was a pretty fair swimmer at the school, and for a time held the state butterfly record.

When he attended Sydney University in 1952, doing engineering and science, as he was good at mathematics and physics, he made the University second team. There was a coterie of outstanding Wallabies playing for University at this time, notably John Solomon, John Blomley, Dave Brockhoff, Brian Piper, 'Max' Elliott and 'Mac' Hughes. Doughty ex-Eastern Suburbs scrum-half 'Barney' Walsh was the coach. He made the first XV in 1953 when the Wallabies left to go overseas. University won the Sydney Premiership in 1953, 1954 and 1955. John, who was a breakaway in the early stages of his career, displaced Dave Brockhoff, who then left the club in 1954 to play for Eastern Suburbs.

John was selected for the Wallaby tour to New Zealand in 1955. John Solomon was the captain, and Alan Cameron the vice-captain. There were some legendary players on that tour: Dick Tooth, Garth Jones, Rod Phelps, Eddie Stapleton, Cyril Burke, Nick Shehadie, Keith Cross and 'Mac' Hughes. The managers were Wylie Breckenridge and Bill Cerutti. John was then 20 years of age.

He remembers his first flight to New Zealand with the good-natured Nick Shehadie seated next to him. John was quite shy, and once glanced at a photograph of his girlfriend that he kept in his wallet.

"What's that?" said Nick.

"My girlfriend," replied John.

"Give me a look," said Nick, adding conspiratorially, "I won't say anything."

In a few minutes everyone on the Wallaby team heard about John's girl. Nick did it all in a very acceptable manner, ribbing the youngster, and making him feel at home.

On that tour, after a harrowing provincial game, the manager, ex-Waratah Wylie Breckenridge, got up at the after-match function and told it like it was: "We tried to play football, pity you fellows didn't."

John made the first test team, the other breakaway being 'Mac' Hughes, a remarkable character who missed the plane to New Zealand as he was too busy doing a university assignment. They had two great players lining up against them, Bill Clark and Peter Jones. It was Jones who scored an unbelievable try to beat the Springboks, and when interviewed for national television said: "Well, ladies and gentlemen, I hope I never have to play a game as tough as today's. I'm absolutely buggered."

The All Black breakaways soon made their presence felt. New Zealand scored four minutes after the start when Peter Jones came round from a lineout and bumped his way through the Australian defence. He passed to Bill Clark, and the big All Black forward appeared to fumble several times before scoring between the posts. Ron Jarden converted the controversial try. It was 5-0, Australia eventually losing the test 16-8 at Wellington's Athletic Park. John Thornett particularly excelled in the match at cover defence. An oddity of the game was veteran scrumhalf Cyril Burke playing at inside centre.

New Zealand won the second test at the Carisbrook ground 8-0, thus retaining the Bledisloe Cup. As they did so often, Australia bounced back to win the third test by 8 to 3. John Thornett played in all three tests, and proved to everyone that he had the right big-match temperament.

The Springboks came to Australia in 1956, the year of the Melbourne Olympics. Second rower Alan Cameron was the new Australian captain, and John Solomon the coach. The tests, both dour and unattractive games, were won by South Africa by identical scores of 9 to 0. Because of injuries to key players Arthur Summons, Ross Sheil and Dick Tooth, the ageless Cyril Burke announced his country's call once again in the second test, and played five-eighth. Again, Thornett played in both tests.

There was a bit of a set-back in 1957 as John was dropped for the two tests against the visiting New Zealanders, 'Chilla' Wilson, Keith Cross and Dave Emanuel getting the nod ahead of him. As Thornett said: "You know, I always started a season slowly. I liked it when winter set in, my play improved somehow."

However, he was selected for the eight-month long 1957-58 tour of the British Isles, France, Canada and the United States. There was great criticism when Australia's captain against the All Blacks, Dick Tooth, experienced halfback Cyril Burke and dynamic breakaway

Keith Cross did not make the squad. The captain was Bob Davidson. The manager was Terry McLenaughan, and the coach was a brilliant player from the thirties, centre-winger Dave Cowper.

It was an unhappy tour, team discipline being awry, the coaching somewhat outdated and on top of that a succession of injuries. There were some outstanding players in the team, such as Jim Lenehan, Terry Curley, Arthur Summons, Des Connor, Tony Miller and Alan Cameron. The team played 41 matches, winning 22, losing 16 and drawing three. They did have some fine wins over Llanelli, Swansea and Munster, but they lost all five internationals. All, except the match against France, could have gone the other way. The Wallabies were particularly unlucky against Ireland and Scotland and it was a highly unsuccessful campaign.

His own tour was not a happy one on the playing field, as he contracted hepatitis and was hospitalised in London for six weeks. His third game back was a test. He played in all but one international, against England.

In 1958 he missed the first test against the visiting Maori team, but made the next two. Then it was off to New Zealand again, the team being hailed as one of the worst ever to leave Australian shores. Queenslander 'Chilla' Wilson was the captain, Charlie Blunt the manager and Bill McLaughlin the assistant manager. Some outstanding Wallabies on the team were Alan Morton, Rod Phelps, Arthur Summons, Eddie Stapleton, Wilson and Terry Curley. Beres Ellwood and Jon White were two newcomers who would make an impact.

John was injured and not considered for the first test, but was back at the side of the scrum for the second and third tests. The Wallabies were taken apart in the first encounter 3-25, but came back to win the second 6 to 3. In the final test Australia lost bravely 8-17.

Thornett reflected later on the second test victory: "Of all the matches in which I have played, one of the most memorable was the second test against New Zealand at Christchurch in 1958. We had left Australia, described by one sportswriter, as the worst team Australia had ever sent away in any code. We had lost the first test by a big score but from there on started to develop well, scoring a good win

against Otago. However, we were still very much the underdogs for the second test. We slogged it out with New Zealand's forwards all through the first half and midway through the second-half it was 3-3. It suddenly dawned on us all that we were such strongly criticised underdogs, that it inspired us. Then Alan Morton scored his brilliant try and we were in front. From then on the forwards literally threw themselves into the rucks, really playing superbly. We came off winners against all the forecasts of the experts and I can still remember the gleeful figures jumping up and down for joy on the top deck of the stand of the Australian reserves who had not played."

The British Lions came to Australia in 1959 for two tests, and they had some superb players with them, such as Tony O'Reilly, Peter Jackson, Bev Risman, Dickie Jeeps, David Marques and Ron Dawson. They were too strong for Australia, winning 17 to 6 and 24 to 3. John played in both games.

In 1961 the Fijians arrived, the Wallabies winning the first two tests handily and drawing the third 3-3. John played in the last test, being united with his brother Dick for the first time in an international match.

The next excursion was a short six-match tour to South Africa in 1961, the talented 21-year-old Ken Catchpole, on his first tour, gaining the captaincy over more experienced hands such as John, Tony Miller and Rod Phelps. Ken had to coach the team as well. Both John and Dick Thornett were in the Wallaby team.

John played his first international match in the front row in the first test at Ellis Park, and Australia was led to the slaughter, 28 to 3. Thornett described the encounter in *This World of Rugby*: "...we were absolutely overwhelmed. I have never had such a feeling of helplessness on a football field as when wave after wave of Springbok players poured through our defences. It was my first test as a front rower and I remember that we were pushed back so fast in some scrums that even when we won the ball Catchpole had to dive to escape being trampled on by our own scrum which seemed to be almost running back. The scrums were like South African charges and near the end, with my shoulders red raw from the pounding my opposite number had given me, I kept telling myself that there couldn't be many more scrums. But in the last minute or two there must have been six. I had a tremendous relief as the whistle went to end the game because it meant South Africa couldn't score any more - the only time I have felt quite like that. They scored seven tries that day, a remarkable feat in a test."

It was a more respectable showing at Port Elizabeth, Australia going under again, however, by 11 to 23. In this match John teamed with his brother in the second row. This move away from breakaway signalled a new era in John's rugby career, and one that extended it. There were lessons for the Australian players that year, and with improved scrummaging that was learned from the 'Boks it heralded a new era in Australian rugby as well, called the 'glorious sixties'.

France toured Australia that year, and Australia lost the single test at the SCG by 8 to 15. John and Dick were again in the second row.

In 1962 Wilson Whineray led the All Blacks on a tour of Australia. It was a strange sight to see former Wallaby Des Connor playing brilliantly behind the New Zealand pack. The Australian selectors could not make up their minds as to the captaincy in this period. Hooker Peter Johnson took over in the first test, won by the All Blacks 20 to 6; and fullback Jim Lenehan was given the nod for the second test, which was another All Black victory, 14 to 5. John was once more in the second row with Dick in the second test.

There were more tests that year, in New Zealand. The leader of the 25-man touring party was now John Thornett, at 27 years of age. He played in the three tests, again partnering brother Dick. The initial test was a hard-fought 9-9 draw, proclaimed a 'moral' victory for the Aussies by the press. The referee penalised Australian forward Geoff Chapman in the dying moments of the game, and the mighty Don Clarke saved the day for the All Blacks with an easy kick in front of the posts. The next test was another All Black win by 3 to 0, as was the last test, by 16 to 8. Australian kicking had let down the team once more. John Thornett, however, had shown leadership skills that had been sadly lacking in the past. He was a born leader of men, never asking anyone to do what he would not do himself.

He wrote of captaincy in *This World of Rugby,* and he fitted the bill perfectly: "The captain should be a player who has the complete respect of his players. He should be one of the most experienced players in the team, not necessarily the most brilliant. Captaining a team from the forwards…has the advantage that one can really stir the work-horses of the side and get them functioning as a determined unit."

He was very proud when called upon to captain his country. He said: "I was low-key about it. I was not a great tactician, and I always let Ken Catchpole organise the backs."

In 1963 there was a test match against a Mike Weston - captained English team. The field was a quagmire for the game, but Australia won handily 18 to 9, despite twelve of the Aussie players coming down with a gastric upset before the game. Ex-New Zealander Greg Davis was the find of the match as breakaway.

Thornett was in the front row when he led the team to South Africa the same year. It was the most successful tour ever to that country. It was a team well selected and well managed by Bill McLaughlin and Alan Roper.

The first test was won by South Africa 14 to 3, Australia being weakened by the loss of Ken Catchpole, Dallas O'Neill, Peter Crittle and Dick Marks.

Then came the second test at Newlands, and Australia recorded an historic 9 to 5 victory. Thornett described it: "We had lost the first test but we had a good record against provincial teams and every man went on confident that we really had a chance this time. In the first few minutes a penalty try was awarded against us. The Springboks converted but this severe setback only seemed to increase the determination of the Australians.

"This was Jules Guerassimoff's first test and with Greg Davis he handed the South African backs a terrific pounding. Ian Moutray, in his only test appearance, tackled like a demon at centre for Australia, and with the Springbok backs taking a hammering throughout we were well on top. Leading 9-5 with 10 minutes to go we closed the game up, throwing the ball in short in the lineouts and kicking it out whenever we got it. The South Africans could do little to prevent it. What a thrill it was to win after such a bad start!"

It was a mighty Wallaby team with no

evident weaknesses. For John Thornett, it was his first win against the Springboks in six tests. He was totally exhausted when the game ended.

Then, in an amazingly gutsy performance, and contrary to the predictions of the pundits, the Wallabies won the third test by 11 to 9. It was an unheard-of situation, with Australia leading 2-1 in the test series, with but one test to go. The 1963 Wallabies had been the first international team to win consecutive test matches in South Africa since 1896. It was a high-point of Australian rugby.

The South Africans deservedly won the final encounter 22 to 6, though the Wallabies were visibly disturbed by a blatant error on the referee's part and a 14-5 penalty count against them in the first half. A riot by the black spectators also unsettled them.

Ian Diehm wrote, in *Giants in Green and Gold:* "The 1963 Wallabies were ably led by John Thornett who proved one of the most popular touring captains ever to visit South Africa. South Africans loved the big fellow, who seemed to epitomise all that was good in Australian Rugby. The side was successful because it had great players in key positions in Jon White (loosehead prop), Peter Johnson (hooker), Rob Heming (lineout) and the two stars of the tour - Ken Catchpole and Greg Davis. Jules Guerassimoff got through a tremendous amount of work as did John O'Gorman who was so effective in the back of a lineout.

"White, Johnson and Thornett became household names in South Africa."

Peter Crittle was one of the great practical jokers on the tour. Some of the team were playing cards, and Crittle got one of the players to go into a cupboard, and put a noose around his head, so that he looked dead. Then he rang for room service. The waiter put down the beer, and Crittle said: "Would you mind getting my money from my pants in the closet."

The waiter opened the door of the closet, screamed, and ran for his life, as all the Wallabies collapsed in laughter.

Thornett was captain again on the 1964 tour of New Zealand, the front row of Thornett, Peter Johnson and Jon White providing the platform that Australia had needed over the years. It was a mixed tour, New Zealand winning the first two tests 14 to 9 and 18 to 3,

then Australia triumphing 20 to 5 at Athletic Park, Wellington.

In 1966 the Lions returned to Australia under Mike Campbell-Lamerton. It was a disappointment for Australia, as they lost the two tests 8-11 in Sydney and 0-31 at Brisbane.

1967 was to be the swan-song for this remarkable Australian. Once more he led his country, on the 1967-68 tour of the British Isles, but failed to reach his own personal standards. He contracted impetigo, a contagious skin disease, from a rival front rower, and when he came back he was struggling. He found himself in the insidious position of having to vote himself out of the tests. Manager Bill McLaughlin voted for him to play in the international against Wales, and coach Alan Roper voted against him. He felt he could not in the circumstances vote for himself. It was all very traumatic. He did not play against England, Scotland and Wales, but did play against France. This was to be his last test, and Australia went down by 14 to 20. One of his greatest memories, however, occurred on that tour, and it was playing against the Barbarians, and defeating them 17 to 11 in an exciting game.

The team lacked consistency, but was strong enough to defeat Wales, the first Wallaby team to do so, and England. One can only speculate what might have happened if the captain had not come down with impetigo and lost form.

There was considerable controversy on the tour as Wallaby hooker Ross Cullen was sent home after an ear-biting incident, though it was provoked. Thornett still believes it was the correct decision. Coach Alan Roper was against it. How much this unsettled the team is uncertain, but there were factions who opposed what had happened. Thornett had the experience of travelling with a relatively undisciplined team ten years previously, and remembered only too clearly the carping criticism of the British press over Australian rough-house tactics.

Thornett feels in reflection that though it was unfortunate that an example had to be set in such an uncompromising manner, the action of the Australian management was totally supported by the British press and was the right thing to do from the viewpoint of international relations.

His career was an exceptional one by any

standards. He played 112 times for Australia, 37 of these tests. He captained Australia a then-record 16 times, since surpassed by Andrew Slack (19) and Nick Farr-Jones (36). He was to receive an MBE for his services to sport.

John Thornett would have made a fortune today in rugby, but this was not as he saw the game or for that matter life itself. Rugby, if anything, interfered with his career. He has, however, successfully occupied middle management positions in various companies, and now lives in the country, tending a farm and running a company that provides advice for those starting up a business.

Bill McLauglin, who was one of Thornett's managers, had this to say of him: "He is quiet by nature, but a very staunch character with the vision to see beyond Sydney football grounds and take in the overall international picture. I doubt he has ever failed to do anything asked of him if he thought it would help rugby - and these demands have been considerable."

# Cyril Towers

Cyril Towers is arguably the greatest centre threequarter that Australia has ever produced, and it is a position where Australia has never taken a back seat. Players like John Brass, Trevor Allan, Rod Phelps, Geoff Shaw, Andrew Slack, Jason Little and Tim Horan come quickly to mind, and though each had special attributes none had the all-round attributes of this all-round Randwick flyer. And no-one could equal him in the tactical sense.

Cyril Towers was the thinking man's centre, a real student of the game who could take one hundred minutes explaining what you should have done in an eighty-minute game. The author remembers him only too well. After graduating as a hot-shot high school player and thinking he had all the answers he gravitated to Randwick in 1945, where Cyril was still playing the occasional game when the club was in need.

The author listened in awe after his initial first grade game as Cyril came up to him and carefully dissected his game. There were points made that were never to be forgotten: how to position your body and hands to limit knock-ons, how to fan to get outside your man, how to draw two men, how to hold the ball when going for the opening, how to run parallel to the sideline on the breakthrough to maximise scoring opportunities, how to position your body on a rolling ball, and so on and so on. It was always an amazing litany, and a new world opened up listening to this erudite man, a world of reason, logic and calculation. His only fault,

perhaps, was that he had to give you the whole works all at once, rather than introduce you to the task gradually and sequentially. Many disdained him as a bore, or dismissed him through the ignorance of youth and the lack of understanding of the value of experience.

He was a very humorous man, being particularly adept at one-liners. One of his favourites was: "Anyone that takes him for a fool is no mug." When speaking of a selector he did not like he once said: "He's a little like the Chinese: if you can't be wise be mysterious." On the appointment of a new Australian coach he remarked: "If he got a bright idea on rugby it would die from solitary confinement."

When sidestepping trouble he offered this sage advice: "Absence of the body is better than presence of mind." If he was ever asked about someone he really did not like, he would quip: "Oh, he's not a bad bloke in his way but he doesn't weigh much."

One of his most used was when someone asked: "How are you, Cyril?"

He would often reply: "Oh, battling on - like dandruff trying to get a head!"

There was nothing he enjoyed more than cooking at a barbeque, with good company, telling stories, and tossing down a few cold ales.

Randwick is what it is today because of three or four men, each convinced of the efficacy of the running game. The men were an astute Waverley College coach by the name of Arthur

Hennessey, who had a profound influence on rugby league as well as rugby union; Waratah halfback Wally Meagher, a prince of a man who preached the gospel of the running game every day of his life; Cyril Towers, a pupil of Hennessey's and a close friend of Meagher's; and Len Palfreyman, a forward who became convinced of the message and was the perfect associate of Meagher and Towers. Hennessey's role was more of mentor and philosopher, and his presence was short-lived. Meagher, Towers and Palfreyman were the heart and soul of the club, operating on a day-to-day basis in a hands-on approach and yet at the same time being the spiritual advisers of the running game, the veritable apostles, their parish Randwick.

After graduating from high school, the author badly sprained his ankle playing basketball, and being then shy and reticent, did not appear at the Randwick pre-season trials except the final one. He went up to Wally Meagher and Len Palfreyman: "Excuse me," he said, "could I get a game this afternoon?"

"Where have you been to this point, son?"

"I was hurt, sir."

"Have you played before?"

"Yes, I was in the Sydney Tech High School team and have been in the Combined High School team the last two years."

"Well," said Wally Meagher, "we'll give you a run in the fourths this afternoon."

"I'm sorry, Mr Meagher", the author said coolly, "I don't play fourths."

"You what, son?" said Wally Meagher, a trifle irritated.

"Do you go to watch the fourths, Mr Meagher?"

"Well, no, I don't!"

"That's why I don't play fourths, Mr Meagher."

Wally said, somewhat exasperated: "That's the best I can do, son."

"That's all right, Mr Meagher, I will come back next year." the author turned and walked down the steps of the Randwick stand, and then walked slowly across the field. He was climbing the fence, when Wally Meagher called out: "Hey, son, we'll give you a run in the thirds."

"Thanks, Mr Meagher", the author called back respectfully.

That afternoon the author knew he had to impress, so every time he got the ball he gave it a go, as they say, passing the ball only in an emergency, playing as a complete and utter individualist.

Everyone lined up at the training session on Tuesday night anxious to hear how they had been graded. Meagher, standing next to Cyril Towers, looked around and fixed his eyes on the author, who instinctively knew he was going to cop it.

"Before I start", said Wally Meagher, "I just want to say that we have one player here, you, young Howell, who did everything that you are not supposed to do at Randwick. You went for the opening every time, you died with the ball, you never set up your wings…you are a complete disaster, as bad as I have ever seen."

The author was completely crestfallen, and figured his rugby days were already over at 18 years of age. "But," Wally went on, "I saw something in your play, and hopefully you learned your lesson. We'll play you in the thirds on Saturday."

The author breathed a sigh of relief, and from then on played Randwick football, the brand of football inspired by Towers, Hennessey, Meagher and Palfreyman.

The essence of the Randwick game, then and today, is to maximise attack and mobility, to move the opponents around, to de-emphasise or completely eliminate kicking, to move the ball with speed and to utilise the extra man from the winger or fullback position at every opportunity, and to get the ball to where the smallest number of people are, the wingers. The mark of a good centre at Randwick was the number of tries the winger scored, and setting up the wings was an art form, at which Cyril Towers had no peer. He understood it all like no Australian player before or since.

Cyril Towers was born in 1906 in Melbourne, and was brought up in an Australian Rules atmosphere. One of the other pupils at Middle Park was future professional runner Austin Robertson, considered Australia's finest in those days. Cyril's great-great grandfather, whose name was O'Callaghan was, during the gold rush, mayor of Ballarat. Cyril's father was killed in the First World War at Gallipoli just before his tenth birthday, so Cyril was sent to stay with Mr O'Callaghan's daughter, who had a farming property at Warracknabeal, Victoria.

There was plenty for young Cyril to do in the country, and he got lots of exercise as he had to walk seven miles to school in the morning and then trudge back in the afternoon. It was a real blessing for the youngster when the school was moved three miles closer.

His mother remarried, and his step-father worked for the Bank of New South Wales, and during the 'flu epidemic the family was moved to Roma, Queensland, where he was exposed to cricket and rugby for the first time. He first of all went to a convent - he remained throughout his life an ardent Catholic, rarely missing a day at church - and then transferred to Roma High School. The headmaster, a man named Thompson, was an interstate cricketer, and Cyril and the others bowled and fielded their hearts and souls out to keep Mr Thompson in the Queensland side.

There was a recording made by Cyril shortly before he died, and it was supplied to the authors by his wife, Rita Towers, who still lives in the house at Maroubra where they spent their married life, just a short distance from Wally Meagher's home. He said: "This was a great experience for me in Roma where I spent three years. We lived about a mile and a half out of town with a paddock, a horse paddock, and a house, on about five or six acres. We kept our own cows and we used to have to feed those and milk them, and four horses of my own, which enabled me to assist people nearby who were drovers of cattle, and they had large herds up there in the backblocks of Roma, and I was able to earn a pound or two for myself assisting a drover who had three sons and a wagon - a kitchen wagon - and we'd get on the road there, on Christmas holidays, and other holidays, and spend a month on the roads more or less. They were barbaric conditions half the time, but it gave me an eye-opener into the way you live in those vast areas."

After leaving Roma, now that the 'flu epidemic had ceased, he had six months at Waverley College, and it was here that he got his first real experience with rugby and came under the tutelage of one of the great Australian rugby theorists, Arthur Hennessey.

After three months with Randwick High School, Cyril did the Bankers' examination and got a job with the Government Savings Bank. He remained with the bank throughout his working life.

While with the Rural Bank that first year he was living at Coogee, and played Kentwell Cup rugby with Coogee. The following year, 1923, he continued with them. There were two new clubs in the senior Sydney competition that season, YMCA and Randwick. The Randwick players who led the way were 'Greg' George, Len Palfreyman, Owen Crossman, Wally Meagher and Ted Greatorex.

In 1924 Cyril had a rather disastrous start to his last season as a junior, for a steel girder from a lorry fell onto his leg while he was walking in Sydney and his broken leg kept him out of action for some eight weeks.

Despite his injury, he made a junior representative team which played a curtain-raiser before a NSW-All Blacks game. Some 30,000 were on hand, and Cyril said: "It was no thrill, it was a decided fright…to be quite honest, I was never so lonely before in my life." The occasion was a big influence on his career, as he sat in the stands afterwards, watching the main game, seeing the "irresistible forward force" of the All Blacks, and watching the two mercurial All Black backs, centre A.E. ('Bert') Cooke and Maori fullback George Nepia.

In 1925 he was asked by Len Palfreyman to try out for the Randwick senior side, gravitating to outside centre, a position he played almost exclusively from this point on. He quickly moved towards higher honours in his first year of grade football, being selected as a reserve for a metropolitan team against New Zealand, and was unlucky not to make the tour to the land of the long white cloud that year.

In 1926 New Zealand was coming back to Australia, and trial games were held to select the NSW team. For the first time Cyril teamed up with Sid King in the centres, their opponents being the veterans 'Johnny' Wallace and 'Tug' Morrissey. The honours of the day went to the youngsters.

As Cyril Towers wrote for the *Sydney Mail* twelve years later: "Reverting to the King-Towers partnership, it had a good run in Australian football, and I do not think I am being an egoist when I say it had a good run in Australian football, and I do not think I am being an egoist when I say it more than held its own with all-comers. On or off the field one could not be associated with a more sincere and courageous personality than Sid King, and on the score of tackling alone he takes second place to no other player known to me in my association with rugby union football."

Cyril made the Waratah team against the All Blacks which, one must appreciate, is now recognised as Australian representation, as there was no rugby in Queensland at the time. He wrote: "To say I was nervous was to put it very, very mildly indeed; the incidents of the play, however, crowded so quickly on the heels of each other as to leave no time for thought other than the task on hand. My personal task was in opposition to that great player 'Bert' Cooke, and that's a handful for anyone."

The Waratahs won that first game. History was made in that match, as scrumhalf Wally Meagher called a mark from a lineout, then kicked a goal. It had never happened before. The second test in 1926 was narrowly won by the All Blacks.

The year 1927 changed Cyril's life for ever, as he was selected for the eight-month tour of the British Isles, France, Canada and the United States. It was the tour of tours, the previous one being in 1908. The *Rugby Union News* came up with an inspired lyric to an old tune:

(To the tune of "Parlez-Vous.")
The "Waratahs" are going away,
    Parlez-vous.
The "Waratahs" are going away,
    Parlez-vous.
The "Waratahs" are going away,
We hope the League won't get them to stay,
    Inky-Pinky, Parlez-vous.

Across the world they're "gonna" roam,
    Parlez-vous.
Across the world they're "gonna" roam,
    Parlez-vous,
But the Army's keeping Duncan at home,
    Inky-Pinky, Parlez-vous.

Of our nation, they are the cream,
    Parlez-vous.
Of our nation they are the cream,
    Parlez-vous.
Of our nation they are the cream,
"John" Wallace will lead this team.
    Inky-Pinky, Parlez-vous.

Yes, they're after John Bull's blood,
    Parlez-vous.
Yes, they're after John Bull's blood,
    Parlez-vous.
Yes, they're after John Bull's blood,
Tancred, Lawton and Big Bruce Judd,
    Inky-Pinky, Parlez-vous.

They're "gonna" cover themselves with glory,
    Parlez-vous.
They're "gonna" cover themselves with glory,
    Parlez-vous.
They're "gonna" cover themselves with glory,
Three cheers for Ross, Ted Thorn and Storey,
    Inky-Pinky, Parlez-vous.

"The Sheik" has got a brand new bride,
    Parlez-vous.
"The Sheik" has got a brand new bride,
    Parlez-vous.
"The Sheik" has got a brand new bride,
He'd like to have her in the side,
    Inky-Pinky, Parlez-vous.

We'll see 'em off at the train,
    Parlez-vous.
We'll see 'em off at the train,
    Parlez-vous.
We'll see 'em off at the train,
And hope they'll soon be back again,
    Inky-Pinky, Parlez-vous.

Of all our players they are the best,
    Parlez-vous.
Of all our players they are the best,
    Parlez-vous.
Of all our players they are the best,
They'll prove so when they win each test,
    Inky-Pinky, Parlez-vous.

I've been talking, it seems, for hours,
    Parlez-vous.
I've been talking, it seems, for hours,
    Parlez-vous.
I've been talking, it seems, for hours,
So we'll end with a cheer for good old Towers,
    Inky-Pinky, Parlez-vous.

There was nothing quite like the boat trips of yesteryear, and for those who went it was an unparalleled experience. Cyril wrote: "Once aboard ship we gradually blended into a happy family and learned to mix with each other and understand and respect the feelings of the various members of the team.

"In a touring party this understanding is of great importance as, broadly speaking, they are cooped together for six months, and a great amount of understanding and tolerance is essential to overcome the 'pin pricks' that will occur from time to time."

They stopped at Colombo and Pompeii. While at Pompeii one of the Aussies complained about the Italian food, the Australian diet being very limited in those days. There was nothing on the menu that sounded palatable to him other than spaghetti in tomato sauce. He said he had eaten many things in his time, but it was the first time he had been reduced to feeding on skipping-ropes.

For three weeks the team trained at Teignmouth, a small Devonshire seaside resort. After playing against Devon and Cornwall, Newport and Wales were next on the schedule. During the Wales game Towers and Bruce Judd tackled the fullback, and the ball shot loose. Judd picked it up and scored. Following the tackle, one of the spectators said: "Say, man, that's not cricket."

Bruce Judd, who had a speech impediment, turned to the spectator and said: "W-w-well, w-who said w-we were p-playing c-c-cricket?"

The game had commenced with the playing of the 'Welsh National Anthem' and 'Advance Australia Fair'. The same spectator said: "I didn't like the Welsh anthem much: but say, what *was* that second tune?"

The first international against Ireland at Lansdowne Road was narrowly won by the Waratahs 5 to 3. One of the Waratahs, Ted Greatorex, was asked to do the radio broadcast, and began by apologising for his Australian accent. He described a Waratah coming across the field to make a tackle, then the Waratah hesitated. Greatorex said: "Come on, you silly bastard, don't stand there looking, tackle him." Recovering quickly, he apologised for his Aussie accent.

There was an old visitor, Burleigh Gorman, who travelled with the team. He kept slipping into the conversation: "I remember in 1892", and of course the players just switched off and shook their heads. However, at a function hosted by Sir Thomas Lipton at the Royal Ulster Yacht Club he went on about what he had remembered in 1892. One of Lipton's old friends remembered a similar incident in 1884, much to Burleigh's disgust, then Sir Thomas Lipton himself recalled an incident in 1878. The team enjoyed Burleigh getting upstaged.

While in Ireland an Irishman told Cyril: "Why, if you go to Dublin you must see the Liffey. The smell from the Liffey, my boy, is one of the finest sights in the town."

Wally Meagher, who was of Irish extraction, was quite disgusted in England as they pronounced his name in countless ways, but not like 'Maher', as it should have been. He could hardly wait to get to the emerald isle, where they knew how to pronounce Meagher. At the Hibernian Hotel the porter insisted on hailing him as 'Meegar'.

The Welsh were even more parochial in those days, many of the people in the valleys scarcely knowing anything about the outside world. There was little excuse for the mayor of Abertillery, however, who expressed a warm welcome for the New Zealand Waratahs, who had come all the way from South Africa to have a run against the locals.

Once in Wales, Cyril had a conversation with a local who asked: "Where do you come from?"

"Australia", Cyril replied.

"Australia? You don't mean Austria?"

"No, Australia."

"They're different places, are they?"

He then went and got an atlas and showed him where Australia was. Then the local asked him how he got to Wales.

"We came by ship," Cyril said.

"My goodness, it's a long trip, isn't it?" said the bemused Welshman.

"A fair one," replied Cyril, and left the local to ponder it all.

The excursion to Scotland was one of the most remarkable, and the atmosphere at Murrayfield incomparable. The participation of captain Johnny Wallace, who had played for Scotland, added to the friendliness of it all. Cyril remembered one particular evening: "A most hilarious dinner was tendered us at Aberdeen, and we enjoyed a grand repast, punctuated with song, laughter, and what goes with it. We had more or less settled into groups late in the night for discussion on general topics, and it appears that during this part of the evening we lost considerable social prestige. Two of the Waratahs were idly stabbing two pineapples with butter-knives for the want of something better to do, and this appeared to cause great consternation amongst the waiters who were doing the honours. One waiter confided to me later, when I made inquiry, that he had never seen such a disgusting practice before, just wantonly mutilating the pineapples, *which were worth from 12/6 to 15/- each*. But the matter of their loss was not the all-important factor. *What mattered most was that they were the only two pineapples in Aberdeen."*

Scotland won a game of great quality, where the issue was in doubt until the final whistle. England also beat the Waratahs four tries to three.

There were social aspects of the tour that lived in the minds of the Waratahs for the rest of their days. These were the receptions by their Majesties, King George and Queen Mary, the Prince of Wales, later to be King Edward VIII, and the Duke and Duchess of York, and on top of this they were taken to see baby Princess Elizabeth. The highlight of the tour was being invited to the King's private estate at Sandringham, and going shooting with him. Each player was presented with a pheasant, many of which were later mounted.

The French part of the tour was next, and the Waratahs won the international by 11 to 8. Cyril won the game with a glorious swerving run from one end of the field to the other. After he had scored his opposing centre came running full speed at him, and Cyril felt he was going to cop one for his efforts. Instead, Cyril got a kiss on both cheeks. The centre thought it was the best run he had ever seen.

While in Bordeaux they went to the Opera and heard the world-renowned Gigli in *La Tosca* and *Pagliacci*. Afterwards they went backstage, had a glass or two, then it was announced that the 'Waratah Quartet' would vocalise. As Towers put it: "The four who had angled for this invitation turned out to be Judd, Greatorex, 'Doc' Tarleton, and Harry Woods, and they inharmoniously rendered *Back to Mortdale*. What a musical treat! Gigli and his operatic cast and that inimitable quartet! Each of these four Waratahs will, in years to come, be able to look his great-grandchildren square

between the eyes and tell them what 'I and Gigli' did for Continental Opera."

The playing part of the tour ended in Canada, after which there were glorious stop-overs at Honolulu, Suva and New Zealand. Then the tour of tours was over: "Our general manager actually shed a tear or two at the final meeting on board where he called us together to express his appreciation of the way we had so happily banded together during our eight months abroad, but there was a general feeling of loss by each of us at the prospect of our disbanding.

"Words failed adequately to express his or our feelings of the happy memories we retained, and I personally, quite apart from any kudos gained on the football field, esteem it an honour to have been associated with such a likeable and companionable band of good fellows as the Waratahs."

Cyril always credited winger and Waratah captain Johnny Wallace for improving his timing of the pass, a feature of his game that later made Cyril famous. Wallace told him firmly: "Give me the ball when I call for it!" When Wallace called, he got it, and Towers started to appreciate the value of the moment when the pass should be given.

Johnny Wallace wrote about this as well. He said: "In Towers, who was unfortunately injured in the first test, King had a partner who had shown himself to be one of the greatest individualists of the day. Towers in attack combined soundness with a highly developed capacity to beat his man. He sidesteps and swerves splendidly. His main weakness is his lack of judgement in timing his pass. He generally slows down a little and delays his pass too long. With King and Towers together, if there was a chance to penetrate the opposing line, they could be relied upon to do it.

"When starting attacks from the loose play Towers is the master…"

Jimmy Carlton, one of Australia's greatest-ever sprinters, told Cyril: "If I had your fast start I would break all records." Cyril appeared to be at his maximum in a few strides, leaving even Carlton behind. He was a fitness fanatic, never catching the lift to the seventh floor where he worked, and delighting in racing up the stairs, a lottery ticket often up for grabs. In the pre-season he would go for the weekends to the Megalong Valley, where he would walk and run. In body-build he was solid, with big hands and strong arms.

After the tour, a journalist wrote: "Cyril Towers is probably the greatest centre the union game has known since 'Dally' Messenger…his service to the wing three-quarters is ideal, as he usually secures the overlap for his supports."

Cyril, it should also be noted, was a sportsman of the old school, as can be exemplified by a club match against Parramatta. The referee made a mistake and awarded Randwick a penalty kick right in front of the posts. He refused to kick at goal, and kicked the ball out for a lineout instead. It was the first time a footballer was seen refusing to take advantage of a referee's error. He was just that kind of man.

Only three of the Waratahs were available for the tour of New Zealand in 1928 where they were, Cyril said, "Beaten by goals and oysters". In the two tests they scored seven tries to four and lost both. As for the oyster reference, like many a team before and since, at Southland they were treated to a fantastic meal of unlimited giant Bluff oysters, plus vinegar and Worcester sauce, aided in their passage by vast quantities of New Zealand beer. The Wallabies were carried home, and crawled on to the field next day, where Southland did them in.

The British team came to Australia in the middle of the depression in 1930 after New Zealand. They man-handled NSW, the great five-eighth Roger Spong being prominent. The test followed, and in an historic match Australia triumphed, 6 to 5. The victory marked the end of the international career of Owen Crossman, rated by Cyril as the finest winger he had seen. Unfortunately, Crossman and Bryan Palmer were unable to go to the British Isles. Cyril's proudest moment came in this game as he saved it for Australia. The brilliant five-eighth Roger Spong broke through, with two centres on his right and a backrow forward, Ivor Jones, on his left. Cyril, who was a great defender, calculated that fullback Alex Ross would get Spong, and by the way he was running Spong would eventually pass the ball to Jones, so he went for the corner flag and hit Jones with such force from behind when he received the ball that Jones knocked on. Australia won the ensuing scrum and the game ended shortly thereafter.

Cyril went north to play with an Australian XV at Brisbane, to find the British team glorying in the sunny weather. The Irish front rower Jimmy Farrell said: "If we could only play our games sitting down, sure this would be glorious." Farrell also loved the pineapples. After finishing his dinner he would say: "Faith, ai'll have four-r-r pineapples." In Brisbane, when asked what he was doing, he was always going to a pineapple 'bust', coming from a pineapple 'bust' or so full of pineapple he'd fear he'd 'bust'.

When the 1931 season came around many great players, such as Jack Ford, Owen Crossman, Jim Tancred, Jimmy Carlton and Wylie Breckenridge departed the scene, but as so often happens their shoes were filled by some pretty neat customers such as Dinny Love, Harold Tolhurst, Bill Hemingway and Harold Herd. The game in Queensland and Victoria was also moving ahead in leaps and bounds.

A fully Australian side toured New Zealand that year, and though there were some imposing figures such as Dave Cowper, their record was only average. In the test at Auckland they were beaten by the boot of Ron Bush, the New Zealand fullback. This was the very first game for the Bledisloe Cup. As well, they were again "beaten by the shellfish" at Invercargill.

At the team's welcome at the Cargan Hotel in Auckland Cyril questioned the president of the NZRFU, Stan Dean, about the wisdom of the team leaving their hats and coats at the hotel entrance-way. With a twinkle in his eye, Dean said: "Oh, that's all right, Cyril, there is really no risk as you people are the only Australians in the place."

Cyril was a great admirer of New Zealand football. As he said: "You get fellows there that instead of pushing pens are swinging axes and they carry that on to the football field." Australia got its players mainly from the cities, whereas the All Blacks came from small towns and were farmers and fishermen.

There were many new faces in the interstate and trial games of 1932, such as 'Jockey' Kelaher, Aub Hodgson, Francis McPhillips, Wal Mackney and Jack Young, with the added incentive of a trip to South Africa. When the team to tour was announced, Cyril's name was not among them. It was one of the shock omissions in Australia's rugby history.

Australian selectors have made some awful decisions in their time, but this was one of the most ridiculous, and was widely criticised. It was held, by some, that Cyril's superior knowledge of the game was a disadvantage, as he might be proferring too much advice to the team and the management. The manager, Dr Wally Mathews, was particularly against the inclusion of Towers.

Cyril kept playing, and well, but the death knell had all but sounded for his international career. He was a remarkable and unusual man, and in 1936 he went off to Europe, purchasing a bicycle and doing it the hard way. He even made it to Berlin for the 1936 Olympic Games, and trained with the US sprint immortal Jesse Owens. Cyril was always fascinated with footwork, and learned much from Owens. From there he went to South Africa. He was a self-educated person, and particularly gloried in seeing ancient sites.

When he came back he captained NSW and Australia in 1937 against the Springboks. The state side played a remarkable game in the mud, to win 17 to 6. The Springboks rallied to win the first test, also in the mud, by 9 to 5. In the third test at Brisbane the Springboks won by 26 to 17. Towers, who was the dominant figure in the first two tests, had to leave the field with a badly gashed forehead. It was to be his last test for Australia.

The final trial in 1939 to pick the team to go to England was Australia versus The Rest, and Cyril captained The Rest that day. They flogged Australia by 48 to 3, wingers Basil Porter and Des Carrick scoring three and two tries, respectively, and Cyril two. He was the dominant player on the field. Basil Porter was to say for years afterwards: "I played outside the master." Despite the fact that the ex-Waratahs Wyle Breckenridge and Jack Blackwood were selectors, Cyril was not picked to go to England. It was said that the manager, Dr Mathews, felt that Cyril was too strong a personality. Cyril retired in 1940, aged 34, and in so doing said: "I'm tired of the union's petty muddling and stupid administration. They've killed my enthusiasm for football."

He kept going as long as he could, filling in wherever they wanted him, and was ever a role model and inspiration at the Randwick club.

He played a record number of games for Randwick, 233, which, like all records, succumbed over the passage of time.

Bill Cerutti and Cyril Towers were the first rugby players to have played fifty games for NSW and Australia. He also, in his time, held the record in the State for the greatest number of tries and the most points.

His career was rejuvenated when asked to do rugby broadcasts for the ABC, and his deep knowledge of the game was only too apparent to his wide audience. Everyone knew who Cyril Towers was, well beyond the time when memories of players' achievements have faded. He became famous in broadcast circles when he announced a game in South Africa while he was in the studio in Sydney. He reconstructed it by a constant flow of cables from South Africa. It is a broadcast masterpiece.

His wife Rita had four children: Tom, who played some 50 first grade games for Randwick; Tim, who played second grade football and first grade cricket for Randwick; and two daughters, Lyn, who married Wallaby Roy Prosser, and Margariete, who married Wallaby 'Jake' Howard. Margariete is probably the world's leading female coach, and the mother of present Wallaby Pat Howard. Margariete is an out-and-out rugby worshipper, and in many ways is more like Cyril than Cyril.

The legacy that Cyril left, as well as Hennessey, Meagher and Palfreyman, is the Randwick club. They were the ones who saw that attractive football can also be winning football. So few have caught on to their message. The 'Towers' or 'Meagher' system that is at Randwick permeates all the grades.

When he wrote "Twelve Years of Rugby Union" for the *Sydney Mail*, he offered his reflections: "What, may I ask, is more pleasant than the pleasure of memory? In looking back over my many games and my pleasant associations with players and clubmen, I feel that in any other branch of sport, or in fact many other avenues, I could not have derived greater pleasure or more character-building benefit. To the rugby union game I sometimes feel that I am indebted for my most sincere thoughts and actions, and if my feelings on this point be correct the game and its associations have done much for me indeed."

# Col Windon

Col Windon was the greatest attacking breakaway in Australia's long rugby history. They called him 'Breeze', and he ran like the breeze, like the very wind. There was nothing he could not do with the ball in hand, and when in full flight he had a distinctive, characteristic style as the defence closed in on him. Ball held tightly in one arm, bent over for contact, eyes on the defender, hand spread ready for a palm, he was action personified. As a winger, he had led the Sydney competition one season in try-scoring. He was also Australia's leading try-scorer for over thirty years, his record being eventually broken by mercurial winger Brendan Moon.

He has photographs in his personal collection of his father playing rugby for Randwick in 1906, 1908 and 1910, well before the acknowledged beginning of the present club. His father, who worked for the railways, was also president of the Coogee Surf Club and the Coogee Swimming Club, so Col and his brother Keith naturally gravitated towards an early life of swimming, surfing and football. A park at Coogee is named after his father and is testimony to his outstanding community contribution.

In the thirties, his father was writing his annual report, and one of his colleagues burst in and said: "What are you doing here? There's one of the best footballers you've ever seen at the Oval." It was Keith.

His brother Keith is five years older than Col, and he has had a tremendous influence on him. Keith went to New Zealand with the Wallabies as a 19-year-old breakaway in 1936, but he had to defer in the tests to the more experienced Aub Hodgson and Owen Bridle.

In 1937 he was the star against the mighty Springboks in Australia, and those who saw him marvelled at his play. He was picked on the Wallaby team to the British Isles in 1939, at the time being acknowledged as one of the best forwards in the world. War broke out after the team arrived in England and the team never played a game. He would have been at his peak then.

He went into the Air Force, and kept playing at every available opportunity. Whenever he got a leave he traded his uniform for a Randwick jersey. When international rugby resumed, the principal candidates for post-war Wallaby captaincy were Keith Windon, Bill McLean, Dr Phil Hardcastle and Ron Rankin. Bill McLean won out, but Keith was good enough to be selected on his own merit to tour the land of the long white cloud. While on tour he developed leg problems, which were diagnosed at the time as gout, and reluctantly ended his career.

About ten years later a journalist picked his greatest team ever, and Keith and Col Windon were the breakaways. Unfortunately, like so many others, his best years would have been in the war period.

Keith was very astute, aptly described as a

'heady' player. When the author was playing for Randwick in the centres and was in the process of creating an opening, there were always two simultaneous calls from the Windon brothers: "I'm with you!" They could smell a try like no others in history.

Col respected his brother, and many of the things that made him stand out as a player were passed on from Keith. One of the most important was to look around before packing down, to study the opposition, trying to 'read' what was happening. Keith also kept stressing one dictum: "Run to the lineout, then rest!"

When Col lists his school attendance, his friends are always surprised when they read Sydney Grammar, though first of all he went to Randwick Public School. Whatever a Grammar-type is in actuality, that image has little resemblance to Col Windon. As he said: "Mum had a little money she'd been left, and the truth is I was a bit wayward and she thought Grammar would be good for me."

In 1940 Col made Randwick's first-grade team, as a winger, and it was that year he led the Sydney competition in try-scoring. There were a few handy men around him in those days, Wallabies Cyril Towers, 'Shirts' Richards and Ron Rankin among them, and they knew how to set up to put wingers across the line. Col could sprint, winning a few Australian championships at 'flags', which combined sprinting, judgment and diving at a flag. One he beat regularly in the event was Johnny Bliss, reputed to be the greatest beach sprinter of all time.

It was Cyril Towers in particular who taught Col how to position himself for the pass, and how to analyse a game while in progress. Randwick beat Manly in the Grand Final that year.

He was off to the Army in 1941, his brother Keith going to the Air Force. Col loved the physical fitness courses, excelling above all others. He had a little luck on the way, as when he found out most of his mates were getting ready to embark he hurried back to his camp to get his kit-bag. He called out to them as he left: "I'll be right behind you!" When he got to his camp all leave was cancelled, and he was, like all others there, confined to quarters. Almost all those who left went to Singapore and became POW's, including Wallabies Roger Cornforth, John Fuller, 'Blow' Ide and Cec Ramalli.

He did get to the Owen Stanley Range at the tail end of the campaign, as a 'runner'. He reflected on those days: "The Japanese took a few shots at me but my zig-zag was just too good."

Lady luck gave him a little nudge again as he was brought back from overseas for training at the Atherton Tablelands. There was a rugby league competition there in 1944 run by the 6th division. So Col organised a team from the 2nd/3rd Infantry Battalion which eventually won the competition. As there were no breakaways in league, Col played five-eighth and captained the side.

Then in 1945 the Battalion went into full war action at Aitape (New Guinea) and walked all the way to Wewak cleaning out many Japanese and releasing many POW's. They were just about to take on the Sepak River and the Torecilli Mountains when they dropped the atomic bomb on Japan, so Col and his Battalion mates were pleased, as the war was over. Even better, he was transferred from Wewak to Avoca St, Randwick.

There was no football from 1940 to 1945, but when the war was over he resumed playing with Randwick in 1946. The experts told him that with Rudy Cornelsen, the father of Greg, 'Mick' Love and his brother Keith he would not make the Randwick firsts. The pundits were way off base, as that year Col was selected for the Metropolitan team, New South Wales and Australia, and was picked, with Charlie Eastes, as one of the five best players of the year by the *New Zealand Rugby Almanack*. Col was now big and fast, and with his brother Keith continually advising him, found he was perfectly suited to the breakaway position.

One of the turning points of his life was the Australia versus the Rest game in 1946. It was the final trial before the Wallaby team to tour New Zealand was to be selected, the first major overseas tour after the Second World War. The teams were: *Australia:* Ron Rankin, Jimmy Stone, Charlie Eastes, Trevor Allan, Paul Johnson, Des Bannon, Cyril Burke, Keith Windon (captain), Bruce Hamilton, George Nosovitch, Kev Hodda, Arthur Buchan, Graham Cooke, Bob McMaster and Eric Tweedale; *The Rest:* Ken Kearney, Jack

McLean, Mal Quartermass, Max Howell, Mal Murphy, Mick Cremin, Roy Cawsey, Col Windon, Alan Livermore, Bill McLean (captain), Eric Davis, Ernie Freeman, Phil Hardcastle and Geoff Gourlay. The Rest won, Col was sensational at breakaway, and was on his way to New Zealand as a result. Because of the defeat, Bill McLean won out over Col's brother Keith for the Australian captaincy.

During the Australia versus the Rest game, the veteran Queenslander Graham Cooke warned Phil Hardcastle about holding and was ignored. 'Cookie' whirled around and let fly. Unfortunately, Hardcastle ducked and they carried Eric Tweedale off the field that day.

So it was off to New Zealand by flying boat for Col Windon, with the first Wallaby team to travel by plane. Keith Windon developed what was diagnosed at the time as gout, so in the first post-war international it was, at the two breakaway positions, Col and Alan Livermore, the father of Ross Livermore, the main force in later years behind the Queensland Rugby League. The All Blacks had opposing them Morrie McHugh and Roy White. Some of the All Black legends in that game were fullback Bob Scott, centres Johnny Smith and Ron Elvidge, five-eighth Fred Allen, winger Wally Argus, lock Jack Finlay and hooker 'Has' Catley. The All Blacks, principally made up out of the famous Kiwi contingent, really rolled over the Aussies by 31 points to 8. Col Windon was the best of the Wallabies on the day.

There was a winger on the 1946 tour, Jimmy Stone, who has always intrigued Colin and who was as competitive as they come. Before the war, when Jimmy Stone had the ball or looked as though he was getting it, the crowd would be on its feet. He was mercurial, for the crowd knew he could score from anywhere. He made the 1946 tour to New Zealand more on reputation than anything else. Injuries and lack of opportunity prevented a real view of him. But everyone remembered his past magic.

In his first game overseas the opposition kicked off, and the ball went almost to the Wallabies' goalline. Jimmy Stone took it, and started running and swerving, his past brilliance returning in all its glory. Defenders were left in his wake as he went right through the opposition and put the ball down between the posts. The home crowd was stunned, the

Wallabies overjoyed.

The author was proudly sitting in the stands that day, in his Australian blazer, when he noticed Jimmy Stone walking off the field. He strode up to the stand and sat down, saying: "I've done me leg in. You ain't got a cigarette, 'ave ya?" That was the end of Jimmy Stone that day. He was different, no disputing that.

On the 1946 tour during one of the games the stuttering Dr Phil Hardcastle, a relaxed character who had an annoying habit of climbing all over his opponents, using his elbows, holding jerseys, and so on, turned to Col in the middle of a line out and said: "C-C-Col, w-w-what are w-w-we g-g-going to b-b-bloody w-well b-be d-doing t-t-tonight, m-m-mate?"

Col gave it to the genial Phil straight: "Forget about tonight, what are you going to do when the ball comes?"

Col liked a good time as well as the next after a game, but when on the field he was all concentration and commitment.

In the second test, the All Blacks won narrowly, 14 to 10. Col Windon was all over the place, setting up Australia's first try after a run from his own 25. He secured from a ruck near touch, moved ahead with that swerving, crab-like run that made him famous, passed to captain Bill McLean, who relayed the ball on to Terry MacBride, and then Charlie Eastes, who scored. In the final minutes of the game Col Windon made another break and passed to Trevor Allan, who was forced out near the All Blacks' goal-line. It was a 'moral victory' for Australia.

As a result of his exploits on the 1946 tour he was, as mentioned, selected as one of the five players of the year by the *Rugby Almanack of New Zealand*. They said of him: "Whether in the tight scrummaging or in the open play, Windon was equally at home, whilst he was adept at linking up with his backs in attack. Probably the feature of Windon's play that impressed most was his determination, which attribute enables him to score tries that others were unable to accomplish. He was the outstanding forward on either side in the first test match, and at Wellington, particularly. His try at New Plymouth was the result of a swerving run after he had accepted a pass from his backs, whilst both tries at Wellington were outstanding efforts, the reward of tireless following up, determination, and the ability to seize opportunities."

When the All Blacks came to Australia in 1947 they were still a pretty fearsome mob. The core of the team was again from the Kiwis, which was lauded in the British Isles during war-time. Among the Freddy Allen-led team was perhaps the greatest centre that ever lived, Johnny, or simply 'JB' Smith. He had strutted his stuff against the Wallabies the year before and shown his class as he left many a Wallaby on the ground.

There was much excitement in the air, for all the players knew that the All Blacks were the ultimate test, and those who made the grade would make the nine-month tour of the British Isles. The first major game was against New South Wales.

The state team was: Brian Piper, Charlie Eastes, Terry MacBride, Max Howell, Alan Walker, Mick Cremin, Cyril Burke, Col Windon, Roger Cornforth, Arthur Buchan, Phil Hardcastle, Joe Kraefft, Doug Keller, Don Furness and Eric Tweedale.

The All Black team was: Bob Scott, Wally Argus, David Mason, Morrie Goddard, Johnny Smith, Jim Kearney, Percy Tetzlaff, Roy White, Charlie Willocks, Lachie Grant, Keith Arnold, Johnny Simpson, Has Catley and Harry Frazer.

The author had to go up against 'JB', and was absolutely terrified. In one of the first movements the ball came out from Tetzlaff to Kearney and then on to Smith. The author moved up quickly, keeping to the inside on an inside-out defence. Smith was sauntering as the author moved in for the tackle, thinking to himself that 'this is easy'. Suddenly Smith exploded, shot to the outside and absolutely flattened the author as he dived at him. He couldn't believe what had happened.

Smith went only about five yards, and Col Windon, coming across in cover defence, took Smith with a perfect tackle, ball and all. The author, who was up through sheer fright almost as soon as he hit the ground, said: "Thanks, Col." Col just nodded.

As well as his offensive acumen, Col was always solid in defence, and had the speed to cut off emerging problems on the field of play. NSW won the game that day 12 to 9, the game ending with a superlative Windon run that resulted in a try. Many of the NSW team started packing for England that day.

Respected writer Eddie Kann wrote: "Col Windon rose to his best form and gave a brilliant display in the open. He showed he is, like Eastes, a player for the big occasion. Windon was the most outstanding forward on the team." Eddie was later to call Col: "The Doyen of Breakaways."

Winston McCarthy in *Rugby in My Time* tells a story about Phil Hardcastle during the second NSW game, which the All Blacks won easily. Holding in the lineouts was not considered the right thing by the All Blacks' 'Iron Man' Johnny Simpson and the NSW players, particularly Hardcastle, were a bit 'over the top'.

"And old John (Simpson) said: 'Look' - he used to mark Phil Hardcastle - 'I'm going to tell Phil'. And of course Phil stuttered and had to listen because he couldn't tell you anything in the heat of the moment - 'I'm going to tell Phil that if he hangs on to my jersey when I go up I'll have to clock him…he can't go upsetting our team.' So they all decide that if these things happen they'll warn them, and if they happen again they'll have to clock them.

"Well, they go into the first lineout, and Simpson goes to jump in the air, and sure enough old Phil's got him anchored. So Johnny turned around and I can almost see the look on his face now from the sideline - you could hear him all over the paddock. 'Hardcastle, if you do it again, I'll clock you.' Old Phil didn't have time to say anything, and they go into the next lineout and it happens again. So then Johnny gave the signal to Wally Argus on the wing to toss it in to Phil. Now every time Phil took the ball in the lineout above his head he used to bring it straight down, with his arms straight between his legs, and he'd stand up and they'd come in behind and take the ball from there. Well, he goes up and down he comes. Down go his arms and the next moment you've got a perfect scrum. It was just like a billiards table, and the only thing sticking up in the centre of it was Hardcastle, his arms pinned to his sides right down and just his torso showing. And Simpson said: 'Now!' And Johnny was a tremendously built man with big hands and everything, and he drew back his fist and let fly. Now just at this moment Charlie Willocks, one of our locks, decided that he'd better put his head up to find out what was going on. And he found out. He got between Johnny and Phil Hardcastle, and Johnny hit him fair in the eye. It split Charlie's eye - seven stitches - and he didn't play again the rest of the tour. Johnny was always a bit wild about that, because he didn't get another chance at Phil Hardcastle for the rest of the tour. And Phil was a bit worried about that one."

Col made the first test team in Brisbane, the All Blacks winning 13 to 5, and was one of the best of the Australian forwards. He was rested for the second test, as the selectors experimented with various players. New Zealand won again, 27 to 14.

When the team to go on the nine-month tour in 1947-48 was announced, Col Windon's name was among them. Many considered him the best breakaway in the world at the time.

There were many personal highlights for Col on the tour, one being at Leicester where, in a fiercely contested game, Australia won 17 to 11. Col was captain that day, the fullback Watkin rattling the Wallabies with two field goals and three penalties. Col had his own reply. He said: "I couldn't let him get away with that!" He scored three tries. He was also captain of the Wallabies at Aberdeen. Col played 11 games in a row at one stage, through injuries to Bill McLean, Jimmy Stenmark, Arch Winning and John Fuller.

The game at Llanelli in 1948 is now part of Australian folklore. The Welsh are among the world's most combative creatures, and as is well known absolutely bonkers when it comes to rugby. The most ardent ones seem to live in Llanelli. As someone once said, there are more people with one eye born in Llanelli than anywhere else in the world. Their record against touring teams has been awesome, a highlight being the defeat of the First Wallabies in 1908. After it, the song 'Sospan Fach' emerged, which is sung whenever the 'Scarlets' play, "we beat the Wallabies in 1908" being the key words.

As soon as the Wallabies got on the boat to go to the British Isles these strange-looking little Welsh fellows would emerge, all resembling scrum-halves and five-eighths who couldn't make the grade in their village, and, disgraced, became nomads, working as stewards and clerks in forlorn corners of the globe. Their fanatical

eyes would glisten as they would sidle up to the Wallabies and say: "Wait till you get to Cardiff and Llanelli." It was a primeval chant, which followed the Wallabies everywhere. They would be standing in the toilet, at last in solitude and peace, and one of the little bastards would wander up and say: "Wait till you get to Cardiff and Llanelli." There were assorted replies from the Wallabies, none of which is very printable.

Anyhow, the Wallabies had a police escort to the game at Llanelli, which was unusual to say the least, and thousands were wending their way to the match. Every time the bus stopped and the crowd realised the Wallabies were on board, there would be violent shaking of clenched fists and rather disparaging remarks to what to all appearances were their mortal enemies, these visitors from the Antipodes.

The teams changed and lined up next to one another waiting for the referee's whistle before running on the field. A few police separated the teams, the boys in scarlet's eyes almost popping out of their heads as they were psyching themselves up to murder these innocent visitors. Max Howell was standing there, nervously running on the spot, when a little old lady reached out from the stands and belted him on the head with an umbrella. He was knocked down to his knees, and saw stars. As he stood up he said a few none-too-endearing words to the toothless hag who had assaulted him, at which time the policeman next to him threw a right to his ribs as he ran out and down he went again. The referee blew his whistle, the author feeling the bump on his head and the soreness of his ribs. And the game hadn't even started.

To say that the game was violent is an understatement, referee Ivor David never refereeing another international game because the game got so out of control. The manager of the Wallabies even jumped over the fence to cancel the game, but burly Bob McMaster pushed him back, saying: "They started it, we'll finish it!"

As they say, it was on for young and old. The veteran Cooke was at the forefront, demonstrating for all to see that he was the uncrowned boxing champion of the world. As bodies were hitting the turf in all directions from Graham's exertions, the referee blew his whistle and pointed towards the stand. Cookie started walking, as well he should, and bumped into Col Windon. It turned out it was Colin that was sent off, for a reasonably innocuous incident. Col was tough enough, but his game was developed by brains rather than brawn. He had taken a meaningless kick at a player who was upending him with a grasp on his groin.

There was an international furore over the incident, and at the time it was believed that Col Windon was the first Australian ever to be sent off the field in an international game. Little did the Wallabies know that three of the Wallabies of 1908 were given their marching orders.

Col scored two tries against England, one ranked among the finest ever seen at Twickenham, and was crucial in the Wallaby victory. As one England reporter described it: "Windon, seizing upon a knock-on by (five-eighth) Kemp, tore through their defence like a red-hot rocket. He had 50 yards to go, and three men after him, but this prince of breakaway forwards had the speed and stamina to get there. Tonkin kicked a goal, and although there was still plenty of fight in the England pack, the game was now lost and won." Col, as was his custom, had looked up to study the opposition before going down in the scrum, and heard Tommy Kemp yell to his scrumhalf, "I don't want it!" The scrum half threw the ball anyhow, and it went loose. Col thought: "If you don't want it, I do", scooped the ball up and was away.

Respected writer Phil Tressider, who was at the game, recalled many years later: "I saw him single-handedly destroy England at Twickenham."

With all his flash and speed, Col was also a work-horse on that 1947-48 tour. He played in 27 games, exceeded only by Trevor Allan, Arthur Tonkin, Terry MacBride and Cyril Burke. He scored nine tries on tour. And he also had guts, as he battled malaria to play the test against Scotland.

The newspapers can recognise real talent, and two of the headlines that have always intrigued Colin are "The Indefatigable Windon" and "The Ubiquitous Windon". Col lays no claims to academic aspirations, and one of his Wallaby cohorts remarked: "Col thought they were swearing at him!"

There is a little larceny in all of us, and many on the 1947-48 tour looked up to Ken Kearney,

who had done a tour of duty in England with the RAAF, and seemed to know all the angles. He took the boys for their first steak in London, and though they found out it was horse steak after they finished, most concluded it was better than kippers.

Anyhow, Ken announced to fellow conspirators that he had just read that there was an electricity strike in France, and the country had completely run out of candles. People were offering all kinds of money in France if they could get their hands on one. So quite a few converted all available cash to candles, and stuffed them in their kit-bags and trunks.

The Wallabies left for France the next morning, each conspirator rubbing his hands in glee and mentally calculating the amount of profit that would come his way. As the team arrived, they were horrified to see lights everywhere. The strike was over, and you couldn't give candles away, and the larcenous ones were last seen dropping candles in the Seine River, tears in their eyes.

The visit to Buckingham Palace was, of course, a highlight of the Wallaby tour, with no incidents to mar the occasion. They tell a story about the legendary Kiwi back Ike Proctor, who was served wine at a royal visit in thousand-year-old glasses.

When the Kiwis got on the train they had a supply of champagne, and though beer was the normal alcohol consumed by the lads they felt they should not waste it, so soon there was the popping of corks and paper cups were confiscated from the train. Ike disdained this, producing a thousand-year-old glass more suited to the champagne. Ike always had this habit of borrowing things in his travels.

The party was soon underway, everyone having a great time. Then suddenly the train came to a screeching halt, and police came clambering into their section. Rather sheepishly Ike produced the centre of the commotion, the thousand-year-old glass, but soon recovered when offered second best, champagne out of a paper cup. The Wallabies, of course, would never resort to such antics, though there was always a mysterious rattling noise as Wallaby second rower Graham Cooke walked out of a dining room.

There were three tests in Australia against the Maoris in June 1949, the Maoris winning the first 12-3, the second being a draw and the third a substantial Wallaby victory 18-3. Col Windon scored a rare triple, as he got a try in each of the matches.

Then it was off to New Zealand for the 1949 tour. 'Tubby' Allan was captain and Col Windon vice-captain. They were a perfect team.

One of Col's memories of the 1949 tour was of the Wallabies' two good humour men, assistant manager Bill Cerutti and second row forward Nick Shehadie, doing the New Zealand haka. It brought the house down wherever they went.

Cerutti was priceless, as always endeavouring to second guess the referee in favour of the Wallabies at every available opportunity. There was a continuous banter: "Free kick, sir! Thank you very much, Mr Referee! No try, Mr Referee, Sir!" And so on. Cerutti was really one of rugby's great characters.

In New Zealand, Col scored a try in each test, but the try he remembers most was one he set up connected with a play called 'Double'. The ball had been going out from Cyril Burke to Neville Emery and thence to John Blomley and Trevor Allan, and Col, who was leading the forwards, could see the cover defence leaving early in anticipation.

He called: "Double, double, double!" and took the ball from the lineout and reversed play to the front of the lineout. "Come with me," he called out to Ralph Garner, drew the fullback as only he could, and Garner was over, for "the easiest try he ever scored in his life".

So, in 1949, Col scored a try in each of the Maori tests, and one in each of the All Black games. It was a remarkable performance.

The Wallabies beat the All Blacks by 11 to 6 and 16 to 9. Despite the fact that thirty of New Zealand's finest were in South Africa, the All Blacks fielded very strong teams, with Maoris such as J.B Smith, Ben Couch, Vince Bevan and Ron Bryers.

In the first test, it was reported that "Windon was always handy in toeing movements, and his great backing-up earned him Australia's only try". After the second test, and he had to have injections of novocaine in his leg to get on the field, it was noted: "Windon raced in among them, grabbed the ball, punted high into NZ territory. Brockoff joined him, and Windon

scored in the corner. The try stunned the crowd, and many NZ forwards stood bewildered on Australia's own goal-line." The two victories meant Australia had won the Bledisloe Cup. They became the first Wallaby team to win the series in New Zealand.

Col Windon stated, after the game: "It was my ambition to play until Australia had beaten the All Blacks in a test series."

In 1950 he played no football, the company he worked for not allowing him time off for representative commitments. This became too much for him, so he came back to the game in 1951, playing against the All Blacks in Australia. Trevor Allan had departed to rugby league, as had Tony Paskins, Neville Emery and Ken Kearney, and the only hold-overs from 1949 were Arch Winning, Nick Shehadie, Cyril Burke and himself. Col had been vice-captain in 1949, so it was presumed he would be Australia's captain in 1951.

Arch Winning, a Queenslander, had been transferred to Sydney and was playing for Randwick, whose captain was Windon. When Windon decided to withdraw from the team leadership to concentrate on his game, 'Arch' took over. Winning returned to Queensland and captained his state, and in a big surprise was selected as Australian captain in 1951.

Australia lost the first match 0-8, and Col was selected as captain in the second and third tests, also won by New Zealand, with scores of 17-11 and 16-6.

Times have changed these days, as the teams rarely consort. Back in 1951 Col had an engagement party, and invited the All Blacks along. The whole team showed up, and every available food item in his house was rapaciously devoured, baked beans, spaghetti, bread, you name it and it went down the throats of the All Blacks. The beer just kept rolling in. Soon the sing-song started, with quarts of beer firmly clenched. "Life is just a bowl of cherries" was followed by:

The bubbles on the beer
Keep haunting me,
Every time I have a drink
I'm happy as can be.
The bubbles on the beer
When on a spree,
Why don't you come
And have a drink with me.

They were all arm in arm, 'Mick' Cremin, Col Windon, J.B. Smith, Percy Tetzlaff, and so on. That was the way it was in those days. You fought one another in the trenches, and then you celebrated with your antagonists. More's the pity that this has all but disappeared in the professionalisation and commercialisation of the modern game. Col played against the Fijians on their first tour of Australia in 1952 and although they were very aggressive, he liked the open style of football they played. During one test the great Joe Levula made a break and was being marked by one of Australia's greatest wingers, Eddie Stapleton. Joe caught Eddie on the wrong foot and started to accelerate. A certain try was on when Col, who had been trailing Stapleton, had the job of tackling this long-striding winger. After the game the three Australian selectors, one being Tom Pauling, came to Col and said that it was the perfect tackle as he did not leave the ground with his legs and so was not palmed off.

In the last test against Fiji, Col scored a try in the dying minutes, and if Australia had converted this try it would have drawn the match at 18-all. Australia lost 18 to 16.

In 1952 Col was off to New Zealand on his third trip, with John Solomon as captain. Australia won the first match at Christchurch 14 to 9, but the New Zealanders fought back to win the second 15 to 8. Shortage of a reliable kicker led to Australia's downfall. Windon scored in the first test, breaking wide on the blindside and shaking off tacklers on the way.

Col always wanted to tour South Africa, and his wish came true in 1953. He was then 32 years of age. While training at the surf club prior to departure he pulled something in the back of his leg, but seemingly shook it off.

Johnny Wallace was the coach of the 1953 tour, and Col was a crucial factor in his determination to open up the attack against the less mobile 'Boks. Wallace told him: "The two greatest forwards ever are you and Jack Ford."

Unfortunately, Wallace's plans were thrown into disarray as, against Pretoria, his leg collapsed, and he became a virtual passenger from then on, and was unable to play in any of the tests. It was a sad end to a brilliant career. He had scored 11 tries in 20 tests, a record until Brendan Moon exceeded it, and played over 100 games for the green and gold. He also managed 98 games for Randwick, thus playing more games for his country than his club.

He retired after South Africa, and was married in 1954. He was asked to coach Randwick in 1954 after Gordon Stone faltered, and then was elected coach in 1955, 1956 and 1957.

In later years Col got into horse-racing, his close friend Ross Cribb getting him involved in a syndicate. He had some outstanding wins with 'Heat of the Moment' and 'Dolceeza'.

Col Windon had superb fitness, seemingly running harder at the finish of a game than at the start. He had unbelievable positional sense that appeared to be intuitive. He had speed to burn, and ran like a gazelle. His swerve was a joy to behold, his palm a thing of beauty.

In the years he played, the magazine *Sporting Life* selected All Australian teams. Col was an All Australian in 1947, 1948, 1949, 1951 and 1952. Rugby league international Jack Reardon picked one team from the best players in rugby union and rugby league, and Col was one of the five union players selected. He was also elected to the Randwick City Council Sporting Hall of Fame. He scored five tries in one interstate game. He was truly indefatigable, ubiquitous and the doyen of breakaways.

# About the Authors

Professor Emeritus Max Howell has two doctorate degrees, one from the University of California at Berkeley and the other from the University of Stellenbosch, South Africa.

He was Foundation Chair of Human Movement Studies at the University of Queensland, and has held distinguished posts in Canada and the United States.

A Wallaby, he toured New Zealand in 1946, played against the 1947 All Blacks in Australia and then in 1947–48 was on the nine–month tour of the British Isles, France, Canada and the United States.

He retired from international rugby at twenty years of age to concentrate on his studies overseas. He played and coached in Canada and the United States and became the Canadian national coach.

He has written 37 books and has over 300 academic publications.

●

Dr Lingyu Xie was born in the People's Republic of China and is a research expert in sport history. She completed her bachelor's and master's degrees at the Beijing Institute of Physical Education and then became a research worker in the China Sport Museum. She was an outstanding volleyball player in China and now participates in aerobics.

Dr Xie and Professor Howell are married, and have been conducting research together on rugby in New Zealand, England, Ireland, Scotland, Wales, South Africa and Australia for this and future publications.